The Complete Guide to HUMAN RESOURCES and the LAW

2000 Supplement

The Complete Guide to

HUMAN RESOURCES and the LAW

2000 Supplement

Dana Shilling

PRENTICE HALL

Library of Congress Cataloging-in-Publication Data

Shilling, Dana.
Complete guide to human resources and the law / Dana Shilling.
p. cm.
Includes index.
ISBN 0-13-011556-8
1. Labor laws and legislation—United States. 2. Personnel management—United States. I. Title.
KF3455.S55 1998 98-5107
344.7301—dc21 CIP

Printed in the United States of America

10 9 8 7 6 5 4 3 2

ISBN 0-13-011556-8

PRENTICE HALL
Paramus, NJ 07652

On the World Wide Web at http://www.phdirect.com

Introduction

The main volume of this work was published in 1998, by and large covering the events up to 1997. This supplement takes over, dealing in large part with 1998's events, with a few detours for late 1997 developments and news from the first quarter of 1999.

This volume includes a new Chapter 31, covering potential areas of employer liability if the corporation merges, is acquired, or otherwise goes through transition. There are also new sections and subsections through the supplement.

What trends emerged between publication of the main volume and the supplement? More Supreme Court involvement, for one thing; a surprising number of cases from the High Court are discussed here. Of course, the lower courts continued to issue decisions, and administrative agencies such as the Internal Revenue Service (IRS) and National Labor Relations Board (NLRB) continued to issue rules.

The emerging areas of discussion and litigation include the Americans With Disabilities Act and Family and Medical Leave Act, especially in the disputed territory where the two statutes interact (and affect other areas of law, such as Worker's Compensation and wrongful termination). Retaliation cases became one of the leading subjects for antidiscrimination suits. The Supreme Court made it more likely that employers will be liable when quid pro quo sexual harassment occurs, thus making it more important than ever to maintain a meaningful program for preventing, detecting, and punishing harassment.

Perhaps the basic issues have been roughed out in the "traditional" areas such as race and sex discrimination, and therefore the spotlight has shifted to what once were marginal areas. However, the Equal Pay Act, and the issue of pay equity for women, has gained new prominence in the past year or so.

The "traditional" pension—the defined benefit plan—is no longer the "conventional" pension. Employers are showing much more interest in market-oriented plans such as the 401(k) and, especially, the cash-balance plan. Such plans shift much of the risk from employer to employee. Health plan trends also show greater employee copayment responsibilities, as well as a continuing shift from indemnity to managed care. However, it has become far more likely than before that managed care plans will be required to answer state-law claims and will not be held entitled to ERISA preemption.

By the time you read this, we'll probably know if Y2K (year 2000) problems led to widespread disruptions of computer systems, including those used for human resources (HR) functions! One trend that emerged is the ever-increasing dominance of HR software, and especially the (public) Internet and corporate intranets in administering payroll and benefits and communicating with employees. Even companies that have no plans to engage in e-commerce are likely to find that many back office functions can be performed more efficiently and less expensively online.

You'll also note that many references and citations are made to online rather than print sources, because a few mouse clicks can bring you powerful information (often at no cost).

Once again, the purpose of this book is to communicate in plain English with nonattorney HR professionals, and to place developments in the legal system in the context of the practical issues faced by your counterparts throughout the United States. To this end, facts, figures, and survey results are covered so you'll be able to see how your plans and your operations compare to those of other companies, and so you can benefit from solutions they have devised.

Contents

Chapter 7 Compensation Planning—29

Chapter 8 Wage and Hour Issues—35

Chapter 9 Employee Group Health Plans (EGHPs)—45

Chapter 10 Fringe Benefits—65

Chapter 11 Early Retirement and Retiree Health Benefits—75

Chapter 12 Substantive Law of Pensions—79

Chapter 13 Plan Administration—91

Chapter 14 Plan Disclosure—95

Chapter 15 Distributions from the Plan—101

Chapter 16 Plan Termination—105

Chapter 17 ERISA Enforcement—109

Chapter 18 Labor Law—113

Chapter 19 Unemployment Insurance—121

Chapter 20 Worker s Compensation—123

Chapter 21 OSHA—127

Chapter 32 Forms—219

Index—277

The Complete Guide to

HUMAN RESOURCES and the LAW

2000 Supplement

Chapter 1

THE HIRING PROCESS

1.5 RECRUITING IN A COMPETITIVE ENVIRONMENT

In a competitive environment within a mobile society, it's not only a challenge to recruit a good workforce, it can be tough to retain employees. Another job offer, the need to move to accompany a spouse, or simple dissatisfaction can trigger high turnover.

Not every employee is a paragon, of course, and it may seem easier to allow employees to drift away than to fire them (and worry about potential liability). But even an employee who earns only $30,000 a year in straight salary costs the company close to $40,000 a year (once taxes and benefits are taken into account), plus recruitment and training costs and the initial period of diminished productivity as the new hire gains expertise. So reducing turnover even of unexceptional employees is helpful.

Companies can improve recruitment and retention by adopting a more structured approach. As new jobs are created, or jobs open up, the manager who will supervise the new hire should complete a formal requisition:

- Job title
- Why it has to be filled
- Why the job is required at all—could the functions be delegated among existing employees, outsourced, or assigned to part-timers or temporary employees?
- Hiring date
- Degree of priority for hiring
- Special qualifications required
- Formal job description, or changes in the existing description

Job descriptions and interview questions should be reviewed for compliance with the American with Disabilities Act (ADA) and other antidiscrimination laws. Before the offer is extended, at least a basic background check should be done, such as checking references provided by the candidate and consulting objective sources of information. (These suggestions come from James T. Ryan, "Avoid Hit-or-Miss Hiring," *HR Magazine*, "Focus," 11/98, p. 23.)

TIP

Remember that, to the extent that credit-related information is investigated, the provisions of the Fair Credit Reporting Act must be obeyed (see ¶1.11 in the main volume).

As more people gain Web access, at home, at the office, or in public places such as libraries and airports, Internet recruiting becomes a greater factor. A truly nationwide (and even worldwide) pool can be accessed.

Many of the costs of recruiting, such as Help Wanted advertising, can be reduced or eliminated. Now that thousands of people have posted their resumes online, the HR department can do a rapid screening of resumes and target the best candidates, without offending anyone or hurting anyone's feelings. In-house recruitment departments can adopt some tactics usually used by headhunters.

Although it might be considered unethical to make an effort to recruit employees from a competitor, there is no ethical problem if the employees have already voluntarily posted their resumes to a job site on the World Wide Web. Sherry Kuczynski makes this point in "You've Got Job Offers," *HR Magazine*, 3/99, p. 51. (Resume posters have taken at least a small affirmative step toward getting a new job, so it is easier to scan the resume database and find a good match than to publish a Help Wanted ad and hope that the right person will read it.)

In fact, an automated voice mail system, known as IVR (for interactive voice response), can mechanize the early stages of the recruitment process. Applicants call a toll-free telephone number and answer a series of questions to indicate whether they have the basic qualifications for the job. If they fit the profile, the system can direct them to send in a resume or schedule an in-person job interview. (See Ruth E. Thaler-Carter, "Reach Out and Hire Someone," *HR Magazine*, 5/99, p. 8.) Applicants like the flexibility of the system (and those who already have jobs can call from home, outside normal working hours!). The HR department will have to review the responses, and the phone time itself can be expensive: The average IVR call costs the employer about $4 (an eight-minute phone call at 50 cents a minute).

Users of Web recruiting tools say that the company's own Web page, listing job openings, is the best tool for this purpose, followed by sites that create a database by allowing candidates to post their resumes, links to the company's Web page, coordination with recruiters, and job listings in Web sites for job hunters. (Ruth E. Thaler-Carter, "Recruiting Through the Web: Better or Just Bigger?" *HR Magazine*, 11/98, p. 61.)

However, the availability of the Web doesn't eliminate the need for headhunters and search services, especially when a top job has to be filled and finding the right candidate is crucial. In those cases, it often makes sense to use the Web to communicate with the search service—and let the headhunters use their own Web tools to narrow down the candidate pool.

Unless you hire only immigrants newly arrived in this country (which carries with it its own set of problems!) or recent graduates with no work experience, at least some of your new hires will come from other businesses. Because you want relevant experience, the odds are that some of your new hires will previously have been employed by competitors, and some of them will have been actively recruited.

In a worst-case scenario, your competitor will charge you with wrongfully inducing employees to leave their jobs and come to work for you—perhaps in violation of covenants not to compete, or perhaps giving you access to confidential customer lists and trade secrets. Recently, for instance, Wal Mart accused amazon.com of luring away skilled merchandisers, and a department store sued an executive recruiter for interfering with employment contracts. (See Joseph E. Bachelder III, "Inducing an Executive to Change Jobs," *New York Law Journal*, 3/29/99, p. 3.)

In the worst part of the worst-case scenario, you might be forced to pay a competitor's lost profits as well as its costs of recruiting its own new executive. But that would require proof that you interfered improperly with an employment contract.

➠ TIP

An important part of any high-level interview (or the screening process performed by a recruiting firm you have retained) is to make sure that either there is no express or implied contract, or that hiring the candidate would not violate it.

There is very little chance that an individual acting on behalf of his or her corporation would be subjected to personal liability for "luring away" a competitor's executive, but the hiring corporation itself might be liable.

Courts recognize the need to stay competitive by attracting top talent. Just make sure that you use accepted channels (including the Internet), not surreptitious targeting of competitors' executives. It's best if the position is open to a wide range of candidates, not the smaller fishpond of competitors' staffs! Make it clear that you are offering a position based on the individual's experience and transferable skills, not his or her potential for industrial espionage.

1.7 NONDISCRIMINATORY HIRING

In a March 1999 article ("Build a Legal Employment Application," *HR Magazine*, 3/99, p.129), Timothy S. Bland and Sue S. Stalcup suggest that it can be worthwhile to indicate on every job application form that the form will be rejected if the applicant includes extraneous information not requested on the application. That's because some applicants use the unwanted information tactically: They include it, then if they are not hired, they use the information as a premise for a discrimination charge. For instance, unsolicited information about union activism could be used against the company, if the inference is believed that the company refuses to hire union activists.

Some states (typically Southern states in which tobacco growing is a major economic activity) forbid employment discrimination on the basis of smoking, so outright asking applicants if they smoke could create legal problems. However, if your workplace is smoke free, or if smoking is restricted to designated smoking areas, it makes sense to disclose your policy and let applicants decide whether or not they can measure up.

1.9 IMMIGRATION AND HIRING PRACTICES

1.9.3 Employment Verification Documents

See 63 FR 5287 (2/2/98) for an Immigration and Naturalization Service (INS) Proposed Rule reducing from 29 to 13 the number of documents that will be accepted for verification of employment eligibility. In some circumstances, a newly hired individual can provide a receipt for a document rather than the original document itself.

Employers can complete the Form I-9 either at the time of hiring or before hiring (once a commitment to hire has been made). However, the form must be completed at the same point in the employment process for all employees.

The Proposed Rule includes a new Form I-9A, for reverification of employment eligibility that has already been established.

The full text of the Proposed Rule can also be found at http://www.ins.usdoj.gov.

1.9.4 [NEW] H-1B Visas

The American Competitiveness and Workforce Improvement Act, P.L. 105-277, increased the number of visas that can be issued in fiscal year (FY) 1999–2001 to highly skilled immigrants undertaking temporary positions. Before P.L. 105-277 was passed, only 65,000 H-1B visas could be issued worldwide per year. Under P.L. 105-277, 115,000 such visas can be issued in 1999 and 2000, tapering down to 107,500 in FY 2001. The 65,000 limit is reimposed as of the start of FY 2002.

The H-1B visa is a nonimmigrant visa for temporary workers in "specialty occupations"—jobs that apply a highly specialized body of knowledge in both a theoretical and practical way. Most H-1B visa holders work in high-tech businesses, such as software development. The initial duration of an H-1B visa is three years, although it can be extended for three more years.

H-1B workers must have at least a bachelor's degree in their specialty or must have equivalent qualifications and expertise. If the job requires a state license, the H-1B visa holder must have the license.

Employers making use of these H-1B visas are required to take steps to protect the jobs of American workers. The employer must apply to the Secretary of Labor for a Labor Condition certification for each H-1B employee. The employer certifies that the worker will not be underpaid; that the working conditions of the temporary foreign worker will not have a negative effect on the working conditions of U.S. citizens and legal immigrants; and that the employer is not engaged in a labor dispute or lockout. The application must be posted within the workplace.

H-1B workers must be paid either the salary the employer would otherwise pay for the job or the prevailing wage in the area. (Of course, this is required to deprive employees of an incentive to hire a foreign workers simply to lower wage costs.) Willful violation of this requirement or violation of the layoff requirement (see later in this chapter) can be penalized by a $35,000 fine and three years of debarment from federal contracts.

If the employer is "H-1B dependent" (more than 15% of its workforce consists of H-1B visa holders), then additional steps have to be taken to protect American jobs. The companies have to certify that they have not laid off an American from the same job in the 90 days before hiring the H-1B worker (and won't, in the 90 days afterward). Placement agencies must certify that they won't refer an H-1B worker to an H1-B dependent company within 90 days of the layoff of an American.

In practical terms, even the expanded number of these visas is less than the demand, so if you want to hire an H-1B worker, it makes sense to start early in the year. The quota is usually filled midway through the year, and visa processing takes several months. (The fiscal year begins in October, so applications can be made as of October 1 for the following year.)

The problem is that employers usually recruit workers from foreign students, who are in this country holding student visas and are about to graduate from a college or graduate program that gives them their specialized skills. But immigration law requires employers to wait until the student graduates before offering him or her a job. You can get around this problem by having the student get permission from the Immigration and Naturalization Services to add a year of PGPT (postgraduate practical training) to his or her student visa, so you can apply for the H-1B visa during this extra year.

Dan Hartsfield, Rodney A. Malpert, and Amanda Petersen's article "H-1B Visas for 'Specialty' Workers" (*National Law Journal*, 4/19/99, p. B5) explains these techniques. Also see "Labor Department Proposal Sets Out Employer Requirements Under the New H-1B Law," 67 LW 2391 (1/12/99).

People with student visas must leave the United States by July of the year in which they graduate, unless they have PGPT authorization. (Of course, many students remain and work in this country illegally, but this is not only unethical but a potential source of liability for the employer.)

The Department of Labor's Proposed Regulations for working with H-1B visas were published in 64 FR 627 (1/5/99).

NLRB Memo

On December 4, 1998, Fred Feinstein, the general counsel of the National Labor Relations Board, issued Memorandum GC 98-15, entitled "Reinstatement and Backpay Remedies for Discriminatees Who May be Undocumented Aliens in Light of Recent Board and Court Precedent." This Memorandum GC 98-15 can be found at http://www.nlrb.gov/gcmemo/gc98-15.html.

The purpose of the memo is to inform NLRB regional directors and their subordinates of current policy for dealing with discrimination charges filed by noncitizens who are not legally permitted to work in the United States. On the one hand, the NLRB is opposed to employment discrimination; on the other hand, the Immigration Reform and Control Act of 1986 makes it unlawful to hire or continue to employ an undocumented alien worker.

The NLRB's basic statement on this issue is *A.P.R.A. Fuel Oil Buyers Group*, 320 NLRB 408 (1995), enforced by 134 F.3d 50 (2nd Cir. 1997). The NLRB allowed undocumented aliens to bring charges of wrongful discharge on the basis of union activity, and awarded them back pay, but also conditioned their reinstatement on their proof of authorization to work in the United States. The NLRB memorandum advises its regional offices to seek an unconditional reinstatement order in similar cases. The exception is the situation in which the employer makes an affirmative showing that the complainant is not authorized to work in the United States. In such cases, it is the NLRB policy to seek conditional reinstatement.

A.P.R.A. did not resolve the situation in which the employer hired, then improperly fired, a person without knowledge of the fired person's employment status. The rule of *Hoffman Plastic Compounds, Inc.*, 326 NLRB No. 86 (9/23/98), is that the fired worker was not entitled to reinstatement (because, as it turned out, he was not authorized to work in the United States). Eligibility for back pay was tolled at the point that the employer discovered the worker's undocumented status.

However, undocumented status, while it reduces the remedies available to the discriminatee, does not exempt the employer from scrutiny of its conduct. According to Feinstein's memorandum, the employer's evidence about the complainant's immigration status is irrelevant to an unfair labor practice hearing and cannot be admitted. In a compliance proceeding, where the issue of reinstatement arises, the employer may be able to introduce evidence about work authorization status. This is permitted only if the employer has a reasonable basis, independent of the compliance proceeding, to claim that the discriminatee is not authorized to work in the United States. The NLRB "would object to the compliance proceeding being used as a fishing expedition to try to determine whether someone is unlawfully in the country." The NLRB's position is that questioning a complainant about immigration status violates IRCA's antidiscrimination provisions (8 USC §1324b(a)(6)).

EEOC, DOJ MOU

See 63 FR 5518 (2/3/98) for the Memorandum of Understanding (MOU) between the EEOC and the Department of Justice's Office of Special Counsel for Immigration Related Unfair Employment Practices. Under the MOU, each agency can act as the other's agents to receive complaints about immigration-related discrimination charges. The two agencies will coordinate to avoid duplication of effort.

In response to immigration-law changes, the two agencies will treat document abuse, intimidation, and retaliation as immigration-related unfair labor practices and will accept pattern or practice charges. The EEOC has agreed not to ask if the charging party is a U.S. citizen, national, or work-authorized alien as a condition for referring charges to the Department of Justice (DOJ). When wage and hour or Office of Federal Contract Compliance inspections are made, I-9 forms will not be inspected. The text of the MOU can be found at http://www.ins.doj.gov/public%5Faffairs/news%5Freleases/laborbg.htm.

➠ TIP

It should be noted, however, that the full Fourth Circuit reversed its earlier three-judge panel decision and now holds that only a citizen, or an alien with a valid work visa, is a "qualified" employee. Therefore, an undocumented alien cannot make out a Title VII prima facie case: *Egbuna v. Time-Life Libraries Inc.*, 153 F.3d 184(4th Cir. 1998).

1.10 ADA Compliance in Hiring

Even if a job applicant is not disabled, he or she can bring suit under the ADA if employment is denied on the basis of the applicant's answers to pre-employment inquiries that are made improperly and in violation of the ADA: *Griffin v. Steeltek Inc.*, 160 F.3d 591 (10th Cir. 1998).

Chapter 2

EMPLOYEE HANDBOOKS

2.2 LEGAL IMPLICATIONS OF THE HANDBOOK

A trend reported in 1998 was for unions to challenge the language of employee handbooks (as well as to challenge workplace rules)—and for NLRB regional offices to view these challenges favorably. The case of *Lafayette Park Hotel*, 326 NLRB No. 69 (1998), shows the way in which a union's challenge to one handbook provision can open the door to NLRB examination of the handbook as a whole. In this case, the handbook included a ban on false, vicious, profane, or malicious statements about the hotel or its employees. The NLRB struck down this rule, on the grounds that employees were not given adequate notice of what constituted improper conduct. But once it looked at that rule, the NLRB also invalidated another rule, requiring employees to leave the premises as soon as they finished their shift. This rule was unacceptable because it denied access to nonwork areas such as the parking lot.

An article by New Jersey attorney A. Michael Weber ("Unions Challenge Employee Handbook Language," *National Law Journal*, 2/8/99, p. S7) also discusses earlier NLRB cases in which the NLRB allowed employees to discuss wage and benefit information with the union during contract negotiations, despite a work rule prohibiting disclosure of confidential information; and a work rule banning "derogatory" statements could not be enforced to prevent the union from making truthful statements that questioned the medical care provided by the employer, a hospital.

Two Indiana workers were fired when a supervisor found them up on the plant roof—and there was a smell of marijuana in the attic through which the roof was reached. The employees said that they had been ordered up to the roof to clean the gutters (and were probably telling the truth). They sued the employer because the grievance procedures set out in the handbook were not observed before firing them. But they lost their case; it didn't even go to trial, because summary judgment was granted.

In Indiana, handbook provisions create a contract only if the employee provided some consideration other than merely taking the job. Anyway, the handbook didn't promise that the procedures would be followed in every case—in fact, it said that immediate dismissals could occur when necessary. [*Orr v. Westminster Village North, Inc.*, 1997 Westlaw 769409 (Indiana 1997)].

A Texas court took a very different view. A newly recruited employee was concerned about whether the job would be permanent. She was told that she could keep the job as long as she continued to perform well. Nevertheless, she was fired. A Texas court said that she had an oral contract permitting termination only for good cause. After her hiring, the employer issued a handbook informing all employees that they worked at will. To the court, this was not determinative, because the handbook itself said that handbook provisions did not have contractual status [*Doctors' Hospital of Laredo Limited Partnership v. Dromgoole*, 1998 Westlaw 75554 (Tex. App. 1998)].

A Washington court ruled that a handbook case was properly dismissed because it was brought too late. The employee claimed that the statute of limitations should have been six years, because the action was based on a written contract (i.e., the handbook itself). The court rejected this argument, because the employee handbook was a general document and did not relate to the specific facts of the employee's job with the company. The employee's next argument was that, because spoken (parol) evidence was needed to interpret the handbook, the statute of limitations should have been three years (the correct one for a partly written, partly oral contract). The court denied this argument too, because even if parol evidence can be introduced to interpret a contract (many contracts have an integration clause that rules out parol evidence), such testimony does not make the contract partly oral. The employee's claim was really one based on a promise of specific treatment in a specific situation. Reliance on a handbook provision is really a tort claim, not a contract claim, so contract concepts don't apply. The case is *DePhillips v. Zolt Construction Co.*, 136 Wash.2d 26, 959 P.2d 1104 (Wash. 1998).

Chapter 4

WORK–FAMILY ISSUES

4.1 INTRODUCTION

Updated Insights from Hewitt

Hewitt Associates' survey, tracking the trends of 1997, shows that 69% of employers allowed employees juggling work and family to work flexible hours: Only 58% permitted this in 1992. When the survey focused in on major employers, it found that 73% offered flextime, 61% allowed a part-time schedule, 24% allowed a compressed work schedule (e.g., four ten-hour days instead of five eight-hour days), 20% allowed telecommuting, and 16% had shortened "summer hours."

Among the major employers, 85% had some kind of child care benefit (versus only 74% five years earlier). Nearly all (97%) offered dependent care spending accounts; 42% had resource and referral services, but only 15% offered emergency child care programs or programs that can care for sick children who can't make use of their regular day care alternative.

Elder care programs were offered by one-third of large employers, consisting of resource and referral services (84%), counseling (17%), and long-term care insurance (24%).

One-fifth of major employers permitted more Family and Medical Leave Act (FMLA) leave than the 12-week minimum; the rest stuck with the statutory amount. Twenty-six percent of major employers gave adoption benefits, averaging $2776. (This information comes from WestGroup Employment Alert 9/3/98, p. 6.)

4.2 CHILD CARE OPTIONS AT WORK

On April 23, 1998, the Department of Labor's (DOL's) Business-to-Business Mentoring Initiative on Child Care was launched. It will be run by the DOL's Women's Bureau. The Initiative intends to promote awareness of the importance of work-related child care and to link up employers that have already implemented successful child care programs with companies intending to do so. The experienced providers will serve as mentors for the novices. The Women's Bureau produces a resource kit, including standards and best practices and information about developing an effective child care program.

➠ TIP

Your company can volunteer to participate as a mentor (if it already has a success story) or link up with a mentor; the Women's Bureau regional staff will help make the link-ups. Application forms can be obtained by telephone, (800-827-5335; by fax, 202-219-5529; or from the Women's Bureau Web site. See http://www.dol.gov/dol/wb/public/childcare/b2bintro.htm.)

In 1998, Long Island's Symbol Technology opened its second corporate day care center; it has 120 day care places for the children of its 1850 employees. (See Diana Shaman, "Corporate Day-Care Centers Grow, But Cautiously," *New York Times*, 3/1/98, p. RE7.) Management of the centers is outsourced to Children's Choice Child Care, a private company. The care cost was $189 a week in 1998; parents paid $141.75 a week, with the employer subsidizing the balance. Manhasset's CMP Publications has a day care center with fees ranging from $142 to $157, depending on the age of the child.

A company called Serendipity operates a 10,000-square-foot child care center. Much of its enrollment comes from 28 member companies, although membership is not a prerequisite. Care costs from $560 to $640 a month, with discounts offered to employees of member companies. Another Long Island company, First Class Child Care, provides day care and back-up care in emergencies, for fees of $730 to $940, discounted to between $635 and $760 for employees of sponsoring companies.

Families and Work's 1998 Business Work-Life Study (BWLS), by Ellen Galinsky and James T. Bond, is order #W 98-03 and costs $59 plus shipping and handling. It can be ordered from http://www.familiesandwork.org/summary/worklife.pdf, where you can also download an Executive Summary. Rima Shore's "Ahead of the Curve: Why America's Leading Employers are Addressing the Needs of New and Expectant Parents" is #D 98-04 and costs $39 plus shipping and handling from the same source.

The 1998 BWLS reports on a sample of about 1000 companies and nonprofit organizations with 100+ employees. The survey's conclusions are not surprising: Better work–family support enhances job satisfaction, loyalty, and employee retention.

BWLS revealed that companies in the sample permitted eight flexible work arrangements. The most common (offered by 88%) was time off to attend family-related events. Eighty-one percent offered a gradual transition back to the workplace after birth or adoption leave. Basic flex-time arrangements were available in about two-thirds of these companies. Over half allow transitions between full- and part-time work, with occasional opportunities to work at home even for employees who are not engaged in a formal telecommuting arrangement. Almost half (46%) of survey respondents believed their work–family arrangements yielded a positive return on investment; about a third thought they were cost neutral; and only 18% thought that the cost of flexible work arrangements was greater than the benefits received.

The survey respondents were generally subject to the FMLA. Many companies provided more leave than the required 12 weeks. Eighty-one percent funded at least some pay for workers on maternity leave under their temporary disability plan. Thirteen percent offered at least some replacement pay for paternity leave, and 12.5% did this in connection with adoption leave. The FMLA requires granting leave to employees whose children are seriously ill; about half of the respondents also allowed time off (without loss of pay or vacation days) when children were mildly ill, for an average of 11 days per employee. One-quarter of employers said that the number of days off varied with the situation; 9% allowed employee parents to take as many days off as they needed to cope with minor childhood illness, and 5% provided care for mildly ill children (e.g., specialized day care centers).

Dependent care assistance plans (letting employees apply pretax dollars to pay for child care) were quite common, found in 50% of survey respondent companies. The only other common child care mechanism was information and referral. Less than 10% provided on-site child care, child care vouchers, reimbursement of employees' child care costs when they had to travel or work late, or other direct care mechanisms.

The BWLS also addressed employer attitudes and corporate culture. Two-thirds of respondents said it was "very true" that the company gave equal support to male and female employees in their family caregiver role; 30% said it was "somewhat true," and 5% said that the statement was not accurate for their organization. Over half (55%) said that supervisors are encouraged to support workers who have family problems and find solutions that are mutually acceptable to families and the organization; 41% said the statement was somewhat true, and only 4% felt it was not very true or not true at all.

When asked if management includes employees' personal needs in the factors behind business decisions, 51% of respondents said that was somewhat true, 31% said it was very true, 18% said it was not very true or not true at all. Forty-four percent believed their organization made an ongoing effort to inform employees of available work-family assistance measures; but only 19% said this was very true, and 37% said it was not true at all. This is a sad commentary—employers should certainly keep employees informed of existing work–family initiatives, even if they don't have the personnel or funds to implement additional programs.

The finance/insurance/real estate sector was the most likely to offer work–family assistance. Wholesale/retail trade was the least generous in this regard.

Understandably, work–family support increases with company size, in that larger companies have more revenue and a broader range of personnel. It can be cost-effective to establish a program for 500 people whereas a program for 50 would not be cost-effective. Furthermore, a broader range of personnel allows more flexibility in finding someone to cover for an employee who needs a few hours, days, or weeks to satisfy a family need.

Support for work–family needs correlated strongly positively with diversity. The more women and minorities in leadership positions within the company, the more likely the company is to provide work–family assistance, especially practical measures such as child care on site or nearby or dependent care assistance plans. The larger the proportion of female employees (even in rank-and-file rather than decision-making positions), the larger the number of work–family options. However, the most costly options tended to be concentrated in companies with a lower proportion of female workers—perhaps to reduce the likelihood that the costlier measures would actually be called upon.

"Ahead of the Curve"

Rima Shore's "Ahead of the Curve" study focuses on three graphics: increase in the number of employed parents with children under six; working parents who report significant work–family conflict; and children's brain metabolism. The metabolism of a child's brain increases rapidly between birth and age three, and then levels off—(i.e., the first three years of life are crucial to intellectual development).

Between 1989 and 1993, the number of parents in the workforce with children under six remained fairly stable (at about 20 million), then shot up dramatically, exceeding 21 million in 1997. Between 1992 and 1997 (the times of greatest growth), the percentage of parents of young children reporting significant work–family conflict went from about 15% to over 30%.

The factors that Shore reports as increasing the stress are as follows:

- New parents' time shortage (62% of mothers of preschool children have paid jobs, and most of the jobs are full time rather than part time)
- Increasing physical, emotional, and time demands of the workplace over the past five years
- Increasing financial worries for new parents; inflation-adjusted income of families has remained more or less level for 20 years
- Unpredictable or erratic work schedules, which increase the difficulty of finding dependable child care
- Lack of information about parenting and combining work and family roles

Shore identifies five corresponding trends for employers:

- Maintaining a supportive corporate culture in order to retain valued employees
- Staying competitive with other employers, when it can be hard to fill mission-critical highly skilled jobs
- Maintaining company morale, especially in the wake of downsizing
- The need to function 24/7 in a global economy
- Public companies' need to satisfy stockholders, especially institutional investors

In Shore's analysis, the solution to work–family problems must begin even before the children are born, including parenthood education (including instruction in breast feeding), substance abuse treatment, and prenatal care. Intervention is required to help high-risk babies early in their development.

Although Shore's study finds that 84% of working parents of preschool children have access to employment-related health insurance, 5% overall (including 11% of single parents and 12% of low-income households) do not have any health insurance at all. Shore adopts conventional recommendations: full utilization of FMLA leave; flexible scheduling; and opportunities to work at home. (Shore refers to The Child Care and Employment Turnover study, which revealed that mothers lacking access to a child care center within a 10-minute drive of their homes were almost twice as likely to quit their jobs as those with a day care center within easy driving distance.)

Even employees who have a workable child care solution during normal working hours are often stymied when they have to work shifts or put in a lot of overtime or weekend work.

Breast feeding for at least six months, and preferably a year, is the medical recommendation for newborn babies. So either new mothers must choose bottle feeding; delay their return to work until they are ready to stop breast feeding; or use a workplace lactation program that either allows them to feed their babies at the workplace or gives them an appropriate private place to pump and store breast milk. (See Kathryn Tyler, "Got Milk?" *HR Magazine*, 3/99 p. 69.)

Workplace lactation programs are extremely productive for employers because they aid employee retention. Furthermore, babies fed with breast milk are often healthier than formula-fed babies, so their parents need less time off to deal with babies' illnesses. The Los Angeles Department of Water and Power found that it got back between $3.50 and $5.00 for every dollar invested in the lactation program, cut absenteeism by 27%, and reduced health care costs by 35%.

The demands of a lactation program are modest. Breast-feeding employees need a private, reasonably quiet and pleasant place to express breast milk and a refrigerator or cooler to keep it cool, plus a sink to wash up. Some employers provide sophisticated, sanitary breast pumping equipment. Typically, employees will need about an hour a day to express milk (two 30-minute or three 20-minute breaks).

However, in May 1999, MSNBC Cable won a case in the Southern District of New York. An ex-employee sued under Title VII and the ADA because she was not given access to a private place to express breast milk during the working day. The judge ruled that lactation is not a disability, so the ADA claim was invalid, and no evidence of sex discrimination was produced. (The plaintiff was not denied the opportunity to pump breast milk; the question was whether the locations in which she was permitted to do so were suitable.) The case of *Martinez v. NBC Inc*, #98 Civ. 4842 (S.D.N.Y. 5/19/99), is discussed in Deborah Pines's *New York Law Journal* article, "Discrimination Found in Lack of Privacy for Use of Breast Pump," available at http://www.lawnewsnetwork.com/practice/employmentlaw/news/A1598-1999May19.html.

4.4 CORPORATE ELDER CARE ACTIVITIES

Corporate awareness of the significant economic impact of elder care is increasing. In June 1997 the MetLife Mature Market Group and the National Alliance for Caregiving performed a major survey, releasing a report, "Family Caregiving in the U.S.: Findings from a National Survey."

TIP

Copies of the report can be obtained by telephoning (203) 221-6580.

According to MetLife's summary paper, "The MetLife Study of Employer Costs for Working Caregivers," in 1996 (when the telephone survey was done) close to one-fourth of all U.S. households (i.e., more than 22 million households) included at least one person with caregiving responsibilities. Almost two-thirds of those caregivers were employed, and over 50% worked full time. Therefore, there were 14.4 million Americans who combine caregiving and employment responsibility. Metlife's conclusion is that U.S. business loses productivity and encounters supervisory costs for resolving caregiving issues, to the tune of **$11.4 billion** per year (to replace employees; cope with absenteeism and partial absenteeism; deal with interruptions during the workday and the need for employed caregivers to drop their work and deal with family crises). The estimated average cost to business, per caregiver employee, was $1142 a year: $69 allocable to absenteeism, $85 to partial absenteeism, $657 for workday interruptions, $189 for crisis tasks, and $141 for supervisory involvement.

In addition, employers spent close to $5 billion a year to replace employees who had to quit their paid jobs because they were no longer able to balance caregiving and employment. Even in the employer's best-case scenario—when a person who wasn't doing a very good job even before caregiving began quits and is replaced by a better-skilled and more productive person—hiring and training someone new is time-consuming and expensive. The worst-case scenario for the employer is losing a superior employee, who is replaced by someone who has a lot less to offer the company.

More than 17% of caregivers at Levels III–V (moderate to fairly intensive caregiving) told the surveyors that they had to take early retirement or quit their jobs because of their caregiving responsibilities—estimated at 4% a year (given the approximately four-year duration of the caregiving obligation). The Conference Board thinks that the cost of recruiting a replacement and bringing him or her up to speed is about 75% of the salary of the replaced employee.

About 10% of the Level III–V caregivers spent six workdays a year or more absent from work for caregiving-related reasons. Fifty-nine percent of employed Level III–V caregivers engaged in partial absenteeism: not missing an entire day of work, but coming in late, leaving early, taking a long lunch break, etc. It has been estimated that at least an hour a week (50 hours a year) is lost this way, over and above what caregivers can make up by staying late on other days, restricting other breaks, etc. Level III–V caregivers were also estimated to lose an hour a week to interruptions during the day, such as receiving or making telephone calls related to the care needs of the elderly parent or in-law. Another three days a year were lost to coping with crises: the elderly relative's hospitalization or move to a nursing home, for instance.

MetLife stresses that the $11.4 billion figure is an extremely conservative estimate, because it takes into account only caregivers who are employed full time and who provide care at Levels III–V (i.e., moderate to very heavy levels of care). If the 8.7 million caregivers who work part time, or who provide Levels I and II of care (very light to light), are considered, the productivity impact could be over **$29 billion** a year.

Furthermore, caregivers add direct costs to the employer's health plan. Because caregiving is so stressful, caregivers are unusually heavy consumers of health and counseling services.

Women Caregivers

A May 1998 white paper, "Work and Elder Care: Facts for Caregivers and Their Employers," was issued by the Department of Labor's Women's Bureau and can be found at the DOL's Web site, http://www.dol.gov/dol/wb/public/wb_pubs/elderc.htm. This is a very useful, free, and public-domain resource; you're free to download it and reprint it for employees who need help with elder care. (It contains useful information about the various kinds of support services available to caregivers.) You can also place it on your HR Web site or intranet.

As the report says, "Women are more likely than men to be caregivers and to receive care, although an increasing number of men have parental responsibility.

Many caregivers are caring for both children and elders. Caregiving impacts on work, causing caregivers to come in late, work fewer hours, and even give up work or retire early."

According to the Women's Bureau, 72% of caregivers are female. The typical caregiver is a 46-year-old woman; the typical care recipient is the caregiver's 77-year-old, chronically ill mother. Caregiving lasts an average of 4.5 years (until the person receiving the care dies, enters an institution, or—in rare cases—recovers enough not to need care).

The Women's Bureau notes that 41% of caregivers are responsible for children under 18 as well as for elderly persons. On the average, they provide eight hours a week of direct, hands-on physical personal care to the elder, plus 3.7 more hours of indirect care tasks such as shopping and cooking. Women caregivers spend an average of 19.9 hours a week on caregiving, versus an average of only 11.8 hours for male caregivers.

What Employers Are Doing

It's not hard for corporate management to understand both the devastating impact of illness and frailty on a family (especially if the managers themselves are caregivers)—and of caregiving on corporate productivity. Although we don't have complete, current figures, it seems that approximately one-quarter to one-third of U.S. workers, at least in large companies, have access to some degree of employer assistance with caregiving. Providing intensive or comprehensive services is likely to exceed the pocketbook of nearly all employers, but there are many simple, cost-effective steps that an employer can do that will be extremely useful to caregiver-employees.

Information and referral (I&R) is the most popular employment-related caregiving service; 79% of employers offering elder care provided I&R, versus 25% providing long-term care insurance (usually on an employee-pay-all basis). Since much productivity is lost when employees have to do their own research into available elder care resources, providing complete, accurate information yields an immediate improvement in productivity. Other benefits offered by at least some employers include the following:

- Seminars about relevant topics (such as Medicare, Medicaid, and state- and charity-run programs available in the area)
- Support groups for caregivers
- Hotlines with elder care information
- Subsidized phone consultations with resource or elder care experts (including those in the parent's geographic area, if the caregiver child lives far away)
- Directories and other publications

- Caregiver fairs, with exhibits from the Social Security Administration and other public agencies as well as voluntary organizations and for-profit service vendors
- Counseling from a psychologist or clinical social worker
- Subsidies for adult day care for the parent
- Respite care
- Emergency care (including care in the home of the elderly person)
- Paratransit, such as wheelchair-compatible vans, to provide transportation to doctors' appointments and other trips that otherwise would require the employee's chauffeur services
- Subsidizing the cost of pagers that the parent can use to contact the employee in an emergency
- Case management—services of social workers or geriatric care manager (GCMs), who advise the employee about creating and managing a complete elder care plan for the parent's current and foreseeable future needs
- Adding elderly dependent parents to the coverage of dependent care accounts

In the unionized workplace, the AFL-CIO has prepared a worksheet titled "Bargaining for Eldercare," available from www.aflcio.com. It's worth a look so you can see the kinds of issues that are likely to be brought to the bargaining table.

Although it is quite costly for the employer to add LTCI as an employee benefit (especially if employees can get coverage for their parents), employee-pay-all LTCI coverage costs the employer little. There are many excellent free or low-cost elder care resources already available, and a basic I&R program can be created very inexpensively by collecting, indexing, and distributing these resources and working closely with local philanthropic and government organizations benefiting the elderly.

What Employers Can Do

In a spring 1998 speech to the Northern Illinois Society for Human Resource Management and Northwest Human Resources Council, Joy Loverde suggested criteria for a compassionate, cost-effective corporate eldercare program. (See West Employment Alert, 5/14/98, p. 7.) An optimal program

- Educates employees
- Alerts employees to responsibility they can be taking for their parents' (or other recipients') elder care
- Teaches employees to share caregiving and create an informal network

- Motivates employees by focusing on caregivers' needs rather than elders' needs
- Provides employees with psychological tools for discussing sensitive matters with family members

As the main volume notes, employers can provide long-term care insurance. Even if employees pay the full premium cost themselves, this is a valued benefit—especially if the employees can get coverage for their parents under the same plan. Note that the amount of benefits that can be received tax-free under an LTCI policy increased from $175/day (for 1998) to $180/day (for 1999).

BWLS Results

The Business and Work Life Study also covered employers' elder care activities. I&R was the major corporate activity, provided by 23% of the survey respondents and under consideration by another 5%. Nine percent allowed coverage of family members in the LTCI plan, and another 12% were considering adding this. Only 5% offered direct financial support for local elder care programs, and only 2% were contemplating doing so in the future. Most respondents (60%) considered their elder care investment cost neutral; 19% thought costs outweighed benefits, and only 21% viewed the elder care investment as offering positive economic benefits.

Chapter 5

Diversity in the Workplace

5.4 ENGLISH-ONLY RULES

As of early 1999, almost half the statutes (most of them in the South or Northwest) had passed statutes declaring English to be the official language of the state. (This information comes from Alejandro Bodipo-Memba, "Wage Gap Widens in 'English Only' States," *WSJ* 2/25/99, p. A2.) Such laws were present in Alabama, Alaska, Arkansas, California, Colorado, Florida, Georgia, Hawaii, Illinois, Indiana, Kentucky, Louisiana, Massachusetts, Mississippi, Missouri, Montana, Nebraska, New Hampshire, North Carolina, South Carolina, North Dakota, South Dakota, Tennessee, Virginia, and Wyoming. The statutes usually include exemptions in certain situations, such as the criminal trial of a non-English-speaking person, or when promotion of health and safety requires communication in another language. About 40 municipalities also had similar laws of their own.

According to the Federal Reserve Bank of Atlanta, in states with English-only laws, men who were not fluent in English earned an average of 9.3% less than fluent English speakers (Hispanic males with limited English skills earned 10.3% less in states with English-only laws than in the other states). However, the wages of women who were not fluent in English did not differ significantly in the two groups of states (perhaps because many women for whom English is not a first language work in domestic or factory jobs where little communication with the public is required).

The Arizona Constitution forbids state officers and employees to use any language other than English in their jobs, but the Arizona Supreme Court struck this down as a violation of the First Amendment and of the Fourteenth Amendment's Equal Protection guarantee [*Ruiz v. Hull*, 66 LW 1683 (Az. Sup. 4/28/98)].

According to the EEOC's David Lopez, 32 challenges to English-only rules were filed by the EEOC in FY 1996, with 14 more in the first quarter of fiscal 1997 alone. (See 66 LW 2375.)

5.5 PROMOTING DIVERSITY

The Society for Human Resource Management (SHRM) 1998 survey discussed in *Employment Alert* (8/20/98, p. 12) showed that 75% of the *Fortune* 500 had structured diversity programs, and only 36% of a general sample of companies did so. This is understandable—smaller or less-established companies have less money available for nonemergency, non-bottom-line projects. The survey costs $39.95 for non-SHRM members, $29.95 for members, and can be purchased from http://www.shrm.org/shrmstore or (800) 444-5006.

Three-quarters of survey respondents were satisfied with their diversity programs, but only about half of *Fortune* 500 companies, and about one-third of other companies, actually had metrics to gauge program success. Few companies (about a quarter of *Fortune* 500, a tenth of other companies) make success in promoting diversity a factor in top executives' compensation.

Ten percent of the *Fortune* 500 and 5% of other companies consider diversity skills in assessing performance, but not in setting compensation; 6% and 1%, respectively, consider diversity performance for compensation only; and 58% of the *Fortune* 500, 79% of other companies, do not use diversity as a criterion for judging managers at all. (See Patricia Digh, "The Next Challenge: Holding People Accountable," *HR Magazine*, 10/98, p. 63.)

Nearly all firms with diversity programs considered employee diversity training an important component of the program. *Fortune* 500 and smaller firms provided about equal amounts of diversity training: an average of 8.63 hours a year for middle managers, 7.3 hours/year for top managers, and 5.3 annual hours for nonexecutive employees.

The good news is that commitment to diversity often translates into improved performance. A survey done by the American Management Association (AMA) and the Business and Professional Women's Foundation (BPW) showed that the average 1997 sales growth rate for companies led by white males was an impressive 13%. Does this mean that companies need a traditional Caucasian male leadership to succeed? No, because the average sales growth rate was 20.2% where senior management included African-, Asian- and Hispanic-Americans, and 22.9% in companies where the majority of top management was female. The survey can be ordered from AMA's Eric Rolfe Greenberg, (212) 903-8052, or Gail Shaffer (BPW), (202) 293-1100; the survey is discussed in Robert W. Thompson, "Executive Briefing," *HR Magazine*, 4/99, p. 10.

Chapter 6

The Role of the Computer in HR

6.1 INTRODUCTION

Large-scale enterprise resource planning (ERP) software cannot only handle routine HR tasks, but can add immense power to interpret data about the corporation's workforce. At first, this power was available only in very expensive proprietary products, beyond the reach of all but the *Fortune* 500 and requiring extensive user training. Today, software vendors like SAP and PeopleSoft are not only offering smaller-scale, easier-to-use, more affordable packages—they are moving from proprietary standards to simple Web interfaces. So the products can be put to use right away, with little or no training cost. (See Jim Meade, "Adapting to the Shifting Software Market," *HR Magazine*, "Focus," 5/99, p. 3.)

See Chapter 1 for a discussion of the impact of the Internet on hiring practices.

6.2 DOING RESEARCH ON THE NET

Significant human resources/benefits information is available online. Most of it is free, although some sites include a members-only component, sell publications for which there is a charge, or require a paid subscription.

Nearly all federal agencies have at least one Website. To say the least, these vary in quality, attractiveness, and comprehensiveness. They also tend to be somewhat crash-prone, so be sure to close all your desktop files before pointing your browser at a government site. At least that way, you won't lose any data if you have to reboot your computer.

The best government sites (such as http://www.irs.ustreas.gov) are cornucopias of useful forms, explanations, and news summaries about, as well as the text of, new regulations. It's worth checking on a regular basis to see, for instance, if the Pension and Welfare Benefits Administration (PWBA) or Occupational Safety and

Health Administration (OSHA) has proposed or implemented any new rules; if there will be hearings nearby at which you will want to testify; or if new forms and publications are available.

Also note that the National Labor Relations Board (NLRB) makes its forms for unfair labor practice charges and election petitions available at its Web site (http://www.nlrb.gov), so you may face additional charges or organization drives in light of the increased availability.

The following sites are worth looking into:

- Society for Human Resource Management (SHRM): http://www.shrm.org, SHRM Online. This superlative site features a library; job bank; many links; a bookstore; significant features for members (including information about local chapter activities); a directory of consultants; white papers; and news coverage (including international issues). The research resources include an index to *HR Magazine* and some stories; over 150 white papers; government affairs backgrounders on regulatory and legislative issues; and numerous newsletters. Some publications from other publishers are also available at this site, but access is usually limited to SHRM members.
- BNA Human Resources Library, part of http://www.bna.com; trial subscriptions are handled through http://subscript.bna.com/trialref (no www). In addition to primary sources such as federal and state laws, this site contains analysis and model forms.
- BenefitsLink. A really fine and comprehensive site, put together by David Rhett Baker, with lots of interactive features (message boards and Q&A columns with experts); a directory of services and products for the HR department; and information about HR software as well as a great deal of software and many documents that can be downloaded right from the site: http://www.benefitslink.com/index.shtml.
- Employment Law Links. For information about sites dealing with various legal issues, see http://www.contilaw.com/links.html. Another "links list" is found at http://www.mtsu.edu/~rlhannah/employee_benefits.html.
- RIA InsideHR HR Wire (http://www.insidehr.com/HRwire/default/asp. Weekly print newsletter linked to a Web site; trial subscriptions are free. As of February 1999, the regular price for a year's subscription is $500. The HR Wire news service deals with laws, regulations, and compliance strategies.
- Cornell University's Workindex, http://www.workindex.com. Indexes sites dealing with subjects like human resources, labor relations, child and elder care, employee communications, and the labor force and labor market.
- Department of Labor eLaws, http://www.dol.gov/elaws/. eLaws stands for Employment Laws Assistance for Workers and Small Business; it's an interactive compliance assistance tool made up of chapters called "advisors." There are 18 advisors. Most of them can be read from your browser, but some have

to be downloaded and installed on your hard drive. The advisors deal with employment standards; mine safety; occupational safety; veterans' affairs; and pension and welfare benefits. The Small Business Retirement Savings Program Advisor, created by the Pension & Welfare Benefits Administration (PWBA), is a detailed comparison chart about simplified employee pensions (SEP) and SIMPLE IRAs (an IRA-type plan offered by the employer rather than set up by the individual), 401(k) plans, and conventional pension plans, comparing their advantages, which employers are permitted to offer them how they are funded the employer's role etc.

- OSHA Expert Systems: http://www.osha.gov/oshasoft. OSHA furnishes free software to help employers identify hazards and estimate the cash benefits of implementing a sound safety program.
- Ross Runkel's Employment Law Page: http://www.rossrunkel.com. Runkel, a labor law professor, has great resources on his site, including e-mail newsletters about the EEOC and the NLRB.
- Work and Family from the *Wall Street Journal.* Jan Wilson hosts a radio talk show on Saturday morning, 10 A.M. to noon Eastern time (toll-free at 800-WSJ-TALK). The show is "Webcast" (broadcast on the Internet) at http://www.wsjradio.com/affils.html#family.
- www.hr-esource.com. A group of related sites, including HR Wire, EEO Advisor, Compensation & Benefits Advisor, and Human Resource Advisor.
- As its name suggest, Lawnewsnetwork is aimed at attorneys. However, its free daily e-mail newsletter and subscription-based employment law site are written clearly enough to offer the HR professional tremendous insights into the evolving law of the workplace. See http://www.lawnewsnet.com.

The company HR Direct, which sells personnel products such as paper forms for the HR department HR software training and motivational materials and HR software has a mail order catalog, (800) 346-1231, and a site at http://www.hrdirect.com.

6.4 CREATING AND MANAGING AN INTRANET

A large workforce, or even a smaller workforce disseminated among several work locations, can make it expensive to send communications by mail or memorandum. Employees don't always like getting a memo blizzard; they often prefer to have access to a centralized bank of information, then decide what to read. (Naturally, the employer must continue to deliver all legally mandated notices, whether or not any employee actually bothers to read them! For information about using electronic media to give plan participants notices or secure their consent to elections, see 63 FR 70071 [12/18/98]: IRS Notice of Proposed Rulemaking, "New Technologies in Retirement Plans.")

When Sedgwick Noble Lowndes talked to 327 midsized companies in the fall of 1998, the majority of them (60%) either already used an intranet for HR and benefit communications (including a comprehensive benefit statement disclosing all of the employee's benefit elections and costs) or anticipated doing so in the future. Only one-fifth planned to use a Web site for similar purposes—no doubt the disparity is due to the greater privacy and security available on an intranet. About a quarter (26%) used or wanted to use an intranet to instruct employees about benefit elections available to them. Twenty-four percent used or intended to use their intranet to collect personal data about employees and to distribute data to employees; the same percentage showed an interest in using an intranet to enroll employees in benefit programs. One-fifth used or intended to use an intranet for 401(k) and retirement information.

Of course, one limitation on the usefulness of a corporate intranet is limited access on the part of employees. In 41% of the surveyed firms, 80 to 100% of the workforce had access to the company's intranet or were expected to gain access within a year. In 9% of the respondent companies, 61 to 80% of the staff had access to the intranet. In 22% of the companies, intranet access was 20% or below. Note that there are mechanisms for giving employees access to intranet benefits information without putting a computer on every desktop.

➠ TIP

Touch-screen kiosks, or a few dedicated computer terminals, can be placed in the HR office, the employee assistance program (EAP) office, or the cafeteria or breakroom, so that non-computer-using employees can use the intranet for this specific purpose.

Amoco handled its intranet implementation by splitting the intranet into an HR component (comprising HR publications, business unit information, benefits information, volunteer information, and ads posted by employees who wanted to sell personal items) and a benefits component (the employee benefits handbook; personnel policies; and links to relevant Internet sites, such as financial planning sites).

Motorola took a dramatic but risky step: It simply eliminated all paper forms and correspondence related to HR. The upshot was a saving of $1.5 million, but there were hard-to-estimate losses with respect to employees who needed additional technical support. This information comes from "Intranet Delivery of HR and Benefits Information," WestGroup Employment Alert, 2/19/98, p. 2; and "More Midsized Firms Communicate Benefits Information Through Intranets," *RIA Compensation & Benefits Update*, 10/7/98, p. 6. Sedgwick's site is http://www.sedgwick.com; the survey is called the 1998 Employee Benefits Minisurvey.

In April of 1998, the International Foundation of Employee Benefit Plans looked at the use of Internet and intranet technology to communicate about employee benefits. The Foundation got 433 respondents to its survey; 125 respondents were already employing Internet and/or intranet communications. Of that small group, only a quarter had been using the Internet/intranet for over one year; a third had been online for less than six months. Three-quarters of the users cited the speed of transmitting information and getting feedback as an advantage of Net communications; two-thirds favored the ability to reduce distribution of printed materials; and about half cited increased efficiency and ease of administration. The respondents were worried about some aspects of online benefits communications, though: for example, limited access by employees to computers, their lack of familiarity with the technology, and issues of privacy, security, and liability. Forty-three percent of users implemented more than one security measure; 185 used passwords, 10% had a firewall, 7% required PIN numbers, and only 1% used encryption; 15% had no security measures in place at all.

Twelve percent of Internet users said they were very satisfied with its performance; 32% were satisfied, 29% somewhat satisfied, and 115 neutral. Only 6% were "very dissatisfied" with the Internet communications experience.

The Net was frequently used in connection with both health benefits and pensions. Two-thirds of the Net users posted summary plan description (SPDs) for health plans on an intranet (but only 2% used the Internet for this purpose); 19% permitted intranet viewing of current benefit elections, versus only 3% using the Internet. One-fifth used the Internet to post directories of physicians participating in the health plan, and 12% used an intranet for this purpose. Understandably, Internet use is limited in an area that can involve both proprietary corporate information and employee privacy.

Pension plan SPDs were on view on 47% of the intranet sites (5% used the Internet for this purpose). Quarterly reports and fund balances could be seen on 14% of intranets and 19% of corporate Internet sites. Viewing Frequently Asked Questions could be done on 21% of intranet and 6% of Internet sites. Furthermore, 48% of the intranet sites posted the employee handbook.

Two-thirds of those not already online for employee benefits expressed a desire to do so in the future. For 23% of the nonusers, the limiting factor was employees' lack of Internet access; 10% were stymied by the cost of implementation, and 9% couldn't find the time for implementation. IFEBP's survey report, "Communicating Employee Benefits Via the Web," is available from the IFEBP, (414) 786-6700, www.ifepb.org.

One advantage of a corporate internet is that it can combine some of the advantages of the broader public Internet while limiting improper or nonproductive online use by employees. SurfWatch Software (Los Altos, California) reports that, based on data supplied by the CheckNet software program, which measures Internet use at work, almost 25% of the time that employees spend online is not work related. The top five nonwork areas are general news; sex; investment; entertainment; and sports. (See Bill Leonard, "Nearly a Quarter of Time Online is Nonwork Related," *HR Magazine*, 11/98, p. 26; SurfWatch's Web address is http://www.surfwatch.com.)

6.6 [NEW] HR IMPLICATIONS OF Y2K

Y2K problems—those caused by computer systems that display dates with two rather than four digits, making it unclear whether "00" or "01" represents 1900–1901 or 2000–2001—affect every part of the enterprise. Computer systems may have difficulty processing information relating to long-term contracts that extend past the turn of the century. There are some problems specific to the corporation's HR functions. Even before January 1, 2000, problems are likely to arise: For instance, when workers present health-plan cards with expiration dates in the twenty-first century, hospital or pharmacy computer systems may reject them, resulting in problems securing treatment.

Pension plans are especially likely to be affected because of their mission of providing long-range financial security to workers. The plan (and its administrators) may fail to live up to their fiduciary obligations to participants and beneficiaries—and such fiduciary failures may be the occasion of liability. The Pension and Welfare Benefits Administration (PWBA; part of the Department of Labor) has issued a useful document, available on the Internet at http://www.dol.gov/dol/pwba/public/pubs/72kgui~1.htm. Also see the Y2K Q&A on the PWBA site.

According to the PWBA, fiduciaries have an obligation to participants and beneficiaries to see that the plan's computers are Y2K compliant. (Noncompliance is very likely to lead to payment problems, or at least delays.) Investment decisions must also be taken with Y2K in mind—(e.g., it is not prudent to retain an investment advisor who is not ready for Y2K). The plan, its sponsor, its service providers, and companies in which it invests should all be compliant.

Of course, plan fiduciaries aren't supposed to tinker with the computer software themselves (unless they have the necessary skills); prudence frequently dictates retaining a qualified Y2K consultant. It may even be necessary to replace the entire computer system. The fiduciary should also create a contingency plan in case it becomes impossible to carry out normal pension plan operations.

Any company that becomes the subject of a PWBA civil investigation will automatically be subjected to Y2K review, and a warning will be issued if PWBA deems that Y2K problems are a risk for the plan's participants and beneficiaries. For instance, the plan will be queried as to who in the organization is responsible for Y2K compliance; who the Y2K contractor is (if any) and how the contractor was chosen; if there is a compliance assessment and contingency plan; and what information participants have been given about potential Y2K impact.

➠ TIP

OSHA also warns of the necessity to check devices with embedded computer chips: everything from respirators to construction site elevators, if workers could be endangered if the devices stop working or function erratically after 1/1/2000.

Chapter 7

Compensation Planning

7.1 INTRODUCTION

It is sometimes assumed that stock prices follow one inevitable trend: upward. This is not, of course, a rational assumption. Stock options are awarded to all employees, or to especially valued employees, as an incentive, so that they can buy stock at an artificially low price and eventually earn a large capital gain profit by selling the stock.

This scenario won't work (and the incentive effect won't be present) if the options are "underwater": that is, the price at which the employee is permitted to buy stock is actually higher than the market price of the shares. Therefore, companies—especially companies that have to recruit crucial employees in a highly competitive market—have an incentive to reprice their options by canceling a grant of options and issuing a new grant that can be exercised profitably.

The big problem with repricing is that the company's stockholders usually oppose repricing, because it benefits corporate executives but not the stockholders themselves. In fact, it can harm stockholders directly, by sending a signal to the market that the company itself doesn't think its stock price is going to improve. Two major surveys, released in December 1998, showed that about 90% of companies would not reprice their options, even though most of them had at least some options that were above the market price. However, in a highly competitive industry, once one company decides to reprice, other companies may feel constrained to follow.

One way to balance stockholder against executive interests is to modify the stock option plan in connection with repricing: Executives could get a smaller number of lower-price options, or accept an extended vesting period (length of time between grant of the option and the date it can be exercised).

Option repricing is discussed in Stephenie Overman's article, "Stock Options: Reprice or Hold Fast?," *HR Magazine*, 4/99, p. 82.

7.4 INNOVATIVE PAY SYSTEMS

Almost three-quarters of U.S. companies have at least some variable pay element in their compensation system. A variable pay plan gives employees access to performance-based awards reflecting that year's performance but that do not get built into base pay. In 1990, companies devoted only 4.2% of total payroll to variable pay; the corresponding figure forecast for 1999 is 7.8%. Furthermore, in 1997, 85% of employees eligible to receive an award got one, so implementing a plan, or adding to the number of eligible employees, can be expected to have a significant impact on payroll. Variable pay is an important part of executive compensation, but many organizations allow variable pay for rank-and-filers.

However, only 22% of companies that offer such plans feel that they more than satisfied their business objective for implementing the plan. About half are neutral, and 28% report that the plan did not meet the business objectives that inspired it. The most successful measure (90% of companies offering it cited positive business results) was calculated on the basis of financial and operating results for the company, the employee's business unit, or his or her own results. Employers attributed positive results to cash variable pay plans 84% of the time—much better than stock options, which were considered to improve business results only 63% of the time.

Because the plans are supposed to create incentives for better work, communication is key. Formal annual review explaining how the award was calculated is useful in pinpointing areas in which employees succeeded and those in which more work is necessary. The most effective plans had "moderate stretch" (i.e., they asked employees to achieve targets that were not comfortably in view but were far from impossible).

The Hewitt survey is discussed in "Variable Compensation Plans Increasing and Improving, But Still Delivering Mixed Results," http://www.hewitt.com/news/pressrel/1998/10-07-98.htm, and "Variable Compensation Plans Often Miss the Mark," RIA *Compensation & Benefits Update,* 3/25/98, p. 6.

Speaking of bonuses, ECS/Watson Wyatt Data Services reported in 1998 that about two-thirds of a large (10,000+) sample of top managers got at least some of their compensation from bonus awards. The typical bonus award was about one-third of base pay. Over four-fifths of executives whose bonuses were premised on satisfying a target achieved the target and received a bonus award.

Just over half (51.6%) of respondents also provided deferred compensation plans for top management—and usually only top management were eligible for the deferred compensation plan.

To order the "1998/1999 ECS Survey of Top Management Compensation," contact ECS/Watson Wyatt Data Services at http://wyattconsult.com (no www) or (201) 843-1177; see "Bonuses, Deferred Compensation Typify Pay Plans for Top Management," *Compensation & Benefits Update,* 8/12/98, p. 5.

Although variable compensation is often disappointing to the company offering the plan, broadbanding has been much more successful. A broadbanding plan eliminates finely tuned salary grades and groups several job titles into one pay band. The most common factor in setting compensation for each band is comparison with market salaries for similar work.

Eighty-seven percent of those surveyed by ACA/Hewitt were pleased with the outcome of broadbanding (although hardly any of the companies had a formal tracking procedure; they reported a subjective belief). Almost a third of respondents planned to expand the use of broadbanding for compensation. ACA/Hewitt noted that few companies have a formal training program to explain broadbanding, and its place within general career development, to employees. Whatever communications occurred tended to be via passive print materials, such as brochures, not face-to-face discussion. The study "Living With Broadbanding in 1998" is reported in RIA's *Compensation and Benefits Update*, 5/20/98, p. 10. Call the American Compensation Association (ACA), (602) 922-2020, for ordering information.

7.5 BENEFITS AS AN ELEMENT OF COMPENSATION

What differentiates the companies that *Fortune* anoints as the "100 Best Companies to Work For in America" from 100 other companies that came close but didn't make the cut? *Fortune* studies ten areas of HR practice, including worklife programs; financial incentives; how personnel are hired and trained; and how the organization's culture functions. The top companies get almost twice as many applications as next-level companies of comparable size, so they have a better talent pool to choose from. The top companies lose about one-eighth of their employees each year to voluntary quits, which sounds pretty bad until you realize that companies on the next level have a 26% turnover rate.

Two-thirds of the 100 Best companies are public companies, so corporate stock can be a potent motivator. (In the other third, perhaps a family atmosphere makes up for lack of access to stock market riches.) Sixty percent of the publicly traded 100 Best had broad-based stock options or grant programs—significantly more than the 43% of next-tier companies that had them. In half of the 100 Best companies, more than 80% of employees owned stock in the company (whether awarded or purchased on the open market).

The 100 Best companies provided a median of a full day more of training—40 versus 32 hours in the next-tier companies—and both administrative/support staff and managers had access to training on more equal terms than in the next tier of companies. The 100 Best were much more likely to provide career counseling, mentoring, and academic courses.

Above all, the 100 Best companies attract and retain employees with superior working conditions, including generous benefit packages. The report lists nine health and wellness benefits (e.g., health club discounts; workout facilities on site;

stress reduction programs). All of them were much more commonly found in the 100 Best than in the next tier. The same was true of convenience and personal benefits, such as an in-plant cafeteria or meal subsidies; take-home meals; assistance with buying a home; and discounts on entertainment for those precious (and perhaps rare) off-duty hours. Fifty-six percent of the second-tier companies allowed casual dress every day—61% of the 100 Best companies did this. (This information comes from "Hewitt Associates Shows How the 100 Best Companies Get Their Edge," http://www.hewitt.com/news/pressrel/1998/12-28-98.htm.)

7.6 SEVERANCE PAY

Section 7001 of the IRS Restructuring and Reform Act of 1998, P.L. 105-206, provides that, when deciding whether money constitutes "deferred compensation" under Code §404(a), the money is not considered to be paid or received until it is actually received by the employee. Although the statute has its greatest applicability in the context of nonqualified deferred compensation plans for executives, the statute was passed to overturn *Schmidt Baking Co.*, 107 Tax Court 271, a case involving a company's accrued liabilities for severance and vacation pay.

A settlement award to a laid-off employee, reflecting his age, years of service, and earnings impairment, constituted "wages" for income and FICA tax purposes, according to the Eighth Circuit [*Mayberry v. U.S.*, 151 F.3d 855 (8th Cir. 1998)]. The court did not accept the employee's contention that the sum was a nontaxable personal injury award because it replaced wages and was not the product of settling tort claims.

Severance and Separation Benefits, published by Lee Hecht Harrison (Woodcliff Lake, N.J.), is a study designed to answer questions about severance policies and their competitive effects. Free copies are available from the company at (800) 611-4544; Lee Hecht Harrison's Web site is http://www.ihh.com. (See "How Does Your Severance Policy Stack Up?" *RIA Compensation & Benefits Update*, 2/10/99, p. 5.)

Over 1800 companies responded to the survey. Most of them (83%) have a formal, written policy that entitles all full-time employees to a severance benefit (calculated using base pay and number of years of service) if they are RIFed or their job is eliminated by downsizing. Almost half of respondents (48%) also granted severance benefits to part-timers, and 7% even provided severance to temporary and contract workers. Almost all respondents continued medical benefits posttermination, and close to half of them continued life insurance benefits. Exempt employees, or at least some exempts, were offered outplacement assistance by about three-quarters of responding companies.

Severance was much less commonly offered when the employee's conduct was a factor in termination: 26% provided severance after a termination for poor performance, 13% in other terminations for cause, and 14% when an employee was asked to relocate but refused.

The most common allocation was one week of severance pay per year of service—a measure used for 70% of nonexempt employees, 66% of exempt employees, 57% of executives, and 51% of corporate officers. Next most common was two weeks per year of work, offered in about 20% of plans.

About a quarter of respondents allow appeals if employees feel their severance benefits have not been calculated correctly. To avoid future problems, about 70% of survey respondents condition severance payments on signing a release of employment-related claims. (But see §26.3 for a discussion of how to draft acceptable ADEA releases.)

Chapter 8

Wage and Hour Issues

8.1 INTRODUCTION

According to the Bureau of Labor Statistics (http://stats.bls.gov), in 1997 wage and benefit costs rose 3.3%, as compared to 2.9% in 1996 and 2.7% in 1995. The 1997 figure was made up of a 3.8% increase in wage costs but a much lower increase in benefit costs (2.1%). If private industry was broken out from the economy as a whole, its costs increased somewhat more—3.9% increase in wage costs, 2.3% in enhanced benefit costs. Service workers scored the largest wage gain, at 4.0%, trailed by 3.8% for white collar and 2.6% for blue collar workers.

A mid-1998 Massachusetts statute, H.B. 5746 (signed August 7, 1998), imposes higher criminal penalties for wage and hour violations (violations of laws about minimum and prevailing wages, overtime pay, and classification of employees). The new penalty structure permits a fine of up to $10,000 and/or six months' imprisonment even for a nonwillful violation ($25,000 and/or one year for subsequent nonwillful violations). Initial willful violations can be penalized by a fine of up to $25,000 and/or six months' imprisonment, subsequent willful violations by up to $50,000 and/or two years in prison. Furthermore, the state's Attorney General has the power to impose civil penalties by citation in wage law cases, and intent affects only the size of the penalty. Penalties of up to $25,000 per violation can be imposed.

The Fair Labor Standards Act (FLSA) allows the pay of hourly workers—but not salaried workers—to be docked for absenteeism. DOL Opinion Letter No. 89 (discussed in *Employment Alert*, 3/5/98, p. 11) says that making a deduction from a paycheck to reflect unpaid leave under the Family and Medical Leave Act does not convert an otherwise exempt person into a nonexempt wage worker. However, this relief provision is limited to FMLA leave, where both the worker and the employer firm are subject to the FMLA.

8.2 MINIMUM WAGE

➠ TIP

If you require uniforms to be worn during working hours, and employees must supply their own, make sure that the cost of the uniforms doesn't drive their overall compensation below the minimum wage. This point comes from Simon J. Nadel, "Employers Relaxing Dress Standards But Potential Pitfalls Remain in Workplace," 67 LW 2195 (10/13/98).

8.4 THE CONTINGENT WORKFORCE

In December, 1997 the EEOC published guidance on contingent workers as part of its internal compliance manual. (See http://www.eeoc.gov/press/12-8-97.html, discussed at 66 LW 2359.) Based on information from the National Association of Temporary and Staffing Services showing that more than 2.3 million workers are employed by the temporary help industry, the EEOC stated that agencies and employers are both generally liable for civil rights violations committed in the placement of contingent workers.

If both the staffing firm and its client have control over the worker, then both are joint employers. The staffing agency has the burden of taking immediate and appropriate action (such as refusing to assign any more workers) if it finds that a client company has practiced discrimination against a temporary worker.

➠ TIP

The guidance also notes that individuals in welfare-to-work programs are covered under federal antidiscrimination laws.

The important case of *Bronk v. Mountain States Telephone & Telegraph Inc.*, 98-1 USTC ¶50,316 (10th Cir. 1998), holds that, although ERISA forbids excluding employees from the plan once they have satisfied minimal age and service conditions, it is permissible to draft the plan to deny participation to leased employees, even if they are common-law employees. The Tenth Circuit's position (which is not exactly the same as that of the Ninth Circuit; see later) is that IRC §414(n)(1)(A) merely requires that leased employees be treated as employees—it does not require them to be offered plan participation. The decision quotes IRS Notice 84-11, Q&A 14, to support the permissibility of keeping leased employees out of the plan.

The Ninth Circuit reversed the trial court in *Burrey v. Pacific Gas & Electricity*, 1998 WL 727284 (9th Cir. 1998). According to the appeals court, people who had worked at Pacific Gas & Electricity (for 12 years!) through a temp agency were not §414(n) leased employees.

For FLSA purposes, a staffing company and its client companies do not become coemployers. The staffing company is the FLSA employer of temps provided to client companies, because the staffing company hires and controls the workers, assigns them to job sites, and controls their schedules [*Baystate Alternative Staffing Inc. v. Herman*, 67 LW 1480 (1st Cir. 12/30/98)].

In contrast, the Occupational Safety and Health Review Commission decided that an employee leasing company was *not* subject to the Occupational Safety and Health Act, because the workers were not their employees. In this reading, employees work in the employer's "business," and here the leased workers were assigned to a factory where the leasing company did not exercise significant control over them [*Sec'y of Labor v. Team America Corp.*, 1998 WL 733708 (OSHRC 1998)].

¶10.2 of the main volume discusses the *Vizcaino v. Microsoft* case. On May 12, 1999, the Ninth Circuit rendered another *Vizcaino* decision, #98-71388, 99-35013. Originally, in 97 F.3d 1187 (9th Cir. 1995), aff'd 120 F.3d 1006 (9th Cir. 1997), the Ninth Circuit decided that members of the class action were really Microsoft employees, not independent contractors, and therefore entitled to participate in Microsoft's stock purchase plan. (For background on Microsoft's very large contingent workforce, see Steven Greenhouse, "Equal Work, Less-Equal Perks," *New York Times*, 3/30/98, p. D1.) The case was sent back to the District Court to sort out the rights of individual plaintiffs. The District Court narrowed down the plaintiff class to certain temp agency employees and workers reclassified as common-law employees by the IRS, and who worked at Microsoft between 1978 and 1990. Microsoft tried to narrow the class down even further, and plaintiffs and potential plaintiffs tried to widen it.

The May 1999 decision by the Ninth Circuit held that temp agency workers could still be common-law employees of Microsoft (and thus entitled to participate in the stock plan) if they also satisfy the common-law control tests. The Ninth Circuit remanded the case to the District Court *again* but required a broader class definition. Microsoft had to prove any reason why a particular person who either came from a temporary agency or was reclassified by the IRS should not have been allowed to participate in the stock purchase plan.

An article by Frederick D. Baron, Carrie Battilega, and Mitch Danzig, "Workforce 2000: Alternative Staffing Arrangements," http://www.lawnewsnetwork.com/practice/employmentlaw/papers/lawfirm/A1487-1999May14.html, gives some practical suggestions for problem-free use of temporary workers:

- Have a written contract with the temp agency, clarifying the status of the workers.
- Don't train the temporary workers at your site; make sure that the temp agency provides any needed training.
- Check to make sure the temporary agency maintains appropriate Worker's Compensation coverage for its staff.

- If you ask your employees to sign confidentiality agreements, you can impose the same requirement on temps—but use a separate form that refers to their status as such.
- Want to hire a temp for your permanent workforce? Make it clear to the new hire that his or her start date is the date he or she became permanent (unless your counsel advises you that the new hire must be counted as an employee as of an earlier date).

Baron et al. discuss an emerging form of staffing: the Professional Employer Organization, or PEO. The PEO and its client are joint employers, and therefore have joint responsibility for the people who work under this arrangement. The PEO takes care of HR tasks, while the client trains, manages, and supervises the staffers referred by the PEO. (They are joint employers because each has meaningful employer-type responsibility, albeit in different roles.)

It's vital to make sure that you pay your appropriate share (e.g., of employment-related taxes and Worker's Compensation) and monitor compliance by the PEO of its obligations. In a 1996 bankruptcy case, the PEO client was considered responsible for payroll taxes, even though the contract with the PEO made the PEO responsible [*In re Earth Movers, Inc.*, 1996-2 USTC ¶50,549 (M.D. Fla. 1996)]. In short, a potential PEO arrangement should be scrutinized by your tax advisers, and any necessary adjustments should be made to your payroll system if you adopt the PEO as one of your staffing mechanisms.

8.5 WORK SCHEDULING

Boeing required new hires to go through an unpaid orientation period. A class action in Washington State court accepted the plaintiffs' contention that the orientation period was really work. The lower court required payment at the minimum wage for the orientation period; the Washington Court of Appeals required pay at the normal contract rate for the job [*Seattle Professional Engineering Employees Association v. Boeing*, 963 P.2d 204 (Wash. App. 1998)].

8.5.3 Fewer Hours, Same Pay

Compensation and Benefits Update's 10/7/98 issue (p. 3) gives a thorough treatment of the pros and cons of the 9/80 work schedule, where each work week runs from noon on Friday to noon on the next Friday and includes 40 working hours. However, the employees work nine hours a day on Monday through Thursday, eight hours on the first Friday in the pay period. The second Friday in the pay period is a day off. (It may be necessary to hire temps to cover the second Friday, or to pay employees overtime for working this day in addition to their normal 9/80 work schedule; and 9/80 won't work for customer service or managers who are expected to be available for client contact during normal 9-to-5, Monday-to-Friday times, and perhaps on weekends.)

Under California law, as long as the work week does not exceed eight hours, overtime pay is not required for the 9/80 schedule. A single shift can last up to 12 hours. However, the employer must hold a secret ballot and get consent of two-thirds of the workforce before changing the schedule.

According to the *Compensation and Benefits Update* article, cyclical companies with a strong orientation toward the needs of their clients are the best prospects for the 9/80 schedule. Another helpful factor is moving from separate programs for vacation days and sick days to a unified program for paid absences with no need to document the reason for the absence.

8.6 TELECOMMUTING

Although computer and Internet use has continued to grow, telecommuting has not achieved the predicted degree of success. FIND/SVP says that there were 8.5 million telecommuters in 1995, 9.7 million in 1996, and 11.1 million in 1997. At-home personal computer users added up to 5 million in 1995, 6.7 million in 1996, and 8.3 million in 1997, and e-mail users were 1.6 million, 2.7 million, and 3.4 million, respectively. (These figures come from Lin Grensing-Pophal's article, "Training Employees to Telecommute: A Recipe for Success," *HR Magazine*, 12/98, p. 76.)

The Olsten Center for Workforce Strategies reports that half of the businesses in the United States and Canada have a pilot or permanent project that allows at least some telecommuting, but many programs are being scaled back for failure to achieve efficiency and cost savings. Employees working at home can get burned out. Just knowing how to use the necessary technology isn't enough for a productive telecommuting experience; employees also need to learn how to schedule and coordinate work.

Managers back at the office need to know how to measure telecommuters' productivity—and keep in-house employees from becoming jealous of what seems to be a sweet deal for the telecommuters.

TIP

Some large companies have taken the pragmatic step of creating an in-house simulation lab to replicate telecommuting conditions. (Smaller companies can join forces to create a shared facility.) Some employees discover that they absolutely hate telecommuting conditions or can't be productive; it's best to find that out in advance, before disrupting everyone's schedule to allow and then phase out telecommuting for that person.

8.8 OVERTIME AND OVERTIME PLANNING

The Department of Labor's Wage and Hour Division handles about 40,000 complaints a year, and 70% of its investigations stem from employee complaints. In 1997, U.S. industry paid $63 million for back wages and penalties affecting over 125,000 employees. The DOL sued Iowa Beef Processors over 14 minutes of setup/cleanup work required of each employee each day. The suit resulted in an award of $7.1 million in back wages and interest. (See Carla Joinson, "Keeping Time," *HR Magazine*, 10/98, p. 120.)

In a similar case, the Tenth Circuit found that meat packers who were paid on "gang time," from the first animal part arriving at the workstation to the last, had to spend at least 10 minutes of compensable time before shift (to put on protective gear) and after shift (to clean up). Because this was not a trivial amount, and because the company was on notice because of other violations, the three-year statute of limitations for willful violations was applied, and the company had to pay $1.5 million in compensatory damages, plus pre- and postjudgment interest [*Reich v. Monfort, Inc.*, 144 F.3d 1329 (10th Cir. 1998)].

Many employees, especially those with family responsibilities, prefer comp time to overtime pay. However, the law requires comp time to be used in the same week as the overtime it compensates. If a nonexempt employee works more than 40 hours a week, overtime pay is required, even if the overtime was unauthorized. (The unauthorized work is a disciplinary, not a wage-and-hour, issue.) If supervisors are pressured to finish a certain amount of work in a certain amount of time, the company probably won't be able to claim that overtime was unauthorized. Raising output requirements or adding new projects may create an inference that overtime was required.

Wage-and-hour investigators look at real responsibilities and tasks and are not impressed by "title inflation," which makes a person sound like a manager when in fact he or she is really doing routine nonexempt tasks. A merger or acquisition could lead to reshuffling of titles and responsibilities and might result either in a promotion that makes a nonexempt person exempt or a demotion that has the contrary effect.

The following are some items that may require compensation or overtime:

- Rest breaks under 20 minutes
- Down time or on-call time that prevents the employee from pursuing personal business
- Preparation before shift; cleanup after shift
- Classes, meetings, and conventions that are mandatory rather than optional
- Unscheduled, or even unauthorized, work actually performed by the employee
- Travel time when the employee is away from home on business or moving between job sites (but not normal commuting)

If overtime is required, it must be paid at a rate of time-and-a-half, including shift differentials and call pay. If substantial bonuses are paid on a regular basis, they must be included in the hourly rate calculation.

Rig welders hired to work on particular projects sued for overtime pay—and won—in *Baker v. Flint Engineering & Construction Co.*, 137 F.3d 1436 (10th Cir. 1998). The Tenth Circuit viewed the economic realities of the job as characterizing the welders as employees rather than independent contractors, although they supplied their own tools. The tools were of fairly low value compared to the rigs they worked on, and they were told what and where to weld, making them more like employees than independent contractors.

An Alaskan's usual work schedule was two weeks on the job, two weeks off—but when he was working, he put in seven-day weeks averaging 14 hours a day. The employer's position was that, after a promotion, the plaintiff had become an exempt supervisor. Both the trial and the appellate courts agreed that the plaintiff was nonexempt, so there was a hefty overtime bill to be paid. The only question was *how* hefty. The trial court deducted 40 hours of straight time from the 98-hour work week, coming up with 2940 hours: 1200 hours straight time, 1740 hours overtime, adding up to $72,627.60 in unpaid overtime. But the appeals court said this was the wrong method. Instead, the worker's regular rate should be the basis for calculating total earnings for all hours actually worked; then the actual payments should be deducted. So the employee should have been paid $72,627.60 overtime, but he should also have been paid $33,396.00 for straight time, adding up to $106,023,60 overall. He was in fact paid $66,780 in total compensation, so the company actually owed him $39,243.60 for unpaid overtime. That's a big bill—but only about half of $72,627.60 [*Piquniq Management Corp. v. Reeves*, 1998 WL 775243 (Alaska 1998)].

As ¶23.8 shows, retaliation cases are a growing part of the employment discrimination caseload. In 1998, the Ninth Circuit tackled an FLSA retaliation case, in *Lambert v. Ackerly*, 156 F.3d 1018 (9th Cir. 1998). The plaintiffs used to work selling tickets for the Seattle SuperSonics. Initially, they were paid a $13,000 base salary plus commissions. The team made a $2000 allowance for overtime; after that, employees were told either to take comp time or stop working overtime. A productive sales rep could earn as much as $90,000 a year. The team changed the compensation system, telling the sales reps to work from 8:30 to 5:30 without overtime. The reps, not unnaturally, didn't like the new system and contacted the Department of Labor for information about overtime compensation. One of the plaintiffs claimed that the team's controller threatened her with firing if she kept up with the overtime issue. She, and five other people, were discharged. They sued under FLSA §215(a)(3)(the antiretaliation provision), which forbids discrimination against employees who file complaints or institute or testify at FLSA proceedings; they also claimed that their discharge violated the public policy of the state.

They did very well at the trial court level, getting not only compensatory damages but punitive damages and emotional distress damages. The Ninth Circuit dismissed the FLSA retaliation charges because the employees had not filed a complaint or testified at a hearing. Contacting the DOL doesn't reach the level of participating in formal legal proceedings.

Washington State law is more generous to employees: It bans retaliation against anyone who has complained to the employer or is "about to cause to be instituted" a wage and hour proceeding. Complaints by the plaintiff group therefore entitled them to protection against retaliation under state law, but not to punitive damages (because state law does not make this remedy available in wrongful termination cases).

8.12 TRUST FUND TAX COMPLIANCE AND THE 100% PENALTY

What is the status of nonqualified deferred compensation (e.g., "top hat" plans for executives) for Federal Insurance Contributions Act (FICA) and Federal Unemployment Tax Act (FUTA) purposes? IRS Final Regulations issued January 29, 1999, dealing with Code §3121, provide the answers. In general, wages are subject to FICA and FUTA when they are paid, or when they are considered "constructively" paid. Welfare plan benefits and severance pay are not considered deferred compensation. "Window benefits"—early retirement incentives that are available only for a limited time—are not considered deferred compensation if they are paid after January 1, 2000; before that, employers could elect to treat them as deferred compensation.

Nonqualified deferred compensation counts for FICA and FUTA either when the work giving rise to the compensation is done or when the right to collect the deferred amounts is no longer subject to a substantial risk of forfeiture—whichever comes later.

The Code includes "nonduplication" rules to make sure that the same amount is not subjected to FICA and FUTA both when the work is done and when the funds are actually paid out. Stock options are not considered deferred compensation as long as compensation is actually or constructively received in the year the option is exercised.

8.13 TAX DEPOSITS: PAPER FORMS

As a general rule, the IRS Web site is an excellent source of beautifully clear PDF forms that you can print out and file (The URL is http://www.ustreas.gov; click on the silly mailbox graphic, then scroll down the next page until you reach "Forms" at the bottom. What really happens then is that you are sent to http://ftp.fedworld.gov/pub/irs-pdf, an archive of tax forms that use the File Transfer Protocol, or ftp.)

However, several employment-related forms carry a notice that they appear on the site for information only and that printouts cannot be filed to satisfy compliance obligations. Some tax forms are printed in a special scanner-friendly machine-readable format using special links. You can order the machine-readable copies by calling 1-800-TAX-FORM (829-3676). IRS Publication 1167, "Substitute Printed, Computer-Prepared, and Computer-Generated Tax Forms and Schedules," and Publication 1179, "Specifications for Paper Document Reporting and Paper Substitutes for Forms 1096, 1098, 1099 Series, 5498, and W-2G," give the full story.

Chapter 9

Employee Group Health Plans (EGHPs)

9.2 CONTENT OF THE PLAN

A unionized company that wants its employees to pay 30% of the premium thereby has an obligation to release information to the union about the health care claims of nonunion employees and their dependents. Such information is not confidential, because the employer has opened up the issue of health care costs and cost containment [*U.S. Testing Co. v. NLRB*, 160 F.3d 14 (D.C. Cir. 1998)].

The Pension and Welfare Benefits Administration issued a major statement on the SPD requirements for health plans [62 FR 48376 (9/8/98)], dealing not only with the pension plan SPD (see Chapter 14) but with disclosures health plans must make with respect to Comprehensive Omnibus Budget Reconciliation Act (COBRA), Health Insurance Portability and Accountability Act (HIPAA) portability, and the Newborns' and Mothers' Health Protection Act.

Group health plan SPDs must include the following:

- Participants' cost-sharing obligations, such as premiums, deductibles, coinsurance, and copayments
- Caps (lifetime or annual) on plan benefits, or other benefit limits
- Coverage of preventive services
- Coverage (if any) of existing and new drugs
- Coverage of medical tests, devices, and procedures
- Which health care providers are inside the network
- Circumstances under which network providers must be used; coverage, if any, of out-of-network services
- How primary care and specialty providers must be selected

- Conditions for getting emergency care
- Requirements for preauthorization of treatment and utilization review

It's permissible for the SPD to include only a general description of the provider network, as long as the SPD discloses the availability of a separate document (furnished without charge) that lists all the network providers.

The Summary Plan Description for a health plan must describe the rights and responsibilities of employees and their families with respect to COBRA continuation coverage (see later)—(e.g., what constitutes a COBRA qualifying event; premiums ex-employees must pay for continuation coverage; notice procedures; how to make an election; and how long coverage will last). EGHP SPDs must either describe the plan's procedures with respect to qualified medical child support order (QMCSO) determination, or must inform participants and beneficiaries that, on request, they can get a free copy of the plan's QMCSO procedures. The description should be ample enough to assist potential alternate payees in enforcing their rights.

➠ TIP

A manual drafted for the administrative staff of a welfare benefit plan was not an SPD, even if the employee relied on it, because it was designed as an internal plan document, not a tool for employees to understand their benefits better [*Cooperative Benefit Plan Administrators Inc. v. Whittle*, 66 LW 1304 (M.D. Ala. 9/19/97)].

9.2.1 Mental Health Parity

Extensive, significant interim regulations on implementation of the mental health parity rules were jointly published by the IRS, Department of Labor, and Department of Health and Human Services on December 22, 1997. The rules begin at page 66931 of Volume 62 of the *Federal Register.* The mental health parity requirement took effect for plan years beginning on or after January 1, 1998. It is scheduled to expire for services provided on or after September 30, 2001 (unless Congress chooses to extend it).

Under these rules, an EGHP that provides both medical and mental health benefits can satisfy the parity requirements in various ways:

- Not having any lifetime limit or annual dollar limitation on mental health benefits
- Using the same aggregate lifetime or annual dollar limits for physical and mental treatments

- Setting separate limits, as long as the mental health limit is not smaller than the limit for physical ailments
- Using a weighted limit for mental health benefits, to reflect the plan's differential treatment for different categories of physical illness

➠ TIP

Note that if there is a separate limit for mental health benefits, benefits for treating substance abuse cannot be counted toward that limit.

The interim rule provides assistance in calculating the "increased cost" exception (parity is not required if it would increase the cost of the plan by 1% or more). It is estimated that 90% of plans will encounter cost increases of less than 1% and thus would not be entitled to exemption. Plans that claim this exemption must disclose to the Department of Treasury the notice that they give their plan participants and beneficiaries. (The interim rule provides model notices that can be used to comply with this requirement.)

In the same issue of the *Federal Register*, on page 66967, the IRS indicated that the text of those interim rules would also operate as IRS temporary regulations.

9.2.2 Maternity Stays

Interim and Proposed rules to implement the 1996 Newborns' and Mothers' Health Protection Act were issued jointly by the IRS, Pension and Welfare Benefit Administration, and Health Care Financing Administration. See 63 FR 57,545 for the interim rules and 57,565 for the proposed rules; both were published on October 27, 1998. The interim rules make it clear that, when a baby is delivered in the hospital, the stay begins at the time of delivery (or the last delivery, in a multiple birth). If the mother is admitted to the hospital after delivering elsewhere, the stay begins at the time of admission.

The new rules forbid health plans to punish health care providers for complying with the Health Protection Act. It is improper to make payments or incentives to either a mother or a health care provider to induce an earlier check-out from the hospital. However, it is permissible to offer postdischarge follow-up after an early discharge, as long as the services obtained do not exceed those that would be provided during the 48- or 96-hour stay required by the Health Protection Act. Plans are not permitted to offer benefits that are less generous during an extended than during a normal maternity stay, and they may not increase the mother's copayment obligations during the extended period.

9.2.4 Domestic Partner Benefits

A state university's denial of health insurance benefits to the same-sex domestic partners of family members has been held to violate the Oregon state Constitution. *Tanner v. Oregon Health Sciences University*, 971 P.2d 435 (Ore. App. 1998) holds that unmarried same-sex couples constitute a true class. They are not permitted to marry, and therefore discrimination against them represents unconstitutional discrimination on the basis of sexual orientation and not, as the university claimed, a distinction on the basis of marital status.

9.2.7 [NEW] Women's Health and Cancer Rights Act

The Women's Health and Cancer Rights Act of 1998, P.L. 105-277, became law on October 21, 1998. If an EGHP covers mastectomies, the Act requires it also to cover reconstructive breast surgery if the patient wants it and her attending physician prescribes it. This includes reconstruction of the mastectomized breast; surgery on the other breast to balance the patient's appearance; prostheses; and treatment of physical complications of mastectomy. The deductibles and coinsurance imposed on reconstructive surgery must be comparable to those imposed on other benefits under the plan. The Act is effective for plan years beginning on or after October 21, 1998.

EGHPs (and the insurers and HMOs that provide the medical and surgical benefits) are required to provide two forms of notice to plan participants. There was a one-time, "start-up" notice requirement that had to be satisfied by January 1, 1999. There is also an ongoing obligation to notify new plan participants of their rights under this Act, as soon as they become participants; notice must be renewed annually.

The notice must satisfy the Department of Labor requirements for Summary Plan Descriptions (see 29 CFR §2520.104b-1). The notice describes the types of reconstructive surgery covered, the applicable deductibles and coinsurance, and the fact that copayments for reconstructive surgery may not exceed those required for other types of care. It is not necessary for both the EGHP and the insurer or HMO to furnish the notice, as long as one of them does.

Health Promotion Measures

According to Hewitt Associates, 91% of U.S. companies undertake at least some health promotion efforts in the interest of keeping down health costs. Only 62% did so in 1992 and 89% did in 1996, so this is clearly a trend. The older and more stable an industry's workforce, the more likely it is to add health promotion to the plan. The two most popular health promotion measures are health screening (for blood pressure or cholesterol levels), offered at 78% of respondent companies, and education and training (offered by 76% of survey respondents)—(e.g., seminars and workshops; substance abuse counseling). Over one-third of respondents (39%) used financial incentives or disincentives (e.g., raising or lowering health premiums based on health or disease factors in the employee's lifestyle). About one-quarter (27%) gave employees questionnaires or risk appraisals.

This information comes from the Hewitt Newsstand online newsletter, http://www.hewitt.com/news/pressrel/1998/11-19-98.htm. The full study, "Health Promotion/Managed Health Provided by Major U.S. Employers in 1997," can be ordered for $50 a copy from Hewitt Associates Publications Desk, 100 Half Day Road, Lincolnshire, IL, 60069, (847) 295-5000.

9.5 CLAIMS PROBLEMS

The Eastern District of Wisconsin found that it was arbitrary and capricious for a plan to deny coverage of a medically necessary feeding tube, for a patient who was unable to swallow, on the grounds that meals were available in the hospital: "An administrator is not free to give ordinary words bizarre or obscure interpretations." See *Schneider v. Wisconsin UFCW Unions,* 66 LW 1432 (E.D. Wis. 12/4/97).

Even if symptoms begin earlier, a disease is not a "preexisting condition" if it was not diagnosed until the policy is in effect. A Wisconsin woman made two emergency room visits in May 1996 when she experienced stomach pains. On both occasions, she was told her condition was trivial and sent home. Her health insurance policy became effective on June 18, 1996. In late June, she was admitted to the hospital, where she was finally diagnosed with advanced cancer that killed her a few weeks later. The insurer in *Ermenc v. American Family Mutual Ins. Co.*, 1998 Westlaw 484640 (Wis. App. 1998), took the position that her cancer was a preexisting condition, so her hospital bills were not covered. The court was unimpressed—although she had some illness before the policy became effective, the actual cancer diagnosis occurred after the effective date.

In the view of the Tenth Circuit [*Healthcare America Plans Inc. v. Bossemeyer*, 166 F.3d 347 (10th Cir. 1998)], there is no ERISA violation when an EGHP administrator denies benefits for high-dose chemotherapy for breast cancer on the grounds that the treatment is experimental. The plan at issue defined experimental treatment as treatment not generally accepted by the medical community. Because that is a discretionary standard, the standard of review of plan decisions is whether or not they are arbitrary and capricious. To the Tenth Circuit, the exclusion for high-dose chemotherapy was reasoned and valid and therefore survived court review.

The Eleventh Circuit upheld a requirement in a self-insured health plan that all suits protesting internal appeals decisions be filed within 90 days. Although this is a short time frame, it was not inappropriate, in that the health plan had procedures for expediting decisions. (The court would not make a general ruling that a 90-day limitation would be permissible in all cases, only under the facts of this particular case.) See *Northlake Regional Medical Center v. Waffle House Sys. Employee Benefit Plan,* 1998 Westlaw 792150 (11th Cir. 1998).

9.5.1 [NEW] PWBA Proposed Rule

The Pension and Welfare Benefits Administration proposed a rule for claims procedures. To say the least, it has been controversial. The lengthy text was published at 63 FR 48390 (9/9/98). ERISA §503 requires all employee benefit plans to provide adequate written notice of claims denial. Once a claim is denied, the participant must be given a reasonable opportunity to have the denial reviewed by the appropriate fiduciary. But, of course, reasonable people may differ as to what constitutes adequate notice or reasonable appeals procedures.

The current proposal stems from a Request for Information that the PWBA published in the *Federal Register* on September 8, 1997. More than 90 comment letters came from benefit plan professionals, employers and their law firms, managed care organizations and health providers, and beneficiary groups. The claimant groups expressed a need for significant procedural changes, closer to the National Association of Insurance Commissioners model acts (for health insurance) and Health Care Financing Administration (HCFA's) Medicare rules. The position of the other constituencies, however, is that major changes are not required.

Based on the comments, the PWBA decided to make major changes in claims procedures, especially with regard to health benefits, bearing in mind the technological developments since ERISA's initial passage and the emergence of managed care as the dominant delivery system for employee health benefits. The PWBA was greatly influenced by the recommendations of the President's Advisory Commission on Consumer Protection and Quality in the Health Care Industry, as embodied in the November 20, 1997 report, "Consumer Bill of Rights and Responsibilities."

The estimated impact is great: The DOL's cost analysis shows 51,000 health plan claims a year (40,000 in large plans, the rest in small), for 56 million plan participants whose claims are handled by service providers and 14 million whose claims are handled in-house by the employer. Under the Proposed Rule, time limits for processing claims begin to run when a claim is initially filed with the plan, or with a third party who has authority to make a decision about the claim. In other words, the PWBA recognizes the legitimacy of employing a Third-Party Administrator (TPA) or otherwise outsourcing claims processing, but outsourcing does not change the plan's underlying timing obligations.

Plans are not permitted to inhibit or hamper claims filing—for instance, by imposing a fee for making a claim or appealing a denial. Plans that require preauthorization are not permitted to reject claims in instances where it was impossible to obtain preauthorization (e.g., emergency treatment of an unconscious person).

The central concern of the Proposed Rule is the timing of claims decisions. The general rule is that any period of over 90 days is unreasonable for giving beneficiaries written notice of claims denial. A 90-day extension can be obtained if special circumstances require longer processing time, but the claimant must be notified of the extension within the original 90-day period.

Under the current rule, once notice of denial has issued, the plan has the right to limit the period of time during which the denial can be appealed. However, the period must be reasonable; related to the benefit that has been claimed; and must reflect the other factual circumstances of the plan. Claimants must be given at least 60 days to appeal. Review decisions must be made promptly, normally within 60 days of the request unless special circumstances require an extension of another 60 days.

The proposal would extend the 60-day period during which claimants can appeal to 180 days. The Proposed Rule imposes the 180-day period only for health and disability plans, but the PWBA is considering generalizing it to all pension and welfare benefit plans.

The Proposed Rule requires health plans to determine claims on a schedule depending on whether the claim is for urgent or nonurgent health care (i.e., whether or not the patient is at risk by delaying treatment until the coverage status of the claim is resolved).

In general, the plan administrator's obligation is to make a decision about nonurgent claims within a period that is appropriate under the circumstances—but is definitely not more than 15 days after filing. Extensions of time are no longer allowed. Claimants must be notified within five days of the receipt of an incomplete claim, so they can provide the missing information; they must be given at least 45 days to do this. Review decisions about nonurgent care must be made within 30 days of receipt of the review request.

Urgent care is defined by §2560.503-1(j)(1) to mean situations in which applying the ordinary timing requirements could seriously jeopardize the life or health of the claimant or his or her ability to regain maximum functionality. It also includes cases, certified by a physician who has knowledge of the claimant's condition, in which denying or deferring the treatment would subject the patient to severe pain that cannot be managed without the treatment. Plans are given a maximum of 72 hours (or a shorter time, if that is reasonable) to process claims involving urgent care.

Who decides whether a claim involves urgent or nonurgent care? Generally, a plan representative, who is required to abide by the standards of a reasonable layperson (not a reasonable health professional). However, claims certified by a physician as urgent must be treated as urgent.

Under the proposal, an EGHP satisfies the requirements of having a "reasonable" claims procedure only if the procedure is described in detail in the Summary Plan Description (SPD). The definition of claims procedure extends to all filing procedures; notifications of benefit determinations; reviews of denials; and utilization review measures (e.g., preauthorization and other approvals).

All managed care arrangements for preapproval or precertification are deemed part of the plan, and therefore must be disclosed. (If a plan fails to have a reasonable appeals procedure, then dissatisfied participants can proceed straight to federal court; they will not be required to exhaust administrative remedies if appropriate remedies are not available within the plan.)

Also subject to disclosure are internal plan documents (rules, guidelines, protocols, etc.) used as a basis for denying an initial claim. This includes the plan's usual and customary fee schedules, because these are relevant if only part of a claim is allowed because it exceeds the schedule.

The SPD must also give a full explanation of the plan's review processes, including disclosure of the right to sue under ERISA §502(a). The proposal extends disclosure to "pertinent documents," all the documents, records, and information relevant to the claim, whether or not the plan actually used them in the determination. The PWBA is considering, but has not yet adopted, a requirement that plans disclose the ability of claimants who bring ERISA suits to receive reasonable access to records of up to 50 plan claims, for a five-year period, involving other plan participants with the same diagnosis and treatment. (For insured rather than self-insured plans, the insurer would be subject to the same disclosure requirements.)

The proposal also implicates ERISA §503's notice requirement. The plan must give notice when incomplete claims are submitted. If a health care benefit is to be provided over a period of time, notice is required when the benefits are reduced or terminated. Such reductions or terminations are treated as if they were adverse claim determinations and must be treated as urgent claims if the participant's health could be jeopardized by the change.

Denials must be reviewed by a named fiduciary who did not make the initial determination and is not a subordinate of the person who did. The initial adverse determination is not entitled to deference when it is reviewed. The review must consider all information submitted by the claimant—including new information that the claimant did not submit initially. If the determination was based on a medical judgment, another health care professional, independent of the first one, must be consulted. Appeals of urgent-care claims must be expedited, and necessary information can be telephoned or faxed to speed things up.

No plan can require more than one level of mandatory appeal: Claimants can't be forced to take up the same matter over and over. The PWBA forbids plans to impose compulsory arbitration either as part of the single level of appeals, or at a later time, although voluntary arbitration is permissible.

These rules are supposed to apply to all plans. The proposal eliminates the special treatment given to collectively bargained plans and HMO-based plans under prior law.

9.8 HEALTH CARE COST TRENDS

A study by William M. Mercer Inc., published in January 1999, shows that 1998 was a year in which health care trends turned around. Between 1994 and 1997, health care costs remained more or less level (rising 2.5% in 1996, and only 0.2% in 1997); but in 1998, average health care costs went up a painful 6.1%.

For the first time, HMO membership declined: In 1998, 47% of employees got their coverage from HMOs or point-of-service (POS) plans, versus 50% in 1997. The 1998 HMO enrollment was 29% of the insured workforce; POS plans covered 18% of insured workers. However, enrollment in preferred provider organizations (PPOs) went up: 35% in 1997, 40% in 1998. (The percentages can exceed 100%, because employers can offer multiple plan options.)

In 1998, the average cost of health coverage (including both active and retired workers) was $4164 per person per year. Since the 1997 figure was $3924, the Mercer survey showed that health care costs were on the rise again. A key factor in the increase was a 13.8% jump in costs of covering prescription drugs; a trend predicted for 1999 was employer requirements of higher copayments for prescriptions. These figures come from Ron Winslow, "Measure of HMO Membership Falls for First Time," *Wall Street Journal*, 1/26/99, p.B7; "Growth in Health Plan Costs Held to 0.2 Percent in 1997," *Compensation and Benefits Update*, 3/11/98, p. 4. Also see Ron Winslow, "Health-Care Inflation Kept in Check Last Year," *Wall Street Journal*, 1/20/98, p. B1, and "Co-Payments Rise for Prescriptions," *Wall Street Journal*, 1/12/99, p. B1, tracing CIGNA Corp.'s experience with rising drug costs.

In 1995, the average prescription cost $18 to fill ($25 for a brand-name rather than generic drug). In 1997, the corresponding figures were $26 and $48. Therefore, participants in plans insured by CIGNA went from a 1995 $5 copayment for generic approved drugs—but $15 to $20 for "preferred" brand-name drugs, and up to $40 for a prescription involving a nonpreferred, nongeneric drug. (In both years, patients had to pay the full cost of drugs outside the formulary.)

Managed care firms face increases of as much as 16% a year in prescription drug prices—and prescription drug costs can represent as much as 14% of the plans' overall bills. The plans say that the increased copayments are designed to make consumers more economical in their drug choices. But drug prescriptions are controlled by doctors, not patients; and it doesn't seem fair to require sick people to take a drug that is not the most therapeutically effective, to save money for the managed care plan.

The low-hanging fruit has been harvested. One perspective is that employers, by switching from indemnity to managed care, have already taken the simplest step to reduce costs. Another perspective is that insurers that offer managed care plans have now more or less eliminated the competition and are in a position to raise premiums.

RIA's *HR Wire* looked at surveys performed by Towers Perrin, Hewitt Associates, and Buck Consultants and predicted that, in 1999, health care costs would go up somewhere between 6 and 15%. Towers Perrin expected retiree health costs to go up 6% in 1999 (for early retirees) and 10% (for Medicare-eligible retirees). Hewitt predicted a 1999 average cost for insuring an active employee of between $4300 and $4400. Hewitt expected cost increases to be highest for indemnity plans, lowest for POS and PPO plans. See http://www.insidehr.com/HRwire/hrwire_story.asp/99011801.htm.

As predicted, small employers faced significant cost increases in 1999, described by the *New York Times* as "some of the steepest price increases for health insurance in almost 10 years" (see Jennifer Steinhauer, "Health Insurance Costs Rise, Hitting Small Business Hard," *NYT*, 1/19/99, p. A1). January 1999 increases for businesses with over 100 employees averaged 6% nationwide, but small businesses faced increases from 10 to 13%. Some small New York firms were told to pay 30% increases to maintain coverage—with the result that many of these businesses changed carrier, increased the employee share of the premium, or dropped coverage.

Not everyone who lacks health insurance is unemployed—or even employed by a company that does not have a health plan. Employers who offer health plans sometimes find that workers, especially lower-paid workers, are offered health coverage but decline to accept it. See Peter T. Kilborn, "Poor Workers Turning Down Employers' Health Benefits," *NYT*, 11/10/97, p. A24, and Laurie McGinley, "More Workers Drop Employer Health Policies," *WSJ*, 11/10/97, p. B2. Employee Benefit Research Institute (EBRI) figures show that, in late 1997, the average worker would pay $396 for health insurance coverage for him- or herself under an employer plan—and would pay about $1600 for family coverage. A person earning $7 an hour (i.e., not a minimum-wage worker) would have to devote 11% of gross pay just to purchase family coverage.

Nor does mere enrollment in an EGHP always solve an employee' s health-care-cost problems. A study by Consumers Union shows that in 1996, per capita health care costs for Americans were $3778. Families earning between $30,000 and $40,000 had average out-of-pocket health care costs of about $1500 (e.g., about 4.5% of earnings). But there were over two and a half million families that spent more than 30% of their earnings for out-of-pocket health care costs. More than 11 million families spent "only" 10% or more of their income on health costs—and 9 million of those families had insurance coverage for every member. (These figures come from a news item, "Health Policies Don't Cover Many Expenses," *WSJ*, 1/23/98, p. B7B.) The problem, then, is not just the large number of uninsured persons, but those who have nominal insurance coverage that imposes severe financial burdens both on them and on their employers.

9.10 MANAGED CARE

William M. Mercer figures, quoted in Nancy Ann Jeffrey' s article "Test Over Time," *WSJ*, 10/23/97, p. R6, show that, although the market share of HMOs has remained fairly constant since 1994 (23% in 1994, 27% in 1995 and 26%), other forms of managed care have grown. In 1993, for instance, HMOs had a 19% market share; point-of-service (POS) plans were a minor player, at 7%; PPOs had a 27% share; and traditional indemnity plans captured almost half the market, at 48%.

The established principle under which employers escaped liability—because the HMO provided the actual treatment—and the HMO escaped liability—because

ERISA preempts state law but says virtually nothing about the obligations of HMOs to employees who are denied care or who are injured by negligent care—is beginning to erode.

Early in 1999, the Supreme Court, in *Humana Inc. v. Forsyth*, #97-303, 67 LW 4085 (Sup. Ct. 1/20/99), permitted EGHP members who alleged that they were overbilled as part of a conspiracy to force them to make excessive copayments to sue for insurance fraud under RICO. (Therefore, treble damages became a possibility.) The defendant, naturally, claimed that the McCarran-Ferguson Act precluded the RICO suit, but the Supreme Court held that RICO does not invalidate or supersede state insurance laws, so the RICO suit is not barred by the McCarran-Ferguson Act.

The Supreme Court returned to EGHP ERISA issues in April 1999. The decision in *UNUM Life Insurance Co. of America v. Ward*, #97-1867, 67 LW 4243 (Sup. Ct. 4/20/99), is that ERISA does not preempt state "notice-prejudice" laws. A notice-prejudice law prevents an insurer from denying a claim based on late filing, unless the delay was prejudicial to the insurer's interests. But this decision, although a setback for insurers, doesn't harm employers who administer EGHPs, because it says that although the employer is the insurer's "agent," the employer's role "relates to" an ERISA plan and therefore is preempted by ERISA.

ERISA doesn't preempt an employee's state-law claims against an insurer who denied benefits under an individual disability policy that had been converted from a group policy. The employer was no longer involved, so ERISA was no longer the governing statute [*Demars v. CIGNA Corp.*, 67 LW 1656 (1st Cir. 4/6/99)].

In early January 1999, Aetna U.S. Healthcare announced a new national policy permitting outside review of denials of coverage (in addition to review of denials performed by the plan itself). The outside reviewer's decision would be binding on Aetna but would not preclude litigation by dissatisfied plan beneficiaries. About 6 million beneficiaries of Aetna HMO and POS plans, in about 30 states, would be subject to the external-review provision.

Other managed care organizations, such as UnitedHealthGroup, Kaiser Permanente, and Pacifi-Care Health Systems, announced plans to add outside review of their decisions later in 1999. The issue is not a simple one. Not only do insurers want to control the cost of care (and patients want freer access), doctors want greater autonomy in practicing medicine without interference from managed care companies. (About one-third of the states have legislation requiring some kind of external review for HMO decisions.)

At the heart of the debate is whether doctors should be allowed to prescribe any medications, operations, or treatments they think are prudent and beneficial to the patient's health—or whether they should be restricted to absolutely necessary, life-saving care.

Several 1999 articles from the *Wall Street Journal* bear on these issues. See Nancy Ann Jeffrey, "Aetna to Set Reviews for HMO Coverage Disputes," 1/12/99, p. B6; Laurie McGinley, "Managed-Care Industry Body May Back Right to Appeal Denials of

Treatment," 1/20/99, p. B6; Ron Winslow and Rhonda L. Rundle, "Aetna Reels in Wake of $116 Million Damages Verdict," 1/22/9, p. B4; Laurie McGinley, "HMO Fracas Moves to Who Makes Medical Decision," 2/18/99, p. A24. Milo Geyelin's "Courts Pierce HMOs' Shield Against Lawsuits," 4/30/99, p. B1, summarizes the trend toward greater HMO liability when patients are harmed by delayed or denied care.

Washington State's statute, requiring HMOs to provide acupuncture, massage, chiropractic, and other alternative medical treatments, is not preempted by ERISA [*Washington Physicians Service Association v. Gregoire*, 147 F.3d 1039 (9th Cir. 1998)].

ERISA does not preempt a surviving spouse's medical malpractice, breach of contract, and breach of fiduciary duty suit against an HMO primary care doctor who delayed referring the decedent to a medical specialist [*Nealy v. U.S. Healthcare*, 67 LW 1586 (N.Y. App. 3/25/99)].

A similar result was reached in *DeLucia v. St. Luke's Hospital*, discussed in Shannon P. Duffy's article, "When Quality, Not Quantity of Care Is at Issue, ERISA Doesn't Apply," http://www.lawnewsnet.com/stories/A1763-1999May25.html. In this case the parents of a deceased premature infant went to state court and sued the HMO that denied coverage of a breathing monitor. The HMO tried to remove the case from state to federal court, claiming ERISA preemption. The ERISA argument was unsuccessful, because the case involved a simple allegation of improper medical care—a classic state-law medical malpractice case. The employer plan had no meaningful involvement in the case.

A tragically similar case, *Bauman v. U.S. Healthcare Inc.*, U.S. Dist. Lexis 4110 (D.N.J. 1998), involves the death of another newborn. HMO policy called for discharge within 24 hours (but see ¶9.2.2 for current law about mandated coverage of longer maternity stays). The baby died of meningitis shortly after discharge. The parents sued the company that owned the HMO, the hospital, and the doctor who discharged the baby without detecting the soon-to-be-fatal infection. The claims against the HMO included negligently adopting a policy that encouraged or required premature discharge, with reckless indifference to the risks of the policy. According to the District Court for the District of New Jersey, these claims were not preempted by ERISA, because ERISA §502(a) (claims for benefits due under the plan) was not involved. The parents' claim was not for plan benefits, but was based on negligence in crafting the structure of the plan. However, the court did dismiss the parents' claim (on ERISA preemption grounds) that the plan promised them a home visit that was not delivered.

When a patient of a Medicare HMO dies, the Medicare Act does not preempt state-law claims of wrongful death or negligence or misconduct on the part of the HMO [*Wartenberg v. Aetna U.S. Healthcare Inc.*, 1998 Westlaw 185416 (E.D.N.Y. 1998)].

See Nancy Ann Jeffreys' article, "Test Over Time," *WSJ*, 10/23/97, p. R6, for criticism of HMO handling of the needs of chronically ill enrollees. People suffering from asthma, diabetes, kidney problems, or other chronic ailments may find that the plan offers inadequate coverage for medications and devices needed to control symptoms, as well as cuts back on physician visits needed to monitor their condition.

The Center for Studying Health System Change, in collaboration with the Robert Wood Johnson Foundation, suggests that employers need to take the next step: not just having managed care plans, but a coordinated "managed competition" strategy that impels competition among insurers. (See "Study Suggests Few Employers Use Managed Competition Principles," *Compensation and Benefits Update*, 7/29/98, p. 5.) Over 20,000 firms were surveyed in this massive study [see http://www.hschange.com, or call (202) 554-7549]. Only 17% of companies offered more than one plan for employees to choose among (although because of the distribution of employees, 41% of covered employees had a choice of plans). Managed competition creates incentives for employees to select the plan that best suits their needs—and for insurers to offer consumer-friendly plans, because they risk loss of enrollment if customers are dissatisfied.

Managed competition advocates suggest that employers adopt a policy of "equal dollar contribution" (i.e., to determine the amount they will contribute toward employees' insurance). Employees who want a more expensive plan have to pay the difference themselves. Only about one-quarter of companies (28%) used the equal dollar contribution methodology. Thirty-one percent simply paid the full premium for coverage, and 34% paid a given percentage of the premium, with the employee responsible for the balance.

For managed competition to be effective, employees must have detailed information about competing plans. The survey criticized employers' performance in this regard. Even among the large (over 500 employees) companies, the ones with the greatest HR resources, only 22% gave employees information beyond basic plan descriptions.

9.10.8 Employer Liability for HMO Actions

According to an Information Letter issued by the Department of Labor on February 19, 1998, it may be a breach of fiduciary duty for health plan trustees to choose health care providers merely based on cost considerations, without considering quality. In this context, quality involves issues such as the number and qualification of doctors in the health plan; employees' access to those doctors; the provider's past record; ratings and accreditation; and consumer satisfaction. Therefore, merely accepting the provider that posts the lowest bid is not necessarily appropriate fiduciary conduct, if the low-cost provider is not also a quality provider. This DOL letter is discussed in the RIA *Compensation and Benefits Update*, 3/25/98, p. 3.

9.10.9 State Regulation of Managed Care Plans

In 1998, Ohio passed the Physician-Health Plan Partnership Act, H.B. 361, effective October 1, 1998. This legislation forbids "gag clauses" (provisions in managed care plans that forbid participating physicians from discussing treatment options not covered by the plan with patients who might benefit by the treatments).

It is unlawful for plans to offer financial incentives to health care providers for limiting or reducing necessary medical services.

Under the Act, doctors cannot be penalized by the plan for furnishing needed care; blowing the whistle on improprieties committed by the plan; or helping patients with claims or claims appeals. If a provider offers treatment in good faith, and the treatment is approved by the plan, the plan will not be able to deny coverage for such services retroactively. Emergency services must be covered without preauthorization in any situation in which a prudent layperson would reasonably deem emergency care to be required.

When care is recommended by a physician, the plan must delegate coverage determinations to qualified medical professionals using documented scientific evidence. These professionals must not receive financial incentives based on the number of claims they deny. Plans must have a formal procedure for reviewing new drugs and procedures for safety and effectiveness. The plan must provide (and pay for) independent professional review of claims denied as experimental.

Determinations as to the need for referral to a medical specialist must be made within three business days of the time a patient or primary care doctor requests the determination. Referral must be made within four business days. Primary care physicians must be permitted to make "standing" referrals to specialists for patients who need follow-up care. However, it is permissible for a treatment plan to limit the number of specialist visits or the period of time during which specialist visits will be authorized.

Although managed care plans can maintain a formulary of approved drugs, doctors must be permitted to prescribe other prescription drugs if the formulary drugs are ineffective or potentially harmful to a particular patient. The patient cannot be charged extra for the nonformulary drugs.

The Ohio managed care bill is discussed in "New Ohio Managed Care Law Effective Oct. 1," *Compensation and Benefits Update*, 9/9/98, p. 5. For a history of state regulation of HMOs, see Laurie McGinley, "Broad Battle to End HMOs' Limited Liability for Treatment-Coverage Denials Gains Steam," *WSJ*, 1/12/98, p. A22, and Peter T. Kilborn, "Bills Regulating Managed Care Benefit Doctors," *NYT*, 2/16/98, p. A10.

Two very similar cases, involving individuals who claim that they would not have suffered paralysis if their HMO had certified treatment more rapidly, reached different results. To the Eastern District of Louisiana, ERISA preempts the claim [*Benoit v. W.W. Grainger Inc.*, 67 LW 1271 (E.D. La. 10/21/98)]. But a Pennsylvania state court ruled a couple of months later that ERISA does not preempt the suit; HMOs should be prepared to suffer financially if they operate negligently [*Pappas v. Asbel*, 67 LW 1416 (Pa. 12/23/98)].

9.14 TAX IMPLICATIONS OF HEALTH PLANS

A partnership sought an IRS Private Letter Ruling as to the status of its plan for "medical consumer cards" issued by a managed care company to the partners and employees of the partnership. The consumer cards provided discounts on noncore items (e.g., dental and vision care) that were not part of the basic health plan. There would be a fee for the card, although it was not clear whether the partnership or the individual users would pay the fee. The company had no financial risk stemming from use of the cards.

In PLR 9814023, the IRS ruled that the partnership' s distribution of the cards constituted a fringe benefit. Employees would not have gross income because of the issuance of the card, because for them, the cards were part of an accident and health insurance plan excluded from gross income by Code §106(a). When the employees use the card to get a discount, they do not have compensation income. After all, the employer doesn't pay them; the participating health care providers extend them a discount.

At the partnership level, the cost of buying cards for partners was not deductible, because the plan did not conform to the definition of "insurance." The partnership didn' t ask the IRS about the tax status of cards provided to employees, but probably those costs would be deductible, because the plan had been ruled to fit the insurance definition for employees although not for partners. See "Mixed Tax Results for Employee Medical Discount Cards," *Compensation and Benefits Update*, 4/22/98, p. 4.

9.15 COBRA CONTINUATION COVERAGE

In 1998, the Supreme Court resolved an important COBRA question, in *Geissal v. Moore Medical Corp.*, #97-689, 118 S.Ct. 1871 (6/8/98). Under *Geissal*, it is legitimate for an employer to terminate COBRA coverage if and when the employee gains access to other coverage subsequent to making a COBRA election. However, it is not permitted for the employer to terminate COBRA eligibility on the basis of coverage that the employee had access to prior to the election.

If an individual elects COBRA coverage and becomes disabled during the continuation period, the Fifth Circuit allows extension of coverage as long as the individual complies with the requirements set out in the health plan's SPD. Coverage cannot be denied based on limitations that appear in the formal text of the plan (or even in the COBRA statute or regulations) but are not included in the SPD.

According to the plan text (and COBRA), an additional 11 months of COBRA coverage would be provided based on notice that the Social Security Administration had ruled the applicant was disabled before the initial 18-month COBRA continuation period ended. But the SPD, the document available to the employee and his wife, said that the COBRA period could be extended based on notice to the employer within 60 days of the Social Security Administration determination of disability. The couple met this requirement, so the Fifth Circuit found them entitled to a COBRA extension even though the disability occurred after the employee terminated employment and initially became COBRA eligible. The case is *Fallo v. Piccadilly Cafeterias Inc.*, 1998 Westlaw 239020 (5th Cir. 1998).

An employer that mistakenly extended continuation health benefits after the collectively bargained date was not estopped from terminating the coverage as soon as it discovered the mistake—even though the ex-employee's wife had racked up a $45,000 hospital bill in the meantime. The Seventh Circuit, in *Coker v. TWA*, 165 F.3d 579 (7th Cir. 1999), decided that it was not reasonable for the plaintiff to rely on the mistaken communications from the employer, given that the employee was given written materials at the time of the layoff, explaining the benefits.

Even a plan that allows retirees continued coverage at their own expense for an indefinite period of time (i.e., after the COBRA period expires) still has an independent obligation to issue COBRA notice at retirement, because retirement is a COBRA event [*Mansfield v. Chicago Park District Group Plan*, 1998 Westlaw 128061 (N.D. Ill. 1998)].

The employer's business records, showing that COBRA notice was mailed, are adequate evidence to prove notice, even though the employer couldn't find a copy of the actual letter that was sent to employees. (The plaintiff didn't dispute receiving a standard notice form.) See *Roberts v. National Health Corp.*, 1998 U.S. App. LEXIS 446 (4th Cir. 1998).

COBRA Regulations

On January 7, 1998, the IRS published a Notice of Proposed Rulemaking at 63 FR 708. The proposals conform COBRA to HIPAA, the Small Business Job Protection Act, and various other statutes. As a result of these changes, qualified beneficiaries can get 29 months (rather than the original 18) of COBRA coverage with respect to the same qualifying event if

- They are all qualified with respect to a termination of employment or a reduction in hours
- They became disabled, within the Social Security Act definition, within the first 60 days of COBRA continuation coverage
- They have given the plan administrator a copy of the determination of disability, within the initial 18-month COBRA period and also within 60 days of the date the determination was issued

During the extended period (after 18 months, before the 29 months have expired), the employer can charge a premium of 150% of the applicable premium, rather than the normal 102% limit. Charging the 150% premium will not violate the IRC §9802(b) prohibition on premium discrimination on the basis of health status. If a second qualifying event occurs during a disability extension, then COBRA coverage can last for 36 months; the 150% premium can lawfully be charged until the 36-month period ends.

HIPAA creates entitlement to COBRA coverage for children born to or adopted by covered employees during a period of COBRA coverage. The maximum coverage period for the child runs from the date of the employee's qualifying event—not the child's birth or adoption. The effect is that the child's COBRA coverage ends at the same time as other family members' coverage.

The January 7, 1998 rule makes it clear that Medical Savings Accounts are not subject to the COBRA continuation coverage obligation. Neither are plans substantially all of whose coverage is for "qualified long-term care services," as defined by IRC §7702B; the plan can use any reasonable method of deciding whether it falls into this category.

In February 1999, the IRS went ahead and finalized COBRA regulations first proposed in 1987. The 1999 final rule, found at 64 FR 5160 (2/3/99), is fairly similar to the 1987 proposal. However, the final rule implements *Geissal*. It allows a measure of employer discretion in defining how many "plans" are maintained for COBRA purposes. It includes rules for coping with EGHPs in corporate transitions (see Chapter 31). It clarifies that COBRA does not apply to most medical flexible spending accounts. If the EGHP provides both core health coverage and noncore coverage (e.g., vision and dental), it is no longer necessary to allow qualified employees to elect only the core coverage.

Taking leave under the Family and Medical Leave Act (FMLA) is not in and of itself a COBRA qualifying event. But if an employee who was covered by the EGHP before or during the FMLA leave fails to return to work after the FMLA leave, there is a qualifying event for this person (and any dependent who is at risk of losing health coverage) as of the last day of the FMLA leave. The employer is not allowed to require the ex-employee to reimburse the employer for health premiums paid during the leave.

These regulations apply to qualifying events that occur in plan years beginning on or after January 1, 2000. In the interim, plans are required to comply in good faith with reasonable interpretations of Code §4980B (the statutory provision governing continuation coverage).

9.16 HEALTH INSURANCE PORTABILITY

The mental health parity rules discussed previously also affect HIPAA. See 62 FR 66957-66961 (12/22/97) for the Pension and Welfare Benefit Administration's amendments to 29 CFR Part 2590 Subpart B, explaining the portability implications of mental health parity.

Also at the end of 1997, the IRS, the Department of Labor's Pension and Welfare Benefits Administration, and the Department of Health and Human Services jointly published a "clarification of regulations" that appears at 62 FR 67688 (12/29/97). This document makes it clear that health insurance portability is not required for certain health flexible spending arrangements (FSAs). In technical terms, such FSAs are "excepted benefits" under ERISA §§732 and 733(c) and IRC §§9831 and 9832(c). Another implication is that FSA coverage is not "creditable coverage" that triggers portability rights under HIPAA.

According to this document, a health FSA is a "benefit program that provides employees with coverage under which specified, incurred expenses may be reimbursed (subject to reimbursement maximums and any other reasonable conditions) and under which the maximum amount of reimbursement that is reasonably available to a participant for a period of coverage is not substantially in excess of the total premium (including both employee-paid and employer-paid portions of the premium) for the participant's coverage." As the document notes, FSAs usually cover medical expenses excluded by the primary EGHP.

The FSA is excepted from HIPAA if the employee's maximum FSA benefit for the year is not greater than twice the employee's salary reduction election under the FSA for the year, as long as the employee has other EGHP coverage and provides at least some benefits that are not excepted benefits.

What about employees or dependents of employees who, prior to HIPAA, were turned down for group health plan coverage because of health status? Another IRS/DOL/HCFA clarification, also published in the *Federal Register* on December 29, 1997 (62 FR 67689), forbids group health plans and group insurance coverage to continue excluding those people from plan enrollment or coverage.

Plans are not allowed to establish rules for initial or continued eligibility based on "health status-related" factors—(e.g., health status; medical condition; claims experience; receipt of health care; medical history; genetic testing; insurability; or disability). Employees and their dependents cannot be required to pass a physical examination in order to enroll in the health plan, even if they are late enrollees.

A person who enrolls post-HIPAA cannot be treated as a late enrollee if he or she was previously denied enrollment for health status-related reasons, or if he or she thought it was futile even to apply.

Slightly earlier, Proposed and Temporary Regulations were issued: 62 FR 60165 and 60196 (11/7/97), dealing with changes in cafeteria plan elections, as well as HIPAA conformity for plans dealing with COBRA, medical child support orders, and Medicare/Medicaid eligibility. The effective date of this rule was delayed until 12/31/98.

9.17 MEDICAL SAVINGS ACCOUNTS

In late 1998, the General Accounting Office (GAO) was supposed to report on its survey of the market effectiveness of medical savings accounts. It may tell you something about said market success if you see that GAO/HEHS-99-34, "Medical Savings Accounts: Results From Surveys of Insurers" (12/31/98), is a remarkably brief document that reports that the GAO could only survey insurers, because it was unable to locate enough employers and MSA participants to arrive at any valid conclusions!

9.19 MEDICARE AS SECONDARY PAYER (MSP)

Hewitt Survey: Employers React to Medicare Managed Care Changes

Before 1999, the Medicare system made provision for managed care, but generally in the form of HMOs (already familiar to benefit professionals because of their role in the EGHP). As of January 1999, the federal government planned to phase out Medicare HMOs in favor of an assortment of Medicare+Choice (M+C) managed care plans. Senior citizens would have a choice between getting their care through the conventional Medicare program or from an M+C plan.

In August 1998, Hewitt Associates received survey responses from 350 employers dealing with their reactions to the new program. Most of the employers said that they were aware of the transition to Medicare's new managed care format, but only 17% had even a tentative policy for communicating with employees and retirees about the new program or changing their retiree health plans. About a third of them plan to give their employees written information about Medicare+Choice; about 10% planned to outsource employees' and retirees' questions about M+C to an outside contractor.

About a third of the survey respondents had experience in sponsoring a Medicare risk HMO for older employees and retirees. Two-thirds of survey respondents planned to sponsor at least some medical coverage for individuals who retired at or after 65. Three-quarters of respondents considered offering M+C HMO coverage for this purpose in the future; 60% considered offering a POS HMO. PPOs were under consideration by 55% of respondents, but very few were interested in offering the other M+C alternatives (private fee-for-service plans; provider-sponsored organizations [PSOs]; or medical savings accounts [MSAs]).

Chapter 10

Fringe Benefits

10.4 INSURANCE FRINGE BENEFITS

On January 13, 1999, the IRS issued a proposed revision for the PS 58 "table rates" used to determine if employees have taxable income due to the employer's payment of insurance premiums over and above the pure cost of insurance. For most employees, the new rates are significantly lower—the older the employee, the more marked the effect. The IRS decided to lower the insurance costs to reflect increases in life expectancy. The new rates became effective on July 1, 1999; see T.D. 8821.

Employee's Age	Current Law	Proposal
>25	.08	.05
25–29	.08	.06
30–34	.09	.08
35–39	.11	.09
40–44	.17	.10
45–49	.29	.15
50–54	.48	.23
55–59	.75	.43
60–64	1.17	.66
65–70	2.10	1.27
>70	3.76	2.06

A September 1998 case, *Cehrs v. Northeast Ohio Alzheimer's Research Center*, 155 F.3d 755 (6th Cir. 1998), involves an employer that had a life insurance plan. A disabled employee was told that he did not fit the plan's definition of disability, so the employer would not maintain his life insurance coverage. However, the employer did not give any reason for the determination or how to appeal it. After the ex-employee's death, his family sued under ERISA §503. The employer's litigating position was that the employee failed to mitigate (reduce) his damages by investigating and discovering that the employer's position was incorrect. The Sixth Circuit rejected this argument, taking the position that when a plan fails to provide statutorily mandated notices, employees essentially can't mitigate their damages; and requiring them to do so would reward plans for failure to provide the required notices.

10.5 CAFETERIA PLANS

Proposed and Temporary Regulations for bringing cafeteria plans into conformity with HIPAA were published at 62 FR 60165 and 60196 (11/7/97); their effectiveness was delayed until 12/31/98. The rule deals with the way cafeteria plan participants can change their elections during the plan year. The basic rule is that elections can be changed only in response to changes in family status. However, an employee who separates from service can revoke existing benefit elections and agree not to receive benefits for the rest of the coverage period. An employee who does this and is later reemployed by the same employer will not be permitted to make new benefit elections for the rest of that coverage period.

10.6 FLEXIBLE SPENDING ACCOUNTS (FSAS)

At the end of 1997, the IRS, the Department of Labor's Pension and Welfare Benefits Administration, and the Department of Health and Human Services jointly published a "clarification of regulations" that appears at 62 FR 67688 (12/29/97). The document makes it clear that health insurance portability is not required for certain health flexible spending arrangements (FSAs). In technical terms, such FSAs are "excepted benefits" under ERISA §§732 and 733(c) and IRC §§9831 and 9832(c). Another implication is that FSA coverage is not "creditable coverage" that triggers portability rights under HIPAA.

According to this document, a health FSA is a "benefit program that provides employees with coverage under which specified, incurred expenses may be reimbursed (subject to reimbursement maximums and any other reasonable conditions) and under which the maximum amount of reimbursement that is reasonably available to a participant for a period of coverage is not substantially in excess of the total premium (including both employee-paid and employer-paid portions of the premium) for the participant's coverage." As the document notes, FSAs usually cover medical expenses excluded by the primary EGHP.

The FSA is excepted from HIPAA if the employee's maximum FSA benefit for the year is not greater than twice the employee's salary reduction election under the FSA for the year, as long as the employee has other EGHP coverage and provides at least some benefits that are not excepted benefits.

According to Hewitt Associates (call 847-295-5000 for more information), about 17.5% of the workforce participates in health care FSAs. Ninety-one percent of the employers who implement FSAs have forfeitures in the plan, averaging $136 per employee per year. The survey of about 500 employers showed an average 1997 FSA contribution of $744 per employee for health care accounts, $2848 for dependent care accounts.

10.8 DISABILITY PLANS

Corley v. Kimberly-Clark Tissue Co. Pension Plan, 1998 U.S. Dist. LEXIS 9381 (S.D. Ala. 1998), involves a pension plan that limited disability retirement benefit eligibility to persons unable to hold any paying job, with medical certification that the inability is expected to be lifelong. The plaintiff's own doctor said that the plaintiff could not do heavy manual labor but could do light to medium work. In light of this, his application for disability retirement was rejected. The doctor revised his opinion but never indicated that the plaintiff was completely unable to work. The pension plan's physician opined that the plaintiff was unable to perform any job currently available with the employer—which is not the same thing as complete inability to undertake paid work. The District Court upheld the denial of benefits. The plan did not act arbitrarily or capriciously, and there was no abuse of discretion. The evidence did not show eligibility for the benefit—only inability to retain the preinjury job.

An attorney had heart surgery and was unable to return to work. Although six doctors said that he couldn't work, one doctor said that his inability to work was motivational in nature. The employer cut off his disability benefits based on that one opinion, and the insurer affirmed the denial, describing litigation as a "sedentary" occupation. The attorney sued under ERISA §502(a)(1)(B), the cause of action for recovery of benefits due under a plan.

In *Kearny v. Standard Insurance Co.,* 66 LW 1678 (9th Cir. 4/21/98), the Ninth Circuit ruled that the plan, which required "satisfactory written proof of disability" as a prerequisite to paying benefits, did not explicitly give discretionary authority to the plan administrator. Therefore, the administrator's decisions should be reviewed on a de novo basis, subject to objective standards. Since there were certainly material issues of fact as to what a litigator's job entails and the plaintiff's ability to perform the job, the lawyer's claim should have proceeded to trial.

Disability benefits that are reduced on the twenty-fifth anniversary of the former employee's hiring, to the level of the pension he or she would have received after retiring with 25 years of service, remain disability benefits and do not become pension benefits as a result of the reduction. Therefore, under *Picard v. Comm'r,* 165 F.3d 744 (9th Cir. 1/26/99), benefits received under the plan remain tax-free under IRC §104(a)(1).

On February, 17, 1998, the Israel Discount Bank filed a settlement with the EEOC, under which the bank agreed to parity between mental and physical disabilities in its long-term disability plan: See 66 LW 2519. The case's docket number is 95-CV-6964 (S.D.N.Y.).

If the employee pays all the premiums for long-term disability insurance, and the employer's only role is to administer the payments (without endorsing the policy), then ERISA does not preempt a suit by the employee against the insurer, claiming that benefits were cut off in bad faith after the employee refused to take an independent medical examination. There are three tests for deciding whether ERISA preempts litigation about a disability policy:

- Was there a "plan, fund or program"? In this case, a plan was clearly present—but it was not an ERISA plan.
- Does the arrangement qualify for the ERISA safe harbor? It does if the employer does not make any contributions to the plan; the plan is completely voluntary; the employer does not profit from the plan (other than receiving a reasonable administrative fee); and the employer allows one or more insurers to publicize the availability of the program, but does not endorse or recommend it.
- Is the employer's sole function under the plan collection of premiums, or is there deeper employer involvement?

In the judge's view, in the case of *Bagden v. Equitable Life Assurance Society of the United States*, an employer can be neutral even if it is involved in program administration. The most important criterion is whether a reasonable employee would believe that the program was part of the employer's own benefit package, or that the employer controlled the program. But in this case, the employer properly gave information about the program but did not endorse it. Since ERISA preemption was not triggered, the employee is at liberty to sue the insurer for terminating her disability benefits.

Bagden is discussed in Shannon P. Duffy's article, "Employee-Paid Disability Policy Falls Under ERISA Safe Harbor," from *The Legal Intelligencer.* The article is available at http://www.lawnewsnetwork.com/practice/employmentlaw/ news/A1399-1999May12.html.

Nor does ERISA preempt an employee's state-law claims about an insurer's denial of benefits under an individual disability policy converted from a group policy [*Demars v. CIGNA Corp.*, 67 LW 1656 (1st Cir. 4/6/99)]. The employer is no longer involved, so neither is ERISA.

A plan participant who was denied benefits under a long-term disability plan brought suit under ERISA §502(a)(3) and got a default judgment covering disability expenses, medical benefits, prejudgment interest, and attorneys' fees [*Rogers v. Hartford Life & Accident Insurance Co.*, 167 F.3d 933 (5th Cir. 1999)]. When the plan got the court to reopen the case, the Fifth Circuit reduced the damages, on the grounds that the cost of medical treatment lay outside the disability plan's contract. The *Mertens* case [508 U.S. 248 (Sup. Ct. 1993)] says that §502(a)(3) remedies are purely equitable; compensatory damages are unavailable.

See 63 FR 48389 et. seq., especially p. 48394 (9/9/98), for the timing requirements for claim resolution in disability benefit programs. This Proposed Rule shortens the time that plans have to rule on disability claims and also extends (to 180 days) the period of time that employees are given to appeal an adverse determination.

If an incomplete claim for disability benefits is submitted, the plan must notify the claimant that the claim is incomplete within 15 days. An initial determination must be made as to complete claims within 30 days. If the initial determination is adverse to the claimant, and the claimant appeals, the appeal must be processed within 45 days.

Although the general rule is that the Mental Health Parity Act, 42 USC 300gg (see ¶9.2.1), does not cover disability plans, employers must beware of the argument that distinguishing between physical and mental disabilities violates the Americans With Disabilities Act. The argument pro and con can be found in "Post-Employment Fringe Benefits and the ADA: Suing for Differential Disability Coverage," *WestGroup Employment Alert*, 7/9/98, p. 1.

There's an outside chance that the distinction will be penalized under Title III of the ADA (the ban on discrimination in public accommodations). However, cases such as *Ford v. Schering-Plough Corp.*, 1998 Westlaw 258386 (3rd Cir. 1998), *EEOC v. C.N.A. Insurance Co.*, 96 F.3d 1039 (7th Cir. 1996), and *Parker v. Metropolitan Life Ins. Co.*, 121 F.3d 1006 (6th Cir. 1996) either find that there was no discrimination or find that the discrimination, if any, is between different classes of disabled individuals, whereas the ADA only bans discriminating between disabled and nondisabled persons.

ADA Title IV immunizes insurer and benefit plan decisions based on underwriting, classifying, or administering risks, as long as the decisions are not a subterfuge to escape ADA compliance. Therefore, decisions that have actuarial support are likely to qualify for this safe harbor. However, *Lewis v. Aetna Life Ins. Co.*, 7 F.Supp.2d 743 (E.D. Va. 1998), does not allow safe harbor characterization for a distinction between physical and mental disabilities for which actuarial support was not proven.

Nancy Hatch Woodward's article, "Supplemental LTD Plans Can Reduce Executive Discrimination," *HR Magazine* ,12/98, p. 68, points out that most long-term disability (LTD) plans have maximum benefits of $5000 a month. Even though their maximum replacement level is 60% of prior income, this amount is still uncomfortably small for highly compensated employees—especially since an LTD plan replaces only salary income, not bonuses or stock options.

An employer that has only minimal LTD protection may be at a disadvantage when trying to recruit employees in a market that offers much higher benefits. It's true that executives tend to work in "safe" jobs where there are few industrial accidents, but 90% of disability stems from illness rather than accident, so this argument is not very compelling.

> **TIP**
>
> No doubt your workforce would prefer you to respond by increasing the limits on the disability plan for everyone—but that's expensive. A good compromise is to offer individual supplemental disability policies over and above the group plan. A supplemental plan can have higher limits and replace all compensation, not just salary.

Usually, employers pay for the base plan (generating taxable income for the employee), but employees pay for the supplements; group premiums are 5 to 20% lower than individual premiums, so employees still benefit. If the employee pays all, the employer can open up the plan to everyone, not just executives, although executives tend to have more disposable income and therefore find such plans more appealing than rank-and-file workers do.

See §10.14, later in this chapter, for the *Parker-Hannifin* case.

Although it involves an individual policy, a 1999 case from the Eastern District of New York may provide some guidance. The issue in *Mossa v. Provident Life & Casualty Insurance Co.*, #96-5996 (E.D. N.Y. 2/11/99) (see Bill Alden, "Disability Policy Clause Interpreted by Federal Judge," *New York Law Journal*, 2/17/99, p. 1), was when benefits can be terminated on the grounds that the person can engage in "any gainful occupation." The opinion requires consideration of the individual's earnings history and availability of jobs in the relevant geographic area—a position shared by most of the courts that have had to interpret such clauses.

10.9 EDUCATION ASSISTANCE

A Hewitt Associates survey of 460 companies revealed that about half (46%) imposed a maximum on the educational assistance they would provide an individual in any year; the median figure was $3000, but some paid quite a bit more, in line with the rising cost of tuition. A number of companies raised their reimbursement levels to encourage employees to take two courses a semester rather than one (so they could complete their coursework faster). On the other hand, few companies reimburse for more than two classes a semester—a heavy course load is likely to cut into workplace productivity.

Many companies offer higher reimbursement for graduate than for undergraduate courses. Reimbursement is the key word: Only 5% pay in advance, and 76% wait for the employee to finish the course (and almost two-thirds reimburse only if the grade is C or better; some offer a base level of reimbursement, and enhance it if the employee gets an A or a B). Most companies reimburse the related cost of books and school fees, but 23% limit reimbursement to the actual cost of tuition. There is an increasing trend for employers to require that the courses be work related.

Traditional on-campus university courses are not the only option. Many employers see the benefit of using television, video, or the Internet for distance learning, which is much more adaptable to employees' work and family schedules. See Dale K. DuPont, "Tuition Aid That Makes the Grade," *HR Magazine*, 4/99, p. 75.

10.14 VOLUNTARY EMPLOYEE BENEFIT ASSOCIATIONS (VEBAS)

An employer could deduct only the part of the VEBA contribution that was used to fund long-term disability benefits. The portions that funded postretirement benefits and medical benefits for union members were not deductible, because the employer failed to satisfy the IRC §419A(c)(2) requirements for accumulating assets to prefund the benefits [*Parker-Hannifin Corp. v. Comm'r*, 139 F.3d 1090 (6th Cir. 3/23/98)].

10.15 VACATIONS AND VACATION BANKING

The "group emergency pool" technique can be used to maintain the paycheck of sick employees who would not otherwise be entitled to pay. It works especially well in smaller companies that can't afford a short-term disability plan. Employees donate unused vacation days, and the donor's salary is contributed to the sick employee. Theoretically, at least, employees who benefit from the pooling system will donate some of their own time when they get better.

Many variations and administrative structures are possible. There can be an anonymous pool, or the donors can be identified so the recipients can thank them. The company can allow pooling of vacation time only, sick leave only, or both. Usually, the maximum donation is 80 hours, because there are sound reasons for requiring employees to take at least some vacation time. A person who never takes vacations could be a workaholic who needs to slow down before he or she burns out—or an embezzler who has to keep watch over a dishonest scheme.

A donation plan can be calculated on an hour-for-hour basis; or, if employees with widely disparate wage scales are involved, on a dollar-for-dollar basis. Employers who want to implement a plan of this type should be sure to communicate it to employees and maintain written policy guidelines. Employees should not be put under pressure to donate; it should be a voluntary program. To avoid potential liability, make sure that pregnancy-related and HIV/AIDS-related requests are handled on a par with other sick day requests. For information, see Carla Joinson, "Time Share," *HR Magazine*, 12/98, p. 104.

Not only can vacation days be donated; they can also be purchased and sold. In 1994, Hewitt Associates surveyed about 500 companies and found that 15% allowed buying and selling of vacation days; 24% allowed this in 1997. After all, from the corporate viewpoint, the same number of work days are put in; all that changes is the identity of the people doing the work. Eighteen percent of the survey respondents allowed selling of vacation days, and 12% allowed buying. Where both are permitted, there are more would-be buyers than sellers: 25% of employees want to buy more vacation days, and only 10% want to sell. Even if the program has no net cash effect on payroll, it can be effective, because it's an incentive for employees to feel more in control of their schedules. (These figures come from Kate Walter's "Time For Sale" on p. 131 of the October 1998 issue of *HR Magazine.*)

Typically, vacation-sale plans allow the purchase or sale of up to five days. Employees get a monthly or quarterly statement of their vacation "balances." IRS regulations call for the purchase/sale decision to be made at benefit enrollment time. They also require employees to use up their regular days off before their purchased days.

If regular vacation days are on a "use it or lose it" basis, the same can be true for purchased days; or unused days can be banked toward a sabbatical or cashed out. (Year-end extra cash is especially welcome for holiday purchases.) The employer can deduct the cost of purchased days from the purchaser's paycheck, and the cost can be spread out over the entire year. Vacation day sales can be added to a flexible benefit program that includes flex credits and cash.

In the 1998 Eighth Circuit case of *Mange v. Petrolite Corp.*, 135 F.3d 570 (8th Cir. 1998), the plaintiff employees took voluntary retirement or voluntary separation as part of a reduction in force. The company's vacation policy treated vacation benefits as vesting at the end of the fiscal year. The plaintiffs claimed that their vacation vested on the last day of employment, and therefore they're entitled to be paid for unused vacation days. Their claim did not succeed in court, because the RIF programs didn't cover pay for unused vacation days, and the employees waived their claims under the regular plan by accepting the RIF incentives.

10.18 ERISA REGULATION OF WELFARE BENEFIT PLANS

A brokerage firm created an association of small firms (those with under 225 employees) so the members could maintain a self-funded health benefit plan. The Third Circuit ruled that the members lacked the requisite commonality of interest, and therefore the plan was not an "employee welfare benefit plan" as defined by ERISA [*Gruber v. Hubbard Bert Karle Weber Inc.*, 159 F.3d 780 (3rd Cir. 1998)].

Where failure to make complete disclosure could be harmful to benefit participants, a benefit plan administrator has a fiduciary duty to give complete and accurate information about the plan; it's not enough simply to answer participants' questions, if it's clear that the participant is unaware of important features of the plan [*Krohn v. Huron Memorial Hospital*, 67 LW 1619 (6th Cir. 4/1/99)].

Chapter 11

EARLY RETIREMENT AND RETIREE HEALTH BENEFITS

11.1 INTRODUCTION

In 1997, only about 10% of corporations surveyed by Charles D. Spencer & Associates Inc. offered incentives for early retirement. This is noticeably lower than the 13.2% of respondents who coped with recession in 1991 by offering early retirement as a way to reduce their employee census. Only 6.1% of retirement decisions in 1997 resulted from the early retirement incentives, whereas over one-third did so in 1991 (37.6%).

However, the 1997 incentive offers were not only more selective (typically, made to a targeted group, not a broad swathe of employees) but more attractive, because over half of eligible employees accepted the offer in 1997, versus less than one-third in 1991 (52.3% and 32.7%, respectively). In 1997, close to 9% of the surveyed workforce was eligible for the incentives—less than 1% of the workforce qualified in 1997.

Far fewer employers offered to supplement the Social Security benefit in 1997 than in 1991 (remember, Social Security benefits are reduced if a nondisabled person retires prior to normal retirement age). Otherwise, incentive plans were more or less the same in both years. Typically, persons over 55 with 10 years of service were eligible for early retirement and were offered three to five years of additional age or service credit in the computation of their pension.

However, as this chapter shows, retiree health coverage is declining greatly. In 1991, 41 of the 50 employers surveyed provided retiree health insurance, and 26 of those provided lifetime coverage. In 1997, only four of 21 private companies surveyed offered lifetime health coverage; only five extended coverage from the time of retirement to age 65 (i.e., the age of initial Medicare eligibility). See "Drop in Early Retirement Incentive Offers Reflects Boom Times," *Compensation and Benefits Update,* 7/15/98, p. 7.

In early 1999, the Sixth Circuit adopted the Third Circuit rule, previously expressed in *Fischer v. Philadelphia Electric Co.*, 96 F.3d 1533 (3rd Cir. 1996): A revised early retirement incentive has received "serious consideration," and therefore must be disclosed to potential early retirees, once senior managers discuss the proposal for purposes of implementation. Thus, *McAuley v. IBM Corp.*, 67 LW 1480 (6th Cir. 1/22/99) permits retirees to sue for breach of fiduciary duty when their ex-employer adopts an early retirement plan more favorable than the plan they accepted.

In the view of the Seventh Circuit, it does not violate ERISA to deny early retirement to employees who are deemed especially valuable, if the plan gives management discretion as to whether early retirement is in the company's best interests. A company's standards (as opposed to rules) are supposed to be applied flexibly and with discretion, and implementation of this standard was not so arbitrary or capricious as to violate ERISA [*McNab v. General Motors*, 162 F.3d 959 (7th Cir. 1998)].

Another General Motors case, this time in the Third Circuit, says that the LMRA and NLRA do not preempt early retiree's claims under state law that the employer fraudulently induced them to accept early retirement. [*Voilas v. General Motors*, 67 LW 1538 (3rd Cir. 3/3/99)].

An early 1998 case arose because a plant closed, then was re-opened by a new owner who required the former employees to re-apply for their old jobs, cut wages, reduced benefits, and changed the seniority schedule. According to the Tenth Circuit, there was no "permanent shutdown" of the plant, and therefore the original employer's "forced termination" provision did not come into play, and the plaintiffs were not entitled to early retirement benefits [*Dycus v. PBGC*, 133 F.3d 1367 (10th Cir. 1998)].

A "suspension" of benefits (for exceeding the plan's limitation on postretirement employment) is not considered a "reduction" in benefits subject to the ERISA anti-cutback rule. Therefore, tougher limitations on post-retirement employment, adopted six years after the plaintiff retired, permitted the employer to suspend retirement benefits without violating ERISA [*Spacek v. Maritime Association*, 134 F.3d 283 (5th Cir. 1/22/98)].

It is a breach of fiduciary duty to inform potential early retirees that lump-sum payouts are available, without also disclosing the IRC §415 limitations on rollovers and pointing out that failure to make a rollover will result in immediate taxation. See *Farr v. U.S. West Communications, Inc.*, 58 F.3d 1361 (9th Cir. 1998). The fiduciaries' common-law duty of loyalty requires them to deal fairly and honestly with plan participants, so it is a violation to give them incomplete information.

11.2 EARLY RETIREMENT INCENTIVES: ADEA ISSUES

See ¶26.3 for the EEOC's Final Regulation on how to draft a waiver that is valid under the Older Workers Benefit Protection Act.

Although the Older Workers Benefit Protection Act mandates a 21-day period during which employees can consider whether or not to accept an early retirement offer, the offer need not remain irrevocable during that period. The employer retains the option of canceling the offer [*Ellison v. Premier Salons Int'l Inc.*, 164 F.3d 1111 (8th Cir. 1999)].

11.3 RETIREE HEALTH BENEFITS

A study of 612 Fortune 1000 companies, performed by Watson Wyatt Worldwide, showed that 83% of manufacturing companies and 61% of service companies provided some retiree health benefits in 1997. However, only 205 of the companies pre-fund the retiree health benefit, and only 25% of the accumulated obligation for retiree health benefits was pre-funded. The study can be found at http://www.watsonwyatt.com, and is discussed in Bill Leonard's article, "Retiree Health Plan Funding Stagnates," *HR Magazine*, "Focus", 12/98, p. 3.

In 1998, and again in 1999, the Clinton Administration, in view of declining availability of retiree health coverage, and concerned about the growing number of uninsured people, suggested lowering the Medicare eligibility age, so that "near-elderly" people over 55 could "buy in" to Medicare coverage. That suggestion was not adopted. In fact, there was some support in Congress for raising the age of Medicare eligibility on the same schedule as eligibility for Social Security benefits, with the eventual result that Medicare eligibility would be delayed until age 67.

See GAO/HEHS-98-133, "Private Health Insurance: Declining Employer Coverage May Affect Access for 55- to 64-Year Olds," (6/1/98), describing the effect of declining employer participation in retiree health coverage on the access of the "near elderly" to health insurance.

This report notes that, according to the consulting firm Foster Higgins, the average cost to the corporation of providing retiree health coverage was $5210 for 1996 (a figure that hadn't changed much since 1993). Peat Marwick figures show a fall in the cost of early retirement coverage, from $5748 in 1993 to $5460 in 1995. Other Foster Higgins data shows that, in 1997, 12% of survey respondents said that, during the two years prior to the study, they had raised the plan contribution required of retirees; 6% had increased retirees' deductibles and copayments; 4% restricted eligibility; and 8% moved retirees from an indemnity to a managed care plan.

Peat Marwick looked at the amount that retirees had to pay toward the cost of their own family benefits. In 1995, the percentage contributed by retirees ranged from 41 to 53% (analyzed by size of firm—200 workers or over 5000 workers; the smaller the firm, the larger the retirees' responsibility), an average of $2040 to $3048 a year. The overall nationwide average was 45%, or $2340 a year. The number of retirees who declined to enroll in COBRA plans went up between 1994 and 1997, often because of the expense.

To the extent that employers provided retiree benefits at all, they were likely to subject the obligation to some sort of "cap" (i.e., a yearly or lifetime maximum); they also tended to make eligibility requirements stricter. The decline in employment-related retiree health coverage opens up some opportunities for sale of acute health insurance to the near elderly. Such clients then become a good market for Medigap insurance once they reach the age of Medicare eligibility.

A William Mercer study shows that the annual cost of providing retiree health benefits actually dropped in 1997, going from $3182 in 1996 to $3149 the next year. According to this study, 46% of employers provided coverage for early retirees—a percentage that dropped to 38% in 1997. In 1993, 40% of retirees who were over 65 or otherwise eligible for Medicare had coverage under an employer plan, but this was true of only 31% of Medicare-eligible retirees in 1997. Another important trend was the decline in indemnity coverage of retirees, in favor of a shift to managed care—especially Preferred Provider Organizations (PPOs). The William Mercer survey, "Growth in Health Plan Costs Held to 0.2 Percent in 1997," is discussed in *Compensation and Benefits Update*, 3/11/98, p. 4.

The GAO notes that in the 1980s, about two-thirds of companies offered retiree health benefits, a percentage that had declined below 40% in late 1998. Retiree health benefit plans reflect the same trends as plans for active employees (more managed care and increasing copayment responsibilities for plan participants), but the easy gains have already been made in both types of plan. See Stephenie [sic] Overman, "Keeping Retiree Health Benefits Afloat," *HR Magazine*, 12/98, p. 114.

According to the Northern District of Illinois, given that retirement is a COBRA event, a plan has an independent duty to issue a COBRA notice at retirement, even if retirees are given access under the plan to health coverage for an indefinite period of time, not limited by the COBRA period: *Mansfield v. Chicago Park District Group Plan*, 1998 Westlaw 128061 (N.D. Ill. 1998).

In a unionized environment, when the Collective Bargaining Agreement determines retiree benefit rights "for the term of the agreement," it is not an ERISA violation to terminate retiree health and life insurance benefits after a contract ends. In other words, it's a new ball game each time the CBA is re-negotiated. See *Pabst Brewing Co. v. Corrao*, 161 F.3d 434 (7th Cir. 1998).

ERISA fiduciary duty was not breached by transferring the obligation to provide some retiree health benefits to a new company formed when a corporate division was spun off: *Sengpiel v. B.F. Goodrich Co.*, 1998 Westlaw 637159 (6th Cir. 1998). To the Sixth Circuit, the new entity's reduction of retiree health and life insurance benefits was lawful, because the power to alter benefits was retained in the plan documents. The reduction should be analyzed as a plan amendment, modification, or termination—that is, a business decision—rather than a fiduciary decision involving discretionary issues in plan administration.

Chapter 12

SUBSTANTIVE LAW OF PENSIONS

12.1 INTRODUCTION

The IRS announced 1998 plan limits in IR-98-63 (10/23/98), retaining the 1997 figures. The maximum defined benefit plan benefit remains $130,000 a year. The limit on annual contributions to a defined contribution plan is still $30,000; the 402(g) elective deferral is still limited to $10,000. A highly compensated employee (HCE) remains one earning $80,000 a year, and the SIMPLE limit is still $6000.

For a look at the fixed annuity, a major funding mechanism for pensions, see Jeremy Alexander's "Fixed Annuities Play Major Role in Pensions," *National Underwriter*, 9/28/98, p. 21. A fixed annuity is an investment contract that guarantees a particular rate of return. Alexander reports that, of 295 fixed annuities studied by Beacon Research, about half could be used to invest corporate pension contributions, and nearly all (94.1%) accepted IRA rollovers.

Plan sponsors favor fixed-annuity investments because they are safe and predictable. Furthermore, defined benefit plans take the risk that they will have to contribute more to satisfy the funding obligation as interest rates rise; fixed annuities eliminate this risk. It should also be noted that, if a defined benefit plan is fully invested in guaranteed-rate contracts, Pension Benefit Guaranty Corporation (PBGC) insurance will not be required because of the shift of risk to the insurance company.

The insurance companies that sell fixed annuities can perform many administrative chores, and they make it easy to annuitize the pension obligation when the employee retires. (The insurer may even perform the annuitization at no charge to the plan.) To the extent that the plan still wishes to make minimum distributions to participants who have reached 70 1/2 (or is obligated to do so, in the case of employee-stockholders), "withdrawal without liquidation" (permitted by about one-third of the fixed annuities studied) can meet this need by receiving set payments under the fixed annuity, usually deriving from interest, at stated periods.

The Beacon Research study also shows that 60.5% of fixed annuity plans require funding with a single premium, 33.1% set the premium flexibly, and 6.4% use a basis of a single premium but allow enhancements.

In the view of the Third Circuit, it is not a breach of fiduciary duty for an employer to buy GICs for individual accounts from a company that later was seized by regulators. *In re Unisys Savings Plan Litigation,* 67 LW 1640 (3rd Cir. 3/22/99) holds that the employer did not fail in its duty of prudence. Investment responsibility was delegated to appropriate parties, who made an adequate investigation prior to purchase. The bad result was unfortunate, but not a fiduciary breach.

12.4 PENSION PLAN STRUCTURES

A state cannot use its Disposition of Unclaimed Property Act to seize unclaimed benefits from a defined benefit plan. *Commonwealth Edison v. Vega,* 67 LW 1646 (7th Cir. 4/13/99) says that ERISA preempts the state law, because states do not have the power to take over pension plan operations by recouping unclaimed benefits.

A "floor-offset" plan is a hybrid plan, where the defined benefit portion of the plan guarantees a floor level of benefits, offset by the annuity the retiree could purchase at retirement with the balance in the defined contribution portion of the plan. *Lunn v. Montgomery Ward & Co. Retirement Security Plan,* 67 LW 1496 (7th Cir. 1/26/99), holds that an employee who retired four years after normal retirement age was not entitled to additional retirement benefits to make up for the reduced duration of benefits. The court upheld the general floor-offset structure, finding that it does not violate ERISA's antiforfeiture provisions or benefit accrual requirements.

12.4.3 401(k) Plans

The 401(k) plan, also known as a CODA (for "Cash or Deferred Arrangement"), is a form of deferred compensation under which employees are given the choice either to receive up to $10,000 of their compensation in cash immediately or have the compensation placed into an account where it will accumulate until retirement. The incentives for employees to do this are freedom from taxation on the appreciation in the value of the account until retirement, and the practice of many employers to match part of the employee contribution (although tax law does not require employers to do this). Typically, the plan will place the responsibility for allocating the employee contribution portion of the fund on the employee, who is given a choice of several investment alternatives, such as stock and bond funds. The employer will determine the investment of its own matching contribution.

401(k) plans have gained a great deal in popularity. The Profit Sharing/401(k) Council of America (PSCA) did a study of 401(k) plan sponsorship in the cities of Atlanta, Chicago, and Los Angeles. They found that 401(k) plan sponsorship soared between 1994 and 1998, especially in companies with 100 to 499 employees, where the number of plan sponsors approximately doubled in those four years.[1]

The PSCA survey shows that close to three-quarters of companies that have 100 or more employees sponsor 401(k) plans (71.5%). Dividing these companies by size shows that 78.3% of companies with over 500 employees are 401(k) sponsors, versus 70.1% of companies with over 100 but under 500 employees. Nearly all companies with over 100 workers do have some kind of retirement plan (87.4%; 95.9% of companies with over 500 workers).

For the 1997 plan year, other PSCA studies show that 609 401(k) and profit-sharing plans surveyed covered more than 1.8 million participants and held over $179 billion in assets. Two hundred forty-seven of these plans were 401(k) plans, and 265 combined 401(k) and profit-sharing features.[2] In 1991, only 71% of employees eligible to participate in 401(k) plans actually did so; this percentage increased dramatically, to 84.6% in 1996 and 88.4% in 1997. In both 1996 and 1997, higher-paid employees contributed 6.1% of their pay to the plan, as compared to 5.02% in 1996 and 5.2% in 1997 for their lower-paid counterparts. This is as expected: The more an employee earns, the more discretionary income he or she has for purposes such as investment and funding retirement.

According to the PSCA survey, in 1997 87.6% of 401(k) plans gave employees at least five investment alternatives to choose from; 30.6% allowed 10 or more options. (However, it can be counterproductive to offer so many options that employees are unable to do enough research to make an informed choice.) The most common investment choices were actively managed domestic equity funds; stable value/guaranteed investment contract funds; funds that balanced stock and bond investments; indexed domestic equity funds (for risk-averse people who want to make sure that their account does not underperform the index); and investment in the employer company's own stock.

In 1996, the average contribution by the employer was 4.8% of payroll, which increased to 5.5% in 1997. More and more companies made their matching contribution each payroll period, rather than in a single annual payment.

Another PSCA survey, available at http://www.psca.org/eligible.html, looks at eligibility for 401(k) plan participation in 384 companies varying in location, size, and industry. Of these companies, 280 sponsored both 401(k) and profit-sharing plans, as compared to 53 with only a 401(k) plan and 51 with only a profit-sharing plan.

About a quarter of the 401(k) plans allowed employees to participate as soon as they were hired, or within a month of hiring; eligibility for profit-sharing plans often occurred later. But most 401(k) and profit-sharing plans required a year of employment prior to participation. It was fairly unusual for 401(k) plans to limit enrollment to a particular "window" period during the year.

EBRI's Plan Profiles

The Employee Benefit Research Institute and the Investment Company are developing what they intend to be the most comprehensive database about 401(k) plans and their participants to be found anywhere. The database already includes

1996 data about 23,000 plans covering more than 2.5 million participants, with $75 billion in assets. Data for 1997 are being compiled, but preliminary indications are that the number of plans and the number of participants increased significantly. You can find survey results at http://www.ebri.org/dc_project/account_balances.htm.

As you would expect, the average account balance increased steadily with age: about $6000 for persons in their twenties, over $67,000 for plan participants in their sixties. The average account balance for all accounts was about $29,000, although the largest balances were found in plans offering both investment in the company's own stock and guaranteed investment contracts (GICs), the lowest in plans that offer only GICs or only other investment media, but not GICs or company stock.

The allocation of all account balances was 42.4% in equity funds, 19.5% in company stock, 16.7% in GICs, 9.3% in balanced or mixed funds, 6% in money market funds, 4% in bond funds, and 1.6% in all other. Younger participants tended to favor equity investments; older participants, who as you would expect tended toward fiscal conservatism, tended to favor GICs. The larger the number of participants in the plan, the greater the share that employer stock plays in 401(k) plan investments—which is also intuitive, because large companies are the most likely to have the kind of blue-chip stock that would work well in a retirement plan.

Trends and Predictions

In March 1998, David L. Wray of the Profit Sharing 401(k) Council of America and securities analyst Kathleen Hartman identified more than a dozen directions that they predict the 401(k) market will take,[3] such as

- Continuing increase in 401(k) participation rates
- Higher percentages of salary being saved
- Even greater investment of 401(k) balances in equities
- Higher balances for participants
- Near-universal permission for employees to direct the investment of their own contributions; majority permission of employees to allocate employer matches
- More use of Internet/intranet in 401(k) management and communications
- Lower fees thanks to market pressures
- Legislative changes (such as increasing the percentage that can be contributed to a defined-contribution plan) that will benefit lower-income employees

Nondiscrimination Tests

401(k) plans must not discriminate in favor of highly compensated employees. There are various technical requirements for satisfying the nondiscrimination test, but safe harbors are also permitted to simplify plan administration. If safe harbor matching or nonelective contributions are made on behalf of all eligible rank-and-file employees, and if employees are given adequate notice of their rights, then the plan will probably be held to satisfy the Actual Deferral Percentage (ADP) test and Actual Contribution Percentage (ACP) test and thus to be nondiscriminatory.

See IRS Notice 98-52, 1998-46 IRB 16, for safe harbor rules for plan years beginning after 12/31/98 (including companies that offer more than one 401(k) plan). Notices to employees do not have to be issued before 3/1/99. If the employer just makes the basic, safe harbor matching contributions, the plan will automatically qualify as nondiscriminatory. If it makes additional matching contributions, however, the contributions must be limited as described in the Notice to prevent discrimination in favor of highly compensated employees.

Under the safe harbor, the employer has to match $1 for every $1 deferred by the employee, up to 3% of the employee's compensation. If the employee chooses to defer 4 or 5% of compensation, the employer can match 50 cents for each $1 deferred at this level but cannot offer any further match after matching $3 for the first 3% and $1 for 4 to 5%—the maximum employer match is thus 4% of compensation. Nonelective nonmatching contributions by the employer must contribute 3% for all participants, whether or not the participants are highly compensated.[4]

Notice 98-52 permits the company to defer amending the plan to comply with the safe harbor requirement until it makes other plan amendments to phase in changes based on the Small Business Job Protection Act of 1996.

401(k) Plan Fees and Management

The Department of Labor's Pension and Welfare Benefit Administration (PWBA) has released guidance about 401(k) plan fee structures, which can be found at http://www.dol.gov/dol/pwba/public/pubs/401kfe~1.htm. The purpose of this document is to improve investment decision making by 401(k) plan participants, so you may wish to print it out and distribute it to employees (or make it available on your HR Internet or intranet site). The checklist for 401(k) fees on page 5 of this six-page document is especially handy.

The PWBA report groups fees into three categories: plan administration fees; investment fees (the major component); and individual service fees for optional features, such as plan loans or investment advice. The fees may be payable to the employer, if it furnishes services directly, or to outside service providers. In a bundled arrangement, all fees are funneled through one provider that coordinates the services. In an unbundled arrangement, the fees of the trustee, communications firm, investment manager, or other provider will be charged separately.

12.4.6 [NEW] Cash-Balance Plans

A cash-balance plan is a hybrid plan that is somewhat similar to both the defined benefit and defined contribution form. Despite its hybrid nature, the cash balance plan is required to meet the regulatory requirements for defined benefit plans. Although in some ways the cash-balance plan resembles the 401(k) plan, the employer retains the investment risk in a cash-balance plan, and the cash balance plan trustee manages investments for all of the accounts. Cash-balance plans are PBGC insured; 401(k) plans are not.

The first cash-balance plan, at the Bank of America, received IRS approval in 1985. By the spring of 1999, about 7 million employees were covered by cash-balance plans. Twenty-two of the *Fortune* 100 companies, as well as 400 to 600 medium-sized to large companies, had cash-balance plans. In 1998 and 1999, several extremely large companies adopted this form of plan, including Citigroup, Aetna Inc., IBM, Avon, and SmithKline Beecham PLC.[5]

In March 1999, CBS shifted from a defined benefit to a cash-balance plan, announcing that all employees would have access to a 401(k) plan; workers over 55 whose age and service added up to 70 could remain in the old plan; and new hires would not be eligible for pension coverage at all, but would receive stock options instead.[6]

See http://www.ebri.org/fundamentals/chpt10.htm for an excellent introduction to this form of plan. Basic information, and a pro-cash-balance-plan discussion, can be found in "Addressing Today's Workforce Needs," LA-99/2 (4/23/99), published by the APPWP Benefits Association; see http://www.appwp.org/la42399.html.

The cash-balance plan is structured so that the corporation's books reflect an individual account for each participant, funded by the employer each year, based on a percentage of pay and subject to the IRC §415 limits. The final pension reflects two elements: an annual benefit credit, defined as a percentage of pay, and an annual interest credit at the rate specified by the plan.

The presence of individual accounts makes cash-balance plans more portable than conventional defined benefit plans. If the employee leaves (it's typical for employees, especially younger employees, to make several career changes), the balance can be received in a lump sum immediately, not at retirement age.

Each participant's account also accrues interest until retirement, but the interest rate is specified in the plan and does not reflect actual earnings on the account. The employer therefore assumes the investment risk but also is entitled to retain investment rewards—which, in the current investment climate, have been quite substantial. A high rate of return can permit the employer to reduce its contributions.

In that the cash-balance plan is primarily a defined benefit plan, the employer does not commit to a particular level of contribution. Instead, it makes contributions based on the actuarial valuation of the account. Defined benefit vesting and minimum funding requirements apply. The employer must therefore contribute the normal cost plus amortization of unfunded accrued liability, subject to the full-funding limit. PBGC premium and termination requirements apply to cash-balance plans.

At retirement, the employee's annuity is based on the participant's vested account balance. In addition to making the required qualified joint and survivor annuity (QJSA) and qualified preretirement survivor annuity (QPSA) payments, cash-balance plans are more likely to offer a lump sum election than conventional defined benefit plans. However, there is little IRS guidance for structuring or operating a cash-balance plan.[7]

On July 30, 1998, the Third Circuit decided a lawsuit by Bell Atlantic employees by holding that it was not a violation of ERISA fiduciary duties to convert a conventional defined benefit plan to a cash balance plan, but the court did not allow publication of its opinion.

The differences between cash-balance plans and conventional defined benefit plans have significant practical consequences both for the plan and for its retirees. Most conventional defined benefit plans are structured so that accrual increases in the later years of employment. In contrast, accrual is greater in the early years of a cash-balance plan. It is common for defined benefit plans to subsidize early retirement, but rare for cash-balance plans to do so.

Therefore, cash-balance plans are much more attractive to a corporation's younger or more mobile, shorter-service employees than its long-service employees who are close to retirement age. (According to the Employee Benefits Research Institute, less than 10% of workers spend 20 years or more in the same job.)

From the employer's perspective, a cash-balance plan can be attractive if there are many employees with long tenure, who are accruing pension entitlement at a high rate because of their long service. One option would be to switch to a defined contribution plan, but cash-balance plans usually cost the employer less than similar defined contribution plans, because extra investment earnings and plan forfeitures can be included in the actuarial calculation, thus reducing the cash-balance plan contribution.

It's one thing if a start-up company adopts its first plan, in which case employees understand the plan and its implications. Conversion to a cash-balance plan can be difficult for employees to understand and can have the effect of "freezing" older employees' balances and requiring older employees to work for several years to catch up (because of changes in interest rate assumptions).

There are several approaches to moving from a defined benefit to a cash-balance plan. The defined benefit plan can be "grandfathered" for a period of time, or until the retirement of employees who put in most of their career under the old arrangement. The employer can supplement the cash-balance accounts of long-tenure workers or increase the 401(k) match for those workers, so they do not lose out in the long run.

12.5.1 Taxation of Participants of Nonqualified Plans

In 1996, the Tax Court decided that §83(a) requires inclusion in income as soon as vacation and severance pay benefits are secured with a letter of credit, because the employee is deemed to have received those amounts [*Schmidt Baking Co. v. Comm'r*, 107 TC 271 (1996)]. Congress overturned that result by legislation, passing §7001 of the Internal Revenue Service Restructuring and Reform Act of 1998 (IRSRRA), P.L. 105-206, adding a new IRC §404(a)(11). The new section makes it clear that deeming is not proper—amounts are not included in taxable income until they are actually received. See IRS Notice 99-16, 1999-13 IRB 10, for information about how to make accounting changes to conform to the IRSRRA requirements.

12.6 FACTORS IN CHOOSING A PLAN FORM

IRS Announcement 99-2, 1999-2 IRB 44 (12/29/98), encourages employers that do not have plans to permit employees to invest, via payroll deductions, in either regular or Roth IRAs. The Announcement explains how to adjust withholding taxes to compensate for deductible IRA contributions.

12.10 EMPLOYEE CONTRIBUTIONS

On January 25, 1999, the Supreme Court decided the extremely significant case of *Hughes Aircraft Co. v. Jacobson*, #97-1287 (67 LW 4122). The case involved Hughes Aircraft Company's defined benefit retirement plan. Unlike most defined benefit plans, this one mandated employee contributions, and a large part of the plan was attributable to employee contributions.

The Hughes plan operated at a surplus, and the employer suspended its contributions in light of the surplus. It also amended the plan to provide for early retirement benefits and to add a new benefit structure for new participants. Under the new structure, employee contributions were not required; the plan was funded with the surplus from the older plan.

The plaintiff employees contended—unsuccessfully—that the employer had an obligation to share the plan surplus with the employees who contributed to it, rather than using the surplus to reduce the employer's future obligations. In the view of the Supreme Court, the very nature of a defined benefit plan is that the employer assumes and controls the risk. If the plan operates at a surplus, it is not improper for the employer to apply that surplus toward other obligations—because the employer is always obligated to provide the vested benefits specified in the plan. In this analysis, Hughes did not violate ERISA, because it did not cease to furnish vested benefits as defined by the plan.

Nor did the Supreme Court accept the employees' argument that Hughes improperly terminated the old plan. Instead, the court held that an amendment creating a new benefit structure is permissible—and should not be treated as the creation of a second plan—if there is only one pool of assets used to fund both obligations. The old plan was not terminated merely because an additional benefit structure was added, because payments would continue to be made to longer-serving employees on the basis of the original plan.

For a later case dealing with pension surplus, see the Second Circuit's April 1999 ruling that New Coleman Holdings Inc., a unit of Sunbeam Corp., was entitled to the surplus (approximately $14 million) in the pension plan of one of its controlled companies. The surplus derived from investment gains. The investment was intended to fund future benefits, and the District Court held that plan participants were entitled to the money. The Second Circuit reversed, on the grounds that participants in the defined benefit plan would get their promised benefits, and so were not harmed; the corporation was entitled to reap the benefit of the investment success.[8]

12.11 LEASED EMPLOYEES

According to *Bronk v. Mountain States Telephone & Telegraph Inc.*, 98-1 USTC ¶50,316 (10th Cir. 1998), ERISA does require that employees be permitted to participate in the plan once they have satisfied the plan's age and service requirements. However, it does not violate ERISA to draft the plan in such a way that leased employees—even leased employees who are common-law employees—are excluded from all participation. See IRS Notice 84-11, Q&A 14: "[IRC]§414(n)(1)(A) requires only that a leased employee be treated as an employee; it does not require that a leased employee be a participant in the recipient's qualified plan."

12.13 WHICH PLANS ARE MOST POPULAR?

The Small Employer Retirement Survey (SERS), performed by the Employee Benefit Research Institute (EBRI), the American Savings Education Council, and market researchers Mathew Greenwald & Associates, was released in June 1998. The survey shows that small employers that do not offer retirement plans are often ill-informed about small business alternatives and overestimate the cost and difficulty of maintaining a plan. See http://www.ebri.org/sers/SERS.htm.

Nearly all small business plans are defined contribution plans: 92% of companies that offer plans offer this form of plan; 15% offer defined benefit plans; and 8% have both defined benefit and defined contribution plans. The 401(k) plan is the most common defined contribution mode for the survey respondents (61% of plans). Thirty-one percent of respondents who offer plans offer profit-sharing plans; 12% have a SIMPLE plan (a savings incentive match plan).

Close to half of the small businesses with pension plans use a third-party administrator (44%); brokerages are involved in plan administration in 31% of the cases, 29% use mutual fund companies, 25% involve insurance companies, and 14% use banks. (The numbers add up to more than 100% because of the strong potential for using several kinds of advisors and administrators in the same plan.) Of the small businesses that do offer pension plans, 20% have done so for two decades or more; 24% have had a plan for 10 to 19 years; another 24% had a plan for one to five years; and 8% had a plan for a year or less. (Of course, it's possible that some short-term plans are in new enterprises, rather than established enterprises that took a long time to set up a plan.) One-sixth of small companies that already offer a plan intend to add a new plan type within two years; only 4% anticipate terminating one or more of their existing plans.

Although companies without plans claim to be familiar with many popular plan types, two-thirds or more of the survey respondents that did not offer pension plans had never heard of thrift savings plans, 403(b) plans, or money purchase plans.

Understandably, financial factors were significant in the decision not to adopt a plan. Fifty-one percent of non-plan-sponsoring respondents said that their revenues were too uncertain to maintain a plan; 45% said that the required employer contributions are prohibitively expensive; 42% felt that the vesting requirements force unfairly large contributions on behalf of short-term employees. The expense of starting and maintaining a plan and the burden of government regulation were each cited as factors in their decision by 35% of respondents. Here again, the response is well over 100%, because multiple factors are involved in the decision.

What distinguishes small businesses that offer pension plans from those that don't? Fifty-three percent of companies with plans have revenues over $1 million a year, versus only 36% of companies that do not provide plans. Two-thirds of survey respondents without pension plans are family owned, as compared to 47% of companies offering plans. Companies with plans tend to have more over-30 employees, to have a better-educated workforce, and to pay more than companies that don't have plans. They tend to retain employees for longer (although high turnover is not necessarily an evil if a company requires little training of its workforce and can bring new employees on line quickly).

Companies that offer pension plans tend to offer more of other employee benefits as well. Survey respondents that provide pensions almost universally (99%) provide paid vacations; 97% provide health insurance; 79% offer life insurance; 72% pay employees on sick leave; and 62% offer disability insurance. However, tuition assistance and child care assistance were only offered by a minority. Companies without pension plans provide paid vacation in only 88% of the cases; only 70% offer health insurance. Less than half of the companies without pension plans provide paid sick leave, insurance, or other benefits.

The survey involved four true-false questions about plan operations: whether a plan can be set up for under $2000 (which is true); whether employer matches of 401(k) contributions are legally mandated (false); whether a plan, once created, can be terminated (true); and that employees can be required to contribute to administrative costs (true). Only 28% of respondents answered all four questions correctly, and 19% were correct about only one or two.

12.14 PBGC PREMIUMS

Although concerns have been voiced about the long-term viability of the PBGC, it achieved its third straight surplus year in 1998 (following 20 deficit years). For the year ending 9/30/98, the PBGC single-employer program had assets of $17.6 billion versus $12.6 billion in liabilities. The agency covered about 42 million employees; 209,300 of them received $848 million in insurance payments in FY 1998. 1998 was a year in which comparatively few plans terminated, so the PBGC was not stressed by major new obligations.[9]

In October of 1998, the GAO studied the long-term prospects of the agency in a Letter Report, "Pension Benefit Guaranty Corporation: Financial Condition Improving, But Long-Term Risks Remain," GAO/HEHS-99-5, dated 10/16/98. The GAO's conclusion was that most insured, underfunded plans have strengthened their financial status, which is hopeful for the PBGC's long-run stability. The PBGC's forecasting methodology has become more sophisticated, so there will be fewer surprises. However, there are still some large underfunded plans that might make large calls on the PBGC in the future.

Over time, many small plans have terminated, so that although the number of participants has increased since the 1980s, the number of PBGC-insured plans has been cut in half.

REFERENCES

[1]"401(k) Plan Sponsorship Growth 1994–1998," performed with Booz-Allen & Hamilton Inc.; see http://www.psca.org/grow401k.html.

[2]PSCA's "41st Annual Survey of Profit Sharing and 401(k) Plans"; see http://www.psca.org/surv41st.html.

[3]"Trends in the 401(k) Market," *West Employment Alert*, 4/16/98, p. 4.

[4]For safe harbor modifications of Notice 98-52, see "Recent IRC Changes Make 401(k) Plans, SIMPLEs More Attractive," *Compensation and Benefits Update*, 12/30/98, p. 1.

[5]Paul Beckett, "Citigroup Makes Move to Change Pension Benefits," *WSJ*, 4/2/99, p. A4; no byline, "Pension Shift at Citigroup," *NYT*, 4/6/99, p. C2; Ellen E. Schultz, "SmithKline and Aetna Are Latest Firms to Make Big Changes in Pension Plans," *WSJ*, 4/8/99, p. A6.; no byline, "IBM Ready to Adopt 'Cash-Balance' Plan for Pension Program," *WSJ*, 5/4/99, p. A8. For background, see Ellen E. Schultz, "'Cash' Pensions Trigger Protest of New Allies," *WSJ*, 1/22/99, p. C1, and "Older Workers Fight 'Cash Balance' Plans," *WSJ*, 2/11/99, p. C27.

[6]Ellen E. Schultz and Kyle Pope, "CBS Is Replacing Its Pension Program With Cash-Balance Plan, Stock Options," *WSJ*, 3/24/99, p. B10.

[7]The main guidance comes from Notice 96-8, IRB 1996-6 (2/5/96). It requires that the lump sum distribution from a cash-balance plan must be computed by determining the hypothetical balance in the plan projected out to normal retirement age, then making sure the employee receives at least the present value of that sum. There were earlier

regulations in 1991, amended in 1993. See Colleen T. Congel, "Cash Balance Pension Plan Growth Fuels Congressional, Regulatory Action," 67 LW 2531 (3/16/99).

[8]Frances A. McMorris, "Sunbeam Unit Is Entitled to Surplus in Pension," *WSJ*, 4/5/99, p. B2.

[9]"Pension Benefit Posts a Surplus of $5 Billion," *WSJ*, 3/30/99, p. A17.

Chapter 13

Plan Administration

13.2 CREATING A PLAN

Qualification failures can be handled by the IRS by methods other than disqualification of the plan. See Rev. Proc. 98-22, 1998-12 IRB 11, for the details of EPCRS program (Employee Plans Compliance Resolution System). EPCRS is a unified program that consolidates the Voluntary Compliance Resolution and Administrative Policy Regarding Sanctions programs. The IRS's goal is to create incentives for plan sponsors to undertake corrective steps as soon as possible, preferably voluntarily before enforcement actions are commenced. EPCRS is not available if the qualification failure deals with diversion or misuse of plan assets. The program took effect on September 1, 1998.

EPCRS allows plan sponsors to resolve voluntarily, with no need for IRS approval, any qualification failures that stem from the plan's failure to follow its own provisions. Minor operational failures can be corrected without user fees or sanctions. At any time before an audit occurs, a plan can pay a small user fee for IRS approval of corrective measures. Once an audit occurs, however, Rev. Proc. 98-22 requires sanctions to be imposed that are reasonable in light of the seriousness of the violation and any ameliorative measures already taken.

➡ TIP

Rev. Proc. 98-22 Appendix B includes a checklist plan sponsors can use when preparing to make a request under one of the EPCRS subprograms (VCR, SVP, and Walk-in CAP, depending on the timing and seriousness of the violation).

13.3 CLAIMS PROCEDURE

A self-insured health plan imposed a 90-day time limit for filing suits based on internal appeals of claims denials. The Eleventh Circuit found this requirement to be valid [*Northlake Regional Medical Center v. Waffle House Sys. Employee Benefit Plan*, 1998 Westlaw 972150 (11th Cir. 1998)]. The court declined to impose a general rule that a 90-day limitation is always permissible, but under the facts of the case, and given that the plan had procedures for expediting decision making, the limitation was appropriate and not overreaching.

13.4 STANDARD OF REVIEW

The main question is whether decisions are reviewed de novo, based on objective standards, or whether deference is granted and the inquiry is merely whether the administrators acted in an arbitrary and capricious fashion.

According to the Ninth Circuit, a disability plan that requires "satisfactory written proof" of disability, but does not say in so many words that the plan administrator has discretionary authority, is subject to de novo review of the objective correctness of the administrator's decisions [*Kearney v. Standard Insurance Co.*, 66 LW 1678 (9th Cir. 4/21/98)].

In contrast, the Seventh Circuit case of *McNab v. GM*, 162 F.3d 959 (7th Cir. 1998), involved an early retirement plan that gave management discretion to reject early retirement applications from employees who were deemed especially valuable and therefore whose early retirement was contrary to the company's best interests. The court interpreted this as a standard rather than a rule (i.e., something that can be applied flexibly and with discretion). Denial of early retirement to the plaintiffs was not sufficiently arbitrary or capricious to constitute an ERISA violation.

13.5 ADMINISTERING THE CLAIM

See §9.5 of this Supplement for a discussion of the Pension and Welfare Benefits Administration's September 9, 1998 Proposed Rule (63 FR 48390). Although the most controversial features of this proposal relate to EGHPs, and therefore are discussed under that heading, the proposal also applies to pension claims.

The PWBA estimated that 690,000 pension claims would be affected (629,000 from small plans, the rest from large plans). The agency also estimated that 65 million participants and 518,000 pension-plan procedures would be affected that would be handled by service providers, as compared to 22 million participants and 173,000 pension-plan procedures handled in-house (see 63 FR 48403).

The proposal retains most of the timing requirements imposed on pension and welfare benefit plans (although it makes significant changes in the timetable

EGHPs must use to handle claims and appeals). However, plan administrators are required to notify pension and welfare benefit claimants within 45 days of receipt of an incomplete claim. They must also inform the claimant what information is needed to complete the claim. Claimants must be given 180 days to furnish the needed data, and the plan must resolve the claim no later than 45 days of receipt of the missing information, or 45 days after the end of the 180-day period, whichever comes first [Prop.Reg. §2560.503-1(d)(1)]. See 63 FR 48393.

A 1998 case from the Northern District of California [*Bankamerica Pension Plan v. McMath*, 1998 Westlaw 422323 (N.D. Cal. 1998)] finds that it was proper for a plan to give effect to an unsigned form that changed a beneficiary designation. The employee didn't know that the form was not signed, and otherwise complied with the plan's requirements, so it was not arbitrary or capricious to carry out his wishes even though the technical requirements of the plan were not satisfied.

13.6 PLAN AMENDMENTS

As a general rule, Code §411(d)(6) prevents plans from adopting amendments that eliminate optional forms of benefits, but the Secretary of the Treasury has the power to permit exceptions to this rule. A recent example is found in IRS Notice 98-29, 1998-22 IRB 8. In mergers, for instance, the surviving plan may find itself saddled with a confusing variety of optional plans, which can be time-consuming and expensive to administer. The IRS is considering a relief provision, under which a defined contribution plan could be amended to pare down the number of payment options, as long as participants would have a choice of at least one lump sum and one multipayment form of distribution. Another possibility is to allow cancellation of payment options that are extremely unpopular with participants, or those that affect only a very small portion of the benefit.

13.9 ACCOUNTING ISSUES FOR PENSION PLANS

➠ TIP

Check the PBGC's Website each month, at http://www.pbgc.gov/interest.htp, for updated interest rates used each month for

- Valuation of lump-sum payments from the plan
- Variable-rate premiums
- Valuation of annuity benefits
- PBGC charges on employer liability, unpaid contributions, and unpaid premiums

Rates are updated on the fifteenth of every month.

13.11 ROUTINE PBGC COMPLIANCE

The current basic flat-rate premium for single-employer pension plans remains at $19 a year for each participant. Underfunded plans are subject to an additional variable-rate charge of $9 for every $1000 of unfunded vested benefits. For premium payment years beginning on or after January 1999, the required interest rate under 29 CFR §2006 is 4.30%. See http://www.pbgc.gov/premiums.htp.

On January 14, 1999, the PBGC established a toll-free telephone hot line (800-736-2444) for the assistance of plan administrators who have questions about plan coverage, premiums, or plan terminations. See the PBGC's press release, http://www.pbgc.gov/1999form.htm.

A PBGC Final Rule appearing in the *Federal Register* on December 14, 1998 (63 FR 68684) amends 29 CFR Part 4007 to provide that the final filing due date for a calendar-year plan's premium declaration will be October 15. In other words, the date is the same for the declaration as for the extended due date for Form 5500. The Final Rule makes corresponding changes in the treatment of the declaration for fiscal-year plans, which are now due on the fifteenth day of the tenth full calendar month of the premium payment year. (Adjustments are made if the plan changes its plan year, or if it is a new or newly covered plan.)

Proposed PBGC regulations, published in the *Federal Register* on April 27, 1999, give defined benefit plan sponsors an incentive to catch up on underpaid PBGC premiums before the agency detects an underpayment. The monthly penalty for a late premium payment is only 1%, not the standard 5%, if the company corrects the underpayment itself, prior to PBGC notice.

For some plans, the issue is whether or not they have 500 participants and therefore have to make an estimated PBGC premium payment by February 28. The April 27 proposal allows the determination to be based on either the actual number of plan participants in the previous year or the number reported, whichever is lower. The proposal removes the requirement that an employer seeking the safe harbor pay the balance of the premium by October 15. However, the safe harbor relates only to underpayment penalties, not interest accrued because payment is late.

Chapter 14

Plan Disclosure

14.2 SPD

The Pension and Welfare Benefits Administration proposed amendments to the SPD regulations, which appear at 63 FR 48376 (9/9/98). These proposals have already been described in Chapter 9, to the extent that they deal with group health plans. Under the proposal, the SPD must specify the type of pension plan administered by the plan administrator, especially whether defined contribution plans are intended to comply with ERISA 404(c)'s fiduciary duty provisions.

The SPD must also specify the circumstances that may lead to denial or loss of benefits that would otherwise reasonably be expected—including the extent to which plan termination will affect accrual and vesting of pension benefits, and how the plan's assets will be disposed of upon termination. Such discussion must be prominently visible, not "minimized, rendered obscure, or otherwise made to appear unimportant."

PBGC-insured plans must disclose the fact of insurance, must summarize the guarantee provisions of ERISA Title IV, and must mention that more information about guarantees is available from the PBGC or the plan administrator.

A plan's claims procedure will not be "reasonable" unless it is laid out in the SPD, which must describe all of the plan's claims procedures and their time limits [all procedures for filing claim forms; all notifications of benefit determinations; all reviews of denied claims; and dissatisfied claimants' right to sue under ERISA §502(a)].

Reviews of claim denials must be made by a named fiduciary, who did not make the initial determination and is not supervised by the person who made it. The review must consider all information submitted by the claimant (including new information not presented as part of the initial claim). The initial denial is not entitled to deference; it is simply another element in the decision.

Adverse determinations must cite the section of the plan that justifies the denial, including internal rules, guidelines, and protocols. These internal rules can affect benefit eligibility and therefore must be disclosed to plan participants; the plan and the employer cannot assert their confidentiality. Documents (e.g., expert reports) created during the review process are also subject to disclosure.

The PWBA is considering adoption of an express requirement that claimants who lose a review decision be given an express right to information about the plan's handling of other claims, but the PWBA has not yet required this. Information about other claims would help claimants decide if arbitrary and capricious determinations have been made, and thus to assess the validity (if any) of ERISA §502(a) claims that they might assert.

According to the Middle District of Alabama, a manual for a welfare plan's administrative staff was not an SPD because it did not contain enough comprehensive information, even if the plaintiff relied on its provisions, because it was designed as an internal plan document rather than guidance for employees. Therefore, the plan was able to enforce the terms of the manual even though it was not published as an SPD [*Cooperative Benefit Administrators Inc. v Whittle*, 66 LW 1304 (M.D. Ala. 9/19/97)].

Also note that, in *Fallo v. Piccadilly Cafeterias Inc.*, 1998 Westlaw 239020 (5th Cir. 1998), an employee was entitled to an 11-month COBRA extension (after the normal 18-month period) because his wife became disabled during the 18-month period. The terms of the plan itself echoed the COBRA statute, requiring that notice of the Social Security Administration's determination of disability be given before the initial 18-month period expired. But the SPD merely required that notice be given to the plan within 60 days of the SSA disability determination and did not rule out extensions for disabilities beginning late in the initial 18-month period. The SPD was the document given to the employee, and therefore it was the document that was given effect by the Fifth Circuit. The moral? Make sure that the SPD is an accurate reflection of all facets of the plan, including its limitations.

14.4 OTHER NOTICES

FASB Changes

In 1998, the Financial Accounting Standards Board (FASB) revised three of its existing statements (No. 87, "Employers' Accounting for Pensions," No. 88, "Employers' Accounting for Settlements and Curtailments of Defined Benefit Pension Plans and for Termination Benefits," and No. 106, "Employers' Accounting for Postretirement Benefits Other Than Pensions"). The new statement, No. 132, "Employers' Disclosures About Pension and Other Postretirement Benefits," streamlines the reporting process by eliminating some noncritical disclosures but increases the amount of information that must be disclosed about changes in the employers' benefit obligations and the fair values of plan assets. Another objective is to increase the standardization of retiree benefit disclosures.

The statement is effective for fiscal years beginning after December 15, 1997. If a company includes comparative information about pre-1998 years, it must restate the disclosures for earlier periods as long as the information is readily available.

Notice of Amendments Reducing Benefits

The IRS issued Final Regulations on December 14, 1998 (T.D. 8795; see 63 FR 68678) explaining the requirements of ERISA §204(h) (for defined benefit plans) and ERISA §302 (for certain individual account plans), with respect to the plan administrator's obligation to give notice of plan amendments that significantly reduce the rate of future benefit accruals. (The Final Regulations replace the Temporary Regulations of T.D. 8631, which appeared at 60 FR 64320 on 12/12/95.) The Final Rule is effective for amendments adopted on or after December 12, 1998.

Under ERISA §204(h), the administrator is obligated to give written notice to participants, alternate payees, and unions (in a unionized workplace) of plan amendments that significantly reduce the rate of future benefit accruals (i.e., that have the effect of changing the annual benefit that will eventually be paid when the employee reaches normal retirement age; for an individual account plan, that have the effect of changing the amounts allocated to participants' accounts in the future). Notice, disclosing the text of the plan amendment and its effective date, is due after the amendment is adopted and at least 15 days before its effective date. The notice requirement applies even if the amendment also triggers the need for a summary of material modifications (SMM), which is in fact provided to the employees.

The plan administrator can use any method reasonably calculated to get the notice to employees: hand delivery; first class mail to the employee's last known address; or delivery in combination with any other required notice.

The plan amendment will not become effective as to *any* plan participant if the administrator intentionally omits to provide the necessary notice. If some but not all persons who were supposed to get the notice were notified, the amendment does not become effective as to those who were not notified.

Example 2, Question 5 of the Final Rule says that, if a plan is amended to modify the actuarial factors used to convert an annuity to a lump sum distribution, the amendment does *not* affect the annual benefit commencing at normal retirement age. Therefore, notice is not required.

Question 6 defines the plan provisions that must be taken into account in determining whether the rate of future accruals has been reduced:

- Dollar amount or percentage of compensation on which benefit accruals are based
- Amount of disparity in a plan using permitted disparity
- Definition of service or compensation taken into account in accruing benefits
- Method of calculating average compensation

- Defined benefit plan's definition of normal retirement age
- Denying future participation to current participants
- Benefits offsets
- Minimum benefit provisions
- Individual account plan formulas for contributions and forfeitures
- Target benefit plan actuarial assumptions

Proper Use of Electronic Media

As Chapter 5 shows, corporations are turning more and more to computers, the Internet, and their own intranets as effective, cost-efficient distributions mechanisms for communicating with employees. Some employer-employee communications are simply an internal policy matter, so the corporation can adopt any communications medium that it chooses. However, others are government mandated, such as required communications about tax and employee benefit matters.

In late 1998, the IRS proposed rules for transmitting information about plan distributions and securing employee consent to elections via electronic media. See 63 FR 70071 (12/18/98).

Code §411(a)(11) does not allow involuntary cash-outs of plan balances over $5000. However, employees can consent to a lump sum distribution. Regulation §1.411(a)-11(c)(2) imposes a prior-notice requirement (i.e., for the employee's consent to be valid, he or she must have received an explanation of the distribution options under the plan and have been notified of the right to defer the distribution and also defer taxation). Code §402(f) mandates notice of the income tax withholding requirements that apply to eligible rollover distributions, and §3405(e)(10)(b) requires notice to recipients of distributions that are *not* eligible rollover distributions of their ability to direct that income tax not be withheld from the distribution.

The Taxpayer Relief Act of 1997 (TRA '97) directed the IRS to start coming up with rules for integrating computer technology into plan administration and the disclosure process. The December 1998 proposals make it clear that a plan [or a 401(k) plan] will not lose its qualified status merely because it uses paperless electronic methods to give notice and secure consents—provided, of course, that proper standards are satisfied.

A satisfactory electronic notice

- Is at least as comprehensible to the average participant as the written notice it replaces
- Contains as much information as the paper version
- Is written (e.g., e-mail or Website) rather than oral (e.g., automated telephone system) if it is complex enough to require writing; the §3405(e)(10)(B) notice is simple enough to be given via telephone, whereas the others require writing

- Advises its recipient that, if he or she wishes, a paper version of the notice will be furnished at no charge; the paper version must be the employee's own copy, which can be saved for reference; posting to a corkboard will not suffice
- Uses any currently available technology, or technology that will be developed in the future, that satisfies the standards

A consent form under §411(a)(11) can be either a written paper document or "an electronic medium reasonably accessible to the participant" (although the latter opens up questions of signature and authentication). The proposal suggests that passwords and/or PINs can be used to make sure that only the participant, and not an unauthorized person, renders the consent.

The IRS declined to use the 12/18/98 proposal as a means of responding to suggestions about electronic media for waivers of the QJSA and QPSA, or for notices rendering a 401(k) plan nondiscriminatory under the safe harbor provision, but noted that guidance will be provided in the future. Guidance will also be issued as to proper electronic handling of the Form W-4P (withholding certificate for pensions).

Chapter 15

DISTRIBUTIONS FROM THE PLAN

15.1 INTRODUCTION

T.D. 8794, published at 63 FR 70335 (12/21/98), contains IRS Final and Temporary Regulations for implementing the TRA '97 increase in the possible "cash-out" from $3500 to $5000. That is, although a plan can permit retirees to take their entire interest in the plan in a lump sum, a plan cannot "cash out" (force acceptance of a lump sum) except for very small amounts: IRC §411(a)(11).

> **TIP**
>
> T.D. 8794 generally applies to distributions made on or after 3/22/99, but most of the requirements can be applied retroactively to plan years beginning on or after 8/6/97.

The "look-back" rule is eliminated for most distributions. The look-back rule allowed cash-out of a present value that does not exceed the cash-out limit at the time of the current distribution, without regard to the value of the benefit at an early distribution. But the T.D. 8794 temporary regulations provide that a participant who has commenced distributions of an optional form of benefit is entitled to at least one more payment; and if the present value was greater than $5000 at the beginning of the distribution of the optional form of benefit, then cash-out of the remaining nonforfeitable accrued benefit is not required. The present value is calculated with the interest rate and mortality tables that the plan uses on the annuity starting date.

The calculation of the accrued benefit under §411(a)(7)(B)(i) does not have to include any service with respect to which the employee has already been cashed out at a level below $3500, and that cash-out occurred in connection with the termination of the employee's plan participation. T.D. 8794 temporary regulations provide that a cash-out of up to $5000 can be treated as part of termination of participation, if it could have been made due to termination of participation at a time when the present value was between $3500 and $5000.

It's permissible for a plan to be amended for plan years beginning on or after 8/6/97 to permit cash-out of up to $5000 with respect to benefits accrued before the amendment—even if the plan did not permit cash-outs before the amendment.

Beneficiary designation is a very important aspect of plan administration, and the plan's administrators need to know the appropriate party to receive distributions. According to the Northern District of California, it is permissible, and not arbitrary and capricious, to give effect to an unsigned form for changing the beneficiary. In *Bankamerica Pension Plan v. McMath,* 1998 WL 922323 (N.D. Cal. 1998), the lack of signature was clearly an oversight; the participant didn't know that the form wasn't signed, and otherwise followed the requirements for changing the beneficiary.

15.2 QJSA/QPSA PAYMENTS

T.D. 8794, 63 FR 70335 (12/21/98), discussed previously, also affects QJSA/QPSA payments. Consent is required for distribution of any accrued benefit (including QJSA/QPSA); the look-back rule (discussed previously) is repealed.

T.D. 8796 promulgates Final Regulations, effective 12/18/98, for giving notice and receiving consent and elections under Code §§411(a)(11) and 417. It appears at 63 FR 70009 (12/18/98). T.D. 8796 finalizes (at long last!) regulations proposed in 1995.

Before the proposal, Regulation §1.411(a)-11(c) required the participant to be notified of rights at least 30, but not more than 90, days before the annuity starting date. Absent such notice, the participant's consent to a §411(a)(11) distribution would not be valid. The same timing requirement was imposed on waivers of the QJSA.

The Proposed Regulations allowed participants to elect distributions after receiving late notice; the plan would not fail in compliance just because a distribution is made less than 30 days after provision of the notice. In 1996, the Small Business Job Protection Act (P.L. 104-188) amended the Code to permit QJSA explanations to be given *after* the annuity starting date.

The Final Regulations unite the two approaches: It is permissible to start distributions less than 30 days after notice (but more than seven days after the notice). QJSA disclosure can be deferred until after the annuity starting date. However, a participant's election of form of distribution remains revocable until the annuity starting date or seven days postnotice—whichever comes later.

Also see 63 FR 70071 (12/18/98), discussed further in Chapter 14, for a proposed rule for use of electronic media to convey necessary information about plan distribution options and get consent to lump sum distribution.

15.7 QDROS

If a qualified domestic relations order (QDRO) satisfies ERISA, the plan administrator is required to abide by it, without inquiring as to its acceptability under state law. If the employee is opposed to the terms of the QDRO, he or she must litigate with the ex-spouse in state court, but the plan administrator is not liable for complying with the QDRO [*Blue v. UAL Corp.*, 160 F.3d 383 (7th Cir. 1998)].

The case of *Emard v. Hughes Aircraft Co.*, 153 F.3d 949 (9th Cir. 1998), involves the common situation in which a divorced employee failed to change the beneficiary designation to reflect remarriage. When the employee died, her surviving husband sued in state court on constructive trust and community property theories. According to the Ninth Circuit, ERISA did not preempt the state-law claims alleging that the failure to change the beneficiary was a mistake. Nor, in this analysis, does California community property law conflict with ERISA, so the widower's claims were allowed to proceed.

The Sixth Circuit took a somewhat different view of a similar case in *Hendon v. DuPont*, 1998 U.S. App. LEXIS 7573 (6th Cir. 1998). The separation agreement required the employee spouse to change the beneficiary designation, but this was not done. The Sixth Circuit said that breach of contract claim involving waiver of plan benefits was preempted by ERISA. Therefore, the plan was justified in distributing the benefits to the ex-spouse.

The Fourth Circuit, in *Metropolitan Life Insurance v. Pettit*, 67 LW 1409 (4th Cir. 12/31/98), also deemed ERISA to preempt suits to enforce agreements that are not QDROs but that purport to affect life insurance benefits under qualified plans. The Fourth Circuit specifically rejected the constructive trust theory that succeeded in *Emard.*

A footnote in the PWBA's September 9, 1998 Proposed Rule on claims processing states that questions about determining the qualified status of, or administering, QDROs should be handled under ERISA §206(d)(3), and that ERISA §503 is not applicable. See 63 FR 48393.

Chapter 16

PLAN TERMINATION

16.2 THE PBGC'S ROLE

The PBGC's *Pension Insurance Data Book 1997*, a 74-page booklet, is available online from http://www.pbgc.gov/databk97.pdf. It has much to say about PBGC operations and posttermination benefit availability.

In 1997, the PBGC was operating with a surplus, not a deficit—the second year of surplus after two decades of deficits (bottoming out at $2.9 billion in 1993). One-quarter of U.S. workers (33 million participants of more than 43,000 defined benefit plans) were eligible for PBGC insurance; the insurance covered $1 trillion in pension-plan liabilities. Although most trends increase over time, the number of plans covered by the PBGC has declined significantly; in 1985, there were 112,000 plans subject to PBGC insurance.

About half the PBGC-insured plans are in manufacturing (50.2%); finance, insurance, and real estate make up another 12.5% of insured plans; with services at 12.2%, public utilities at 7.6%, and all other industries making up the other 17.5%.

As of March 1998, a total of 2510 underfunded plans had gone through termination, and 465,000 workers and retirees had received PBGC benefits. (See Fact Sheet, "Terminations," http://www.pbgc.gov/termfact.htm.) As of that time, the maximum PBGC guarantee for participants who retire at age 65 was $2880.68 a month, or $34,586.16 a year. (The corresponding 1999 figure is $3051.14.)

In 1997 alone, the PBGC paid benefits of $823 million to more than 200,000 participants and beneficiaries in terminated plans. Another 260,000 people were in deferred pay status, so that the PBGC had a future obligation to pay their pension benefits when due. However, this group of close to half a million people was actually less than 1.5% of all participants and beneficiaries. In 1997, the PBGC made $823 million in benefits payments.

The *Pension Insurance Data Book* estimates that there are only one or two distress or involuntary terminations for every hundred standard terminations, and the number of standard terminations has been below 4000 in every year since 1993. This is far less than the late 1980s–early 1990s, when standard terminations were around 11,000 to 12,000 a year.

Furthermore, PBGC payments were quite concentrated, not only in certain industries but in connection with a few very large failed plans. In 1997, 18.6% of all PBGC payments were made just to air transportation industry participants and beneficiaries. In 1997, 20.9% of payments were made in the primary metals sector, which sounds like a lot—until you realize that in 1987 more than one-third of payments were made in that sector. Also in 1997, machinery and computer equipment participants and beneficiaries were 11.4% of those receiving PBGC benefits; all industries other than those three made up less than half the total.

Although the PBGC guarantee extends much higher, in fact most participants and beneficiaries who receive payments from the PBGC get a small check. For 1997, the median monthly payment was only $217. The largest age group of PBGC payees is 70 to 74 (which makes sense in a retirement-related program, after all), and there are far more male than female payees. Female payees are more likely to receive PBGC benefits as widows than as workers in terminated underfunded plans.

Perhaps surprisingly, very few of the firms that file for bankruptcy protection make claims on the PBGC (i.e., have underfunded defined benefit plans). Between 1980 and 1995, of the publicly traded companies that filed for bankruptcy, less than 4% had underfunded defined benefit plans. Almost three-quarters didn't have defined benefit plans (so the PBGC wouldn't be involved), and one-quarter had defined benefit plans but had fully funded them.

This information comes from the PBGC itself, so negative features are not stressed. In March 1999, the PBGC itself was held up to the scrutiny of its internal Inspector General. (See David Cay Johnston, "Pension Fund Agency Is Being Scrutinized," *NYT*, 3/28/99, p. A30.) The agency was charged with failing to notify about half of the beneficiaries of plans taken over by the PBGC about their benefit entitlement. (This group includes close to half a million people.)

There are about 200,000 people covered by failed plans who are waiting for an initial determination of benefits—and, in some cases, the determination is 18 years late. The Inspector General also criticized the PBGC for lacking computer system safeguards to prevent fraud.

16.3 TERMINATION TYPES

The case of *Hughes Aircraft Co. v. Jacobson*, #97-1287, 67 LW 4122 (Sup. Ct. 1/25/99), discussed in connection with several other pension issues, also affects plan termination. *Hughes* involves a plan partially funded by mandatory employee contributions. At a time when the plan had a surplus, the employer suspended its own contributions and created a new, noncontributory plan for new plan participants. Participants in the existing plan charged the employer with ERISA violations in amending the plan. However, the alteration in plan structure did not constitute a voluntary termination under ERISA §4041(a)(1), and employees were not entitled to an order terminating the plan involuntarily.

The employees tried—but failed—to use a "wasting trust" theory: that the original plan was, in effect, wound up because it satisfied all of its objectives. The Supreme Court pointed out that this theory is inconsistent with ERISA's elaborate termination provisions.

Neither a standard nor a distress termination is appropriate as long as a plan continues to provide benefits to participants and accumulate funds for future benefit payments. The Hughes plan could not be characterized as "an enfeebled plan whose membership has dwindled to a mere remnant that would no longer benefit from the Plan's administration." Even though management exercised permissible discretion to change the plan terms, a viable plan remained.

A Final Rule, applicable to amendments adopted on or after 12/12/98, is published at 63 FR 68676 (12/14/98). It contains an example showing the application of ERISA §204(h) to some situations of defined benefit plans that cannot be terminated on the proposed termination date because of failure to satisfy all ERISA Title IV requirements.

If all of the requirements of Title IV are not satisfied, accruals will still cease if an amendment has been adopted that ceases accruals as of a specified date and §204(h) notice of that amendment, including a statement of its effective date, is given.

Question 16 in the Final Rule's Q&A explains that an amendment providing for the cessation of benefit accruals on a specified future date and for the termination of a plan is subject to §204(h). If the plan is terminated in accordance with ERISA Title IV, it is deemed to have satisfied §204(h) no later than its termination date, so no additional benefits have to accrue after the date of the termination. But if the amendment reducing future accruals is effective earlier than the termination date, then §204(h) does apply.

Also see 63 FR 38305 (7/16/98), explaining how to implement the increased "cash-out" that is now permitted when a plan terminates. That is, very small balances under $5000 (not just the earlier limit of $3500) can be distributed in lump sum form even if a lump sum is not requested by the participant.

16.9 DISCLOSURE TO PARTICIPANTS

63 FR 48376 (9/9/98) amends the SPD requirements of 29 CFR §2520-102-3(1). Information must be disclosed about circumstances under which the plan can be amended to reduce or eliminate benefits. If the plan includes any provisions that give the plan sponsor or other party the right to terminate the plan or eliminate

some or all of the plan benefits, participants must be informed of the circumstances permitting plan termination or benefit changes. Disclosure is required of the accrual and vesting provisions for the plan benefits upon termination of the plan. The provisions for allocation and disposition of plan assets posttermination must also be disclosed.

Chapter 17

ERISA ENFORCEMENT

17.2 WHO IS A FIDUCIARY?

ERISA does not permit a fiduciary's investment client to sue the fiduciary for drafting a contract containing a noncompete clause that keeps an ex-employee of the fiduciary from providing independent services for the plaintiff [*Frank Russell Co. v. Wellington Management Co.*, 154 F.3d 97 (3rd Cir. 1998)].

The case arose when an investment capital manager quit his job to open up his own, competing firm. His employment agreement with the former employer barred him from doing business with the ex-employer's clients for five years. The plaintiff was a company that canceled its contract with the former employer in order to have the capital manager take care of its account. The plaintiff sought an injunction against enforcement of the noncompete clause.

Although the District Court granted a preliminary injunction, the Third Circuit reversed, finding that the plaintiff was unable to prove it was at risk of irreparable harm. The plaintiff charged the ex-employer with a violation of its ERISA fiduciary duty in accepting the plaintiff as a client without informing it of the noncompete clause. The Third Circuit was not persuaded by this argument and refused to impose additional fiduciary duties in situations not involving employees.

An investment broker and investment partnerships are not fiduciaries of a profit-sharing plan, and therefore are not liable for unanticipated taxes on the plan investments in a suit brought by the plan trustee. *Pedre Co. v. Robins*, 66 LW 1448 (S.D.N.Y. 12/15/97), reaches this result because the broker's role was purely administrative, with no fiduciary duties. In any event, there could have been no breach of fiduciary duty, because the broker made legal investments and the taxes were not attributable to fraud.

A plan participant who claims that his or her lump sum benefits were miscalculated can only sue the employer for ERISA equitable relief if the employer was a fiduciary vis-à-vis the plan (e.g., performed administrative functions, not just sponsoring the plan). And if the plan, not the employer, has the primary responsibility for making the payments, it's inappropriate to sue the employer to collect additional benefits. See *Esden v. Bank of Boston*, 1998 Westlaw 241855 (D. Vt. 1998). That is, equitable relief can only be ordered against a fiduciary.

17.3 FIDUCIARY DUTY

According to a letter issued by the Department of Labor on February 19, 1998, it may constitute a breach of fiduciary duty for health plan trustees to select health providers purely because they place the lowest bid, without consideration of quality. In this context, quality refers to issues such as the scope of the provider; the qualifications of its doctors; how easy it will be for plan beneficiaries to get access to the doctors; ratings and accreditation; appeals of coverage denials; and consumer satisfaction scores the provider has achieved elsewhere. (See RIA *Compensation and Benefits Update*, 3/25/98, p. 3.)

"Serious consideration" of a new early retirement plan, requiring disclosure to potential early retirees (who need this information to decide whether to accept retirement incentives under existing plans or to hold out for a superior new package), occurs when senior managers discuss the proposal for purposes of implementation.

Using this test, which derives from *Fischer v. Philadelphia Electric Co.*, 96 F.3d 1533 (3rd Cir. 1996), the Sixth Circuit permitted a lawsuit for breach of fiduciary duty by a group of retirees who alleged that they were deprived of information about a later, superior retirement plan [*McAuley v. IBM Corp.*, 67 LW 1480 (6th Cir. 1/22/99)].

➠ TIP

If silence could be harmful, a benefit plan administrator has a fiduciary duty to give complete and accurate information about the plan, even if the beneficiary hasn't asked for the information [*Krohn v. Huron Memorial Hospital*, 67 LW 1619 (6th Cir. 4/1/99)]. Similarly, it is a fiduciary breach for a plan to inform potential early retirees that lump sum distributions are available, without also giving them information about the Code §415 limitations on rollovers and disclosing that amounts not rolled over are subject to immediate income taxation [*Farr v. U.S. West Communications Inc.*, 58 F.3d 1361 (9th Cir. 1998)]. The fiduciaries' common-law duty of loyalty requires honest, fair dealing with plan participants, so complete rather than partial information must be given.

However, fiduciaries are not liable merely because an adverse consequence ensued under their stewardship. An employer's purchase of Guaranteed Investment Certificates (GICs) for individual pension accounts, from a company that was eventually seized by regulators, was not a breach of the employer's fiduciary duty. *In re Unisys Savings Plan Litigation*, 67 LW 1640 (3rd Cir. 3/22/99) holds that the employer acted with adequate prudence in that it delegated investment responsibility to appropriate parties, who made an adequate investigation before recommending the ill-starred purchase. *Bussian v. RJR Nabisco Inc.*, 1998 Westlaw 639320 (S.D. Tex. 1998), reaches a similar conclusion for annuities purchased from an insurer that later became bankrupt.

Well, that's why they put erasers on pencils. If the sponsor is unaware of the error, it is not a breach of fiduciary duty for the sponsor to cite incorrect benefit figures from an actuary's report in a letter to a participant. If the participant knew the figure was inaccurate, but the sponsor didn't, it's permissible for the sponsor to make payments based on the actuary s figure rather than the (higher) true figure. See *Easa v. FTD Ass'n*, 1998 Westlaw 245726 (E.D. Mich. 1998). As the proverb says, "Love thy neighbor—but cut the cards." Double-check all figures and assumptions, even if a mistake won't land you in court.

In that retiree health benefits do not vest at retirement, it is not a breach of fiduciary duty to transfer the benefit obligation to a new company formed in the spin-off of a corporate division [*Sengpiel v. B.F. Goodrich Co.*, 1998 Westlaw 637159 (6th Cir. 1998)].

17.6 PENALTIES FOR FIDUCIARY BREACH

A late 1997 case, *Schmidt v. Sheet Metal Workers' National Pension Fund*, 128 F.3d 541(7th Cir. 1997), arose when a plan employee mailed the wrong form to a participant. Without the correct form, the participant was unable to designate the desired beneficiary. The Seventh Circuit ruled that the plan's trustees were not guilty of fiduciary breach. They weren't responsible for the mistake, and the plan documents and SPD were correct.

17.14 ENFORCEMENT UNDER ERISA SECTION 502

A lawyer employed as a litigator underwent heart surgery and was unable to return to work. His disability benefits were terminated when one doctor said that his inability to work was motivational in nature, not physical. Several other doctors certified his disability. The insurer affirmed the benefits cut-off, on the grounds that litigation is sedentary work suitable for a recuperating heart patient. The Ninth Circuit, in *Kearney v. Standard Insurance Co.*, 66 LW 1678 (9th Cir. 4/21/98), treated the plan, which required "satisfactory proof" of disability but did not explicitly give discretionary authority to the plan administrator, as one subject to objective standards and de novo review. Because there were material issues of fact as to the nature of a litigator's job, and the plaintiff's ability to perform it, the case had to proceed to trial; it could not be resolved by summary judgment.

According to the Third Circuit, a grant of interest on benefits wrongfully withheld for a while, but eventually paid, constitutes "other appropriate equitable relief," which can properly be the subject of an ERISA §502(a)(3)(B) suit [*Fotta v. Trustees of UMW Health Retirement Fund,* 165 F.3d 209 (3rd Cir. 1998)].

When benefits are denied under a long-term disability plan, and the participant sues under §502(a)(3), the participant cannot recover the expenses of medical treatment, because these are extracontractual, compensatory damages of the type ruled out by *Mertens* [*Rogers v. Hartford Life & Accident Ins. Co.*, 167 F.3d 933 (5th Cir. 1999)].

17.16 OTHER ENFORCEMENT ISSUES

Schleibaum v. Kmart Corp., 153 F.3d 496 (7th Cir. 1998), involves a claim that the employer breached ERISA by failing to give adequate notice of benefit denial when it ceased payment of life insurance on behalf of an ex-employee whom the employer claimed was not permanently and totally disabled. After the ex-employee's death, his family sued under ERISA §503 (failure to provide mandated appeal information).

The defendant prevailed at the District Court level; the court took the position that the plaintiff should simply have bought his own insurance after the denial. The Seventh Circuit, however, found for the plaintiffs. The Seventh Circuit's position was that the employee should not have been forced to purchase the coverage.

Furthermore, the Seventh Circuit held that a plaintiff in such a situation is not required to mitigate (reduce) damages by investigating his or her rights, given that the employer controls information about the benefit plan. The case was remanded for determination as to whether the decedent was, indeed, disabled when the life insurance benefits were cut off. If so, the Seventh Circuit held the damages to be the face value of the insurance policy that should have been provided, not just the premiums the ex-employee would have paid under an individual conversion policy.

Chapter 18

Labor Law

18.1 INTRODUCTION

The year 1997 followed an ongoing trend: reduction in the number of unionized workers, and the percentage of the workforce that is unionized, despite large union expenditures for organizing. On the decline in union membership, see Glenn Burkins, "Union Membership Fell Further in 1997," *WSJ*, 3/18/98, p. A2, although the trend turned around in 1998, when over 100,000 persons became union members.

Although LMRA §301 says that labor unions can "sue and be sued" in federal court, that provision does not provide automatic federal jurisdiction when a union wants to sue in federal court. The union must abide by the normal rules of civil procedure, bringing suit in the federal courts only if a federal question is involved or only if the parties are citizens of different states and substantial amounts of money are involved [*K.V. Mart Co. v. United Food & Commercial Workers*, 67 LW 1635 (9th Cir. 4/14/99)].

What is a federal question, anyway? The Supreme Court decided, in mid-1998 [*Textron v. UAAAIW*, #97-463, 118 S. Ct. 1626 (Sup. Ct. 5/18/98)], that an allegation that an employer violated a collective bargaining agreement presents a federal question. But an allegation that the employer fraudulently induced the union into entering into a contract, and getting a no-strike pledge, by promising not to subcontract out work did not come under LMRA §301 and did not present a federal question.

18.3 EMPLOYEE STATUS

Because "supervisors" are not allowed to organize, it often becomes important to determine if a particular person is a supervisor or a rank-and-file employee. Two cases involving employees of the nursing home chain Beverly Enterprises reached different conclusions. To the Fourth Circuit, licensed practical nurses (LPNs) are supervisors because they supervise nursing assistants; must use independent judgment at work; and, for two of the three shifts, are the most senior personnel available [*Beverly Enterprises v. NLRB*, 165 F.3d 307 (4th Cir. 1999)].

But the D.C. Circuit says that LPNs are not supervisors. They have mere paper authority and are not really able to exercise authority over the nursing assistants. Therefore, they are not supervisors and are entitled to unionize if they want [see also *Beverly Enterprises v. NLRB*, this time 67 LW 1460 (D.C. Cir. 2/2/99)]. The Seventh Circuit reached a similar conclusion in a non-Beverly case [*NLRB v. Gran Care Inc.*, 67 LW 1539 (7th Cir. 3/3/99)].

Two pro-union workers in *Dreyer's Grand Ice Cream, Inc. v. NLRB*, 1998 Westlaw 138775 (7th Cir. 1998), held the job of "super-coordinator," in charge of several work teams (including interviewing job applicants, recommending hiring and pay raises, and disciplining team members). The super-coordinator job was eliminated after a year, and the two kept their increased salaries but were not promoted to the newly created position of "facilitator."

The former super-coordinators were fired after an attempt to unionize Dreyer's failed. The NLRB ordered reinstatement, and Dreyer's sought review on the grounds that even after the super-coordinator positions were eliminated, the two workers were supervisors who didn't belong in a bargaining unit. The employer lost: The Seventh Circuit upheld the NLRB, because the two did not continue to exercise authority after their demotion.

18.4 ELECTIONS, CERTIFICATION, AND RECOGNITION

In some recent cases, employer behavior was deemed to taint an election:

- Delivering paychecks at the voting site for a decertification election, rather than at the employees' workplaces [*United Cerebral Palsy Ass'n of Niagara County*, 327 NLRB No. 14 (1998)]. The NLRB requires a legitimate business reason for changing paycheck delivery within 24 hours of an election. Usually, increasing voter turnout is good—but in a decertification election, increased turnout favors the employer rather than the union.
- Telling workers that their yearly merit raises would end if the company unionized [*LaSalle Ambulance, Inc.*, 327 NLRB No. 18 (1998)]. The correct statement would have been that the yearly raises were a term or condition of employment, that could not be altered without bargaining, not a new issue which could not be implemented without bargaining.

- Telling employees that unless they returned to work the next day without a union contract, the business would be closed down, and its equipment sold or leased, was a threat—an unfair labor practice—rather than a permissible prediction of future events. It was a threat because it referred to events wholly within the employer's control [*NLRB v. Gerig's Dump Trucking Inc.*, 1998 Westlaw 75942 (7th Cir. 1998)].

The Second Circuit ruled that it is permissible speech, and therefore not an unfair labor practice, for an employer to increase the amount of information available about existing benefits (information that the employer previously refused to disclose, on the grounds of "saving labor costs") just before the election. *Beverly Enterprises Inc. v. NLRB*, 66 LW 1569 (2nd Cir. 3/9/98), distinguishes improved access to information from actually increasing benefits just prior to the election.

The D.C. Circuit refused to invalidate an election on the basis of unlawful surveillance even though pro-union employees photographed and videotaped other employees. The court did not find that they were acting as union agents who had a probable effect on the election outcome. Nor did the court find that the employees created an atmosphere of fear and reprisal such that a fair election would be impossible [*Overnite Transportation Co. v. NLRB*, 140 F.3d 259 (D.C. Cir. 1998)].

Also on the subject of surveillance, *National Steel & Shipbuilding Co. v. NLRB*, 156 F.3d 1268 (D.C. Cir. 1998), holds that the employer's videotaping of employees at union rallies outside the plant constituted interference with protected activities, because the employer failed to provide reasonable objective justification for the surveillance. Is this a double standard? The employer is in a more powerful position than a union seeking to organize, which probably explains the differing results.

➠ TIP

Undocumented aliens are employees entitled to vote in representation elections—even if their status has been challenged under the IRCA [*NLRB v. Kolkka*, 67 LW 1568 (9th Cir. 3/17/99)]. The NLRB's position is that undocumented workers can also be awarded back pay when they fall victim to an unlawful layoff, up to the date the employer discovered the undocumented status (and, at least theoretically, would have dismissed the worker) [*Hoffman Plastics Compounds, Inc.*, 327 NLRB No. 86 (1998)].

In 1998, the NLRB eased up the rule in its case handling manual. The manual allows balloting by mail only if it is "infeasible" to hold the election via normal in-person balloting. The holding of *San Diego Gas & Electric*, 325 NLRB No. 218

(1998), is that voting by mail should be allowed not only in the fraught situation of an election during a strike or picketing, but when the potential voters would have to travel a significant distance to the polls and are so scattered that simply relocating the polling place wouldn't be effective. Another signal for mail balloting is a workforce with varying schedules that rule out assembling workers in one place at any particular time.

When several unions engage in joint picketing as part of an organization drive, one union will not be vicariously liable for unfair labor practices of another union merely because they share the common goal of organizing the workplace [*Washington v. HCA Health Services of Texas Inc.*, 152 F.3d 464 (5th Cir. 1998)].

January 1999 marked the first time that the NLRB made petition forms for representation cases available online (on its Web site, http:www.nlrb.gov). A June 1998 pilot project for online access to charge forms for unfair labor practices was considered a success, leading to expansion of the program. The usefulness of making the representation petition available from the site will also be assessed after a six-month trial.

18.4.4 Access by Nonemployees

The NLRB found that a grocery chain can permissibly bar nonemployee labor organizers from a public snack bar and could have them leave front sidewalks that the grocery chain was responsible for maintaining. Federal labor was not violated, because the company maintained a consistent ban on solicitation (union solicitation was not singled out). Furthermore, a nearby parking lot was available for solicitation, so the grocery chain's actions did not completely preclude the union from getting its message across. See *Farm Fresh Inc.*, 326 NLRB No. 81 (8/27/98).

18.5 PREVENTIVE LABOR RELATIONS

J. Derek Braziel's white paper, "Avoid the Union Label: How to Fight Organizers Without Violating the Law," http://www.lawnewsnetwork.com/practice/employmentlaw/papers/lawfirm/A1667-1999May21.html, provides some insights about labor's sometimes successful new push to organize. According to Braziel, in 1998 unions won more representation elections than they lost (whereas in other years in the 1990s, the majority of organization drives failed). Unions are targeting new workplaces and new employee groups and are also using new media tactics to make their message seem more appealing (and to publicize alleged employer improprieties).

The practice of salting, mentioned at ¶1.7, involves job applications by confessed union organizers, who then claim to be the victims of antiunion animus if their applications are not accepted. If the application is accepted, of course, the activist will try to convert other employees to the pro-union cause.

➡ TIP

If you're asked to "review" a petition signed by employees, or union authorization cards—don't do it! The result could be authorization of the union without an election.

Although it is an unfair labor practice to threaten employees or punish them for pro-union sentiments, it is perfectly permissible and fair to communicate to employees your honest opinion about why continued nonunion operation serves everyone's best interest, and to publicize facts about the union that could serve as dinsincentives to joining up.

18.6 THE COLLECTIVE BARGAINING PROCESS

"Regressive bargaining"—withdrawing an offer if the union is unable to meet the employer's time frame—has been upheld by the NLRB in *White Cap, Inc.*, 325 NLRB No. 220 (1998), unless it is done specifically for the purpose of avoiding a contract. Where the employer has a legitimate business reason for wanting to resolve the issue quickly, regressive bargaining is permissible.

During the course of unproductive negotiations, a union adopted a "work to rule" slow-down strategy. The employer's response was a lock-out. The NLRB, in the matter of *Central Illinois Public Service Co.*, 326 NLRB No. 80 (1998), agreed with both sides. The slow-down was deemed to be protected activity, but the employer was not out of line either. The lock-out was not inherently destructive of union rights and was motivated by a desire to get the negotiations back on track, rather than by antiunion animus.

The Third Circuit found it to be an unfair labor practice for an employer to refuse to complete a questionnaire about its utilization of nonunion personnel (during scheduled plant shutdowns for maintenance purposes) to perform work otherwise covered by the collective bargaining agreement. Under *NLRB v. PSE&G*, 157 F.3d 222 (3rd Cir. 1998), the union needs this information to represent its members.

18.7 UNION SECURITY

Under a late-1998 Supreme Court decision, *Marquez v. Screen Actors Guild*, #97-1056, 119 S.Ct. 292 (11/3/98), a union does not breach its duty of fair representation if it enters into a collective bargaining agreement that contains a union-security clause that reproduces the wording of NLRA §8(a)(3).

The plaintiff, an actress, claimed that she should have been notified of her right not to join the union and to pay the union only for its representational activities. The plaintiff also challenged the 30-day grace period in the collective bargaining agreement (CBA), but the Supreme Court upheld the Ninth Circuit: Claims of this type fall within the NLRB's primary jurisdiction and cannot be originated within the federal court system.

18.9 LABOR ARBITRATION

An employer demonstrated improper antiunion animus by firing an employee who disobeyed an order that forbade him to change his lunch hour to attend a co-worker's arbitration hearing. The discharged employee helped his co-worker prepare for the arbitration hearing, and therefore had a legitimate interest in attending even though the case did not fall under *Ohmite. Ohmite Manufacturing Co.*, 290 NLRB 1036 (1988), says that refusal to allow an employee to attend an NLRB hearing is unlawful only if the employee has a real need to attend the hearing, or if the employer acts out of an improper motive. The D.C. Circuit did find an improper motive in the case of *Cadbury Beverages Inc. v. NLRB*, 67 LW 1352 (D.C. Cir. 11/17/98): animus against the union.

LMRA §301 permits a federal District Court to enforce a subpoena duces tecum (for production of documents) issued by a labor arbitrator to a person or entity that is not a party to the collective bargaining agreement [*AFTRA v. WJBK-TV*, 164 F.3d 1004 (6th Cir. 1999)]. However, the labor arbitrator cannot order non-parties to appear and testify, only to produce documents.

18.10 STRIKES

A restaurant supervisor who was friendly with, and liked by, employees was fired. The Seventh Circuit held [in *Bob Evans Farms Inc. v. NLRB*, 163 F.3d 1012 (7th Cir. 1998)] that employees who went out on strike in sympathy were overreacting to management's action. Therefore, the strike did not constitute protected concerted activity.

It's hard to accumulate evidence that dozens or hundreds of employees weren't really sick when they claimed to be, but if you have the evidence, it's proper to impose discipline on employees who falsely claim illness. Be sure, however, that discipline is applied fairly and uniformly. Don't target members of a particular ethnic group or union activists while allowing sick-out violations by others.

If you have already experienced a sick-out, a sensible response is to add a uniformly enforced policy that employees who take sick days will be charged with a personal day unless they have a doctor's note diagnosing an actual illness.

TIP

Strikes are not the only hostile labor activity you may encounter. An article by Emily Nelson and J. C. Conklin, "Leery of Strikes, More Workers Stage Sickouts," *WSJ*, 1/12/99, p. B1, deals with job actions in which workers (especially public employees and others who are not supposed to strike because their jobs affect the public interest) agree to call in sick on particular days in lieu of a strike. The article quotes labor law professor Marina Angel, who says that a sick-out is really an unlawful partial strike. It can be especially damaging to employers, who could simply bite the bullet and hire permanent replacements in the wake of a lengthy strike but can't replace employees when a day off is taken here and there.

18.11 THE WARN ACT

WARN Act notice must be given to laid-off employees who have a legitimate expectation of recall. *Kildea v. Electro-Wire Products Inc.*, 66 LW 1731 (6th Cir. 5/13/98), says that such employees fall under the definition of affected employees because of the likelihood that plant closing will lead to job loss.

A company's entire sales force was brought to several centralized locations cross-country and fired. Before their discharge, the salespersons worked all over the United States, with an administrative center in Virginia. The District Court treated the Virginia center as a "single site of employment" from which there could have been a WARN Act mass layoff.

However, on appeal, the Third Circuit found that there were real issues of fact as to whether all sales staffers took orders from, and reported to, the Virginia location. The relevant regulation, 20 CFR §639.3(I)(6), defines three categories of employment sites: home bases; places from which work is assigned; and places where reports are received. So the appeals court in *Ciarlante v. Brown & Williamson Tobacco Corp.*, 1998 Westlaw 209211 (3rd Cir. 1998), sent the case back to the District Court for a factual determination.

Back pay and damages that are awarded under the WARN Act are not "wages" that are subject to a West Virginia statute mandating timely wage payments [*Conrad v. Charles Town Races Inc.*, 67 LW 1220 (W. Va. 7/15/98)]. The state court took this position even though WARN Act damages are described in the WARN Act itself as back pay.

18.13 SHARED LIABILITY

In the view of the Sixth Circuit, vested benefits under a collective bargaining agreement are transferable when the employer transfers employees to another one of its locations, which is covered by another collective bargaining agreement with another union. [In this case, *Anderson v. AT&T Corp.*, 66 LW 1760 (6th Cir. 6/2/98), the benefit was a special wage-incentive payment that was due as long as the employee continued to be employed.]

18.14 EMPLOYER DOMINATION

Once again, the NLRB found employee participation companies formed by the employer to be "labor organizations" improperly dominated by the employer [*EFCO Corp.*, 327 NLRB No. 71 (12/31/98)]. Committees dealing with employee benefits, employee policies, and safety issues were forbidden, but the employee suggestions committee was permitted to stand, because it did not deal with management on subjects that fall under the ambit of collective bargaining. The text of the decision can be found at http://www.nlrb.gov/slip327.html.

Chapter 19

Unemployment Insurance

19.1 INTRODUCTION

HR consulting firm Laurdan Associates Inc. reports that the amount per employee paid by employers for federal and state unemployment taxes decreased slightly between 1997 and 1998. In 1997, the figure was $210, versus $207 per employee in 1998. In 1996, the average duration of unemployment benefit payments was 14.9 weeks, and this too dropped slightly, falling to 14.6 weeks in 1997. In 1996, 33.4% of claimants exhausted their benefit eligibility, versus 33.1% in 1997. See Robert W. Thompson, "Unemployment Insurance Costs Dropped From 1997 to 1998," *HR Magazine*, 12/98, p. 12.

For unadjusted and seasonally adjusted data on the number of unemployment insurance claims, with an analysis of trends in high-unemployment states, you can check out the Department of Labor's Web site, http://www.dol.gov/dol/opa/public/media/press/eta/ui, or call (202) 219-6871 for the Unemployment Insurance Weekly Claims Reports.

19.2 ELIGIBILITY FOR BENEFITS

In a 1998 Missouri appellate case, a truck driver was fired after failing a drug test. When he applied for unemployment benefits, his employer said that benefits should be denied because he was fired for good cause. The ex-employee's argument was that the drug test lab report was just hearsay and not admissible. The employer's rebuttal was that evidence law makes documents kept in the course of business admissible under the "business records" exception.

The trial court agreed with the fired employee, because the report was prepared in the course of the lab's business, not the trucking company's business. But the appellate court said the trial court misread the business records hearsay exception. According to the appellate court [*Associated Wholesale Grocers v. Moncrief,* 970 S.W.2d 425 (Mo. App. 1998)], *anybody's* business records can be introduced, as long as they were kept in the normal course of business, were made close enough after the event to be reliable, and there are other reasons for considering the records to be reliable.

Chapter 20

Worker's Compensation

20.1 INTRODUCTION

On March 3, 1999, the Supreme Court decided a Worker's Compensation (WC) case, *American Manufacturers Mutual Insurance Co. v. Sullivan*, #97-2000, 67 LW 4158 (Sup. Ct. 3/3/99). Under Pennsylvania's WC Act, once liability is no longer contested, the employer or its insurer has an obligation to pay for all reasonable or necessary treatment. However, an insurer, or a self-insured employer, is permitted to withhold payment for disputed treatment pending utilization review by an independent third party.

The *Sullivan* plaintiffs brought a civil rights suit claiming violation of the Due Process clause of the Constitution. They sued state officials, WC insurers, and a self-insured school district, charging that benefits had been withheld without notice, thus depriving the employees of a property right.

Their claims did not succeed. In the Supreme Court's analysis, private insurers are not "state actors" subject to the Due Process clause when they use the utilization review process. The employees do not gain a property right until the treatment has been found reasonable and necessary. Therefore, there was no requirement of giving the employees notice, or holding a hearing, before withholding the benefits until the review had been completed in favor of the employees.

20.3.1 Compensable Injuries

An unusual "mental injury" award was upheld in Pennsylvania in early 1999, for an employee who was falsely blamed for theft by an employer whose books and records were in disarray, with the result that the plaintiff suffered so much stress that she was institutionalized in a mental hospital and unable to work. See Danielle N. Rogers, "Mental Injury Wins Rare Comp," *National Law Journal*, 3/1/99, p. B2;

the case is *Miller v. WC Appeal Board*, PICS Case #99-0130 (Pennsylvania Commonwealth 1/27/99).

Schmidt v. Smith, 155 N.J. 44, 713 A.2d 1014 (1998), says that bodily injury caused by sexual harassment is covered by the employer liability section of the Worker's Compensation insurance policy, because this section of the policy is designed to make funds available to compensate employees for their work-related injuries, even those for which Worker's Compensation payments are not available.

20.6 ALTERNATIVES FOR INSURING WC

Employers have been rejoicing in much lower WC premiums in recent years, although rates may increase in the future if losses trend upward sharply. The reduction in rates has had a severe impact on insurers. The WC insurance industry expects to lose at least $1 billion in 1999. Business written through reinsurance pools may cost insurers as much as $2.5 billion. Some important reinsurance companies are bowing out.

American International Group Inc. has sued reinsurers Unicover and ReliaStar Life Insurance Co. in New York Supreme Court, charging them with repudiating reinsurance contracts with American International. American International wants the reinsurers to be ordered to abide by the contracts and to pay damages. See Deborah Lohse, "Decline in Workers' Compensation Rates Leaves Insurers With Billion-Dollar Tab," *WSJ*, 3/5/99, p. A4.

20.8 BAN ON RETALIATION

The Washington State case of *Warnek v. ABB Combustion Engineering*, 67 LW 1558 (Wash. 3/4/99), permits an employer to refuse to rehire employees who made WC claims against the same employer in another state. In this reading, the antiretaliation statute applies only within a state, not outside it. The court also drew a distinction between refusing to rehire, on the one hand, and discrimination during employment or discharge, on the other. Only the latter would be unlawful.

An employees' retaliatory wrongful discharge claim survived summary judgment in *Newell v. Kmart Corp.*, 1998 Westlaw 230966 (D. Kan. 1998). The plaintiff was fired, allegedly for excessive absenteeism, after she asked to take a vacation day and thought her request was approved. To prevail, the employee must be able to show a connection between filing a WC claim and the discharge. (However, ERISA claims were dismissed for lack of evidence, and the employer's conduct was not outrageous enough to support a claim for intentional infliction of mental distress.)

20.10 WORKER'S COMPENSATION IN RELATION TO LAWS ON OTHER SUBJECTS

A person injured on the job might take FMLA leave in addition to, or instead of, collecting WC benefits, and might be (or might claim to be) a qualified person with a disability for ADA benefits. "When Regs Collide: The ADA and Workers' Compensation," WestGroup *Employment Alert*, 11/25/98, p. 1, tackles the interface issues for these statutes.

The right to get WC benefits is considered a privilege of employment for ADA purposes [see, e.g., *Harding v. Winn-Dixie Stores, Inc.*, 907 F. Supp. 386 (M.D. Fla. 1995)], so an argument that a person suffered discrimination in this area can be litigated. WC statutes do not violate the ADA just because they cover physical disabilities but exclude mental disabilities [*Hensley v. Punta Gorda*, 686 So.2d 714 (Fla. App. 1997)].

But the ADA doesn't have the strong preemptive power that ERISA has to eliminate state-law claims. Recently, for instance, state-law claims were allowed to proceed, even though the ADA's standard of proof is higher for employees with preexisting conditions [*Baley v. Reynolds Metals*, 153 Ore. App. 498, 959 P.2d 84 (Ore. App. 1998)].

A person injured at work might be entitled to WC benefits yet able to work with reasonable accommodation. But a WC judge's determination that the individual could not work even on a reduced schedule is proof that the person was not a qualified individual with a disability [*Dush v. Appleton Electric Co.*, 124 F.3d 957 (8th Cir. 1997)]. An employee who enters into an agreement stating that he or she needs a stress-free work environment isn't qualified for a high-stress job like being a safety police officer [*Jackson v. County of Los Angeles*, 60 Cal. App. 4th 171, 70 Cal. Rptr.2d 96 (1998)].

Testimony or findings from an ADA case can have powerful evidentiary effect in a WC case. A person who sued under the ADA because of a past injury can't deny that the injury involved in the suit was a preexisting disability vis-à-vis the later injury that is the subject of a WC case [*Cobb v. Coyne Cylinder Co.*, 1998 Westlaw 45320 (Ala. App. 1998)].

An employee's answers to questions that the employer should not have asked (because the questions violated the ADA) can be legitimate evidence in a WC case—for instance, where a person lies about past medical history; see *Dureoun v. C&P Production Specialist*, 718 So. 2d 460 (La. App. 1998), and *Caldwell v. Aarlin/Holcombe Armature Co.*, 267 Ga. 613, 481 S.E. 2d 196 (1997).

Chapter 21

OSHA

21.1 INTRODUCTION

A visit to OSHA's Web site, http://www.osha-slc.gov, is worthwhile, especially for the smaller enterprise that is subject to OSHA jurisdictions but can't afford a full-time staffer who is specifically involved in occupational safety and health issues.

Three vital OSHA forms (Form 101, the Supplementary Record of Occupational Injuries & Illnesses; Form 200, the Log and Summary of Occupational Injuries & Illnesses; and Form 174, the Material Safety Data Sheet) are available online, through the OSHA publications server, http://www.osha-slc.gov/OshDoc/Additional.html. This is also the place to locate online versions of significant OSHA documents, such as

- All About OSHA (publication 2056)
- Assessing the Need for Personal Protective Equipment: A Guide for Small Business Employers (publication 3151)
- Concepts & Techniques of Machine Safeguarding (publication 3067)
- Consultation Services for the Employer (publication 3047)
- Employee Workplace Rights (publication 3021)
- Handbook for Small Business (publication 2209)
- How to Prepare for Workplace Emergencies (publication 3088)
- Industrial Hygiene (publication 3143)
- Materials Handling and Storing (publication 2236)
- Safety and Health Guide for the Microelectronics Industry (publication 3107)
- Small Entity Compliance Guide for Respiratory Protection Standard (no publication number)

- Training Requirements in OSHA Standards and Training Guidelines (publication 2254)

> **TIP**
>
> Many of these documents use the Adobe PDF format; the software for reading PDFs can be downloaded free from many government and private sites.

The Occupational Safety and Health Review Commission (OSHRC) decided in 1998 that an employee leasing company was not subject to the OSH Act, because the workers in question were not their "employees" who worked in their "business" as defined by the OSH Act. The leased employees worked in a factory, and the leasing company failed to exercise significant control over them. However, OSHA released a draft of its multiemployer worksite policy, providing that the controlling employer (e.g., the general contractor) can become liable for site hazards if it has sufficient control over employees of the other companies working at the sites. The policy, which applies to both the general and construction standards, defines sufficient control as contractual authority to require subcontractors to prevent or correct violations; or as failure to exercise reasonable care, with the result that employees are placed at risk.[1]

Workplace Violence

According to the Department of Justice's Bureau of Justice Statistics (BJS), there were about 2 million incidents in each year between 1992 through 1996 in which workers were threatened by, or became victims of, violent crime in the workplace. About three-quarters of those incidents involved simple assaults; there were also about 1000 homicides a year; 51,000 rapes and other sexual assaults; 84,000 robberies; and 396,000 aggravated assaults. About one-eighth of violent workplace incidents resulted in injury; only half of the injuries required medical attention. Two-thirds of those victimized were male. One-third of violent workplace incidents took place between people who knew each other (e.g., co-workers).

Understandably, the occupations at highest risk of assault included police and corrections officers and cab drivers. However, many violent incidents occurred in the retail workplace: about 330,000 incidents per year, including 84,000 robberies. However, fortunately, in the period 1992–1996, violent crime rates as a whole went down 17%, and workplace incidents declined by 21%.[2]

21.3 OSHA REGULATIONS

OSHA doesn't regulate employees' exposure to their own tobacco smoke. Permissible exposure limits (PELs) apply only to a situation in which an employee is obligated to enter a contaminated area in order to perform work for the benefit of the employer.[3]

21.3.1 [NEW] Bathroom Breaks

Theoretically, both the OSH Act and state occupational health laws require employers to provide an adequate number of toilets for the size of the workforce. The OSHA general industry sanitation standard (29 CFR §1910.141) requires the presence of toilet facilities in the workplace.

However, until recently, there was little or no regulation of workplace practices that affect employees' access to bathroom breaks. This emerged as an issue of concern, and especially of union activism, in 1998. It's easy for management (who can take breaks anytime they want) to forget that access to restrooms is not just a matter of comfort or dignity, but of health. Employees who are denied bathroom access can suffer bladder or kidney infections or dysfunction. If they restrict their liquid consumption, they can suffer the ill effects of dehydration.

Although the average worker needs to use the restroom two to three times a day, female workers need more bathroom breaks than male workers (other than older male workers, who need to use the restroom more often because of prostate enlargement), and pregnant women need to use the restroom more often than nonpregnant women. If the employee's increased need for elimination is due to a health condition, the Americans with Disabilities Act may require reasonable accommodation. For instance, the worker might be allowed more breaks during the day, but short breaks suitable for bathroom visits, not longer breaks. Or the employee might be assigned to the workstation closest to the restroom, so he or she can return to work quickly.

An April 6, 1998 letter from OSHA forbids employers to impose unreasonable restrictions on bathroom use. OSHA inspectors who receive worker complaints on this issue are directed to investigate the reasonableness of the employer's policy, including the length of time that employees are expected to defer calls of nature.

Union activists point out that lack of bathroom breaks is associated with a speeded-up work schedule that deprives employees of all sorts of needed breaks. Activists also point out that uncomfortable, resentful, or exhausted workers are not only at risk of injury but also likely to experience declining productivity. See 66 LW 2579 (3/31/98) and 2636 (4/21/98).

21.5 USE OF PERSONAL PROTECTIVE EQUIPMENT

A Proposed Rule, published at 64 FR 15401 (3/31/99), requires the employer not only to require personal protective equipment where appropriate, but also to pay for all such equipment, other than prescription eyeware, safety-toe shoes, and logging boots (i.e., items that employees can use in private life, away from the worksite—unlike things like gas masks that have no general usefulness).

21.5.1 Respiratory Protection

OSHA adopted a new respiratory protection rule, published in the *Federal Register* on January 8, 1998, that took effect October 5, 1998. The standard, known as 1910.134, covers respirator use in general industry, shipyards, longshore work, and construction—but not in agriculture. Nor does the standard deal with the issue of tuberculosis prevention (e.g., in health care workplaces).

For guidance to employers, OSHA issued compliance directive CPL 2-0.120, explaining how to select respirators and analyze workplace hazards, when to change the chemical cartridges in respirators, and how to make sure that respirators are properly fitted. Private-sector workers engaged in firefighting must be relieved from the fire site on a "two in-two out" schedule. The respiratory protection directive is explained in an OSHA news release dated 9/24/98; text of the directive can be found at http://www.osha.gov, Library/Reading Room, Directives.

21.8 ERGONOMICS

Congress's appropriations bill for OSHA for the years 1996–1998 forbade the agency to adopt ergonomics standards. Shortly after it became free to do so, OSHA published a draft ergonomics regulation on January 6, 1999. The document was, to say the least, controversial. The OSHA draft (which is certain to be modified in light of the flood of negative public comments received) requires employers (other than construction, maritime, and agricultural employers, who are not covered under the draft) to maintain ergonomics programs if they engage in manufacturing or materials handling. Approximately 25 million workers would be covered because their jobs involve lifting, pushing, pulling, or bending—possible triggers of musculoskeletal injury.

Furthermore, the most controversial portion of an already contentious document requires even nonmanufacturers that do not handle materials to implement an ergonomics program in response to reportable musculoskeletal disorders that occur in the workplace. This requirement has drawn heavy criticism as being vague enough to be impossible to comply with.

In this context, hazards are physical work activities and workplace conditions that are causing, or are reasonably likely to cause or contribute to, musculoskeletal disorders. OSHA estimates that over 640,000 workers suffer musculoskeletal disorders (e.g., carpal tunnel syndrome; low back pain; sciatica) each year. This category of disorder is estimated to cause about one-third of serious workplace injuries and to result in $15 to $20 billion in annual Worker's Compensation expenses and additional billions of dollars in lost productivity.

Once an employer falls within the scope of the proposal, it must identify hazards; analyze them; and train employees to avoid them. A small business panel estimated that carrying out the proposal would cost small business ten or twenty times as much as OSHA estimated. OSHA head Marthe Kent agreed to revise the agency's economic impact analysis accordingly, reflecting, for instance, the need to retain consultants. OSHA's final rule is not expected to be issued prior to September 1999.[4]

A revised Working Draft was issued on March 12, 1999: See http://www.osha-slc.gov/SLTC/ergonomics/backgroundinfo.html for a press release giving background on the working draft. The draft itself, marked "Do not cite or quote," appears at http://www.osha-slc.gov/SLTC/ergonomics/ergoreg.html.

OSHA's position is that ergonomic programs work; they pay for themselves by reducing Worker's Compensation, medical, and disability costs. Under the working draft, the ergonomics standard would apply to all manufacturing and material handling operations, and other general industry jobs where a work-related stress injury problem has been demonstrated. OSHA notes that, although manufacturing and materials handling companies employ 28% of the general-industry workforce, they are the site of about 60% of all work days lost due to repetitive stress injuries.

The working draft uses an "incident trigger" for other general industries (i.e., work-related stress disorders trigger the need for job hazard analysis), although employers can use an even more sensitive trigger that requires ergonomics action at a lower threshold level.

The March 12 draft reflects OSHA's Plain Language Initiative, so it is designed to be user friendly. The standard is clearly written, in a question and answer format, with tables showing the appropriate response to various scenarios. However, in that it is a working draft, there is no formal opportunity to comment on it; the deadlines for notice and comment are related to official publication in the *Federal Register*.

All companies subject to the ergonomics requirements would be required to identify hazards, inform employees, and unite management leadership and employee participation for a safer workplace. If workplace injuries have been reported, or known hazards exist, then job hazard analysis; medical management; prevention and control; training; and program evaluation would be required. However, a manufacturing/materials handling company that had no problem jobs for three years would merely have to maintain controls and training.

Engineering controls are the preferred way to control hazards. OSHA defines engineering controls as physical changes to jobs that control exposure to hazards—(e.g., modifying or redesigning workstations, tools, equipment, facilities, and processes). Work practice and administrative controls are also considered an important part of the ergonomics program, but personal protective equipment (PPE) cannot be considered a permanent control if other controls are feasible. Furthermore, employees must be given PPE at no charge. The Working Draft requires retention of ergonomics program records for three years (medical management records must be retained for the duration of the employee's tenure, plus three years).

OSHA expects the ergonomics program to be phased in. Medical management would have to be commenced for each stress injury after the effective date of the final regulations (when they are adopted), but employers would get an extra year from the effective date to develop hazard identification and management leadership programs. A two-year phase-in period would be given for job hazard analysis, interim controls, and training. Permanent controls, program evaluation, and improving problem jobs would be phased in over three years.

OSHA returned to the subject of musculoskeletal injuries in May 1999, sending letters to close to 12,500 employers with high injury rates and where employees were at risk of injuries from lifting heavy objects (e.g., nursing homes, warehouses, and trucking companies).[5] The letter directs the targeted employers to improve job-site safety. However, some of the recipients (e.g., United Parcel Service and nursing home chain Beverly Enterprises) believe the initiative is unnecessary, because they are already working on improved lifting safety.

For another perspective on the business implications of ergonomics, see Kathryn Tyler's "Sit Up Straight," *HR Magazine*, 9/98, p. 146. Tyler cites a GAO estimate that repetitive stress injuries add $60 billion a year to the private sector's Worker's Compensation claim load. The Bureau of Labor Statistics believes that repetitive motion injuries have increased almost 800% in the past decade. In 1986, 6.4 full-time employees per 10,000 had a repeated-trauma disorder; by 1995, the incidence was 37.2 per 10,000.

➠ TIP

Employees are more likely to file a borderline (or invalid) WC claim if they feel that the employer doesn't care about them, and they are less likely to file a claim without true support if they feel that the company has their best interests at heart. Ergonomics programs can reduce WC claims by 50 to 60%. But be sure that employees are aware of the presence of newly purchased ergonomic tools and are adequately trained to use them properly.

On another ergonomics issue, the New York Court of Appeals permitted a plaintiff to sue a keyboard manufacturer for aggravation of the worker's repetitive stress injury (RSI), even though the plaintiff didn't start to use the defendant's keyboard until 18 months after her first RSI symptoms appeared, which was also 13 months after her RSI diagnosis [*Edmond v. IBM Corp.*, 66 LW 1688 (N.Y. App. 4/7/98)]. But the Eastern District of Pennsylvania ruled, in *Howard v. Digital Equipment Corp.*, 67 LW 1400 (E.D. Pa. 11/25/98), that computer keyboard manufacturers have no duty to warn users of potential RSI risks, because the risk comes from repeatedly striking the keyboard, not from the keyboard itself.

21.9 DIVISION OF RESPONSIBILITY

Under the "peculiar risk" doctrine, someone who hires an independent contractor to perform inherently dangerous work is liable for damages for torts committed by the independent contractor against others in the course of doing the work. However, in California, this doctrine cannot be used by employees of a subcontractor, injured by the subcontractor's negligence, to sue the general contractor [*Toland v. Sunland Housing Group Inc.*, 18 Cal. 4th 253, 74 Cal. Rptr. 2d 504, 955 P.2d 504 (Cal. 1998)].

21.10 OSHA ENFORCEMENT

It does not constitute double jeopardy to impose administrative penalties on an employer after it has been convicted of criminal OSHA violations, because the administrative penalties are clearly civil and cannot result in imprisonment [*S. A. Healy Co. v. OSHRC*, 138 F.3d 686 (7th Cir. 1998)].

The Fourth Circuit ruled that it does not violate the Fourth Amendment prohibition of unreasonable searches and seizures for OSHA to perform off-site videotaping of the worksite, showing that workers 80 feet above ground level did not have safety cables. (The inspector got permission to tape from a hotel rooftop across the street.) See *L. R. Willson & Sons Inc. v. OSHRC*, 66 LW 1476 (4th Cir. 1/28/98) (affirming the decision in the main volume).

29 USC §666(e) imposes penalties whenever a willful violation of an OSHA standard leads to the death of "any employee."

TIP

An early 1999 decision permits the penalty to be assessed against the culpable employer on a multiemployer worksite, even though the deceased employee worked for one of the other employers [*U.S. v. Pitt-Des Moines Inc.*, 67 LW 1523 (7th Cir. 2/18/99)].

OSHA is attempting to defuse the often hostile and antagonistic relationship between the agency and industry. It held its first partnership conference on November 13, 1998, in Washington, D.C. The conference's title was "Partner with OSHA: New Ways of Working." A number of partnerships were already in place by the time of the conference, including a Texas project where OSHA compliance training yielded $2 million in direct cost savings in addition to reduced injury rates; and a ten-point construction program for reducing homebuilding accidents.[6]

In spring 1999, however, the D.C. Circuit ruled that the cooperative compliance program was improper, because OSHA should have promulgated it as a rule, subject to notice to affected parties and with an opportunity for them to comment. See *Chamber of Commerce of the U.S. v. OSHA*, 67 LW 1622 (D.C. Cir. 4/9/99), discussed in Glenn Burkins' article, "Court Rules OSHA Improperly Started Program for Dangerous Workplaces," *WSJ*, 4/12/99, p. A4.

An employee who is injured at work cannot sue OSHA inspectors for failure to detect the hazard at the inspection, because OSHA inspections are "discretionary functions" that are entitled to exemption from the Federal Tort Claims Act [*Irving v. U.S.*, 162 F.3d 154 (1st Cir. 1998)].

Roy G. Stoops, owner of a steel company in Indiana, was sentenced to four months' imprisonment for willful OSHA violations that resulted in the death of a worker. Stoops' company had already had a substantial history of violations. Many dangerous conditions were present at the site, and subcontractors had warned of the risks. Stoops was placed on one year of supervised release and was ordered to pay $6000 toward the funeral expenses of the deceased worker. The company was placed on probation and made jointly liable for the restitution. For more on the Stoops conviction, see WestGroup *Employment Alert*, 11/25/98, p. 10.

Prevention and Planning

In an October 16, 1998 interview with BNA, Marthe Kent, Director of OSHA's Office of Regulatory Analysis, said that OSHA intended to promulgate a regulation, not a standard, to govern workplace safety and health programs. The agency was willing to be held to the tougher standard of analysis that applies to standards. An OSHA standard must address a significant risk; be technologically and economically feasible; be cost effective; and substantially reduce the risk. A regulation is acceptable as long as it is not arbitrary or capricious. Standards can be more specific than regulations because standards are aimed at specific hazards; regulations are not. See 67 LW 2316.

REFERENCES

[1]*Sec'y of Labor v. Team America Corp.*, 1998 Westlaw 733708 (OSHRC 1998); but see 67 LW 2249.

[2]Greg Warchol, "Workplace Violence: 1992–1996," NCJ-168634; see http://www.ojp.usdoj.gov/bjs/pub/press/wv96.pr.

[3]Re tobacco smoke: see *Employment Alert*, 12/23/98, p. 5.

[4]See 67 LW 2443 and 2461; Robert Pear, "Labor Department Acts to Stem Epidemic of Job-Related Aches," *NYT*, 2/20/99, p. A1; Glenn Burkins, "Business Groups and Allies in Congress Seek to Block OSHA Ergonomics Plan," *WSJ*, 2/22/99, p. B18. The draft itself can be found at http://www.osha-slc.gov/SLTC/ergonomics/index.html.

[5]"OSHA Urges Firms to Increase Safety of Lifting Jobs," *WSJ*, 5/11/99, p. B6.

[6]News Release USDL 98-455, 11/12/98; see http://www.osha.gov/media/oshnews/nov98/partner.html and http://www.osha-sk.gov/OshDoc/Directive_pdf/TED_8-0_2.pdf, containing guidelines for developing partnerships at the local, regional, and national levels.

Chapter 22

Privacy Issues

22.1 INTRODUCTION

Although many employers take advantage of the simplicity of using Social Security numbers as employment ID numbers, this is not always sound policy. Many people are concerned about the privacy implications of having too many computerized records tied to the same ID number (and vulnerable to unauthorized access). Legislation has been introduced in Congress (and has attracted significant support) to require organizations other than the Social Security Administration to get advance written consent before using Social Security numbers for any purpose. See Susan J. Wells, "You've Got Their Numbers—And They Want Them Back," *HR Magazine*, "Focus," 12/98, p. 3.

To an increasing extent, business is becoming internationalized, so a U.S. company may find that it has employees and contractors outside the United States. These people won't have Social Security numbers. Don't forget that the European Union's privacy requirements are much stricter than U.S. federal law and will become a factor in operations outside the United States.

Wells' article suggests adopting an identification system that does not use Social Security numbers. It's best not to use a nine-digit number (to avoid confusion with the Social Security number). Most companies will find a six-digit number perfectly adequate: After all, that allows 999,999 options, so even if a 5000-person workforce has a lot of turnover, the ID numbers won't run out for a while. Shorter numbers call for fewer keystrokes, so there's less risk of error—but a large company might need more numbers than a five-digit system will permit.

It's better to assign numbers at random rather than sequentially. If the numbers are assigned based on the order in which employees are hired, it's easy to breach security by getting one number and extrapolating from the hiring dates. Check the format requirements of your payroll and database programs; it may be necessary to start each ID number with a digit, not a zero, a blank space, or a character such as an asterisk or ampersand. Formatting needs also determine whether you can mix letters and numbers or include dots, dashes, or underscores.

22.3 DRUG USE IN THE WORKPLACE

According to the Fourth Circuit, neither imposing a drug testing requirement nor firing two workers for refusal to take the test violated the National Labor Relations Act. (The fired employees claimed that they were really fired because they were union activists.) Even though the testing program was implemented one week after a strike, all employees were required to take drug tests. Furthermore, since 6 out of 20 employees tested positive, the employer had a valid concern about drug use in the workforce. Drug testing policies are valid as long as they are not disparately enforced (e.g., based on race or union membership). This policy required all employees to take the test, and therefore passed muster [*Eldeco Inc. v. NLRB*, 132 F.3d 1007 (4th Cir. 1997)].

In a First Circuit case, an arbitrator said that an employee who failed a drug test should not be fired and should be reinstated if he passed a second drug test. The employer sued the union to get the arbitration award set aside. The First Circuit's decision was that the Collective Bargaining Agreement required just cause for disciplinary determinations. However, the arbitrator's decision couldn't be enforced because it violated the well-established public policy against letting drug users maintain safety-sensitive jobs [*Exxon Corp. v. Esso Workers' Union*, 118 F.3d 841 (1st Cir. 1997)].

Connecticut's statute, §31-51x, prohibits urine testing for drugs unless the employer has a reasonable suspicion that the employee is using drugs or alcohol in a way that does or could adversely affect job performance. *Poulos v. Pfizer*, 711 A.2d 688 (Conn. 1998), is a suit brought by a discharged employee for violation of that statute. The employee was caught stealing from the factory where he worked, and a drug test was ordered because of his suspicious behavior. Cocaine use was detected. He consented to drug testing because he was trying to reduce the consequences of the workplace theft.

The trial court found that the employer did not have reasonable suspicion of drug use and therefore awarded damages to the terminated employee. The appellate court reversed and ordered a new trial, because §31-51x deals with tests required by the employer, not those to which the employee consents. In this reading, an employee's consent does not become invalid merely because he or she faces hard choices when confronted with a threat of termination. Thus, the case was remanded for a determination of the reasonableness of asking for a drug test in such circumstances.

Under California law, an employer can test job applicants even if there is no particular reason to suspect them of drug use, but suspicion is required to test active employees. In a 1998 case, a job offer was extended conditional on the applicant's passing a drug test. The applicant had to move in order to take the new job, and logistics kept him from actually taking the drug test (which he failed) until after he was actually on the payroll. The employer fired him; he claimed that a suspicionless drug test was improper because he was already an employee. The California Court of Appeals didn't buy the employee's argument. In the court's view, the distinction between job applicants and employees exists because employers have a chance to observe their active employees and detect signs of drug use. The plaintiff in this case had not yet given the employer a chance to observe his behavior, and therefore the employer could treat him as an applicant for drug testing purposes [*Pilkington Barnes Hind v. Superior Court,* 66 Cal. App. 4th 28, 77 Cal. Rptr. 2nd 596 (Cal. App. 1998)].

Sherlock Holmes might have called it "The Case of the Pharmacist's Drugs." *Zenor v. El Paso Healthcare System, Limited,* #98-50063 (5th Cir. 5/24/99), discussed at http://www.lawnewsnetwork.com/practice/employmentlaw/authority/cases/G1864-1999May27.html, involves a hospital pharmacist who was also a marijuana user and cocaine addict. One night, he was unable to come to work because he was still dizzy from an earlier cocaine injection. He told his supervisor that he couldn't come into work because of drug side effects. His supervisor asked if he would use the EAP. The pharmacist agreed.

The pharmacist went to the hospital for emergency treatment and then spent nine days in an in-patient detox program; his employer didn't know where he was or why he missed work. The hospital's HR director told him he could take a twelve-week FMLA leave, and his job would be protected until he finished rehab. However, he was fired, in part because his job gave him access to pharmaceutical cocaine.

He sued, charging ADA and state human relations law violations, as well as fraud, breach of contract, promissory estoppel, and intentional infliction of emotional distress. At the trial court level, all of the claims were dismissed except the promissory estoppel claim. The plaintiff won and was awarded significant damages by the jury, but the trial court knocked out some of the grounds on which promissory estoppel was found.

The case got to the Fifth Circuit to challenge the dismissal of the ADA claims (as well as the breach of contract and promissory estoppel claims). As §12.2 in the main volume discusses, being a current drug user is not an ADA disability. The Fifth Circuit cited this provision and took the position that a cocaine user is not qualified for the job of hospital pharmacist, and so could not take advantage of the ADA.

What is the time frame for determining if someone is a "current user"—the date of firing, or the date of entering rehab? The Fifth Circuit's view is that the adverse employment action occurs when someone is told that he or she will be terminated, not the actual effective date of the termination. Otherwise, employers would be penalized if they allowed medical leaves of absence for substance abusers.

The *Zenor* case defines "current" drug use as use recent enough to make it reasonable for the employer to conclude that drug abuse is an ongoing problem. Drug use several weeks prior to termination can fit this definition: See, for example, *Shafer v. Preston Memorial Hospital,* 107 F.3d 274 (4th Cir. 1997); *Collings v. Longview Fibre Co.,* 63 F.3d 828 (9th Cir. 1975).

A brief rehab program is not enough to make it unreasonable for an employer to fear that an addict will resume the use of illegal drugs. Relapse is always a meaningful risk even after a treatment program has been completed.

The ADA has a safe harbor [42 USC §12114(b)] for people who have completed a rehab program, but just entering a rehab program is not enough—the safe harbor is intended for people with a history of staying clean. *Zenor* cites *Baustian v. Louisiana*, 901 F. Supp. 274 (E.D. La. 1996), for the proposition that it isn't enough for an employee to self-report a drug problem before being caught by the employer (although self-reporting is a factor in the employee's favor).

As for the breach of contract claim, the Fifth Circuit considered Zenor to be an at-will employee. There was no public policy reason not to fire him (in fact, public policy might well demand that drug abusers be kept out of hospital pharmacies!).

The hospital's formal policy against workplace drug and alcohol use did not alter Zenor's at-will status. The policy made rehabilitation a condition of continued employment. The policy did say that employees would be reinstated after completion of rehab. However, the employee handbook stressed that employees worked at will. The substance abuse policy itself placed stress on the employer's discretion to discipline employees, including terminating them, for violating the policy. Texas courts do not imply a contractual relationship on the basis of general assurance of job security: See, for example, *Montgomery County Hospital District v. Brown*, 965 S.W.2d 501 (Texas 1998).

Nor did the Fifth Circuit believe that promissory estoppel had occurred. The workplace substance abuse policy was not a promise of reinstatement, only a condition that rehabilitation was a prerequisite for reinstatement. The jury ordered types of damages that are not available under Texas law even if promissory estoppel occurred. So all of the pharmacist's claims were legally invalid.

22.5 GENETIC TESTING

Connecticut passed a statute in 1998 (P.A. 98-1890, effective 10/1/98), forbidding employers to request genetic information from employees or discriminate against employees or applicants on the basic of genetic information. The statute defines genetic information as information about genes, gene products, or inherited characteristics.

22.6 SEARCHES AND SURVEILLANCE

Theoretically, employees will spend their workplace computing and online time carrying out employment-related tasks. In the real world, it's inevitable that employees will waste a certain amount of time on benevolent tasks like personal e-mail, shopping, and playing computer games. This is not necessarily a problem, unless it is prolonged enough to impair productivity, or unless the employee goes to pay-per-view sites at the employer's expense. Many pay-per-view sites are pornographic, so moral issues arise.

Some employee computer use can be harmful to the employer. Employee e-mail can be used to prove that the work environment was sexually or racially harassing, for instance. Does the risk of wasted time or employer liability justify the employer in monitoring employees' e-mail messages or computer use?

A *National Law Journal* article by Cheryl Blackwell Bryson and Michelle Day, "Workplace Surveillance Poses Legal, Ethical Issues" (1/11/99, p. B8), sums up the practical issues and court responses. On the practical front, the American Management Association reports that in fact close to two-thirds of medium- to large-sized companies do in fact perform electronic surveillance, but over half of them limit it to simple nonintrusive measures such as video cameras in the lobby. Only about 15% reviewed the content of employees' e-mail, and 10.4% taped phone conversations (e.g., in order to monitor the quality of customer service). About one-seventh of respondents review computer files, but only a little over 5% reviewed voice mail messages. This report, which reflects 1997 practices, can be found at http://www.ama.org.

Employers might be guilty of torts, and required to pay damages to employees, if they violate employee rights of privacy. However, there are workplace contexts in which employees do not have a reasonable expectation of privacy, so monitoring in those situations is not tortious.

An example is the case of *Bohach v. City of Reno*, 932 F.Supp. 1232 (D. Nev. 1997). To investigate charges of misuse of the police paging system, Reno monitored pagers. The court considered that there was no search, and federal wiretap statutes were not violated, because the pager technology required centralized storage of the messages, defeating any reasonable expectation of privacy.

State and federal wiretap statutes typically include a "provider exception," under which it is permissible for the "provider" of communications to intercept messages on the system. An employer clearly counts as a provider if it owns the equipment on which the employees communicate.

In *Smyth v. Pillsbury Co.*, 914 F.Supp. 97 (E.D. Pa. 1996), an employer was held not to have invaded the privacy of an employee who was fired after sending hostile e-mail messages to a supervisor. The court applied the provider rule because the employer company owned the communications equipment—even though the employees were told that their e-mails were confidential and would not give rise to employee discipline.

➠ TIP

The exception might not be available if an Internet service provider actually handles e-mail service.

Surveillance programs are most likely to survive an invasion of privacy or other employment-tort-based challenge if

- They are created in response to a real problem or real threat (e.g., potential employer liability).
- Employees are accurately informed of the purposes and content of the program—it's definitely a bad idea to tell employees their communications are confidential and turn around and use them against the employees!
- Surveillance is restricted to the least intrusive methods that will get the job done.

Chapter 23

TITLE VII

23.1 INTRODUCTION

Charge Statistics

In fiscal 1997, the EEOC received 80,680 charges; in FY 1998, the corresponding figure was 79,591. (It's not uncommon for a person to allege multiple types of discrimination, so there will usually be more charges than charging parties.) For each of those two years, charges of racial discrimination were the most common, representing 36.2% of all charges for each year (29,199 charges in FY 1997; 28,820 in FY 1998). About 31% of charges alleged sex discrimination (24,728 and 24,454, respectively, for the two years). The next most common allegation was disability discrimination in violation of the ADA: 18,108 claims in 1997 (22.4% of the total) and 17,806 in 1998 (22.4%). Age Discrimination in Employment Act (ADEA) charges were about 20% of the total. In FY 1997, 15,785 ADEA charges were filed, versus 15,191 in FY 1998.

Charges of national origin discrimination were much less common, representing 8.3% of charges for FY 1997 and 8.5% for FY 1998; claims of religious discrimination were rare (1709, or 2.1% of the total, in FY 1997; 1786, or 2.2%, in FY 1998). Equal Pay Act claims were even less common: 1134 (1.4% of the total) filed in FY 1997, and 1071 (1.3% of the total) in FY 1998.

Retaliation claims (nearly all of them involving Title VII rather than one of the other statutes enforced by the EEOC) were made in 22.6% of 1997 cases, and 24.0% of 1998 cases—18,198 and 19,114 cases, respectively. Over time, the relationship among the various charges has changed. In fiscal 1992, for instance, only 15.3% of charges alleged retaliation; by 1998, 24.0% did. In FY 1993 (after the ADA had come into effect), disability discrimination cases represented 17.4% of total charges; in 1998, they were 22.4% of total charges. However, national origin discrimination charges have declined from 10.5% of the FY 1992 total to 8.5% in FY

1998. (Charge figures are from http://www.eeoc.gov/stats/charges.html, updated 1/14/99.)

Additional information about retaliation charges can be found at 67 LW 2259, where the EEOC noted that retaliation claims rose from under 8000 in 1991 to over 18,000 in 1998. The agency pointed out that sometimes juries will award damages on retaliation claims even if the underlying discrimination charges are dismissed.

The September 1998 case of *Gutner v. Cheyney University of Pennsylvania*, #94-7443 (E.D. Pa. 9/23/98), awarded $2.2 million to two white former college professors who claimed they were subjected to systematic reprisals and then forced out of their jobs because they complained about a black department chairman's manipulation of the hiring process.

More detailed information is available about the EEOC's handling of charges of racial discrimination. In FY 1996, 26,287 charges of racial discrimination were received, and 35,127 were disposed of. (This is not a contradiction: Dispositions can involve charges filed in one or more previous years as well as the current year.) In FY 1997, 29,199 charges were received and 36,419 were resolved. Monetary benefits for all successful claimants were $37.2 million in 1996 and $41.8 million in 1997.

➠ TIP

"Successful claimants," however, are only a small segment of all claimants. In both 1996 and 1997, the EEOC determined that there was no reasonable cause for about two-thirds of all charges.

Settlements were obtained in 2.8% of 1996 cases, and 3.3% of 1997 cases. About one-quarter of cases in each year were closed administratively.

Of the small number of remaining cases, reasonable cause determinations were made in 389 cases in 1996 and 918 cases in 1997. Conciliation was successful in 151 cases in 1996, 248 cases in 1997, and was tried but failed in 238 cases and 670 cases, respectively. Merit resolutions occurred in 7% of fiscal 1996 cases (2475 cases) and 8.3% of fiscal 1997 cases. These figures can be interpreted in several different lights. It might be argued that employers have little to fear, because most charges are either determined to be unfounded or are closed administratively. However, the overall amount of monetary relief was substantial in each of these years. Perhaps the answer is that an employer who incurs the wrath of the EEOC is at substantial monetary risk. For details of race cases, see *Employment Alert*, 4/30/98, p. 3, compiled by the Office of Research, Information and Planning from the National Database of the EEOC Charge Data System.

Certainly, the risks are substantial within the court system. In early 1999, United Parcel Service announced its agreement to pay $12.1 million to settle charges of racial discrimination raised in a 1997 class action. Of this amount, $8.2 million was allocated among 12,000 current and former part-time workers, plus

$626,500 to 14 full-time and part-time workers who were original class plaintiffs. Attorneys' fees amounted to some $3.3 million. The class action charged that UPS disadvantaged black drivers when delivery routes were assigned and also deprived black part-time workers of the training necessary for promotion to better-paid full-time status. The UPS settlement is discussed in a news item, *Wall Street Journal*, 1/19/99, p. B8.

EEOC/DOJ Memorandum of Understanding

See 63 FR 5518 (2/3/98) for the Memorandum of Understanding (MOU) between the EEOC and the Department of Justice's Office of Special Counsel for Immigration Related Unfair Employment Practices. Under the MOU, each agency can act as the other's agents to receive complaints about immigration-related discrimination charges. The two agencies will coordinate to avoid duplication of effort.

In response to immigration-law changes, the two agencies will treat document abuse, intimidation, and retaliation as immigration-related unfair labor practices and will accept pattern or practice charges. The EEOC has agreed not to ask if the charging party is a U.S. citizen, national, or work-authorized alien as a condition for referring charges to the DOJ.

23.2 TITLE VII COVERAGE

In August 1998, the full Fourth Circuit reversed its earlier panel ruling. Now *Egbuna v. Time-Life Libraries, Inc.*, 153 F.3d 184 (4th Cir. 1998), holds that it is necessary to be a U.S. citizen, or an alien holding a valid work visa, to be a "qualified" individual. Therefore, an alien who does not have legal worker status in the United States cannot make out a Title VII prima facie case.

In late 1998, the Fourth Circuit joined the Third, Fifth, Seventh, Eighth, Tenth, Eleventh, and D.C. Circuits in ruling that individuals cannot be held liable under Title VII [*Lissau v. Southern Food Service*, 159 F.3d 177 (4th Cir. 1998)].

23.2.4 Race Discrimination

At-will employees can sue under 42 USC §1981 (the prohibition of racial discrimination in the making of contracts), according to the Fifth Circuit [*Fadeyi v. Planned Parenthood*, 160 F.3d 1048 (5th Cir. 1998)] and the Fourth Circuit [*Spriggs v. Diamond Auto Glass*, 165 F.3d 1015 (4th Cir. 1999)]. In this analysis, Congress intended §1981 to provide a remedy for at-will employees of companies too small to be covered by Title VII.

The Tenth Circuit has applied the *Faragher/Burlington* test (see §23.3 of this supplement) to conduct that creates a racially hostile environment. That is, if the conduct is motivated by an intent to serve the employer, it is within the scope of employment. Thus, the employer will be liable for discriminatory conduct by a supervisor reflecting prejudice within the labor force [*Wright-Simmons v. City of Oklahoma City*, 155 F.3d 1264 (10th Cir. 1998)].

Even a single racial slur by a supervisor in the presence of another supervisor can be severe, thus creating a hostile work environment [*Taylor v. Metzger*, 706 A.2d 685 (N.J. 1998)].

23.2.6 The Pregnancy Discrimination Act (PDA)

The plaintiff in *Piraino v. International Orientation Resources*, 137 F.3d 987 (7th Cir. 1998), lost her case under the PDA. She applied for a leave of absence around the time of delivery. This was approved. Two months later, the company changed its policy and refused to guarantee the reinstatement of employees who took leave when they had worked for the company for less than one year. The plaintiff was unsuccessful because the court did not find proof that pregnant employees who had worked for the company for less than a year were treated differently from their nonpregnant peers.

The *Wall Street Journal*'s Sue Shellenbarger took up the topic of light-duty assignments for pregnant workers. ("Pregnant Workers Clash With Employers Over Job Inflexibility," *WSJ*, 2/10/99, p. B1). She noted that pregnant workers may need limitations on the weight they lift or the length of time they must stand—but are otherwise able to work. It's easy to imagine a case in which a pregnant woman can't perform all of the tasks associated with her job but is still healthy and fit enough so that she can't be described as "disabled."

Many mothers-to-be experience problems, because employers seldom make an effort to find light-duty assignments for pregnant workers. Each year, close to 2 million employed women become pregnant, and about 640,000 of those workers have jobs that involve at least some physical exertion. A lot of companies only have a few light-duty slots, and they often prefer to assign them to Worker's Compensation recipients who were injured at work and therefore must be kept on the payroll with or without work assignments.

The Fifth Circuit, in *Urbano v. Continental Airlines*, 138 F.3d 204 (5th Cir. 1998), upholds an employer's policy of limiting light duty assignments to workers injured on the job. In this reading, as long as pregnancy-related disability is treated on a par with other nonoccupational disability, the PDA has not been violated, even if the result is that pregnant workers have to leave work earlier than they would have preferred.

23.3 SEXUAL HARASSMENT

In 1998, the Supreme Court settled the conflict as to whether or not same-sex harassment is actionable under Title VII. *Oncale v. Sundowner Offshore Services Inc.*, 523 U.S. 45 (Sup. Ct. 1998), reached the unsurprising conclusion that same-sex harassment (which can be even more upsetting to the recipient than opposite-sex harassment) is indeed a violation of Title VII.

Two major decisions, *Burlington Industries, Inc. v. Ellerth*, 118 S.Ct. 2365 (Sup. Ct. 1998), and *Faragher v. City of Boca Raton*, 118 S.Ct. 2275 (Sup. Ct. 1998), changed the standard for assessing the employer's burden in providing a harassment-free workplace. The new test, under *Faragher/Burlington*, is whether the action had adverse employment effect on the victim. If so, the employer is absolutely liable. In the absence of adverse employment effect, the employer is still liable—unless it maintained proper antiharassment and grievance policies.[1]

In the *Ellerth* case, a sales representative felt threatened by repeated remarks and gestures from a manager (who was not her immediate supervisor), although she was not deprived of job benefits. She quit her job but did not attribute her resignation to harassment. Three weeks later, she sent a letter to the company explaining that her resignation was due to harassment. She did not report the harassment while it was occurring, although she knew Burlington had an antiharassment policy.

The Supreme Court's decision was that the supervisor's threats of adverse job action created a hostile work environment. The employer becomes vicariously liable for the supervisor's conduct if the employer failed to stop harassment after knowing about it; if the supervisor was able to harass because of apparent authority over the harassment victim; or if adverse job action was actually taken by the supervisor.

The other side of the coin is that the employer can be free of liability if it took reasonable care to maintain a workable complaint procedure, and if the plaintiff failed to use the procedure.

The *Faragher* case involves a lifeguard who sued her municipal employer and two supervisors for a hostile environment (including lewd touching of female employees). The employer did have an antiharassment policy but didn't inform employees of it, didn't supervise supervisors' conduct, and didn't create a procedure for reporting harassment by supervisors to someone other than the supervisors themselves. The Supreme Court's ruling was that the employer was liable for the hostile environment, because it had failed to communicate the antiharassment policy and didn't track the conduct of supervisors.

What's the bottom line? The employer has to make sure that the environment does not become hostile, intimidating, or offensive, so severe and pervasive unwelcome physical and verbal conduct must be prevented. Employees must understand that their complaints will be taken seriously and that there is a chain of command that can bypass the person who is alleged to have committed harassment. Top management should be involved in the process, to signal that the company treats these complaints as serious, and supervisors and managers should be trained to observe and report harassment.

Because the Supreme Court decisions revolve around agency law concepts such as the apparent authority of the supervisor, the employer should not only limit the extent to which supervisors can punish subordinates for not yielding to sexual pressures, but should make it clear that supervisors can only impose workplace discipline for legitimate reasons. It's important to look behind supervisors' write-ups and to check to see not only that the subordinate really did do poor work, come in late, have excessive absences, etc., but that the subordinate was not singled out for sanctions of conduct that was tolerated in other employees who were not sexual targets.

Of course, actual complaints should be given careful investigation, not shrugged off. (See ¶23.3.2 for a discussion of what constitutes appropriate investigation of a complaint.)

Although hostile work environment charges are usually made in the sexual context, the employer might be liable in a racially or religiously hostile workplace. One way to cope is a "mutual respect" policy, which reminds employees not to taunt or insult others or speak slightingly of their culture or religion.

Although by and large employer companies and not individuals will be liable under Title VII and related statutes, *Speight v. Albano Cleaners,* 1998 Westlaw 710438 (E.D. Va. 1998), does permit a Title VII suit against an individual supervisor who had significant degree of control over the plaintiff (and the conduct in question was not plainly delegable). However, in this case, the employer was found not to be liable for quid pro quo harassment in a situation in which the plaintiff was denied a promotion allegedly promised to her. The employer was not aware of the harassment, and the supervisor who committed the harassment did not have authority to promote the plaintiff. Because the employee failed to take advantage of an existing antiharassment policy, the employer could not be held liable for hostile environment harassment either.

In *Corcoran v. Shoney's Colonial Inc.,* 24 F.Supp.2d 601 (W.D. Va. 1998), the employer was held vicariously liable on the plaintiff's hostile environment claim, notwithstanding the employer's prompt investigation followed by separation of harasser and victim. The Western District reads *Faragher/Burlington* to impose vicarious liability, even if prompt remedial action is taken, unless the employee failed to take advantage of the employer's corrective mechanism.

In *Corcoran,* the plaintiff did in fact delay in reporting the harassment, but the court did not find this to be fatal to her case because she did not act unreasonably. Harassment began in June, tapered off, then escalated the following February, at which time the employee complained. The case of *NLRB v. Wehr Constructors Inc.,* 159 F.3d 946 (6th Cir. 1998), imposes vicarious liability on the employer, despite prompt action to separate harasser and victim and despite a reporting delay (which the court deemed to be reasonable under the circumstances).

The Fifth Circuit took up timing issues in *Williamson v. City of Houston,* 148 F.3d 462 (8th Cir. 1998). In that case, a woman police officer reported harassment by a male officer in her squad to her supervising sergeant. After about a dozen unproductive meetings, the sergeant told the woman to report the case to the Internal Affairs Division (IAD). She did so. The City of Houston took the position that it was not on notice of the harassment until she went to the IAD. To Houston, the sergeant was not a member of "upper management," and therefore his knowledge of harassment could not be imputed to the city. The Fifth Circuit disagreed, finding the sergeant to be the plaintiff's supervisor. Therefore, the employer was on notice of the harassment as soon as the plaintiff-employee triggered the complaint mechanism by reporting to her supervisor.

In a quid pro quo case, a series of minor detriments that would not be actionable by themselves can be aggregated to demonstrate tangible job detriment and make out the prima facie case [*Reinhold v. Virginia,* 66 LW 1488 (4th Cir. 1998)]. If the harassment is committed by customers, the Tenth Circuit analyzes the situation as if the harassers were coemployees (not supervisors). The employer will be held liable if its negligence permitted the harassment to continue but will not be held strictly liable for the actions of customers [*Lockard v. Pizza Hut Inc.*, 162 F.3d 1062 (10th Cir. 1998)].

Summary judgment is not appropriate in a hostile environment case where the plaintiff alleges that the sexual comments made in her presence were commonplace, ongoing, and continuing [*Abeita v. Transamerica Mailings Inc.*, 159 F.3d 246 (6th Cir. 1998)].

The Seventh Circuit allows a sexual harassment plaintiff to get punitive damages in cases in which there were no compensatory damages: See *Timm v. Progressive Steel Treating Inc.,* 137 F.3d 1008 (7th Cir. 1998). This might occur, for instance, where a company fails to establish a complaint procedure and then blames the plaintiff for failure to complain. In this case, the plaintiff mitigated damages so effectively that she got a higher-paying job, and therefore could not collect a back pay award.

Interpreting California rather than federal law (FEHA, the state's Fair Employment and Housing Act), the California Court of Appeals ruled that a law firm is directly, not vicariously, liable for failing to protect a staffer against harassment by a partner. The ruling of *Weeks v. Baker & McKenzie,* 74 Cal. Rptr. 2d 510 (Cal. App. 1998), is that the firm employed the partner in conscious disregard of the safety and rights of vulnerable employees. Therefore, $3.5 million in punitive damages could be assessed against the firm. The firm's liability was not limited to the $225,000 punitive damage award against the harassing partner.

Reno v. Baird, 957 P.2d 1333 (Cal. 1998), holds that an individual manager, although potentially liable for harassment, is not an "employer" under the Fair Employment and Housing Act. Nor can the individual manager be sued for wrongful discharge in violation of the public policy expressed in FEHA. The FEHA definition of "employer" includes "any person acting as an agent of an employer, directly or indirectly," but the *Baird* court interpreted this language to have been included in the statute to make employers liable for the actions of their agents, not to subject the agents to personal liability.

According to *Lai v. Prudential Insurance Co.*, 72 Cal. Rptr. 2d 551 (Cal. App. 1998), California's rule is even tougher than the federal rule: The employer remains strictly liable whether the harassment was of the quid pro quo or hostile environment variety. [Contrast this with *Todd v. Ortho Biotech, Inc.*, 138 F.3d 733 (8th Cir. 1998), permitting the employer to get off the hook in a hostile environment case, as long as prompt remedial action was taken.]

The Eleventh Circuit did not permit a "reverse-discrimination" sexual harassment suit, brought by a plaintiff who was denied the promotion that went to the employee who had a consensual sexual relationship with the boss. The holding of *Womack v. Runyon*, 147 F.3d 1298 (11th Cir. 1998), is that an isolated instance of favoring a sexual partner cannot constitute sex discrimination, because the plaintiff class would consist of all of the company's employees (male and female), because they were all equally disadvantaged by such favoritism.

As Chapter 30 shows, it can be difficult to get insurance coverage in sexual harassment cases. The 1998 Fifth Circuit case of *American States Insurance Co. v. Natchez Steam Laundry*, 131 F.3d 551 (5th Cir. 1998), agrees with the insurer that there was no duty to defend, under a commercial general liability (CGL) or umbrella policy, against the EEOC's suit for intentional sexual harassment.

Therefore, the insurance company did not act in bad faith by not providing a defense or insurance benefits. The agency's allegations fit well within the intentional-acts exception of the policy, and the insurer made an adequate investigation before denying the claim. Whether or not there is a duty to defend depends on the language of the complaint, and the EEOC clearly charged intentional acts excluded by the policies.

23.3.2 Required Employer Response

According to the Eleventh Circuit, if the appropriate response to a minor act of harassment is to admonish the harasser, it's permissible for the HR manager to delegate the task of admonition to a co-worker instead of doing it personally, as long as it's clear that the harasser gets the message and the harassed person is satisfied with the outcome of his or her complaint [*Coates v. Sundor Brands, Inc.*, 1998 Westlaw 789169 (11th Cir. 1998)].

The mere fact that an employer adequately investigates sexual harassment claims is not necessarily enough to get the employer off the hook under *Faragher/Burlington*. But an adequate investigation is certainly a valuable first step.

A May 1999 article by attorneys Susan Schenkel-Savitt and Jill H. Turner, of the firm of Winston & Strawn, available at http://www.lawnewsnetwork.com/practice/employmentlaw/papers/lawfirm/A1058-1999Apr30.html, gives some insights into appropriate investigative efforts.

The investigation has further implications. If an employer simply dismisses all accused harassers, this could constitute wrongful termination, in that efforts were not made to determine the validity of the charges. To balance between the interests of accused persons and accusers, the employer must maintain a mechanism for unbiased internal investigations.

The person who conducts the investigation may have to testify later on, so an in-house or outside attorney who normally represents the corporation could be a poor choice. Attorneys are not allowed to serve as witnesses in cases where they are also representing a party. However, choosing an attorney rather than someone else can be a good choice, because communications between an attorney and a client are privileged (opposing parties in litigation can't get hold of them). An attorney's "work product" (materials drafted by the attorney while preparing the case)is also protected. Similar privileges are not extended to nonattorney professionals.

In order to assert confidentiality at the pretrial and trial level, the company must be sure to keep the materials confidential. They must not be given general distribution, and access must be limited to persons involved in the investigation.

The person conducting the investigation must determine the following:

- Person(s) accused of committing harassment, including those contributing to a hostile work environment or participating in a cover-up
- Person(s) who are described as witnesses; the degree to which their recollection tallies with the complainant's
- Any other person(s) who also claim to be harassment victims
- Detailed information about the alleged acts of harassment or the duration and nature of the hostile environment
- Did the acts occur on company property, at company functions, or elsewhere?
- Did the employee make a prompt report of the alleged harassing incident? To whom was it made? If there was no report, was there any justification for failing to report at the time of the incident?

Naturally, the investigator should follow up by contacting witnesses and checking matters of fact. If an incident of harassment was alleged to have occurred on a particular date, for instance, it should be ascertained if the alleged harasser was in the office on that date or was elsewhere.

Interviewing the alleged harasser is very important. It's up to the employer's discretion whether or not to reveal the name of the person making the allegation. To protect the employer against claims by the alleged harasser, the investigator should make it clear that an investigation is being made and that no conclusions have yet been reached as to the validity of the accusations. The accused person should be given a full, fair chance to get his or her own story on the record.

Additional rounds of interviews may be necessary to follow new lines of investigation or confirm disputed facts. The product of the investigation should be a confidential written report rendered to the person with corporate HR responsibility. It's important to indicate whether a particular statement in the report is factual or whether it represents opinion, gossip, or rumor.

The company has an obligation to take at least some action whenever it is determined that a harassment allegation is well-founded. Appropriate action is proportionate to the seriousness of the conduct and has the effect of discouraging future harassment. The action should also be proportionate to actions the employer has taken in similar cases in the past. The harasser's employment record may provide either mitigating (long history of good performance) or aggravating factors (past instances of discipline, especially prior instances of harassment).

If the employer determines that a sanction short of dismissal is appropriate, steps should be taken to keep the harasser and victim apart—but without making it seem that the complainant is being penalized for making a well-founded complaint. The employer should also follow up (and make a written record of the follow-up) to make sure that the disciplinary action has served to prevent future harassment incidents.

In April 1999, the Federal Trade Commission (FTC) raised an explosive issue that few people had ever considered. As ¶1.11 of the main volume explains, employers are limited in the way they can use employees' and job applicants' credit reports, especially under September 1997 amendments to the Fair Credit Reporting Act (FCRA).

The FTC staff answered an inquiry from a lawyer and took the surprising position that an attorney who is paid by a corporation to investigate sexual harassment charges is thereby acting as a "credit reporting agency"—and therefore must conform to FCRA requirements. Failure to satisfy the FCRA can be penalized by a fine of up to $1000, plus punitive damages and the obligation to pay the opponent's attorneys' fees. Another risk is that reports prepared by attorneys in this "credit investigation" role might be denied protection under the attorney-client privilege. This issue is discussed in a May 17, 1999 article by Kevin Livingston, available at http://www.lawnewsnet.com/stories/A1499-1999May14.html.

23.4 RELIGIOUS DISCRIMINATION AND THE ISSUE OF REASONABLE ACCOMMODATION

According to the EEOC, charges of religious discrimination, although still few in number, are increasing: The 1709 charges filed in 1997 were 43% higher than the level prevailing in the early 1990s, for instance. According to the Society for Human Resource Management's 1997 survey, about two-thirds of managers say that their company offers flexible schedules that can be used for religious holidays. However, only 19% included religious issues in diversity training; 18% trained their managers in accommodating religious preference; 15% provided space or time for prayer, study, or discussion; and only 13% accommodated religious attire.

It can be especially difficult to accommodate Muslim employees in a production line environment, because devout Muslims are required to pray five times daily, with several of the obligatory prayers occurring during the work day. Furthermore, part of the prayer obligation is keyed to sunset, so it does not occur at the same time each day, making it even harder to schedule prayers. The need for Muslims to wash their hands and feet before prayer can cause hazardous wet conditions in the washrooms (or hallways, if water is tracked). One simple solution is to install a special self-draining basin, or arrange to have the floors mopped more often.

If possible, flexible scheduling should be permitted—for instance, an employee who wants to leave early on Friday for the Jewish Sabbath or the Muslim prayer service can simply work later on Thursday or start earlier on Friday morning.

Although it is often impossible to provide food in employee cafeterias that fully complies with all religious dietary restrictions, it is a reasonable gesture to provide some vegetarian alternatives (for employees whose religion forbids meat eating) as well as some alternatives to pork and beef dishes (which are shunned by various religious groups). Low-fat vegetarian alternatives can also appeal to health-conscious employees who do not have religious limitations on their food consumption.

Not all religious discrimination claims involve non-Christians. In March 1999, the Eastern District of New York allowed a suit to proceed on a claim that a born-again Christian employee was fired because of "speaking in tongues" at work. The judge found that born-again Christians are entitled to treatment as a protected class.

Easy steps toward religious accommodation include the following:

- Extend the same toleration to religious dress as you accord to "fashion statements".[2]
- If there is a genuine safety risk (such as flowing robes getting caught in machinery), document the risk.
- Discuss the issue with religious leaders: For instance, if the objective is modesty, a female worker could wear a long dress that is not tight, but is narrow enough not to present a hazard; long sleeves might be gathered into bands or gloves to reduce hazards. Such consultation also allows you to find out which holidays merely require believers to attend a religious service or pray and which require days off.
- Workers might exchange their lunch hours for departing early on or before their religious holidays.
- Use bulletin board posting (or your corporate intranet) to get volunteers to cover for workers who need time off for religious observance.
- Diversity can really help everyone in this context: Muslim or Jewish workers can cover the Christmas holidays, for instance, while Christian employees cover the holidays of other religions.
- If you allow optional or floating personal days, these can be used for religious observance.[3]

In the case of *Hernandez-Torres v. Intercontinental Trading Co.*, 158 F.3d 43 (1st Cir. 1998), the plaintiff's claim of a religiously hostile workplace was rejected. Although he received a number of e-mails urging greater productivity, he was not singled out (nonreligious employees got similar messages), and he continued to receive favorable assessments, so he did not suffer job detriment. Since the claim of religious discrimination failed, so did his claim of retaliation.

23.5 THE EQUAL PAY ACT

President Clinton's 1999 State of the Union Address noted that full-time female workers earned an average of 74 cents for every dollar earned by a full-time male worker. The President proposed a $14 million equal pay initiative to be undertaken by the EEOC and Department of Labor; no details of the plan were given. See 67 LW 2567.

In the spring of 1999, the Bureau of Labor Statistics (BLS) released 1998 figures (*Highlights of Women's Earnings in 1998*, Report 928, discussed in a news item, "Women's Earnings Difference Higher After Age 45," *Compensation and Benefits Update*, 5/19/99, p. 5). For 1998, median female earnings for full-time work, $456, were 76% of median male earnings, $598 (up from 63% in 1979). Pay disparities increased with age. Women under age 25 have virtually achieved wage parity, at an average of 91% of the male wage for the same age bracket. But in the 45–54 bracket, women earned only 70.5% of the male median. For women with college degrees, inflation-adjusted income went up 21.7% since 1979, versus only 7.7% for male college graduates for the same period.

Data on job classification of female workers is only available since 1983. In that year, 34.2% of full-time women workers held executive/managerial/administrative positions (i.e., had the potential for high earnings). In 1998, 46.4% of women employed full time held such positions. However, in both 1983 and 1998, about three-quarters of administrative support (e.g., secretarial) positions were held by women. In other words, the "pink collar" sector remains a largely female domain.

In 1998, about one-quarter of women in the paid workforce were part-time workers, earning a median of about one-third the full-time wage for women. The median wage for female part-time workers was actually higher than that for male part-timers, so this is an area in which women have not only reached but surpassed wage parity.

For full-time female workers, median wage increased with age (although parity with male wages declined), as you would expect with enhanced experience and seniority. But wages stayed fairly stable over time for female part-time workers, indicating a lack of mobility and promotion opportunity.

In early 1999, the Paycheck Fairness Act, S.74/HR 541, had been proposed to allow awards of compensatory and punitive damages in EPA cases. The Fair Pay Act, S. 232/HR 1302, had been introduced to extend the EPA to comparable worth situations (i.e., cases in which male and female workers do not perform the same tasks, but the lower-paid tasks performed by females are at least as valuable as the higher-paid tasks performed by males).

The Office of Federal Contract Compliance Programs (OFCCP) announced in late 1998 that it would target EPA compliance. Bernard E. Anderson, head of the Employment Standards Administration, the Department of Labor agency that enforces wage and hour laws, cited major 1998 EPA settlements. In April, Philadelphia's Corestates Bank agreed to pay $1.5 million. In October, Chicago's R. R. Donnelly agreed to pay $425,000. In December, a proposal was made that the OFCCP and EEOC enter into a Memorandum of Understanding that would permit the OFCCP to seek Title VII damages on behalf of employees deprived of equal pay.

The OFCCP's largest EPA case in its entire four-year "glass ceiling" program was settled when Texaco agreed to pay $3.1 million to 186 women executives and professionals who worked in its corporate office between 1993 and 1996. The back pay awards ranged from $1700 to $51,000; the average award was $12,000. The OFCCP performs 30 to 40 "glass ceiling" reviews a year; it checks to see if the company under investigation imposes subtle barriers to the advancement of women and members of minority groups. See 67 LW 2405, 2428. Since 1992, government contractors have ponied up an average of $32 million a year in DOL settlements, usually back pay ordered as a result of routine audits.

Marc Adams' article, "Fair and Square," *HR Magazine*, 5/99, p. 39, suggests some useful resources for auditing your compensation policies for equal pay compliance. The Web site for the DOL's Women's Bureau, http://www2.dol.gov/wb/10step71.htm, suggests ten steps for promoting pay equality. The Equal Employment Advisory Council's site is http://www.eeac.org, and it can be reached by telephone at (202) 789-8650.

Federal contractors can access the audit manual for OFCCP compliance at http://www.dol.gov/dol/esa/public/regs/compliance/ofccp/compdata.htm.

Even satisfying the audit requirements may not be enough to stave off EPA challenges. Your compensation system may have to pass the test of "regression analysis": That is, raw figures may have to be adjusted to reflect differing work experience and performance. It helps to maintain an objective grading system (i.e., Mr. X is at Grade 11; Ms. Y is at Grade 12)—but it also helps to have an objective outside opinion. Pay grades can reflect unspoken assumptions that jobs typically performed by women take less skill than those typically performed by men, even if there is no objective support for such prejudices.

23.6 DISCRIMINATION SUIT PROCEDURAL ISSUES

The EEOC's investigative powers generally end as soon as a Right to Sue letter has been issued [*EEOC v. Federal Home Loan Mortgage Co.*, 67 LW 1608 (E.D. Va. 3/10/99)]. The exception is the case where the EEOC thinks its investigation goes beyond the litigation, in which case it can intervene in the employee's private suit or file its own charges.

Although employers can benefit from situations in which employees delay too long in filing charges, employees may be given additional time to file EEOC charges if the employer actually misleads the employees as to the existence of an investigation by the employer. The doctrine of "equitable estoppel" is applied if, for instance, the employee is afraid to approach the EEOC and imperil the internal grievance proceeding. See *Currier v. Radio Free Europe*, 1998 Westlaw 785623 (D.C. App. 1998).

23.7 AFFIRMATIVE ACTION

See 63 FR 59,629 and 59,657 (11/4/98) for a Department of Labor Final Rule as to federal contractors' affirmative action obligations for hiring and promoting Vietnam veterans and disabled veterans (irrespective of which war disabled them).

The Institute for Women's Policy Research, on behalf of the AFL-CIO, calculated the lifetime earnings lost by women workers who do not receive equal pay for equal work. The lifetime earnings loss is the difference between expected lifetime earnings between the sexes, assuming that women work an average of 47 years. The figures are corrected for actual work experience and education.

If current wage patterns continue, after 40 years in the workforce, an average 25-year-old woman will earn $523,000 less than the average 25-year-old man. (See http://www.aflcio.org/women/about.htm.) Although in a sense underpaying women is beneficial to business, if women workers had an additional $500,000 over the length of a career, they would use most or all of it to invest or purchase goods and services for themselves and their families—so business as a whole would benefit.

23.8 [NEW] RETALIATION

The first step that the EEOC took in its issuance of a revised Compliance Manual (used by EEOC offices) was to issue Section 8, dealing with Retaliation. Volume 2, Section 614 of the earlier Compliance Manual has become obsolete. New Section 8 is found in EEOC Directives Transmittal 915.003, dated 5/20/98.

Under Section 8, there are three essential elements in a retaliation claim that the EEOC will pursue:

- Protected activity by the charging party—opposing discrimination, or participating in the Title VII complaint process
- Adverse action taken by the employer
- A causal connection between the protected activity and the employer's adverse action

If the charging party reasonably and in good faith believed that the employer committed discrimination (even if this belief was incorrect), and if the charging party protested this discrimination to the employer, using a reasonable means of protest, then there is a possible retaliation complaint.

Charging parties are legally protected against retaliation if the charging party, or someone "closely associated" with him or her, participated in any statutory enforcement proceeding. That includes any investigation, proceeding, hearing, or suit under either Title VII or any other statute enforced by the EEOC. It is unlawful for one employer to retaliate on the basis of a complaint against another employer.

Trivial adverse actions are not covered by the compliance manual, but "more significant retaliatory treatment that is reasonably likely to deter protected activity" is banned. The adverse action need not materially affect the terms, conditions, or privileges of employment. Ex-employees have the right to complain of retaliation (e.g., bad references).

The EEOC might seek temporary or preliminary relief (e.g., injunctions) if retaliation places the charging party at risk of irreparable injury and if there is a substantial likelihood that the retaliation claim will succeed. The compliance manual notes that all of the statutes enforced by the EEOC make both compensatory and punitive damages available to victims of retaliation.

Although Title VII retaliation damages are subject to the statutory cap, there is no cap on ADEA or EPA damages. The manual says that punitive damages are "often" appropriate in retaliation cases. For discussion, see "EEOC Issues Retaliation Guidelines," *Employment Alert*, 7/9/98, p. 6.

➠ TIP

An employee who gives a deposition in another person's sex discrimination case is protected against retaliation for the testimony; the employer is not permitted to impose a requirement that the testimony be "reasonable" [*Glover v. South Carolina Law Enforcement Division*, 67 LW 1551 (4th Cir. 3/9/99)].

The Southern District of New York permitted two black employees to maintain a Title VII case alleging retaliation (professional isolation and lack of opportunities for advancement) after they complained about racist jokes in an e-mail on the corporate system. However, the S.D.N.Y. did not permit a class action to be maintained based on those charges [*Owens v. Morgan Stanley & Co.*, 66 LW 1432 (S.D.N.Y. 12/24/97)].

A lateral transfer requiring the employee to perform tasks that the employer knew the employee would be unable to handle (because of phobia), in retaliation for complaining about harassment by a supervisor, is actionable under Title VII.

The transfer involved the same pay, benefits, and status, but the employer knew that the alleged transfer was really a constructive discharge. See *DiIenno v. Goodwill Industries*, 162 F.3d 235 (3rd Cir. 1998).

According to the Eleventh Circuit, protection against retaliation for participation in an investigation is limited to the EEOC investigation. An employer is not liable for retaliation on the basis of participation in the employer's own internal investigation [*Clover v. Total Systems Services Inc.*, 157 F.3d 824 (11th Cir. 1998)].

REFERENCES

[1]For a review of District Court cases on this important issue, see Ronald M. Green and Alesia J. Kantor, "In 1998, Supreme Court Set Standard for Sexual Harassment Liability," *National Law Journal*, 2/8/99, p. S6.

[2]*Liberty Medical Center, American Arbitration Ass'n*, #16-300-00290-96 (8/14/97), required the reinstatement of a Muslim engineer who worked for a hospital that required shirts to be tucked in and banned caps; the engineer's cultural dress included a long tunic and a cap. See Simon J. Nadel, "Employers Relaxing Dress Standards But Potential Pitfalls Remain in Workplace," 67 LW 2195 (10/13/98).

[3]For more on religious accommodation, see Patricia Digh, "Religion in the Workplace: Make a Good-Faith Effort to Accommodate," *HR Magazine*, 12/98, p. 85; Timothy D. Schellhardt, "In a Factory Schedule, Where Does Religion Fit In?" *WSJ*, 3/4/99, p. B1; Bill Alden, "Suit Allowed Over 'Speaking in Tongues,' *New York Law Journal*, 3/10/99, p. 1. The case involved is *Ramprasad v. New York City Health & Hospitals Corporation*, CV 98-1506 (E.D.N.Y. 3/98). Ronald Al. Lindsay and Elizabeth H. Bach's white paper, "Prohibiting Discrimination Based on Religion: An Employer's Obligation," can be found at http://www.shrm.org/whitepapers.

Chapter 24

The Americans with Disabilities Act (ADA)

24.1 INTRODUCTION

During the supplement period, the ADA was one of the main focuses of litigation (including Supreme Court decisions and cases accepted for hearing) and EEOC guidance.

Under *Bragdon v. Abbott*, 524 U.S. 624 (Sup. Ct. 1998), ADA cases are subject to a three-step test:

- Does the plaintiff have an impairment? (As you'll see, this can be a very difficult question to answer.)
- Is the major life activity that is impaired covered by the ADA?
- Does the plaintiff's impairment substantially limit that major life activity?

Bragdon is not an employment case. It arose when a dentist refused to treat an HIV positive but asymptomatic patient in his office, telling her that she would have to be treated at a hospital. The Supreme Court refused to accept the dentist's argument that treating HIV positive patients in the office posed a direct threat, because the medical consensus is that treatment can be safe for patient, dentist, and other patients as long as precautions are followed.

Although this is not an employment case, the court did treat asymptomatic HIV infection as a disability, because it is a physical impairment that substantially limits major life activities such as reproduction. To the extent that reproduction is considered a major life activity, coverage of infertility treatment under health plans might be mandated.

An EEOC Administrative Decision—not a full-scale rule promulgated after an opportunity for notice and comment—says that denying a female employee coverage for infertility treatments and related medical expenses violates Title VII and the

ADA, because the plan covered medically necessary treatments of other kinds of ailments that had a comparable effect on bodily functioning. See 64 FR 22769 (4/27/99).

The Northern District of Illinois ruled, in September 1997, that female infertility is a disability as defined by the ADA, because reproduction can be a major life activity even if it doesn't affect work [*Erickson v. Board of Governors, Northeastern Illinois University*, 66 LW 1304 (N.D. Ill. 9/29/97)]. This contradicts *Krauel v. Iowa Methodist Medical Center*, 95 F.3d 674 (8th Cir. 1996), which holds that reproduction is *not* a major life activity.

One of several major Supreme Court ADA cases in the supplement period was decided in late 1998. *Wright v. Universal Maritime Service Corp.*, #97-889 67 LW 4013 Sup. Ct. 11/16/98, involves an injured stevedore who was denied employment because companies deemed him to be permanently disabled. The plaintiff sued under the ADA without first filing a grievance or going through arbitration under the collective bargaining agreement.

Although the District Court and Fourth Circuit dismissed the stevedore's case, because of his failure to exhaust grievance remedies, the Supreme Court unanimously reversed. *Gilmer* does permit compulsory arbitration of an ADA claim (under the U-4), but to the Supreme Court, this case is different because the employee's claim derived from a statute, not a contract. Although contract claims are presumed arbitrable, that presumption does not apply to statutory claims. For a collective bargaining agreement to preclude litigation of a statutory claim, it must be very clear on that point. A generalized arbitration clause that fails to discuss antidiscrimination statutes will not be enough to keep disgruntled employees out of the court system.

In an ADA case (or an ADEA case), *Papa v. Katy Industries Inc.* 67 LW 1485 (7th Cir. 2/8/99) says that several small affiliates of a larger corporation can have their workforces aggregated when determining the application of the antidiscrimination statute, as long as they are closely related. Aggregation is proper if the corporate veil can be pierced (i.e., the formal organization can be disregarded in favor of practical realities) and the parent company is liable for its subsidiaries' debts, torts, and breaches of contract; if the enterprise was divided with the objective of avoiding employment laws; or if the parent company directed the discriminatory act or policy.

According to the American Bar Association, based on a study of 1200 reported and unreported cases between 1992 and 1998, the employer wins 92% of the ADA cases that are pursued to a final decision (this survey is discussed at 67 LW 2005). In that sample, 440 cases were not yet final; of the 750 decided, the employer won 92.1%. There were some striking differences based on the location of the case. In the Fifth Circuit, employers won 98.1% of the time, versus a comparatively small 83.3% rate of employer victory in the Ninth Circuit.

It should be noted, however, that very few charges ever proceed to litigation. The EEOC's own statistics show that, between FY 1992 (the first year of EEOC enforcement of the ADA; the statute did not take effect until July 26, 1992) and FY 1997, 91,133 ADA charges were filed. The agency reports resolution of 83,664 of the charges, 13.5% of which were merit resolutions. 4.5% of the cases were settled; 6.0% were withdrawn by the complainant after receipt of benefits. About half of the charges (49.6%) were deemed by the EEOC to have been made without reasonable cause, and about one-third (36.9%) were closed administratively.

Good-cause determinations were made in 3.1% of the cases. Conciliation succeeded in about one-third of the good-cause cases and failed in the other two-thirds. In the five years studied, employers were required to pay $162 million with respect to ADA claims.

The most common impairment cited by ADA charging parties was back injury (15,954 cases between 1992 and 1997; 17.5% of the total). The next most common was emotional or psychiatric impairment: 13.2% of the total, or 12,028 charges, followed by neurological impairment (11.0%; 10,004 charges) and injuries to the extremities (9.3%; 8,497 charges). The various other complaints each represented less than 5% of the total.

About half of all ADA charges (52.2%; 47,535 charges) alleged inappropriate dismissal, and more than a quarter (28.9%; 26,319 charges) alleged failure to make reasonable accommodations to a worker's disability. About one-eighth of the claims (12.5%; 11,410 charges) alleged harassment of disabled persons. (The EEOC ADA figures are from *Employment Alert*, 9/3/98, p. 4.)

On the question of who can be sued under the ADA, *Kimel v. Florida Board of Regents*, 139 F.3d 426 (11th Cir. 1998), and *Bledsoe v. Palm Beach County*, 133 F.3d 816 (11th Cir. 1998), hold that states and other public agencies are not exempt from ADA employment and public access suits because of the Eleventh Amendment (although they are exempt from ADEA suits). *Coolbaugh v. Louisiana*, 136 F.3d 430 (5th Cir. 1998), and *Autio v. AFSCME Local 3139*, 157 F. 3d 1141 (8th Cir. 4/9/98), also permit ADA suits against state employers.

The Ninth and Eleventh Circuits are in conflict as to whether employees of state and local government agencies can use Title II of the ADA (which forbids disability discrimination in the services, programs, and activities of public entities) to assert job discrimination claims. The Ninth Circuit says yes [*Zimmerman v. Oregon*, 67 LW 1566 (9th Cir. 3/18/99)]. The Eleventh Circuit says no [*Bledsoe v. Palm Beach County Soil & Water Conservation District*, 133 F.3d 816 (11th Cir. 1998)].

Although individuals are nearly always exempt from being sued under Title VII and other employment statutes, *Alberte v. Anew Health Care Services*, 588 N.W.2d 298 (Wis. App. 1998), does permit an ADA suit against an individual who was president, administrator, and 47.5% shareholder in a company accused of disability discrimination. In this reading, the president was the company's agent and can be held personally liable for both compensatory and punitive damages.

In January 1999, the Clinton Administration proposed initiatives to help disabled people return to work. Although the proposal attracted support from both parties, as of press time no legislation or regulations had been put into place.

Senators Jefford and Kennedy have introduced a bill under which employed disabled persons could buy into Medicaid and would allow Medicare-eligible disabled persons (i.e., those defined as disabled by the Social Security Administration) to retain Medicare coverage for ten years after reentering the workforce.

See Robert Pear, "Proposal Aims at Returning Disabled Workers to Jobs," *NYT* 1/13/99, p. A12, and Laurie McGinley and Bob Davis, "Disabled Workers to Gain Health Care, Tax Benefits Under Bipartisan Plan," *WSJ*, 1/13/99, p. A6. Under the proposal, disabled people would retain Medicare and/or Medicaid coverage for their health needs after returning to the workforce. Such individuals would also be entitled to a tax credit of up to $1000 toward specialized transportation and the cost of assistive devices. The Administration also called for devoting $35 million in the FY 2000 budget (twice the 1999 level) for research into the development of additional assistive technology. The estimated cost of the proposals over a five-year period would be about $2 billion.

24.2 UNDERSTANDING THE DEFINITION OF DISABILITY

A person with an arthritis-like condition could work up to 50 hours a week, as long as he took his medication. When he was terminated, he brought an ADA suit. The Fifth Circuit, in *Washington v. HCA Health Services of Texas, Inc.*, 152 F.3d 464 (5th Cir. 1998), had to decide whether his status as a person with an "impairment" should be measured with or without the daily medication. The Fifth Circuit's answer is that the more serious the impairment, the more likely it is that the plaintiff's condition should be assessed without the ameliorative measure (i.e., the more likely it is that the plaintiff would be treated as a person covered by the ADA). In this case, the impairment was serious enough to be reviewed on a premedication basis.

Substance Abuse as a Disability

The 1999 Fifth Circuit case of *Zenor v. El Paso Healthcare System Ltd.*, (http://www.lawnewsnetwork.com/practice/employmentlaw/authority/cases/G1 864-1999May27.html), discussed in more detail in ¶22.3, takes the position that even though a hospital pharmacist voluntarily reported his cocaine addiction and entered a rehab program, the hospital did not violate the ADA by firing him. He was considered to be a "current user" of an illegal substance, not qualified for the "rehab" safe harbor, because of the risk of relapse. Furthermore, his job gave him access to pharmaceutical cocaine, greatly increasing the risk of future drug abuse.

Nor could a substance abuser be considered a "qualified person" under the ADA for the specific job of hospital pharmacist (although he might have been qualified for many other jobs that required professional skills but did not involve daily contact with controlled substances).

An employee who abuses illegal drugs is breaking the law—an element that is not present when employees encounter alcohol-related disabilities. An article by John P. Furfaro and Maury B. Josephson, "Alcoholism as a Disability," *New York Law Journal* 2/5/99, p. 3, sums up the case law, with an emphasis on New York cases.

Some cases take the view that, once an employee goes through rehab, it constitutes discrimination against the disability of alcoholism to fire or otherwise discipline the employee for pretreatment absenteeism—for instance, *McEniry v. Landi*, 84 N.Y.2d 554 (1994). But even this case points out that employees who flunk rehab, or who are likely to relapse, are not protected from the consequences of a lapse. *Myszczenko v. City of Poughkeepsie*, 239 A.D.2d 584 (2nd Dept. 1997), says that it's OK to fire an employee for misconduct that occurred after a postrehab relapse.

More recently, in *Mercado v. NYC Housing Authority*, 1998 Westlaw 151039 (S.D.N.Y. 3/31/98), the Southern District dismissed a termination case, pointing out that the ADA allows employers to apply the same standards of conduct to all employees, whether or not they have a substance abuse problem. Similar results were reached in other courts [*Williams v. Widnall*, 79 F.3d 1003 (10th Cir. 1996) and *Rollison v. Gwinnett County*, 865 F.Supp. 1564 (N.D.Ga. 1994)].

➠ TIP

Several courts have upheld "last-chance" agreements, under which the substance abuser acknowledges that job-related misconduct occurred in the past and that the employee's reinstatement after rehab is only conditional, based on continued good performance (and perhaps dependent on giving consent for drug/alcohol testing and passing periodic tests). *Marrari v. WCI Steel Inc.*, 130 F.3d 1180 (6th Cir. 1997), treats the last-chance agreement as a reasonable accommodation to the disability of alcoholism. Does someone have to be given more than one last chance? *Evans v. Federal Express*, 133 F.3d 137 (1st Cir. 1998), upholds the termination of an employee who sought a leave of absence to go to an alcohol rehab program; he had already taken leave for drug rehab. He was discharged for absenteeism. The First Circuit's view is that employers are entitled to be skeptical about the success of a second rehab effort after one has failed.

Employers can't penalize rehabilitated individuals based on the mere fact that they are alcoholics or have been addicted to drugs—but it's perfectly legitimate to punish misconduct that happens to be the result of alcoholism [*Brennan v. NYC Police Department*, 1997 Westlaw 811543 (S.D.N.Y. 5/27/97)].

➠ **TIP**

Don't forget that a substance abuser entering rehab (at least an in-patient program) may be entitled to FMLA leave. Additional leave, after the 12 weeks of FMLA leave have been used up, may be required by the ADA as a reasonable accommodation. There are technical legal questions involved, but it's probably true that the employee has to request accommodation in advance. It probably isn't good enough for a person who has already been terminated or disciplined to make a retroactive request for leave.

24.3 PREEMPLOYMENT INQUIRIES

A job applicant who is not hired because the employer was not satisfied with the applicant's answers to impermissible inquiries has an ADA cause of action—even if the applicant is not disabled. See *Griffin v. Steeltek Inc.*, 160 F.3d 591 (10th Cir. 1998).

Questions can be asked about prior Worker's Compensation claims once a conditional job offer is extended, as long as all potential new hires are asked the same question. But the EEOC's position is that it is inappropriate to refuse to hire because of past occupational injury or potential for filing future WC claims.

24.4 REASONABLE ACCOMMODATIONS

Some recent cases say that the employer has no duty to attempt reasonable accommodations (or additional accommodations for a person who has already received some) until and unless the employee takes the first step and requests accommodation. See *Gaston v. Bellingrath Gardens & Home Inc.* (11th Cir. 2/12/99) and *More v. Buckhorn Rubber Products Inc.*, (8th Cir. 2/1/99), both 67 LW 1528.

The employer can select which reasonable accommodation to offer [in the case of *Keever v. City of Middletown*, 145 F.3d 809 (6th Cir. 1998), a desk job at the same pay for a police officer previously assigned to a beat]. It is not obligated to accept the employee's suggestions (e.g., a shift change or promotion to detective).

➠ **TIP**

Finding a job free of stress caused by fellow-employees is not a "reasonable accommodation" to which a clinically depressed employee is entitled [*Gaul v. Lucent Technologies, Inc.*, 134 F.3d 576 (3rd Cir. 1998)].

Smith v. Midland Brake Inc., 138 F.3d 1304 (10th Cir. 3/13/98), says that, if an employee is unable to handle his or her current job, the employer is not obligated to assign him to another job that he or she *can* handle, because the employee is not "qualified" for the existing job.

Malabarba v. Chicago Tribune Co., 149 F.3d 690 (7th Cir. 1998), involved a plaintiff whose multiple physical problems prevented him from returning to his old job as packager (which required several kinds of strenuous physical labor). The company tried to retrain him for the sedentary job of customer service representative, but he failed the exam. The company didn't have any other jobs he could do, so he was terminated.

The Seventh Circuit's position is that the employer was not liable: The plaintiff couldn't do his old job even with accommodation, and whether a person is a "qualified" individual with a disability depends on the job for which he or she was initially hired, not a temporary light-duty reassignment. If an employer's policy is to offer only temporary light-duty assignments for recuperating employees, the ADA does not require creation of permanent light-duty jobs as an accommodation. The employer need only offer a reasonable accommodation, not the accommodation preferred by the employee. When a job involves multiple duties, the employer is not obligated to separate out the duties that the employee can handle after an illness or injury.

In contrast, however, the EEOC position, echoed by several appellate cases, is that reassignment to a job that the employee can handle constitutes a reasonable accommodation: See 29 CFR §1630.2(o). Cases of this type include *Dalton v. Subaru-Isuzu Automotive, Inc.*, 141 F.3d 667 (7th Cir. 1998), and *Aka v. Washington Hospital Center*, 156 F.3d 1284 (D.C. Cir. 1998) (disabled person who cannot do the current job is entitled to ADA relief such as reassignment, with or without accommodation, to a job he or she can perform). The disabled employee in search of accommodation must be able to prove his or her ability to handle the new job [*DePaoli v. Abbott Laboratories*, 140 F.3d 668 (7th Cir. 1998)].

The ADA does not require the employer to discard its existing, nondiscriminatory policies or work rules. For instance, if the employer maintains a rule against demotions, it is not necessary to demote a disabled employee to a position that he or she can handle [*Duckett v. Dunlop Tire Corp.*, 120 F.3d 1222 (11th Cir. 1997)]. If the employer's policy is to give full-time employees greater access to transfers than part-time employees, the policy can be enforced in the ADA context [*Daugherty v. City of El Paso*, 56 F.3d 695 (5th Cir. 1995)]. The *Dalton* case discussed previously says that if the employer had light-duty positions, but wants to reserve them for employees returning to work after a work-related injury, this can be done without violating the ADA.

Employers can lawfully stipulate that light-duty positions are temporary; but if no end date is specified, a court might treat the light-duty job as a permanent accommodation that cannot be terminated without violating the ADA [*Hendricks-Robinson v. Excel Corp.*, 1998 Westlaw 544834 (7th Cir. 1998)]. Furthermore, the employer must volunteer information about potential transfers for which the disabled employee might be suited; it cannot wait for the employee to do research. For a discussion of the reassignment issue, see "Reassignment as a Reasonable Accommodation: How Far Must an Employer Go?" (no byline), WestGroup Employment Alert, 10/1/98, p. 1.

According to *Barnett v. U.S. Air*, 157 F.3d 744 (9th Cir. 1998), the ADA plaintiff's prima facie case includes proof of the existence of an available job he or she could perform with reasonable accommodation. Although the EEOC says that employers are supposed to engage in an interactive process with employees to evolve reasonable accommodations, *Barnett* says that failure to do so is not a separate cause of action under the ADA.

Another case that deals with the ADA prima facie case is *Community Hospital v. Fail*, 969 F.3d 667 (Colo. Sup. 1998). Under *Fail*, once the disabled employee makes the prima facie case, the burden then shifts to the employer to prove, by a preponderance of the evidence, that it either offered the plaintiff reasonable accommodation or was unable to do so because of undue hardship. In this analysis, the employer has greater access to information about the availability of accommodation and therefore should be required to prove this issue.

24.4.3 [NEW] 1999 EEOC Enforcement Guidance

On March 2, 1999, the EEOC released a major document, the 39-page "Enforcement Guidance: Reasonable Accommodation and Undue Hardship Under the Americans With Disabilities Act." This paper, which contains many practical examples of situations and EEOC responses, can be found at the EEOC Web site, at http://www.eeoc.gov/docs/accommodation.html. The document contains a checklist for the use of EEOC investigators assessing ADA charges. For a practice-oriented interpretation, see John P. Furfaro and Maury B. Josephson's article, "New Enforcement Guidance on Reasonable Accommodation Under the ADA," http://www.lawnewsnetwork.com/practice/employmentlaw/papers/lawfirm/A1163-1999May4.html.

A corporation that complies with these guidelines should be free from EEOC enforcement worries. However, since the courts have seldom required corporations to adopt the EEOC viewpoint in every respect, not satisfying all of the EEOC guidelines would not necessarily result in legal liability.

As the document notes, an employer may have to make various kinds of reasonable accommodations to disability (e.g., restructuring jobs; making work facilities and equipment handicap accessible; modifying work schedules; reassigning a disabled worker to a vacant job) but does not have to eliminate essential job functions. Employers do not have to provide items used for both work and nonwork tasks. For instance, employees are responsible for furnishing their own prostheses, eyeglasses, and hearing aids, because these are needed for nonwork functions as well.

Employers are not required to undergo undue hardship, defined by the document as financial difficulty or reasonable accommodations that are unduly extensive, substantial, or disruptive or that would fundamentally alter the nature or operation of the business.

Employees who feel the need for reasonable accommodation must make a clear request but need not use the term "reasonable accommodation"—they can, for instance, ask for time off or adaptive equipment. The request can be made by a representative (family member friend, health professional) on behalf of the disabled individual. Employers must act on reasonable verbal requests but can ask to have them confirmed by a written memorandum, and can demand reasonable documentation of the need for accommodation (e.g., nature, severity, duration of the impairment; which activities are impaired; extent of limitation in employee's functional ability). But documentation cannot be required if the disability and accommodation are obvious or the employee has already provided sufficient substantiating information.

As long as the employer provides an effective accommodation, it can choose its preferred (e.g., most cost-effective) accommodation and need not furnish the one suggested by the employee. Employers can't force an accommodation on an unwilling employee—but someone who rejects an accommodation that would remove a direct threat, or that is necessary to performance of an essential job function, might not be ADA qualified.

Employers must make sure that disabled employees receive equal access to information communicated in the workplace to other employees—(e.g., notices and training). The EEOC regards the obligation of reasonable accommodation as ongoing. Merely making one accommodation doesn't mean that no further accommodations need be made in the future.

The EEOC's position is that an employer can legitimately reallocate essential job functions to accommodate disability but is not obligated to do so. Altering marginal functions is a reasonable accommodation. Using accrued paid leave, or unpaid leave, is a reasonable accommodation, but employers do not have to offer additional paid leave to employees who have a disability.

Employees should be allowed to exhaust their paid leave before going on unpaid leave. The employer must keep the job open during leave, unless this operates as an undue hardship on the employer. In undue-hardship situations, the employer should consider whether the employee with a disability can be transferred to an equivalent vacant position for which he or she is qualified. Furthermore, a leave request need not be granted if the employer can provide an alternative reasonable accommodation that would keep the employee at work.

In the disputed territory where the ADA and FMLA overlap, the EEOC's position is that "An employer should determine an employee's rights under each statute separately, and then consider whether the two statutes overlap regarding the appropriate actions to take."

One example the EEOC gives is an ADA-disabled person who needs 13 weeks of leave. Under the FMLA, only 12 weeks of leave are required, but the ADA does not allow the employer to deny the thirteenth week of leave unless that would be an undue hardship (bearing in mind the impact of the 12 weeks of FMLA leave on the employer's operations). When an ADA-disabled employee returns from leave, the ADA requires reinstatement in the original position (absent undue hardship, or unless the employee has ceased to be qualified for the original position), whereas the FMLA permits reinstatement to any equivalent position.

Offering a modified or part-time schedule is a required reasonable accommodation, unless this would work an undue hardship on the employer. The EEOC's example is an HIV positive employee who has to take medication that induces nausea and wants a 45-minute break to cope with nausea. Employers must consider reassignment to another, vacant position if the requested schedule modifications would be an undue hardship. In "overlap" situations between FMLA and ADA, modified schedules must be offered if mandated by the FMLA, even if the result is undue hardship for the employer that would not be required by the ADA.

Employees need not be offered the chance to work at home unless this would be effective (would not impair essential job functions that have to be performed at the employer's location) and would not cause undue hardship.

If there is a vacant position available for transfer, the employer need not provide training to assist the employee to become qualified, but if training would be offered to a nondisabled employee, it must be offered to the disabled transferee employee. The EEOC's position is that transfer to a vacant position is a reasonable accommodation and therefore must be offered to qualified disabled employees even if the employer does not normally offer transfers. It's not enough that the employee be permitted to compete for a vacant position—the job must go to any qualified disabled employee seeking reasonable accommodation who wants the transfer.

The determination of undue hardship is based on net cost, after accessing potential third-party sources of funds (e.g., state grants). The EEOC does not support the use of cost-benefit analysis in assessing hardship, stating that the cost of the accommodation should be compared to the employer's resources and not to the worker's salary, position, or status. Employers can and should ask employees to contribute to the cost of accommodations that would otherwise not be required because they are too costly.

24.5 WHAT CONSTITUTES DISABILITY?

In April 1999, the Supreme Court heard arguments in three major employment-related ADA cases but had not yet issued its decisions by press time. (April 1999 was also the date of argument for a major ADA case involving the responsibility of state governments to provide facilities for disabled people, but that is outside the scope of this book.)

The first employment-related case was *Murphy v. United Parcel Service*, #97-1992, involving the question of whether a person whose hypertension is controlled by medication is disabled and therefore able to sue under the ADA. *Sutton v. United Air Lines*, #97-1943, copes with the common situation of a person with defective vision whose vision can be corrected with eyeglasses. For both *Murphy* and *Sutton*, then, the critical issue is whether disability is measured before or after corrective measures are taken. *Albertsons v. Kirkingburg*, #98-591, is the case of a one-eyed truck driver whose brain has adapted to provide functional but "different" vision.

The Third Circuit decided in April 1998 [*Deane v. Pocono Medical Center*, 66 LW 1646 (3rd Cir. 4/15/98)], that a person who can perform the *essential* functions of the job without accommodation is qualified, whether or not that person is able to perform other functions of the job (with or without accommodation).

Also according to the Third Circuit, the EEOC's rule found at 29 CFR §1630.2(j)(3) is a reasonable interpretation of the statute that is entitled to deference. Therefore, the determination as to whether a person is limited in the major life activity of working must include consideration of his or her training, skills, and abilities [*Mondzelewski v. Pathmark Stores Inc.*, 67 LW 1393 (3rd Cir. 12/23/98)].

Ross v. Indiana State Teacher's Ass'n Trust, 1998 Westlaw 560238 (7th Cir. 1998), raises some interesting questions. The plaintiff had been on disability for a while, after a hip operation. The plan questioned his continuing need for benefits, so he applied for reinstatement, with a list of requested accommodations. The employer was willing to adopt most, but not all, of them and asked for documentation of the plaintiff's needs. The plaintiff's doctor showed doubt about the plaintiff's ability to work. The employer withdrew the reinstatement offer, and the plaintiff ended up in a bind. Although the Seventh Circuit agreed with the employer that not reinstating a person whose ability to work was dubious was not a denial of reasonable accommodation, the plaintiff was unable to get continued disability benefits. The disability plan's contention was that he was now able to work—he just wasn't able to return to the old job even with reasonable accommodation.

Urinary incontinence was not deemed to be a disability, because it would not debar the plaintiff from holding jobs that permitted her to control her own access to the restroom, even though her teaching position did not allow her to leave the classroom during class periods [*Swain v. Hillsborough County School Board*, 146 F.3d 855 (11th Cir. 1998)].

Somewhat similarly, a person whose physical or mental condition precludes working over 40 hours a week was held not to be ADA disabled by [*Tardie v. Rehab. Hospital of Rhode Island*, 67 LW 1521 (1st Cir. 2/24/99)], given that there are many jobs available that do not require a commitment of over 40 hours a week. Jonathan L. Israel review the question of disciplining employees whose condition prevents regular attendance at work in "When an Employee's Absence From Work is Disability-Related," *New York Law Journal*, 2/8/99, p. S5.

In the view of the Fifth Circuit, not all seizures limit major life activities; the court declined to define "awareness" as a major life activity [*Deas v. River West LP*, 152

F.3d 471 (5th Cir. 1998)]. Also see *LaChance v. Duffy's Draft House Inc.*, 146 F.3d 832 (11th Cir. 1998), holding that a cook's epilepsy made him a direct threat to others (if he had a seizure while using the stove or other kitchen equipment),and therefore not a qualified employee. In this reading, the employee always has the burden of showing that he or she does not offer a direct threat and therefore can perform essential job functions, or that reasonable accommodation is possible. However, the employee did not have to pay the employer's attorneys' fees, because the employee's appeal, although unsuccessful, was not frivolous or unreasonable.

The Sixth Circuit agreed that a grocery store was justified in firing a produce clerk who said that he was HIV positive but neither verified his condition nor took the medical examination requested by the employer. The examination was job related and consistent with business necessity, because minor injuries at work could endanger an HIV positive employee or others [*EEOC v. Prevo's Family Market Inc.*, 66 LW 1486 (6th Cir. 2/4/98)].

For more about workplace HIV issues, including a sample business case and sample workplace policies and training materials, see the HIV/AIDS Workplace Toolkit, http://www.shrm.org/diversity/aidsguide/brta.htm, explaining Business Responds to AIDS (BRTA), a joint venture between business groups and the Centers for Disease Control.

In a somewhat similar Seventh Circuit case, an employee took time off from work because of a claimed back injury. The supervisor thought she was malingering and had an investigation done—revealing that she really was malingering and not disabled. Therefore, firing her did not violate the ADA, because her firing was not related to disability but to deception [*Jasmantas v. Subaru-Isuzu Automotive, Inc.*, 1998 Westlaw 138769 (7th Cir. 1998)].

An employee with chronic obstructive pulmonary disease was not qualified, because even on a flex-time schedule he could not arrive at work early enough to perform essential job functions; the employer had no duty to offer work at home as an accommodation. The Fifth Circuit ruled, in *Hypes v. First Commerce Corp.*, 134 F.3d 721 (5th Cir. 1998), that he was fired on the basis of absenteeism, not age or disability.

The Eighth Circuit accepted an employer's argument that a diabetic sales representative was terminated for cause, not for disability, in that his bad driving record, including a drunk driving conviction, prevented him from holding a valid driver's license, which in turn prevented him from being covered under the employer's automobile insurance policy, which was a requirement of the job [*Mathews v. Trilogy Communications, Inc.*, 143 F.3d 1160 (8th Cir. 1998)].

Four Circuits have ruled that the employer must prove the availability of equivalent jobs in the same geographic area, in order to limit the back pay award of a successful plaintiff who failed to seek other work. Most recently, the First Circuit joined the three other Circuits in saying that it's up to the employee to show that the equivalent jobs were unavailable. In this reading [see, e.g., *Quint v. A. E. Staley Mfg. Co.*, 67 LW 1624 (1st Cir. 3/15/99)], the employee knows why he or she failed to seek other work and thus is the best person to explain it.

The Tenth Circuit requires ADA plaintiffs to articulate, with particularity, the alleged impairment from which they suffer and the major life activity affected [*Poindexter v. Atchison, Topeka & Santa Fe Railroad,* 67 LW 1521 (10th Cir. 2/24/99)].

24.6 DISABILITY AND THE BENEFIT PLAN

Three Circuit Courts (the Sixth, Seventh, and Eleventh) have ruled that a totally disabled retiree or ex-employee is not "qualified" (because he or she is unable to perform job functions) and therefore cannot sue for fringe-benefit discrimination [*EEOC v. CAN Ins. Companies,* 96 F.3d 1038 (7th Cir. 1997); *Parker v. Metropolitan Life Ins. Co.,* 99 F.3d 181, aff'd 121 F.3d 1006 (6th Cir. 1997), *cert. denied* 1998 Westlaw 15861; and *Gonzales v. Garner Food Services, Inc.,* 89 F.3d 1523 (11th Cir. 1996), *cert. denied* 117 S.Ct. 1822].

But that only covers ADA Title I, the employment discrimination portion of the statute. Another front on which employers may have to fight is Title III, the public accommodations title. If an employee benefits plan is considered a public accommodation (and this is far from a settled legal principle!), then excluding a disabled person from it could violate the ADA, even if the disabled person is no longer a qualified employee. See "Post-Employment Fringe Benefits and the ADA: Suing for Differential Disability Coverage," WestGroup Employment Alert, 7/9/98, p. 1.

The argument for bringing disability insurance under Title III is pretty far fetched. The definition of "public accommodation," which is found in 42 USC §12181(7)(F), includes insurance offices, so a few cases say that the policies sold in an insurance office must also be public accommodations—for instance, *Carparts Distribution Center, Inc. v. Automotive Wholesalers' Association of New England, Inc.,* 37 F.3d 12 (1st Cir. 1994), which deals with a cap on AIDS-related insurance coverage.

Most courts do not think Title III is applicable to employment-related disability plans, because they think that all employment-related issues should fall under Title I, or because they limit "place of public accommodation" to mean a physical place like an office or shopping mall that the plaintiff has to attempt to visit physically, or because, as discussed later, they think that Title III requires physical accessibility but doesn't govern the content of services offered to the public. The most significant cases on these issues are *Ford v. Schering-Plough Corp.,* 145 F.3d 601 (3rd Cir. 1998), and *Parker v. Metropolitan Life Ins. Co.,* 121 F.3d 1006 (6th Cir. 1997).

According to "Two New ADA Rules Emerge From Recent Cases," WestGroup Employment Alert, 9/17/98, p. 1, the ADA is being interpreted to prevent employers favoring nondisabled over disabled employees (and job applicants). However, employees who feel that one group of disabled persons is being given an unfair advantage over other groups of disabled persons will probably not be able to use the ADA to sue the employer—(e.g., if physical disabilities are treated more leniently than mental disabilities, or if AIDS is disadvantaged vis-à-vis other diseases). Cases of this type include *Parker v. Metropolitan Life Ins. Co.,* 121 F.3d 1006 (6th Cir. 1997), *cert. denied* 1998 Westlaw 15861, and *Rogers v. Dep't of Health & Environmental Control*, 985 F.Supp. 635 (D.S.C., 1997). However, *Lewis v. Aetna Life Ins. Co.*, 982 F.Supp. 1158 (E.D. Va. 1997), does permit suits for discrimination between classes of disabled people.

Another argument that has often succeeded is that the ADA merely ensures basic access to the goods and services that constitute a public accommodation; it does not cover the content of those goods and services (e.g., the details of a benefit plan). This argument succeeded n *Lenox v. Healthwise of Kentucky*, 149 F.3d 453 (6th Cir. 1998), and *Ford v. Schering-Plough Corp.*, 145 F.3d 601 (3rd Cir. 1998). However, it failed in *Doe v. Mutual of Omaha Insurance Co.*, 999 F.Supp. 1188 (N.D. Ill. 1998), and several recent cases have gone ahead and analyzed the content of insurance policies under the ADA, without specifically ruling on this issue [*Chabner v. United of Omaha Life Ins. Co.*, 994 F.Supp. 1185 (N.D. Cal. 1998); *World Ins. Co. v. Branch*, 966 F.Supp. 1203 (N.D. Ga. 1997)].

ADA Title IV, 42 USC §12201(c) et. seq., provides a safe harbor for insurers and employee benefit plans. They are allowed to underwrite, classify, and administer "risks" as long as they do not violate state law and as long as the risk classifications are not adopted as a way to evade the ADA. It's not too clear how far the safe harbor extends, but *Lewis v. Aetna Life Ins. Co.*, 7 F.Supp.2d 743 (E.D. Va. 1998), says that the ADA is violated by a plan's distinction between physical and mental disabilities unless the distinction has actuarial support that Aetna was unable to produce. [The Mental Health Parity Act, 42 USC §300gg, discussed in ¶9.2.1, is limited to health insurance and does not extend to disability benefit plans; see *Brewster v. Cooley Associates*, 1997 Westlaw 823634 (D.N.M. 1997).]

24.9 INTERACTION WITH OTHER STATUTES

The mere fact of applying for Social Security or employer-based disability benefits will not preclude an ADA suit [see, e.g., *Griffith v. Wal-Mart Stores Inc.*, 66 LW 1487 (6th Cir. 1/29/98)]. However, information provided in the applications for such benefits is admissible as evidence in the ADA case, because it is probative on the question of whether the plaintiff previously requested accommodation [*Whitbeck v. Vital Signs Inc.*, 67 LW 1311 (D.C. Cir. 11/20/98)]. Also see *King v. Herbert J. Thomas Memorial Hospital*, 159 F.3d 192 (4th Cir. 1998), which holds that receipt of disability benefits (as distinct from the mere application) estops an age discrimination plaintiff from claiming she was able to perform the job at the time of her discharge.

A slightly different formulation is found in *Flowers v. Komatsu Mining Systems*, 67 LW 1215 (7th Cir. 1/12/99), which holds that evidence of the Social Security disability determination can affect the plaintiff's damages, by proving the periods of time during which the plaintiff would not have been able to perform the essential job functions even with accommodation.

The Southern District of New York does not accept the EEOC position that distinguishing between mental and physical disabilities in a long-term disability plan violates the ADA. See *EEOC v. Chase Manhattan Bank*, 67 LW 1416 (S.D.N.Y. 12/8/98). The Mental Health Parity Act, 42 USC §300gg, is limited to health insurance—not disability benefits [*Brewster v. Cooley Associates*, 1997 Westlaw 823634 (D.N.M. 1997)].

"Employee Leave and the Law," WestGroup Employment Alert, 9/17/98, p. 4, discusses the interface between the FMLA and the ADA. FMLA leave, although unpaid, is easier to obtain than medical leave as a reasonable ADA accommodation, because the FMLA requires that employers with 50 or more employees grant up to 12 weeks' unpaid leave to any employee who needs the leave because of his or her own illness or the serious illness of a close family member. Reinstatement after FMLA leave is also automatic, but ADA reinstatement requires a showing of ability to perform essential work tasks (with or without reasonable accommodation).

This article also discusses the need for predictable, regular attendance as a fundamental part of job qualification. The article suggests that as long as the employer has a neutral, uniformly applied policy that is actually communicated to employees and enforced, it is in a better position to assert that regular attendance is essential. This argument was raised, for instance, in *Carlson v. Inacom Corp.*, 885 F.Supp. 1314 (D. Neb. 1995); *Fritz v. Mascotech Automotive Sys. Group Inc.*, 914 F.Supp. 1481 (E.D. Mich. 1996); and *Vorhies v. Pioneer Mfg.*, 906 F.Supp. 578 (D. Colo. 1995).

However, *Cehrs v. Northeast Ohio Alzheimer's Research Center*, 155 F. 3d 775 (6th Cir. 1998), does not permit employers to rely on a presumption that regular, predictable attendance is an essential job function. Employers facing this argument should be prepared with additional evidence relating to the need for predictability in this particular job rather than as an everyday part of the working world.

The FMLA, the ADA, and Worker's Compensation have been described as the "Bermuda triangle" for employers. "When Regs Collide: The ADA and Workers' Compensation," WestGroup Employment Alert, 11/25/98, p. 1, discussed in more detail in ¶20.10, explains the interaction among these, especially the ADA and Worker's Compensation.

Chapter 25

FAMILY AND MEDICAL LEAVE ACT (FMLA)

25.1 INTRODUCTION

To qualify for FMLA leave, the employee must have worked at least 1250 hours for the employer in the previous year. An employee had so much leave that he worked only 1037 hours in the relevant time period. Therefore, in the view of the Eastern District of Pennsylvania, he didn't qualify for FMLA leave—vacation and personal days, suspensions, sick days, and holidays don't count toward the required 1250 hours [*Clark v. Allegheny University Hospital*, 1998 Westlaw 94803 (E.D. Pa. 1998)].

25.2 NOTICE REQUIREMENTS

An employee who didn't have a telephone sent a note to her employer saying that she couldn't come in that day because of a pain in her side. She didn't communicate with the employer at all for 12 days, after she had been operated on. This was her fourth unexcused absence in three weeks, so she was fired. The ruling of *Satterfield v. Wal-Mart Stores, Inc.*, 135 F.3d 973 (5th Cir. 1998), is that she did not even give the employer enough notice to trigger a duty to investigate her need for FMLA leave, and her prior unexcused absences made it reasonable for the employer to conclude that she was merely being irresponsible, not in need of medical leave.

If the employee's doctor reports that there is no need for leave, the employer is entitled to rely on that report and deny an FMLA leave request; the plaintiff can't claim that circumstances changed since the medical consultation [*Stoops v. One Call Communications, Inc.*, 1998 Westlaw 142297 (7th Cir. 1997)]. (He or she should have gotten an updated medical certification in such a case.)

However, an employer can't demand certification or recertification without giving the employee the amount of time provided by the FMLA (15 days for an initial certification; recertification no more often than every 30 days) and then fire the employee for failure to provide adequate certification. As *LeGrand v. Village of McCook*, 1998 Westlaw 182462 (N.D. Ill. 1998), points out, reducing the time frame makes it impossible to determine whether the employee didn't have valid evidence—or could have assembled the necessary proof given enough time.

TIP

If an employee provides medical certification of a serious health condition, but you are dubious about its accuracy (or whether the need for leave continues as long as the employee says it does), be sure to ask for a second opinion right away. Failure to do so might make it impossible for you to challenge the medical findings if the case ever comes to court. See *Sims v. Alameda-Contra Costa Transit District*, 1998 Westlaw 208823 (N.D. Cal, 1998).

Sometimes, when it comes to notification, the shoe is on the other foot: The employer must provide notice to employees. The DOL's rule (found at 29 CFR §825.208) is that employers must give advance notice to employees, letting them know when a projected absence from work will be treated as FMLA leave.

This regulation has already been challenged in court. The Middle District of Alabama found it invalid [see *Cox v. AutoZone Inc.*, 990 F.Supp. 1369 (M.D. Ala. 1998)] on the grounds that the regulation extends the availability of FMLA leave past 12 weeks per year if the employer fails to give the notice. In this analysis, the FMLA was drafted to give the employer the right to make employees use up their accrued paid leave before taking FMLA leave—but the statutory purpose was not to give the employee the right to demand FMLA leave instead of paid leave. The Eleventh Circuit heard arguments in the appeal of this case in December 1998.

Effect of Leave

If an employee returns to work after FMLA leave and has been pronounced fit to work by his or her doctor, the employer can require the employee to take another medical examination only if the employee's behavior justifies an inference of ongoing limitations that interfere with the ability to work [*Albert v. Runyon,* 66 LW 1731 (D. Mass. 5/5/98)].

According to *Tardie v. Rehab. Hospital of Rhode Island,* 67 LW 1521 (1st Cir. 2/24/99), the FMLA is not violated by firing an employee who is on medical leave, because the FMLA (unlike the ADA) does not require reasonable accommodation. Reinstatement is not required if the employee is no longer able to perform the essential job functions. And if an employee's work performance is poor enough to justify termination anyway, it's not a FMLA violation to fire the employee while he or she is on leave [*Hubbard v. Blue Cross/Blue Shield Ass'n,* 1998 Westlaw 171831 (N.D. Ill. 1998)].

25.5 FMLA LITIGATION AND REMEDIES

The FMLA became effective August 5, 1993; between then and the end of the DOL's 1998 fiscal year, the DOL served as plaintiff in 29 FMLA suits. As of January 1999, seven of the suits were still pending. The DOL brought most of those cases based on termination of employees who took FMLA leave or refusal to reinstate employees subsequent to FMLA leave.

As in all employment-related contexts, lawsuits were just the tip of the iceberg. DOL received 13,597 FMLA-related employee complaints during that time period. A total of 8364 complaints were resolved by conciliation; 5233 were resolved through investigation. DOL claims successful resolution in 87% of completed cases. Violations were found in 8067 cases, and damages of about $13.2 million were assessed. Back pay recoveries ranged from $1000 to $40,000; the employee who received the $40,000 also got an equal amount of liquidated damages and was reinstated.

At the end of 1997, the Seventh Circuit held that the *McDonnell-Douglas* burden-shifting analysis does not apply in FMLA cases [*Diaz v. Fort Wayne Foundry Corp.*, 131 F.3d 711 (7th Cir. 1997)]. Instead, the FMLA plaintiff's obligation is to prove, by preponderance of the evidence, that his or her discharge violated FMLA rights.

The Courts of Appeals have not yet ruled directly on the validity of DOL's notification requirements (see §25.2, preceding), but the Fourth Circuit applied the requirement in the case of *Cline v. Wal-Mart Stores, Inc.*, 144 F.3d 294 (4th Cir. 1998), without a lengthy discussion that could serve as explanation and precedent.

Also in 1998, the First Circuit decided that an ex-employee (in this case, a laid-off worker who charges that his previous use of FMLA leave induced his employer to refuse to rehire him) is entitled to sue under the FMLA [*Duckworth v. Pratt & Whitney*, 152 F.3d 1 (1st Cir. 1998)]. That is, the right to bring an FMLA case does not depend on current employment with the defendant employer.

The Sixth Circuit allowed FMLA jury trials [*Frizzell v. Southwest Motor Freight*, 154 F.3d 641 (6th Cir. 1998)] on the grounds that, since damages are available, a jury should set them. An additional rationale was the resemblance between the statutory schemes of the FMLA and the Fair Labor Standards Act; FLSA jury trials are well accepted.

At the District Court level, the District of Maryland found that 29 CFR §110(d) (employer is not allowed to challenge eligibility once it has confirmed that the employee is eligible to take FMLA leave) is invalid. To the court in *Seaman v. Downtown Partnership of Baltimore Inc.*, 991 F.Supp. 751 (D. Md. 1998), the regulation goes too far because it usurps Congress's authority to set policy. For discussion of DOL FMLA enforcement, see Deborah Billings, "DOL Rule on Employer Notification Duty to Employees on FMLA Leave Under Attack," 67 LW 2419 (1/26/99).

In late 1998, the Middle District of Florida decided that the Eleventh Amendment precludes FMLA suits in federal court against a state-agency employer

[*Driesse v. Florida Board of Regents,* 67 LW 1268 (M.D. Fla. 10/20/98)]. *Garrett v. Board of Trustees of University of Alabama,* 1998 Westlaw 21879 (N.D. Ala. 1998), says that state employers are free of FMLA liability—and are equally exempt under the ADA.

The statute of limitations is three years for "willful" FMLA violations—a year longer than the normal two-year rule. The Eastern District of Virginia says that, because willfulness is a matter of state of mind, the three-year statute of limitations is triggered whenever the plaintiff alleges willfulness; it is not necessary (at the pleading stage) to support the claim [*Settle v. S.W. Rogers Co.,* 1998 Westlaw 136125 (E.D. Va. 1998)].

FMLA damages are defined by 29 USC §2612 as lost compensation; or, if no compensation was lost, the cost of purchasing care for the person requiring care. The Eastern District of Louisiana ruled, in *Barrilleaux v. Thayer Lodging Groups Inc.,* 1998 Westlaw 614181 (E.D. La. 1998), that a person who sues for lost wages is not entitled to be compensated for care costs as well.

Wright v. Universal Maritime Service Corp., 67 LW 4013 (Sup. Ct. 11/16/98), says that a collective bargaining agreement arbitration clause can effectively bar litigation of statutory claims (such as FMLA claims) only if it is quite specific. A generalized ban on litigation is not sufficient.

The holding of *Albertson's v. United Food & Commercial Workers,* 157 F.3d 758 (9th Cir. 1998), is that a private single-employee employment contract can mandate arbitration of FMLA claims, but a collective bargaining agreement covering an entire bargaining unit cannot.

A (male) state trooper was awarded $375,000 by a Maryland jury because he was denied FMLA leave for the birth of his first child. At that time, Maryland had a law (since changed) that made 30 days of paid leave available to "primary caregivers," but only 10 days available for "secondary caregivers." (Current law has abolished this distinction; all new birth and adoptive parents are entitled to 30 days' paid leave.) The plaintiff's supervisor told him that he could not be a primary caregiver because he could not breast feed his new baby. The case, relating to events in December 1994, was filed in April 1995. By the time it was decided in February 1999, the trooper and his wife had a second child. The second time around, he got his 12 weeks' FMLA leave with no problems. This case is discussed by Tamar Lewin, "Father Awarded $375,000 In a Parental Leave Case," *NYT,* 2/3/99, p. A9.

25.7 FMLA INTERFACE WITH OTHER LAWS

Some tough questions of reconciling FMLA and COBRA were settled by an IRS Final Rule published on February 3, 1999, at 64 FR 5160. The Final Rule provides that merely taking FMLA leave is not a COBRA qualifying event. However, a qualifying event does occur with respect to an employee (and any dependents of the employee who are at risk of losing health coverage) who fails to return to work at the end of the FMLA leave. The typical example is a new mother who does not return to work after her maternity leave has ended.

Under the Final Rule, the COBRA qualifying event occurs on the last day of the FMLA leave. The employer is not allowed to condition the COBRA election on the employee's reimbursement of EGHP premiums paid on his or her behalf during the leave. However, if the employer has actually terminated coverage under the group plan for the class of employees that the employee belonged to before the FMLA leave, it is not necessary to offer continuation coverage to employees who do not return from leave.

Although the two statutes were designed to accomplish different goals, workers sometimes find that FMLA leave is more accessible than taking time off as an ADA "reasonable accommodation." These issues are raised by "Employee Leave and the Law," *Employment Alert*, 9/17/98, p. 4. Remember, FMLA leave is available in the case of the employee's own illness, not just the illness of a family member who needs care.

Furthermore, if the employer company has at least 50 employees and the employee has worked there for at least 12 months, entitlement to FMLA leave is automatic. The employer's discretion as to what constitutes a reasonable accommodation is not a factor. The right to reinstatement is also automatic, and employers are not allowed to raise a defense of unreasonable hardship in the FMLA context, although it is available under the ADA.

An Opinion Letter from the Department of Labor (#89; see *Employment Alert*, 3/5/98, p. 11) takes the position that salaried workers who are exempt from the Fair Labor Standards Act (FLSA) are not brought under FLSA coverage merely because their employer docks their paychecks to reflect unpaid leave under the FMLA. (Normally, pay deductions for absence are characteristic of FLSA-covered wage workers, not exempt salaried workers.) However, the exclusion is limited to FMLA leave taken by employees of companies covered by the FMLA (e.g., those with 50 or more employees).

Chapter 26

The Age Discrimination in Employment Act

26.1 INTRODUCTION

In the view of the Second Circuit, the ADEA applies to employees of the U.S. branch of a foreign corporation that has 20 or more employees throughout the world—it's not necessary that there be 20 employees at the U.S. location [*Morelli v. Cedel*, 141 F.3d 39 (2nd Cir. 1998)].

In the domestic context, the Seventh Circuit allowed employees at several small affiliates of a larger corporation to be aggregated to determine the number of employees (and therefore ADEA coverage) if

- The "corporate veil" can be pierced, and the parent corporation would be liable for its subsidiaries' debts, torts, and breaches of contract.
- An original larger enterprise was split up to avoid employment-related liability.
- The parent company directed the discriminatory act or policy.

This new test replaces an earlier requirement of interrelated operations, common management, common ownership, or centralized control of personnel and labor relations. See *Papa v. Katy Industries Inc.*, 67 LW 1485 (7th Cir. 2/8/99).

Reallocation of duties to several younger workers can be treated as a "replacement" of the demoted employee for ADEA purposes. See *Hindman v. Transkrit Corp.*, 1998 Westlaw 276312 (8th Cir. 1998).

In late 1998, the Eighth Circuit joined the Fifth, Sixth, and Seventh Circuits in ruling that it does not constitute age discrimination for an employer to make reasonable inquiries about an older person's retirement plans [*Watkins v. J&S Oil Co.*, 164 F.3d 55 (8th Cir. 12/30/98)].

Although the nominal range of the ADEA is persons aged 40 and over, in late February 1999, the Supreme Court of New Jersey permitted a 25-year-old to maintain an age discrimination suit and found the New Jersey age discrimination statute to be broad enough to encompass reverse age discrimination (i.e., firing a qualified person who is perceived to be too young for a particular job). This case, *Bergen Commercial Bank v. Sisler*, 67 LW 1560 (N.J. 2/24/99), is discussed in a news item, "State's High Court Lets Man, 25, Sue on Age Discrimination," *NYT*, 2/26/99, p. B8.

Because of *Wright v. Universal Maritime Service Corp.*, #97-889, 67 LW 4013 (Sup. Ct. 11/16/98), a general arbitration clause in a collective bargaining agreement will not preclude litigation of ADEA and other statutory claims. Only a specific clause enumerating the claims can compel arbitration.

Prior to *Wright*, the Third Circuit permitted mandatory arbitration of ADEA (and Title VII) claims of employees who signed the U-4 (securities industry agreement) [*Seus v. John Nuveen & Co.*, 66 LW 1776 (3rd Cir. 6/8/98)].

In other employment-law contexts, all the Circuits other than the Ninth held that the U-4's arbitration provisions were enforceable, because the U-4 was not a contract of adhesion (one that was unfair because it gave one party no chance to negotiate) and because it provided adequate remedies for disgruntled employees. See *Kovalevskie v. SBC Capital Markets Inc.*, 67 LW 1543 (7th Cir. 2/4/99). In contrast, *Rosenberg v. Merrill Lynch*, 66 LW 1471 (D. Mass. 1/26/98), ruled that the Civil Rights Act of 1991 forbids enforcement of the U-4 arbitration clause against employees who want to litigate ADEA or Title VII claims.

See also *Albertson's v. United Food & Commercial Workers*, 157 F.3d 758 (2nd Cir. 1998), which holds that if an employee enters into an individual employment contract (as distinct from a collective bargaining agreement), and the agreement requires arbitration of ADEA claims, that agreement prevents the EEOC from filing suit against the employer for monetary relief. However, the EEOC can still seek classwide injunctive relief against the employer.

Front and back pay awarded to a job applicant who was not hired because of age bias does not constitute "wages" and is not subject to tax withholding [*Newhouse v. McCormick & Co.*, 157 F.3d 582 (8th Cir. 1998)].

26.2 ADEA EXCEPTIONS

The Higher Education Amendments of 1998, H.R. 6, signed 10/7/98, reinstate a traditional ADEA exception. Under the Amendments, it is lawful to require tenured faculty members to retire solely on the basis of age. Although this act affects a small group of individuals—and almost certainly does not include any employees of any of the readers of this book!—it is significant as a possible trend toward cutting back the scope of the ADEA (and other civil rights legislation).

There is a Circuit split on the applicability of the ADEA to state-government employers. The Eleventh Circuit found that the Eleventh Amendment exempts the states from ADEA suits (even though the statute itself includes states in the definition of "employer"): *Kimel v. Florida Board of Regents*, 139 F.3d 1426 (11th Cir. 1998). To the Seventh Circuit, however, the Fourteenth Amendment is more significant in this context. *Goshtasby v. Board of Trustees of the University of Illinois*, 66 LW 1650 (7th Cir. 4/13/98), ruled that the Fourteenth Amendment is broad enough to permit Congress to subject state employers to ADEA coverage.

26.3 THE ADEA PLAINTIFF'S BURDEN OF PROOF

An early 1999 ruling by the First Circuit denies the availability of disparate impact analysis in ADEA cases. *Mullin v. Raytheon Co.*, 164 F.3d 696 (1st Cir. 1999), says that age-related discrimination does not reflect a legacy of past discrimination (as, for instance, racial discrimination does), so disparate impact analysis is inappropriate.

The ADEA case of *Norton v. Sam's Club*, 1998 Westlaw 272630 (2nd Cir. 1998), was dismissed. The evidence showed that the plaintiff was already under suspicion before he was terminated for taking a long lunch hour but claiming only a 30-minute meal break on his time card. The plaintiff lost despite a significant mitigating circumstance: The long lunch was taken in the company of colleagues condoling the employee over his father's terminal illness.

An over-40 store manager was demoted after receiving a warning that, although her personal sales were acceptable, the overall performance of the store was below par. A younger store manager was not demoted despite a similar failure to meet quota—but the employer prevailed, by showing that 35 other managers (34 of whom were under 40) were demoted for failure to meet overall store production standards [*Simpson v. Kay Jewelers*, 1998 Westlaw 196062 (3rd Cir. 1998)].

According to the Fourth Circuit, disparaging comments about age are weaker evidence of discrimination than similar comments about race or sex. Racist or sexist remarks can be made by "outsiders," whereas everyone ages [*Dockins v. Benchmark Communications*, 67 LW 1656 (4th Cir. 3/29/99)].

EEOC Rules on ADEA Waivers

On June 5, 1998, the EEOC published a Final Rule on ADEA waivers, effective July 6, 1998. The rule, affecting 29 CFR §1625.22, appeared at 63 *Federal Register* 30624. The purpose of the rule is to set standards, pursuant to the Older Workers Benefit Protection Act (OWBPA) §7(f)(1), for determining when a waiver is knowing and voluntary, and therefore adequate and entitled to enforcement. All private- and public-sector (including federal) workers are covered.

The June 1998 rule reflects an interesting trend in administrative agency policy: negotiated rulemaking. Instead of an agency promulgating a rule without consulting industry—and very likely having the rule challenged in court by companies that find it unfair or unworkable—negotiated rulemaking involves industry input from the very beginning.

A valid ADEA waiver must

- Be written, and the entire agreement must be in the document (not partially oral, partially written)
- Be written in plain English and be appropriate to the signer's educational level; information about exit incentives must also be understandable
- Be honest and accurate, not misleading
- Specify that it relates to ADEA claims
- Advise the signer to consult an attorney before signing

In general, waivers can release existing claims but not those that might arise in the future. However, the Final Rule allows a waiver that is otherwise valid to include the signer's agreement to retire, or otherwise terminate employment, at a specified future date.

For the waiver to be valid, the person signing must receive valuable consideration specific to the waiver, and more than he or she would receive absent the waiver—(i.e., normal severance pay doesn't count). Nor does it constitute valuable consideration if the employer restores a benefit that was wrongfully terminated. However, it is not necessary to give greater consideration to over-40 employees who sign releases than to under-40 employees, even though younger employees waive non-ADEA claims (e.g., Title VII and Equal Pay Act claims) and older employees waive ADEA claims in addition to such other claims.

If exit incentives are offered to a group or class of employees, the Final Rule contains rules for notifying group members and drafting valid waivers once they have received the mandated notification.

The Supreme Court tackled the controversial issue of "tender-back" in *Oubre v. Entergy Operations Inc.*, 522 U.S. 422 (1998). If a person signs a purported release that is not in fact valid as a "knowing and voluntary" waiver as required by the OWBPA, then he or she can bring suit under the ADEA even without tendering back the severance pay received under the agreement that includes the invalid waiver. The theory is that a defective waiver doesn't qualify for ratification under any circumstances, so it is not necessary to give back the consideration to prevent ratification.

In April 1999, the EEOC returned to the question of tender-back, proposing regulations to implement *Oubre*. The proposal was published at 64 FR 19952 (4/23/99) and also appears on the EEOC Web site at http://www.eeoc.gov/regs/tender.html. You can find a Question and Answer sheet about the proposal at http://www.eeoc.gov/regs/quanda.html.

Naturally, the proposed rule is bound by *Oubre*, so it must provide that ex-employees are not required to tender back consideration before they challenge the validity of a waiver. Nor can employers get around the "no tender-back" rule by using covenants not to sue or other methods to prevent employees from challenging potentially invalid waivers. Such conditions are forbidden either in the actual waiver agreement itself or in separate documents. Nor can employers demand costs, attorneys' fees, or damages for breach of the covenant from employees who sign waivers, because threats of litigation against employees impose a "chilling effect," contrary to public policy, when employees seek to enforce their ADEA rights.

Under *Oubre*, the employer may be entitled to some measure of reimbursement if the employee who received consideration for a waiver gets the waiver set aside and wins an ADEA case. The EEOC takes the position that the maximum reimbursement would be either the consideration given to the employee or the damages that the employee wins after invalidating the waiver, whichever is less. A higher degree of reimbursement would have the same effect as a tender-back requirement: It would deter valid ADEA suits.

According to the EEOC, factors in determining the availability of reimbursement to the employer include the following:

- If the waiver covers other types of discrimination as well as age discrimination, and the consideration for the waiver reflects several categories of rights
- If the ADEA waiver was invalid because the employer erred or acted in bad faith or fraudulently
- How severe the age discrimination was; whether the employer discriminated willfully [if so, the reimbursement to the employer should be calculated after the employee's damages are doubled under ADEA §7(b)]
- Effect on the employee's finances if he or she has to reimburse the employer
- Corresponding effect on the employer's finances
- Whether the reimbursement will serve the public policy functions of punishing ADEA violators and deterring future ADEA violations

If a waiver was offered to more than one employee (e.g., as part of a reduction in force affecting a group of employees), the employer must continue to offer any ongoing consideration, such as payment of health insurance premiums, to employees who signed the waiver and are not participating in the challenge.

Note that, although the OWBPA requires employers to give employees 21 days to think over an early retirement offer, the offer does not become irrevocable for this 21-day period; the employer can still withdraw it [*Ellison v. Premier Salons Int'l Inc.*, 164 F.3d 111 (8th Cir. 1999)].

The theory of "virtual representation" is sometimes used to prevent a second class action once issues have already been raised in another class action. The Seventh Circuit, however, decided that a group of airline pilots challenging an airline's policies for over-60 pilots were not adequately represented by the earlier class action.

The earlier class action dealt with pilots and copilots, who are subject to an Federal Aviation Administration (FAA) policy that requires them to retire at 60. This action dealt with the position of first officer. First officers can be over 60 without violating FAA rules, but the airline refused to employ anyone in that job who could not be promoted to captain status.

Tice v. American Airlines, 162 F.3d 966 (7th Cir. 1998), says that the earlier class action was not res judicata (did not resolve) the current case. ADEA class actions are on an "opt-in" rather than "opt-out" basis (i.e., no one is covered without making a choice of being included). The earlier case dealt with potential employees denied employment because of age; *Tice* dealt with current employees seeking to remain employed by accepting a demotion.

The question of timing in class actions is also addressed in *Armstrong v. Martin Marietta Corp.*, 138 F.3d 1374 (11th Cir. 1998). In this case, some employees were dismissed as plaintiffs from a pending ADEA class action. They brought their own suits. According to the Eleventh Circuit, the statute of limitations is tolled (suspended) while a class action is pending, but the statute of limitations starts all over again as soon as the District Court issues an order denying the certification of the class.

When would-be plaintiffs are thrown out of a class action because they are not similarly situated to the proper class-action plaintiffs, they must file their own suits within 90 days of being removed from the class. Equitable tolling (i.e., permitting an action to continue on the grounds of fairness, although it would otherwise be too late) can be granted only if the EEOC actually misinformed the plaintiffs about the statute of limitations, not if they simply failed to consider this issue or made an incorrect determination of how long they had to sue.

26.5 PENSION AND BENEFIT ISSUES

Receiving disability benefits prevents an ADEA plaintiff from claiming she was able to perform the job from which she was discharged [*King v. Herbert J. Thomas Memorial Hospital*, 159 F.3d 192 (4th Cir. 1998)].

Chapter 27

PROCEDURE FOR DISCRIMINATION SUITS

27.3 ARBITRATION AND ALTERNATIVE DISPUTE RESOLUTION (ADR)

The difficult question of the extent to which employees who allege discrimination can be compelled to arbitrate their claims was resolved by *Wright v. Universal Maritime Service Corp., #97-889,* 67 LW 4013, Sup. Ct. 11/16/98. In this case, an injured stevedore was denied employment because potential employer companies deemed him to be permanently disabled. The plaintiff sued under the ADA without filing a grievance or going through arbitration under the collective bargaining agreement. Although the District Court and Fourth Circuit dismissed his case, because of his failure to exhaust grievance remedies, the Supreme Court unanimously reversed. *Gilmer* does permit compulsory arbitration of an ADA claim (under the U-4, the securities industry agreement), but to the Supreme Court, this case is different because the employee's claim derived from a statute, not a contract.

Although contract claims are presumed arbitrable, that presumption does not apply to statutory claims. For a collective bargaining agreement to preclude litigation of a statutory claim, it must be very clear on that point. A generalized arbitration clause that fails to discuss antidiscrimination statutes will not be enough to keep disgruntled employees out of the court system. However, as you can see, numerous cases have arisen involving extremely specific collective bargaining act provisions.

According to the Fourth Circuit, it is a material breach of the collective bargaining agreement for an employer to adopt arbitration rules that are grossly in its own favor and excessively stringent on the employee. If arbitration rules are unfair, the FAA will not require their enforcement, and therefore the employee will be able to bring suit under Title VII despite the purported arbitration requirement [*Hooters of America Inc. v. Phillips,* 67 LW 1620 (4th Cir. 4/8/99)]. *Gonzalez v. Hughes*

Aircraft Employees Federal Credit Union, 67 LW 1543 (Cal. App. 2/23/99), also strikes down an unfair and one-sided arbitration agreement.

The Ninth Circuit has been quite resistant to claims that employees can be compelled to arbitrate employment claims that they prefer to litigate. At the end of 1998, the Ninth Circuit decided that labor and employment contracts do not fall under the scope of the Federal Arbitration Act. Therefore, an employee can't be forced to arbitrate the portion of a grievance alleging Title VII violations [*Craft v. Campbell Soup Co.*, 161 F.3d 1199 (9th Cir. 1998).]

The Ninth Circuit had already decided, in *Duffield v. Robertson Stephens & Co.*, 66 LW 1692 (9th Cir. 5/8/98), that the U-4 (securities industry form agreement) did not preclude litigation of a Title VII sex discrimination claim, because it is improper to require waiver of the right to sue under Title VII as a condition of employment.

In contrast, the Third Circuit decided that the U-4 arbitration clause is enforceable and precludes Title VII and ADEA suits [*Seus v. John Nuveen & Co.*, 66 LW 1776 (3rd Cir. 6/8/98)]. Indeed, according to *Kovalevskie v. SBC Capital Markets Inc.*, 67 LW 1543 (7th Cir. 2/4/99), all of the Circuits except the Ninth Circuit have affirmed the validity of the U-4 arbitration clause.

The District of Massachusetts agrees with the Ninth Circuit position. It has ruled, in *Rosenberg v. Merrill Lynch*, 66 LW 1471 (D. Mass. 1/28/98), that the Civil Rights Act of 1991 bars enforcement of U-4 Title VII claims. Because the D. Mass decided that the New York Stock Exchange arbitration system is "structurally imbalanced" in favor of employers, it could not be imposed on employees who preferred to litigate their age discrimination claims.

You should also be warned that, in the view of the Sixth Circuit, even if an employee's agreement to arbitrate rather than litigate statutory discrimination claims is valid and enforceable, the EEOC can still sue the employer for money damages and injunctive relief on the employee's behalf. See *EEOC v. Frank's Nursery & Crafts Inc.*, 67 LW 1647 (6th Cir. 4/23/99).

The Ninth Circuit's holding in *Albertson's v. United Food & Commercial Workers*, 157 F.3d 758 (9th Cir. 1998), is that litigation of FMLA claims can be restricted by employment contracts negotiated for an individual worker, but not for an entire collective bargaining agreement.

With respect to yet another employment statute, see *EEOC v. Kidder Peabody*, 156 F.3d 298 (2nd Cir. 1998): An employment contract between the employer and one employee, calling for arbitration of ADEA claims, prevents the EEOC from bringing ADEA claims that seek monetary relief but does not prevent the agency from seeking classwide injunctive relief.

The Fourth Circuit did not accept the argument that an arbitration clause in an employment contract was unenforceable for lack of consideration. The *Johnson v. Circuit City Stores Inc.*, 148 F.3d 373 (4th Cir. 1998), court found that the employer's agreement to be bound by the arbitrator's ruling supplies the necessary consideration.

The Fifth Circuit ruled on a case in which the collective bargaining agreement called for a 30-minute unpaid meal break in each shift. The employer wanted the time to be treated as personal time, but the jury deemed it to be overtime. The employer then challenged the litigation (rather than arbitration) of the claim. The Fifth Circuit said that the Fair Labor Standards Act cause of action was distinct from the collective bargaining act claims. In this context, arbitration is inadequate because it does not grant access to FLSA remedies such as liquidated damages and attorneys' fees [*Bernard v. IBP, Inc. of Nebraska*, 154 F.3d 259 (5th Cir. 1998)].

The National Association of Securities Dealers (NASD) form signed by new employees stipulates arbitration of employment disputes, other than those concerned with "the business of insurance." An employee of an insurance company was fired after he said that he lost some records that were critical to a suit against the employer. He sued the insurer for wrongful discharge and defamation. His position was that the suit involved the business of insurance, and therefore litigation—not arbitration—was appropriate.

The New Jersey Court of Appeals disagreed. The dispute was really about whether the employee violated the employer's document retention policy by disposing of the controversial documents. The dispute could have happened in any workplace—it had nothing in particular to do with insurance. Therefore, any claims brought by the employee would have to go through arbitration [*Fastenberg v. Prudential Insurance Co. of America*, 1998 Westlaw 158826 (N.J. App. 1998)].

The settlement proposal in *Martens v. Smith Barney Inc.*, #96-3779, submitted to the Southern District of New York on November 18, 1997, called for settlement of sex discrimination claims by creating a workplace diversity program; eliminating mandatory arbitration; and establishing an alternative ADR process. The ADR process would involve three steps. First, the claim would be submitted to the Duke Private Adjudication Center. The company would have 60 days to make a settlement offer. Offers rejected by the complaining employee would go to a neutral mediator, paid by Smith Barney. If single-mediator mediation failed, the final step would be a three-member mediation panel. See 66 LW 2355.

A plaintiff sought arbitration to get overtime pay from her ex-employer. The employer characterized her as an executive or administrator and thus an exempt employee not entitled to overtime pay. The Eleventh Circuit enforced an arbitration clause, even though she signed it during her first job with the company, but not during her second when she transferred to another office [*Montes v. Shearson Lehman Brothers*, 128 F.3d 1456 (11th Cir. 1997)].

However, the actual arbitration award was vacated, and the case was sent back for a new arbitration panel. The employer's lawyer urged the arbitrators to ignore the Fair Labor Standards Act, and apparently they gave in to this urging. Although arbitration is supposed to be somewhat less formal than litigation, it should not deprive participants of legal principles and protections available through the court system. Furthermore, arbitration awards can't be reversed based on misinterpretation of law, but can be if the applicable law is actually disregarded. In this case, the facts showed that she was exempt in her first job, but nonexempt and entitled to overtime in her second job.

If an employee loses sex and disability discrimination claims at trial, it is improper for the District Court to issue an injunction forbidding her to arbitrate the claims that have already been struck down. Injunctions can only be granted in situations in which there is no adequate remedy at law. In this situation, the employer could simply appear at the arbitration and get the case dismissed because the issues had already been decided by the court system [*Weaver v. Florida Power & Light Co.*, 67 LW 1634 (11th Cir. 4/13/99)].

27.3.3 EEOC ADR

The EEOC is stressing mediation and other forms of ADR as a means of speeding up resolution of charges. The agency's backlog peaked at 111,451 unresolved charges in June 1995. As of February 1999, the backlog had been approximately 52,000 charges pending. Newly appointed EEOC chair Ida Castro set a goal of 120 days to resolve a charge, but as of February 1999 the average complaint took 276 days to adjudicate. In a December 3, 1998 interview with BNA, Castro said that the EEOC will both use staffers as mediators and will also outsource some ADR functions under contracts with private mediators and mediation associations.

EEOC ADR began in 1997, when 780 cases were settled for a total of $10.8 million; in 1998, there were 1500 settlements aggregating $17 million. The EEOC's goal for FY 2000 is 8000 settlements, according to Steven A. Holmes, "Jobs Discrimination Agency Lightening Its Load," *New York Times*, 2/22/99, p. A1; also see 67 LW 2342.

27.4 THE EEOC CHARGE PROCESS

On December 14, 1998, the EEOC and the Department of Labor (DOL) proposed a new plan for work sharing between the two agencies, giving 30 days for public comment (see Glenn Burkins, "EEOC Gives Labor Department Power to Seek Damages in Worker Bias Cases," *WSJ*, 4/9/99, p. A20). Few comments were received because of the holiday season.

The work-sharing agreement lets the DOL sue federal contractors for remedies, including punitive damages, if the contractors are guilty of race, sex, or religious discrimination. Employees of federal contractors have the option of filing discrimination charges either with the EEOC or with DOL. (About 200,000 companies have federal contracts and thus fall into this category.)

Under prior law, the DOL could review the employment practices of federal contractors (even if no charges were filed), under the Office of Federal Contract Compliance Programs. However, the OFCCP did not have the power to sue employers for damages. The proposal calls for information sharing as well as work sharing, so the EEOC's investigation of a complaint can be supplemented by DOL information about pay and promotion practices in the company.

27.5 ADEA PROCEDURE

See ¶26.3 for a discussion of 1998 and 1999 rules on ADEA waivers.

27.7 LITIGATION

The basic case on the use of after-acquired evidence is *McKennon v. Nashville Banner Pub. Co.*, 513 U.S. 352 (Sup. Ct. 1995). *O'Day v. McDonnell-Douglas Helicopter Co.*, 191 Ariz. 535, 959 P.2d 792 (Ariz. 1998), provides guidance on how to apply *McKennon* in state courts. If the employee sues for breach of the employment contract, seeking lost wages and benefits, the after-acquired evidence can provide a complete defense for the employer as long as the employer can prove that the after-acquired evidence was serious enough to justify firing the employee if the employer had known about it earlier. In a tort suit for wrongful termination, the after-acquired evidence is not a complete defense, but it does have the effect of limiting the remedies available to the plaintiff.

The Fourth Circuit decertified the employee class in a racial discrimination pattern or practice case [*Lowery v. Circuit City Stores Inc.*, 158 F.3d 742 (4th Cir. 1998)]. Individual employees who were once members of the class cannot maintain the pattern or practice case. Each must satisfy the *McDonnell-Douglas* burden-shifting analysis individually. The Fourth Circuit vacated most of the District Court's $4.2 million judgment (of which $3.9 million was attorney's fees). Most of the injunctive relief (e.g., establishment of a department of diversity management; career paths for black employees) was also eliminated, on the grounds of overbreadth.

The Michigan Court of Appeals applied the after-acquired evidence doctrine to a case in which the plaintiff was not hired, rather than one in which a person was hired, fired, sued for discrimination, at which point the defendant employer discovered resume fabrication or other misconduct. *Smith v. Charter Township of Union*, 1998 Westlaw 17798 (Mich. App. 1998), holds that, in failure-to-hire cases, the damage period can extend only from the date of the wrongful denial of hiring until the inevitable point at which the employer would have fired the plaintiff based on the plaintiff's lack of the minimum qualifications that were falsely stated on the fabricated resume.

A defense expert witness should not have been allowed to testify as to the plaintiff's psychiatric credibility. This was not a proper subject for testimony under Federal Rules of Evidence 702, in that it invaded the jury's role of assessing the credibility of testimony. Nor should the defendant have been allowed to introduce evidence of the plaintiff's decade-earlier abortion, because such evidence is prejudicial and not probative. A new trial was ordered in *Nichols v. American National Insurance Co.*, 154 F.3d 875 (8th Cir. 1998), because of the evidentiary improprieties.

The plaintiff's prima facie case in a Title VII failure-to-promote case requires the employee to identify specific positions that he or she applied for but was denied; saying that he or she was qualified for numerous promotions is not sufficient [*Brown v. Coach Stores Inc.*, 163 F.3d 706 (2nd Cir. 1998)].

Two sexual harassment cases a few months apart reach different conclusions as to whether the 90-day filing period should have been tolled. The D.C. Circuit refused to grant equitable tolling to an employee who claimed that severe, continuing harassment rendered her non compos mentis and unable to protect her own interests by filing in time. To the court in *Smith-Haynie v. District of Columbia*, 155 F.3d 575 (D.C. Cir. 1998), the only evidence of the plaintiff's distraction was her own statement. But the Ninth Circuit did permit equitable tolling in *Stoll v. Runyon*, 67 LW 1480 (9th Cir. 1/15/99), where the plaintiff suffered psychiatric disability after repeated sexual abuse, assault, and rape.

Trial lawyer Gilmore F. Diekmann, Jr. tackles the mistakes that employer defendants make in a May 1999 article, "The Top Three Mistakes Employers Make At Trial," posted at http://www.lawnewsnetwork.com/practice/employmentlaw/papers/lawfirm/A1489-1999May14.html. Although the vast majority of claims of employment discrimination wash out (see ¶23.1) and employers can get summary judgment (i.e., dismissal of poorly supported claims without a full trial), the fact remains that of the cases that actually go to a jury, the employee-plaintiff wins about two out of three.

Some of these are cases in which the employer got caught doing something obviously wrong and has to take its medicine. But others are cases that the employer could have won with better trial tactics and a better job of showing its side of the story to the jury.

Diekmann suggests that some cases go to trial because the employer's lawyer got involved too late and failed to identify a losing case that should have been settled. Sometimes the wrong lawyer handles the case: Someone who is essentially business oriented rather than an experienced litigator who is fully cognizant of employment law developments and has handled the case from the very outset.

It's especially important for the trial lawyer to be completely familiar with all the depositions in the case. Depositions not only reflect testimony that was given at a particular time (and can be used to challenge inconsistent trial testimony) but give insight into the witness's character and thought processes (and thus the best way to challenge the testimony).

Juries are usually predisposed to like and sympathize with employee plaintiffs, so it's usually counterproductive for the defense lawyer to seem arrogant, hostile, or bullying. In Diekmann's analysis, the defense lawyer's job is to present a simple story that the jury can understand and accept. Juries have to learn to look at the facts and the legal strategies rather than maintaining their initial sympathy for the plaintiff in situations where, in fact, the employer has the stronger legal arguments and the facts on its side.

27.9 REMEDIES

To the D.C. Circuit, refusal to consider a well-qualified female employee for promotion certainly constituted "intentional" discrimination but was not egregious enough to justify punitive damages [*Kolstad v. American Dental Association*, 1998 Westlaw 226181 (D.C. Cir. 1998), reversing the decision reported in the main volume]. At press time, the Supreme Court had granted certiorari and heard arguments but had not yet rendered a decision.

The Tenth Circuit's test for awarding Title VII punitive damages is the preponderance of the evidence, not proof beyond a reasonable doubt of the employer's willful conduct [*Karnes v. SCI Colorado Funeral Services*, 67 LW 1448 (10th Cir. 12/17/98)].

The Eleventh Circuit declined to impose punitive damages on a large retail company because a low-level manager at one store demoted the plaintiff for discriminatory reasons. *Dudley v. Wal-Mart Stores*, 67 LW 1543 (11th Cir. 2/9/99), holds that imposition of punitive damages requires discrimination by a person high up in the hierarchy or at least knowledge of discrimination by persons in authority. However, you should note that *Deffenbaugh-Williams v. Wal-Mart*, 156 F.3d 581 (5th Cir. 1998), uses a lower standard for imposing punitive damages on corporate hierarchy.

In the Seventh Circuit, a Title VII plaintiff can get both front pay and lost future earnings [*Williams v. Pharmacia Inc.*, 66 LW 1551 (7th Cir. 2/26/98)]. The court found that the two remedies are not duplicative, because front pay substitutes for reinstatement and is ordered for a limited period. It is an equitable remedy, and the judge sets its amount. In contrast, lost future earnings, as authorized by the Civil Rights Act of 1991 (CRA '91), constitute the future pecuniary loss attributable to the effects of discrimination.

Front and back pay awarded under the ADEA to a job applicant who was not hired was not treated as "wages" subject to tax withholding [*Newhouse v. McCormick & Co.*, 157 F.3d 582 (8th Cir. 1998)].

27.9.1 Title VII and the CRA

Because of the Second Circuit decision in *Morelli v. Cedel*, 141 F.3d 39 (2nd Cir. 1998), the Southern District of New York reversed an earlier ruling and held that the damage cap on foreign employers who violate Title VII is based on their total number of employees throughout the world, not just those in the United States [*Greenbaum v. Svenska Handelsbanken*, 26 F. Supp. 2d 649 (S.D.N.Y. 1998)]. Since more employees means a higher damage cap, this decision increases the damage exposure of foreign corporations.

An attorney who wins a mixed-motive Title VII case, proving the role of discrimination in the adverse job action against the plaintiff, performs an important public function (discouraging employment discrimination). In the view of the Tenth Circuit, this function justifies a fee award under 42 USC §2000e-5(g)(2)(B), even if the actual damages awarded to the plaintiff are limited or even nonexistent. See *Gudenkauf v. Stauffer Communications Inc.*, 158 F.3d 1074 (10th Cir. 1998). The Southern District of New York reached a similar conclusion in *Rodriguez v. McLoughlin*, 20 F. Supp. 2d 597 (S.D.N.Y. 1998), and so did the Tenth Circuit in *Brandau v. Kansas*, 67 LW 1500 (10th Cir. 2/16/99).

Federal agencies can't be required to pay compensatory damages under CRA '91 [*Gibson v. Brown*, 137 F.3d 992 (7th Cir. 1998)].

Chapter 28

Wrongful Termination

28.1 INTRODUCTION

In late 1998, the Fifth Circuit permitted at-will employees to sue under 42 USC §1981 (which forbids racial discrimination in the making of contracts) [*Fadeyi v. Planned Parenthood,* 160 F.3d 1048 (5th Cir. 1998)]. The court's position was that Congress planned a §1981 remedy for at-will employees of companies that are too small to be covered by Title VII.

A Virginia man lost his job in a reduction in force. He claimed that the employer told him that a white male had to be RIFed to prevent an inference of discrimination against the many female and minority employees who also lost their jobs. In his wrongful discrimination suit against the employer, the employer requested a jury instruction that would have made it liable only if its sole reason for RIFing the employee was his age, race, and sex. The trial court, upheld by the state's highest court, refused to grant this instruction. The courts held that the proper instruction would be whether the plaintiff was fired *because* of any combination of age, race, and sex [*Shaw v. Titan Corp.*, 1998 Westlaw 190860 (Virginia 1998)]. See *Employment Alert,* 6/25/98, p. 11.

Although Illinois precludes in-house attorneys from suing their employers for wrongful discharge (because of the risk that confidential client matters will be disclosed in the litigation), the rule was not applied to a law firm attorney who was fired for pointing out the firm's practice of filing collection suits in the wrong county, contrary to the state's venue laws. If the discharged attorney works for a law firm rather than a single corporation, a wrongful discharge suit is a possibility, under *Jacobson v. Knepper & Moga, P.C.*, 228 Ill. Dec. 115, 688 N.E.2d 813 (App. 1997).

28.3 EMPLOYEE TENURE

A church employee was fired when the priest observed him receiving illegal anabolic steroids at the church. The employee brought suit, alleging breach of his written contract, which called for 30 days' notice of termination. (Obviously his nerve, as well as his muscles, was pumped up.) Understandably, he lost. The New Jersey court deemed both employer and employee to work subject to a duty of good faith and fair dealing. The employee's serious violation of his obligation relieved the church of its obligation to give him 30 days' notice of termination. See *McGarry v. Saint Anthony of Padua Roman Catholic Church,* 307 N.J. Super. 525, 704 A.2d 1353 (1998).

28.4 PROMISSORY ESTOPPEL

The May 1999 Fifth Circuit case of *Zenor v. El Paso Healthcare Sys. Ltd.* (#98-50063; http://www.lawnewsnetwork.com/practice/employmentlaw/authority/cases/G1864-1999May27.html) involves a hospital pharmacist who entered a rehab program when his cocaine addiction got out of control. In federal District Court, the jury awarded him promissory estoppel damages, but the federal judge threw out most of the award. The appeal to the Fifth Circuit eliminated his promissory estoppel claims altogether. (ADA aspects of this case are discussed at ¶24.2.)

In the Fifth Circuit view, the employee handbook made it clear that the plaintiff was an at-will employee. The Texas rule, as expressed in *Montgomery County Hospital District v. Brown,* 965 S.W. 2d 501 (Tex. 1998), is that at-will employees remain such, even if they have been promised that they can only be fired for "good cause."

The hospital's substance abuse policy made it a necessary condition of reinstatement that a drug or alcohol abuser complete a rehab program—but gave the hospital discretion to reinstate or not reinstate the employee after treatment. The existence of this policy did not change the plaintiff's status as an at-will employee, nor did it entitle him to get his job back postrehab.

Furthermore, promissory estoppel requires detrimental reliance (doing something against the plaintiff's interests). The plaintiff's argument was that the substance abuse policy caused him to disclose his cocaine addiction and seek treatment. But, in fact, he sought treatment after a drug-induced medical emergency, and entering rehab was beneficial and not harmful to him.

The trial court also misunderstood the damages available even if promissory estoppel is demonstrated. Texas law limits damages to "reliance" damages, putting the plaintiff in the same position he would have been if he or she had never relied on the promise. The jury awarded him mental anguish damages and damages for past and future lost earnings, and these are not available in Texas in promissory estoppel cases [*Central Texas Micrographics v. Leal,* 908 S. W. 2d 292 (Tex. App. 1995)].

The plaintiff in *Chieffalo v. Norden Systems, Inc.*, 49 Conn. App. 474, 714 A.2d 1261 (Conn. App. 1998), was previously employed by Norden; quit his job; and was rehired. Five years later, he didn't get a promotion he wanted, and his working relationship with the person who did get the job was poor. The plaintiff refused to participate in a team project and was told that he would be fired if he didn't participate. He continued to hold out, and was fired.

His suit was premised on an implied employment contract. He alleged that one of the company's managers told him at the time of rehiring that he would be employed indefinitely, as long as he returned to prior performance levels. The appellate court ruled that evidence about this statement should not have been admitted. Just because the person who made it was a manager did not give him the power to bind the employer, without proof that the statement was authorized by the employer.

Without that statement in the record, there was no proof that the plaintiff was not an at-will employee subject to discharge at any time, so the employer prevailed.

28.5 PUBLIC POLICY

Where a wrongful discharge violates public policy, California's Fair Employment and Housing Act (FEHA) is violated. However, the individual manager who fired the employee who refused to provide sexual favors is not personally liable under the FEHA. A 1998 California decision holds that, although the FEHA defines "employer" to include "any person acting as an agent of an employer, directly or indirectly," the purpose of this statutory provision is to make employer companies liable for the actions of their managers—not to create personal FEHA liability for the manager [*Reno v. Baird*, 957 P.2d 1333 (Cal. 1998)].

The Pennsylvania workers' compensation statute doesn't say in so many words that it is illegal for employers to retaliate against employees who file Worker's Compensation claims. Nevertheless, employees in this situation are allowed to bring wrongful discharge claims, on the grounds that the legislature didn't rule out a retaliation action—it merely failed to make explicit provisions for one [*Shick v. Shirey*, 716 A.2d 1231 (Pa. 1998)].

Worker's Compensation was also involved in the case of *Lins v. Children's Discovery Center of America, Inc.*, No. 22424-1-II (Washington App. 4/7/99), http://www.lawnewsnetwork.com/practice/employmentlaw/authority/cases/G1431-1999May13.html. The plaintiff was a manager with responsibility for six day care centers. She and five other employees (directors of day care centers) were hurt in a work-related automobile accident. All six filed Worker's Compensation claims. The plaintiff was ordered by her supervisor to fire the other five employees because the supervisor expected the employees to sue the employer.

The plaintiff refused to do so because she knew that Worker's Compensation retaliation was illegal. Unlike Pennsylvania's law, the Washington statute (RCW

§51.48.025) does prohibit employers from firing or otherwise discriminating against a person who has filed or announced an intention to file a WC claim.

The plaintiff, who previously had received good performance ratings, got a bad performance rating and was put on probation, then was fired for neglect of duty and poor performance. She sued for wrongful discharge in violation of public policy, because she refused to perform an illegal retaliatory act. The employer's contention was that although directly firing employees because they file WC claims is illegal, firing an insubordinate employee (even if the disobeyed order was illegal) is not illegal.

The Washington Court of Appeals extended the public policy argument to protect employees who refuse to violate the law. After all, it's in the public interest to provide disincentives for illegal acts, and employees who are not afraid of losing their jobs will be more likely to refuse illegal orders.

28.5.1 Whistleblowers

At the end of 1998, the Supreme Court decided a whistleblower case, holding that an action under 42 USC §1985 (damage to person or property) can be maintained by an at-will employee who alleges that he was fired for assisting a federal criminal investigation of the employer company [*Haddle v. Garrison*, #97-1472, 67 LW 4029 (Sup. Ct. 12/14/98)].

A Texas nurse reported a coemployee's apparent drug use at work and mishandling of prescription drugs. But it wasn't the drug user who got fired—it was the reporting nurse. The nurse lost her whistleblower action in state court. Although the Texas Supreme Court agreed that protection of the safety of hospital patients is part of public policy, it also held that Texas legislators have enacted whistleblower protection in some specific context—but there is no generalized state-law protection for employees discharged for reporting workplace wrongdoing [*Austin v. Healthtrust, Inc.*, 1998 Westlaw 181950 (Texas 1998)]. See *Employment Alert*, 6/25/98, p. 11.

In general, Wisconsin is not hospitable to whistleblower claims. In fact, it permits employers to fire employees for complying with a law (but not for refusing to break one). That precludes whistleblower cases brought by most employees who abide by a legal obligation to report employer wrongdoing. However, in 1997, the state's Supreme Court created a special exemption, allowing wrongful discharge suits only by nursing home whistleblowers [*Hausman v. St. Croix Care Center*, 571 N.W.2d 393 (Wis. 1997)].

The whistleblower provisions of the federal OSHA statute don't prevent state actions for wrongful termination by angry former employees. The OSHA provisions are limited to administrative proceedings and federal suits brought by the Secretary of Labor, not private suits in federal court (which might yield substantial damages). Therefore, according to a Kansas court, the OSH Act doesn't provide an adequate remedy that rules out state-law suits [*Flenker v. Willamette Industries Inc.*, 1998 Westlaw 271624 (Kansas 1998)].

28.7 EMPLOYMENT CONTRACT TERMS

The Statute of Frauds says that a contract that lasts more than a year is only enforceable if it is in writing. In a Washington State case, the employee had an oral five-year contract, allowing either party to end the contract on six months' notice. The employee was fired after he'd spent about eleven months with the company. When he sued for breach of contract, his argument was that the Statute of Frauds shouldn't apply because the contract not only could have been wrapped up in less than a year, that is in fact what happened. But he lost his case. The Washington court said that the Statute of Frauds applies only to employment contracts whose duration is indefinite, not one with a specific term such as five years. Therefore, because he had no written agreement, he also had no case against the employer. [*French v. Sabey Corp.*, 134 Wash.2d 547, 951 P.2d 260 (1998)].

Oral promises to a relocating employee, that she would be fired only for good cause, didn't add up to a contract. Therefore, as an at-will employee, she could be fired even absent cause. Here, the problem for the employee wasn't the Statute of Frauds, but the failure to form an enforceable contract at all [*Montgomery County Hospital District v. Brown*, 1998 Westlaw 107922 (Texas 1998)].

In contrast, a very similar fact pattern in the same state (Texas) resulted in victory for the employee. A newly recruited employee, concerned about job security, was told on at least two occasions that she would not be fired as long as she performed her job well. After her discharge, she was permitted to sue for wrongful discharge under an oral contract theory. In this case, there was an employee handbook (issued after she was hired) that informed the employees that they were employed at will. However, the handbook also stated that it did not create a contract, so the court did not give effect to the at-will provision [*Doctors' Hospital of Laredo Ltd. Partnership v. Dromgoole*, 1998 Westlaw 75554 (Tex. App. 1998)].

An employee was orally promised a bonus equal to a percentage of the employer's profits. Of course, the year would have to end in order to figure out the bonus. The employer said that the Statute of Frauds precluded enforcement of the contract, in that calculation required a period of more than one year. The employee's argument was that he worked at will and certainly could be fired in less than one year. This argument prevailed with a New York court, which allowed enforcement of the oral contract. [*Cron v. Hargo Fabrics, Inc.*, 91 N.Y.2d 362 (N.Y. 1998)].

Contract terms also become significant after the termination of the employment relationship (for instance, if a terminated, retiring, or resigning employee previously agreed to a covenant not to compete with the initial employer).

In a 1998 Minnesota case, a company that hired a person away from a direct competitor was found liable for tortious interference with the covenant not to compete. Furthermore, it was ordered to reimburse the first employer for the $90,000 in attorney's fees it encountered when suing the employee to enforce the covenant. The cite is *Kallok v. Medtronic, Inc.*, 1998 Westlaw 10568 (Minn. 1998).

When the recruited employee got the job offer, he informed the recruiting company about the covenant, which barred employment in a field in which he had worked or had access to confidential information in the preceding year. The term of the agreement was two years. The recruiting company asked its outside attorney if hiring the competitor's employee would create legal problems; the lawyer said that it would be acceptable because the employee worked in a different field and didn't have confidential information.

Once the employee changed companies, the initial employer got a court order forbidding the employee to work for the new company. The competitor was also penalized for interfering with the employment contract. A "tortious interference" case requires proof of five elements:

- Existence of a contract that could be breached
- The defendant's knowledge that the contract existed
- Intentional action breaching or promoting breach of the contract
- Lack of justification for the action
- Damages to the injured contracting party

The Minnesota court decided that the competitor didn't do enough investigation; simple inquiries would have uncovered the real provisions of the noncompete agreement. Therefore, the company was not justified in its actions. Furthermore, the competitor's actions forced the first employer to sue its ex-employee, so the competitor should have to reimburse the first employer for legal fees directly resulting from this wrongdoing.

Cameco Inc. v. Gedicke, 67 LW 1531 (N.J. Sup. 2/18/99), holds that an employee can be liable for breach of the duty of loyalty for assisting the employer's competitors, even without directly competing with the employer. It depends on the nature of the employer/employee relationship and how inappropriate the employee's conduct (i.e., the level of assistance provided to competitors) was. Under this analysis, an employee has a duty to inform the employer of his or her plans before establishing a moonlighting business that could conflict with the employer's business. Damages for breach of the employee's duty of loyalty could include the injury to the employer's business plus the profits the employee earned from inappropriately competitive moonlighting.

28.10.5 EEOC Final Rule on ADEA Waivers

On June 5, 1998, the EEOC published a Final Rule on ADEA waivers, effective July 6, 1998. The rule, affecting 29 CFR Part 1625, appeared at 63 *Federal Register*

30624. The purpose of the rule is to set standards, pursuant to Older Workers Benefit Protection Act (OWBPA) §7(f)(1), for determining when a waiver is knowing and voluntary, and therefore adequate and entitled to enforcement. All private- and public-sector (including federal) workers are covered.

The June 1998 rule reflects an interesting trend in administrative agency policy: negotiated rulemaking. Instead of an agency promulgating a rule without consulting industry—and very likely having the rule challenged in court by companies that find it unfair or unworkable—negotiated rulemaking involves industry input from the very beginning.

A valid ADEA waiver must

- Be written, and the entire agreement must be in the document (not partially oral, partially written)
- Be written in plain English and be appropriate to the signer's educational level; information about exit incentives must also be understandable
- Be honest and accurate, not misleading
- Specify that it relates to ADEA claims
- Advise the signer to consult an attorney before signing

In general, waivers can release existing claims but not those that might arise in the future. However, the Final Rule allows a waiver that is otherwise valid to include the signer's agreement to retire, or otherwise terminate employment, at a specified future date.

For the waiver to be valid, the person signing must receive valuable consideration specific to the waiver, and more than he or she would receive absent the waiver—(i.e., normal severance pay doesn't count). Nor does it constitute valuable consideration if the employer restores a benefit that was wrongfully terminated. However, it is not necessary to give greater consideration to over-40 employees who sign releases than to under-40 employees, even though younger employees waive non-ADEA claims (e.g., Title VII and Equal Pay Act claims) and older employees waive ADEA claims in addition to such other claims.

If exit incentives are offered to a group or class of employees, the Final Rule contains rules for notifying group members and drafting valid waivers once they have received the mandated notification.

28.10.6 Tender-Back

The Supreme Court tackled the controversial issue of "tender-back" in *Oubre v. Entergy Operations Inc.*, 118 S. Ct. 838 (1/26/98). If a person signs a purported release that is not in fact valid as a "knowing and voluntary" waiver as required by the OWBPA, then he or she can bring suit under the ADEA even without tendering back the severance pay received under the agreement that includes the invalid waiver. The theory is that a defective waiver doesn't qualify for ratification under any circumstances, so it is not necessary to give back the consideration to prevent ratification.

See above for the recent EEOC Final Rule that gives additional guidance for drafting a waiver that will *not* be deemed invalid and will *not* permit repudiation of the waiver without tender-back.

28.13 HANDLING A DISCHARGE FOR CAUSE

According to the Minnesota Court of Appeals, an employee who was justifiably discharged (for getting into an argument with one of the residents of a homeless shelter where he worked as an engineer) could not sue the ex-employer on a theory of "compelled self-publication." That doctrine can be used by wrongfully accused employees, not by those who were appropriately dismissed under circumstances justifying the employer's action [*Techam v. People Serving People, Inc.*, 1998 Westlaw 2431 (Minn. App. 1998); see *Employment Alert*, 3/19/98, p. 11].

A California employee could only be fired with just cause. The employer received two sexual harassment complaints about him, investigated and believed the complainants, and fired the employee. He sued, taking the position that he did not in fact harass the complainants.

The California Supreme Court, agreeing with Oregon, Nevada, and Washington courts (but disagreeing with the Michigan Supreme Court), decided that an employer has just cause to fire based on a reasonable inquiry that was appropriately conducted, as long as the inquiry is not used as a pretext for discriminatory or arbitrary discharge. It doesn't matter if the inquiry actually reached the wrong factual conclusion, as long as the employer acted reasonably [*Cotran v. Rollins Hudig Hall International, Inc.*, 17 Cal. 4th 93, 69 Cal. Rptr. 2d 900 (1998)].

A New Jersey casino's hair length policy, requiring pony-tail-wearing male employees to choose between cutting their hair and covering the pony tail with a wig, was upheld by the New Jersey Superior Court. Neither Title VII nor state law forbade a neutrally applied grooming policy that permitted female, but not male, employees to wear pony tails [*Rivera v. Resorts International/Trump Plaza Hotel & Casino*, 702 A.2d 1359 (N.J. Sup. 1997)].

Chapter 29

Corporate Communications

29.2 DEFAMATION

A law firm associate was fired subsequent to receiving a poor performance evaluation. She asked to have that evaluation reviewed, but the results were just as negative. After she was fired, the firm's attorneys merely confirmed her dates of employment and did not give any other information about her tenure at the defendant firm. The ex-associate sued, alleging professional defamation.

The law firm sought summary judgment, which was denied. The firm's theory was that any law firm associate agrees to be evaluated by the employer and that the results of the evaluation are entitled to absolute privilege. The District of Columbia Court of Appeals rejected the claim that evaluations are absolutely privileged, so the case had to go to trial. The law firm was held entitled to a qualified privilege for communications remaining within the firm. The privilege could be forfeited by revealing the information outside the firm, communicating too much information, or having a malicious motivation for communicating information about the former associate—all factual issues that would have to be resolved at the trial. For discussion of privilege re law firm evaluations, see *Wallace v. Skadden, Arps, Slate, Meagher & Flom*, 1998 Westlaw 12571 (D.C. App. 1998); analyzed in *Employment Alert*, 3/19/98, p. 11.

According to the Minnesota Court of Appeals, an employee who was justifiably discharged (for getting into an argument with one of the residents of a homeless shelter where he worked as an engineer) could not sue the ex-employer on a theory of "compelled self-publication." That doctrine can be used by wrongfully accused employees, not by those who were appropriately dismissed under circumstances justifying the employer's action [*Techam v. People Serving People, Inc.* , 1998 Westlaw 2431 (Minn. App. 1998); see *Employment Alert*, 3/19/98, p. 11].

Employees are even less likely to confront and cope with their substance abuse problems if they fear that they will lose their jobs if the employer finds out. Therefore, some employers pledge confidentiality to encourage employees to get treatment.

A Nevada employee claimed that his employer violated his confidentiality with respect to an alcohol treatment program; that other employees jeered at him; and that he was fired when he complained about the employer's indiscretion. He sued the employer, alleging that the employer's breach of confidentiality modified his status as an at-will employee, thus increasing the employer's obligation. But the court disagreed, holding that his at-will status continued. If an employer obligates itself not to fire employees in recovery without just cause, it can be held to that commitment—but this employer didn't make that kind of promise [*Barmettler v. Reno Air, Inc.*, 1998 Westlaw 178459 (Nevada 1998)]. See *Employment Alert*, 6/25/98, p. 11.

29.5 RESPONSES TO REFERENCE CHECKS

Most companies are very circumspect about what they'll say when another company calls to check references. The Society for Human Resources Management (SHRM) reports that only 19% of about 850 HR staffers surveyed explain why an ex-employee had left, and only 13% gave any information about the work performance of the former employee. See Jeffrey L. Seglin, "Too Much Ado About Giving References," *NYT*, 2/21/99, Business, p. 4.

But that's only what goes on the record, in a formal contact such as a call from a lawyer. HR professionals often develop more effective off-the-record communications with people on their own level in other companies.

Of course, the reason for the guardedness is the fear of defamation suits. But Seglin's article cites business school professor C. Patrick Fleener's study of court records for the periods 1965–1970 and 1985–1990. He found reports of a mere 16 defamation cases (covering both federal and state courts)—and 12 of those were wins for the employer. Four plaintiff wins in ten years doesn't seem like a good reason to disrupt the entire practice of using references in hiring. Don't forget that truthful statements are not defamatory, so sticking to the facts, without embroidery, should be a defense in any event.

Chapter 30

Insurance Coverage for Claims Against the Employer

30.2 THE CGL

The CGL exclusion for "employment-related practices" does exclude direct coverage for sexual harassment liability. However, it did not exclude coverage of a sexually harassed employee's claim against the employer for negligent retention of the harassing employee. As the Florida Court of Appeals interpreted the case, charging a company with negligent retention charges it with negligence, not with an excluded claim of intentional injury [*Mactown, Inc. v. Continental Insurance Co.*, 1998 Westlaw 390612 (Fla. App. 1998)].

The CGL exclusion of bodily injury "arising out of and in the course of employment" barred coverage of an age discrimination wrongful termination claim, brought under state (New Jersey) law. The ex-employee alleged that emotional distress resulting from the termination caused physical consequences such as loss of libido, headaches, stomach pains, and eventually a stroke.

Litigation, like politics, makes strange bedfellows, and this time the ex-employee and the employer took the same position: that the bodily injury arose out of the wrongful termination, not out of employment, and therefore should come under the CGL. (The ex-employee, of course, wanted the insurer to be involved so that there would be an additional source of payment of potential damages.) However, the court was not persuaded and did not require the CGL insurer to defend or indemnify [*American Motorists Ins. Co. v. L-C-A Sales Co.*, 155 N.J. 29, 713 A.2d 1007 (N.J. 1998)]. (*Schmidt*, discussed later in this chapter, deals with another kind of policy, not the CGL.)

30.3 NON-CGL POLICIES

In 1997, 1998, and 1999, Employment Practices Liability Insurance (EPLI) attracted significant attention in the HR and legal press.

In 1994, there were only 10 carriers offering EPLI coverage; by 1997, at least 30, and probably about 50 companies, had this coverage for sale. By 1999, over 100 insurers were in the EPLI market, and the Insurance Services Organization (ISO) had at last developed a standard EPLI form. More competition led to increasing comprehensiveness of available EPLI policies, but in most cases, punitive damages and retaliation will *not* be covered, according to Daniel C. Skinner, William T. Edwards, and Gregory L. Gravlee ("Selecting Employment Practices Liability Insurance," *HR Magazine*, 9/98, p. 146).

However, greater availability of policies did not impel the majority of companies or executives to purchase. Aon Risk Services, Inc.'s 1997 survey of 2200 executives found that only about one-third had EPLI coverage; of that small sample, about two-thirds had the coverage as an endorsement to a CGL or directors & officers (D&O) policies, and only 26% owned stand-alone EPLI policies. What did EPLI cost in 1997? Anywhere from $15,000 to $70,000 for $1 million coverage, depending on geographic location and litigation history.

EPLI owners can benefit from the coverage even if they are never sued, because insurers require their insureds to audit their HR functions, improve their procedures, and add new procedures to minimize the risk of suit (e.g., better reporting and investigation procedures for sexual harassment claims). In a sense, this is a counterpart of security measures undertaken to reduce casualty and fire insurance premiums. (This information comes from Simon J. Nadel, "Employment Practices Liability Insurance Makes Some Headway With Employers," 66 LW 2275.)

Insurers are still treating stand-alone EPLI products with caution. Although these policies usually do not cover punitive damages (so the "wild card" multi-million-dollar claims are not covered), it is still difficult to predict what will happen in an employment case. Employers may be driven to settle even a fairly weak case, to resolve the uncertainty and avoid bad publicity and even a small risk of being subjected to a very large judgment.

Furthermore, employers are likely to insist that the insurer having a duty to defend provide them with top-flight, experienced employment defense attorneys. Compensating these skillful attorneys can be a painful task for the EPLI insurer! The insurer's outlook is addressed in Jennifer L. Cox and Bernard E. Jacques, "Risks of EPLI Coverage Prove Difficult to Assess," *National Law Journal*, 12/21/98, p. B14.

The ISO EPLI form modifies the basic claims-made structure in a way that helps employers. A claims-made policy is one that provides coverage when claims are made while the insured still has coverage. But the ISO EPLI form also covers claims made during the 30 days right after the policy expired, unless another insurer is already in the picture. If the same employee makes multiple claims, they are all considered to have arisen on the date of the first claim, so there will be no gap in coverage and it will not be necessary to figure out whether the initial or the later insurer is responsible.

Liability insurance is not very popular among HR professionals. SHRM's 1997 *Employment Litigation Survey* showed that 85% of HR professionals responding to the survey didn't have liability insurance, because they did not feel that they were at high personal risk of being sued. In the small number of cases in which an HR professional might be named as defendant, the employer's CGL would probably cover the HR professional. However, if the employer and the HR professional might find themselves at odds (if the HR professional objects to improper corporate policies, for instance), personal coverage might be worthwhile. See 66 LW 2276.

Employment Law Letter, an online newsletter (see http://www.ulmer.com/events/newsletters/sp99_shop.html), provides valuable guidance in its spring 1999 issue. Stephanie E. Trudeau and William D. Edwards suggest the following questions for evaluating an EPLI policy:

- Does it cover all employees? What about the actions of leased employees and independent contractors?
- Are former employees covered?
- Are claims for breach of explicit or implied employment contract excluded from the policy?
- What coverage (if any) is available for employment-related claims such as infliction of emotional distress or defamation?
- If you are aware of a high-quality employment defense firm, can you require your insurer to select that firm as your counsel, or are you stuck with the insurer's choice of counsel? How much control can you impose on the defense of your cases?
- Does the insurer have to provide you with a defense in adminstrative (e.g., EEOC) proceedings, or only at trial? Remember, very few employment cases actually get to trial—but the employer's life can be made very unpleasant before trial!
- Are you covered for retaliation claims (a growing area of employment litigation), including retaliation against Worker's Compensation claimants?
- Are you covered for injunctive and declaratory relief as well as money damages?
- Is the deductible imposed for each claimant? This is not a desirable provision for the employer, because it could result in having to satisfy the deductible several times a year.
- Does your state forbid insurance against punitive damages? If not, does the policy cover punitive damages?

Schmidt v. Smith, 155 N.J. 44, 713 A.2d 1014 (1998), says that bodily injury caused by sexual harassment is covered by the employer liability section of the Worker's Compensation insurance policy, which is a "gap-filler" designed to come into play when a person suffers job-related injuries, even if that person is not covered by Worker's Compensation.

Providing $1 million in general coverage under a social worker's professional liability policy, but capping coverage of damages for sexual abuse of clients at $25,000, does not violate insurance law or public policy. See *American Home Assurance Co. v. Levy,* Suffolk County Supreme Court, discussed in Bill Alden, "Judge Upholds Insurance Limits for Sex Claims," *N.Y.L.J.,* 2/11/99, p. 1.

In this analysis, therapists are not required to have malpractice insurance, so there is no public policy involved. To the extent that they choose to have the coverage, it is legitimate for the carriers to control the terms of coverage. The social workers argued that such a low cap would deter reporting of sexual abuse, but the court rejected the argument, pointing out that clients seldom know how much insurance their health care providers carry.

Chapter 31

EFFECT OF CORPORATE TRANSITIONS ON LIABILITY

31.1 INTRODUCTION

A qualified plan can change its form for several reasons. As §12.12 (main volume) explains, plans can be amended; see Chapter 16 (main volume) for a discussion of what happens when a plan is terminated. Changes in form also occur as part of a corporate change in form (e.g., when the corporation that sponsors the plan merges with or is acquired by another company, with some or all of the first plan's employees becoming employees of the new or surviving corporation). Sometimes the transition involves the corporation, with its plans trailing behind as an accessory; sometimes the real purpose of the transition is to change the form or operation of the plan (for example, if an employer wants to combine several of its own existing plans for ease of administration or to reduce costs).

➠ TIP

Even if a transition occurs, basic fiduciary principles continue to apply, and plans must be maintained for the sole benefit of participants and beneficiaries. Hence, in 1996 the Supreme Court decided that plan participants and beneficiaries could sue under ERISA §502(a)(3), to get equitable relief for themselves, when a company spun off its money-losing divisions to a new, financially unstable corporation and lied to employees about the safety of their benefits if they transferred to the new corporation.

In contrast, however, given that pension benefits vest but welfare benefits (including retiree health and insurance benefits) do not, ERISA fiduciary duty is not violated by transferring the obligation to pay nonpension retiree benefits to a new company spun off from the former employer. Nor is an ERISA contract claim cognizable. The Sixth Circuit's analysis in *Sengpiel v. B.F. Goodrich Co.*, 1998 Westlaw 6537159 (6th Cir. 1998), is that ERISA requires prefunding of pensions, but not of welfare benefits. The spun-off entity retained the right to reduce benefits in the plan documents, so reducing the benefits had to be analyzed as a plan termination, modification, or amendment (i.e., a business decision, not a discretionary administrative discretion by a fiduciary).

Certainly, part of the due diligence that must be undertaken prior to purchasing another business, or selling a business, is the effect of the change on each corporation's employee benefit plans. For example, if it is discovered that the seller's plan is underfunded, the sales documents might be redrafted so that the seller covenants to correct the underfunding, or the sales price might simply be reduced accordingly. At times, the deciding factor in structuring the deal will be which form offers the desired treatment of the plans.

Changes in corporate structure can have unintended effects on plans, which may violate nondiscrimination, minimum participation, and anticutback rules. The buyer must be particularly careful to find out if defined contribution plans are unfunded or defined benefit plans are underfunded. The presence or absence of golden parachutes, retiree health benefit obligations, and COBRA obligations must be determined. WARN Act notification [see §18.11 (main volume)] may also be required if there is a significant reduction in the workforce after the corporate transition. Last but not least, the tests that establish whether a plan is discriminatory must be repeated after a change of corporate organization.

The test of whether two companies are alter egos (and therefore required to make up for delinquent contributions to a pension plan) comes from basic corporate law. The question is whether one company controls the other so closely that the second corporation has no independent existence, and the second corporation is just a sham used for fraudulent purposes.

In addition to questions involving pension plans, a corporate transition can have other implications: for labor law; for unemployment insurance; and for taxes, for example.

31.2 CHOICE OF FORM

Although the variations are almost infinite, there are several basic ways to structure a corporate transition. Two companies could merge, creating a new successor company or with one company absorbed into the other. One company could buy all of the other company's assets; or one company could buy all of the other company's stock. The consequences of stock and asset purchases are different.

If the deal is structured as either a merger or a sale of stock, the buyer acquires the seller's liabilities as an automatic part of the deal. The buyer will become the sponsor of the seller's employee benefit plans unless

- Action is taken to terminate or freeze the plan. Both corporate action (resolution of the Board of Directors; perhaps affirmation by the stockholders) and pension plan action (plan amendment) will be required.
- The plan is transferred away from the acquired entity (e.g., to a parent corporation that is selling one of its subsidiaries).
- The transaction is set up so the seller retains plan sponsorship.

In this situation, if the plan is *not* assumed, employees might end up forfeiting benefits that had not vested as of the time of the sale. However, if the transaction has the effect of a partial termination of the plan, vesting will be required.

In contrast, in an asset sale, the buyer generally assumes only the specific liabilities it agrees to assume. Thus, the buyer becomes a successor plan sponsor only if it takes action to become one, such as adopting the existing plan or a plan that is a spin-off of the existing plan. (A spin-off divides one plan into two or more; for instance, if a company assigns a spun-off plan to each of several divisions.) There are several reasons why the asset buyer might prefer not to adopt the seller's plan. It might be underfunded, or be associated with other liabilities, or might be inconsistent with the buyer's existing deferred compensation plans.

Nevertheless, companies planning asset purchases should beware: Some recent court cases make them liable for pension liabilities such as the asset seller's unpaid pension contributions and termination liability—even if the asset buyer did not expressly assume them, and even if it is not a successor under general principles governing corporate transitions, if there is continuity of operations and the seller bought the assets knowing that the liabilities existed.

The plans that the seller maintained prior to the transaction could be retained, frozen, or terminated. A buyer who adopts an existing plan could agree to assume liability only going forward, with the seller retaining liability for violations of the plan rules that occurred before the sale. As for plans maintained by the buyer prior to the transaction, there might be a merger between the buyer's and seller's plans. (See §31.3 for a discussion of the anticutback rules and the requirement of crediting prior service to the new plan.)

There are exceptions to this rule. If the transaction is in effect a merger rather than an asset sale, liabilities will be characterized as they would be in a merger. If the buying corporation is a mere continuation of the selling corporation, or if the transaction is a fraud intended to escape liability, the transaction will be disregarded.

If only plan assets, and not the operating terms of the two plans, are merged, then the transaction is not considered a plan amendment that has the effect of reducing plan accruals. However, if the plans merge and one adopts the other's formulas and definitions, the original plan is deemed to have been amended, so if benefits are reduced notice must be given under ERISA §204.

31.3 THE ANTICUTBACK RULE

Code §411(d)(6) forbids amendments that reduce accrued benefits, including early retirement benefits and the availability of additional payout options in addition to the required QPSA and QJSA. If a plan is spun off, the spin-off plan is required to maintain the old plan's payment options as to benefits accrued before the spin-off. In a merger, employees are permitted to retain their premerger payout options. The practical effect is that, if the merged plan wants to have a single payout structure, it must improve the less-favorable plan to equal the options offered under the more-favorable plan.

Section 411(a)(10)(B) requires that individuals who had three years of service before the corporate transition are entitled to keep the old vesting schedule, if it is more favorable to them than the newly adopted one. Employers have an obligation to inform employees of this choice.

Also see §414(l): If plans (even plans maintained by the same employer) merge or consolidate, or a plan's assets and liabilities are transferred to another plan, each participant's benefit immediately after the transition, calculated on a termination basis, must be at least as great as his or her benefit would have been if the plan had terminated immediately before the transition. The regulations for this section say that a transfer of assets and liabilities from one plan to another will be treated as a spin-off followed by a merger. (Therefore, Form 5310-A will probably have to be filed at least 30 days before the merger, spin-off, or asset transfer.)

➠ TIP

Code §414 has separate rules for merging two defined contribution plans; two defined benefit plans; and one plan of each type, to make sure that participants' entitlement to benefits is not reduced by the transaction. There are further requirements to be observed if one of the plans is underfunded and the other one is fully funded.

31.4 THE MINIMUM PARTICIPATION RULE

Initially, minimum participation rules were applied to both defined contribution and defined benefit plans. However, the Small Business Job Protection Act of 1996 provides that, as of January 1, 1997, only defined benefit plans are required to have a minimum number or percentage of participants.

In the transition context, this is significant because it's common for asset buyers to decline to adopt the seller's plan. If the plan is not adopted, there is a risk that the new plan will not cover the mandated 50 employees or 40% of the workforce.

Some relief is available under Code §410(b)(6)(C), which allows one year after an acquisition or the disposition of a corporation to satisfy the minimum participation requirement. After that, however, the plan is likely to become disqualified (unless it has been terminated in the interim).

A possible strategy is to freeze the plan—but that creates difficulties if too many participants choose to cash out. Another option is to merge both (or all) the plans into a larger plan, no later than the fifteenth day of the tenth month after the end of the plan year. The new plan must offer a benefit structure at least as favorable as the most favorable of the merged plans.

31.5 OTHER PENSION ISSUES

If Employer #2 maintains the plan of its predecessor, Employer #1, then service with Employer #1 is credited as service with Employer #2: See Code §414(a)(1). The "same desk" rule provides that separation from service does not occur [with respect to 401(k) in-service distributions or §402(e) lump sums] if the employee holds the same job after the former employer goes through a liquidation, merger, consolidation, or sale of assets.

One fairly common plan provision permits plan participants who have not yet reached retirement age to take plan distributions upon "termination of employment." Courts are split as to whether a change in control of the employer corporation serves as termination of employment for this purpose. It might be worthwhile to draft or amend your company's plan to specify that sale of the business does not operate as termination of employment as long as the employee continues to work for the buyer of the business.

Because the underlying purpose of pension plans is providing postretirement financial security, "in-service distributions" (distributions from the plan while the individual is still working) are severely discouraged by the Internal Revenue Code. There are some special rules governing taxation of in-service distributions when a plan is undergoing transition. Regulation §1.401-1(b)(1)(i) provides that defined benefit plans are forbidden to make in-service distributions to employees before their retirement or termination of employment—unless the plan itself is terminated.

On the other hand, a defined contribution plan other than a 401(k) plan can use the "2 year/5 year" rule: that is, contributions can be withdrawn from the plan after the contributions have been in the plan for two years or the participant has five years of plan participation.

Code §401(k)(10) details the limitations on in-service distributions from 401(k) plans. Absent termination of the plan, participants cannot get distributions until they separate from service, die, suffer disability or hardship, or reach age $59^1/_2$. In-service distributions are permitted incident to termination of the plan, as long as another defined contribution plan is not instituted. In-service distributions are also allowed when substantially all the corporation's business assets and employees are transferred to an unrelated buyer, but the plan's assets and liabilities are not transferred and the seller continues to maintain the plan.

In *Dycus v. PBGC*, 133 F.3d 1367 (10th Cir. 1998), a plant closed and then was reopened by a new owner, who required employees to reapply for their jobs, cut wages, reduced benefits, and changed the seniority schedule. Notwithstanding these changes, employees were not entitled to early retirement benefits under the company's forced termination provision, because the Tenth Circuit ruled that there had not been a permanent shutdown triggering the entitlement to early retirement benefits.

In the view of the Sixth Circuit, a firm's dissolution that makes it impossible for an ex-employee to be reemployed before a five-year break in service elapses does not make the former employee an "affected participant." Therefore, the trustees can lawfully accelerate the forfeiture of his or her non-vested account balance; immediate vesting of the nonvested portion is not required [*Borda v. Hardy, Lewis, Pollard & Page PC*, 1998 U.S. App. LEXIS 3766 (6th Cir. 1998)]. *Borda* concerns a profit-sharing plan to which the plaintiff contributed salary reductions; employer contributions were made.

The vesting schedule for the profit-sharing plan extends over six or seven years. When Borda ceased to be employed by Hardy et al., he was 40% vested in his profit-sharing account. He could have withdrawn that portion, but he elected to leave the funds within the plan. The 60% of the balance that had not yet vested was placed in a suspense account, so if he went back to work for the Hardy PC within five years, he would have been able to earn additional profit-sharing credits.

However, before the five years were up, the firm dissolved. Borda's viewpoint was that dissolution of the firm made him fully vested—but the Sixth Circuit disagreed. He couldn't have been reemployed by a firm that no longer existed, so he could not be characterized as an "affected participant."

Notification

63 FR 68678 (12/14/98), in question-and-answer form, contains rules for giving ERISA §204(h) notice to plan participants. Question 15 says that whether 204(h) notice is required in connection with the sale of a business depends on whether any plan amendment reducing future benefit accruals is adopted.

However, as the four examples given in the Final Rule show, there are circumstances in which the corporation's (or surviving corporation's) obligation to pay pension benefits decreases for practical purposes, even though there has been no amendment adopted that is subject to ERISA 204(h), and therefore there is no obligation to give notice.

Example 4 in the Final Rule concerns a corporation that maintains several plans, including a plan covering employees of a particular division. The plan states that further benefit accruals cease if the employees cease to be employees of the parent corporation. The parent sells all of the assets of the division to another corporation, which also maintains the pension plan, but one with a much lower rate of future benefit accruals than the division's original plan. Then the division's plan is merged into the plan maintained by the corporation that purchases the division. 204(h) notice to the division's employees is not required, because they are no longer employees of the original parent corporation. They are now employees of the purchaser corporation, and future benefit accruals will be calculated under the less generous formula of the purchaser corporation.

The Pension and Welfare Benefits Administration (PWBA) has its own provision for informing employees of the effect of a transition on their pension and welfare benefits. The DOL agency has published a 32-page booklet, "Pension and Health Care Coverage: Questions and Answers for Dislocated Workers." It explains HIPAA and COBRA rights as well as ERISA pension rights. You may wish to add this booklet to your intranet or make copies available in the wake of a layoff or corporate transition. You can suggest that employees call (800) 998-7542 (the PWBA hotline) for free single copies; the text can be downloaded from http://www.dol.gov/dol/pwba.

31.5.1 Tax Aspects of the Transition

Assuming that, after a merger, liquidation, or reorganization, the surviving company maintains the qualified plan of the predecessor corporation, the general rule (under Code §381) is that the original plan's tax attributes are passed on to the successor plan. If two qualified plans consolidate, the deductions taken by each employer before the consolidation will not be retroactively disqualified by the consolidation. Furthermore, the surviving corporation will be able to carry over the predecessor plan's excess contributions and deduct it in its own operation of the plan.

The acquiring corporation can keep up the plan for the benefit of those covered by it under the old ownership—and with no obligation to extend the plan to cover the people who were its own employees before the acquisition.

If the acquirer maintains an existing profit-sharing or stock bonus plan, adds an existing profit-sharing or stock bonus plan to its own preexisting plan, or substitutes a comparable plan for the plan formerly maintained by the acquired corporation, the acquirer can make and deduct "catch-up" contributions equal to the difference between the maintimum contribution to the plan (15% of aggregate employee compensation) and the amount the original employer actually contributed.

TIP

If the buyer makes severance payments to employees of the seller, as part of the transaction, it may have to capitalize those payments instead of deducting them currently. In contrast, severance payments that a company makes in the course of downsizing do *not* have to be capitalized.

➠ **TIP**

If a company acquires a second company that was liable for Federal Unemployment Act (FUTA) tax (and nearly all employers are), the acquiring company can claim a credit against its own FUTA tax for the state unemployment taxes paid by the predecessor.

At the employee level, *LTV Steel Co. v. U.S.*, 42 Fed.Cl. 65 (Fed. Cl. 1998), provides that FICA and FUTA taxes do not apply to payments from a separate trust set up to replace benefits lost because of termination or insolvency of plans. This case arose when the PBGC terminated four LTV defined benefit plans. The PBGC benefits were much lower than the amount that the company promised its workers. LTV entered into a settlement with the United Steelworkers, agreeing to establish a trust to make up the difference.

31.6 REPORTING REQUIREMENTS

In many cases, IRS Form 5310-A will have to be filed 30 days or more before a merger, consolidation, or transfer of plan assets or liabilities, if the transition involves transfer of assets from one qualified retirement plan to another. The exceptions include transactions that come under Regulation §1.414(1)-1(d): defined contribution plan mergers and spin-offs; de minimis mergers and spin-off transactions involving defined benefit plans.

Changes in the ownership or form of ownership of the corporation sponsoring the plan will frequently be "reportable events" that must be reported to the PBGC, as part of the agency's oversight of plans that might be or become unable to pay their benefits. [See §13.12 (main volume).]

Also see ERISA §§4062(f) and 4069(b). The reorganization of a plan's contributing sponsor renders the successor corporation responsible for certain plan liabilities (e.g., the plan's accumulated funding deficiencies, including those previously waived by the IRS).

A party who engages in a transaction within five years before a plan termination, if the intention of the transaction was to evade liability in connection with the plan, thereby becomes a contributing sponsor who is liable for such amounts. (In other words, the transaction has precisely the opposite effect of what was intended.)

An employer who terminates operations at a facility, leading to separation from service of 20% or more of the plan participants, must either fund the plan's guaranteed benefits immediately or make provisions for the funding. [This is also likely to be a WARN Act event; see ¶18.11 (main volume).]

31.7 TREATMENT OF EARLY RETIREMENT SUBSIDIES

Defined benefit plan early retirement subsidies typically call for two forms of qualification: a minimum age, and a minimum amount of service with the employer. What happens in a corporate transition for those who have not met the requirements for the subsidy at the time of the transition but continue to work for the successor employer?

Two cases from 1993 deal with this issue. The Third Circuit case says that if the new employer purchases the old employer's assets and assumes its liabilities, promising to maintain the former benefit package, plan participants can aggregate service with both employers and claim the subsidy as soon as they reach the minimum service.

On the other hand, the Eighth Circuit case involves the sale of a corporate division where the sale agreement made it clear that service with the first employer counted for vesting only, not for any other purposes. Thus, pre- and postsale service could not be aggregated to determine eligibility for the early retirement subsidy.

31.8 TRANSITIONS IN LABOR LAW

At one end of the spectrum, some transitions are clearly legitimate: A firm is failing until someone from outside takes it over, hoping to turn around; a corporation's founder wants to retire and sells the business to someone else; two companies with common interests form a merger. At the other end of the spectrum are paper transactions that have no real practical consequences but are merely a sham to prevent the operation of otherwise-applicable laws or to get rid of an unwanted obligation.

As Chapter 18 in the main volume discusses, it is significant who counts as an "employer" for labor law purposes. "Employees" are entitled to organize and take concerted action to protect their rights against their "employers." Furthermore, if a transaction lacks real substance, the successor may be required to assume the labor-law obligations of its predecessor. The main test is whether there has been a significant practical change, or whether operations in effect continue other than a nominal change in ownership.

31.8.1 Labor Law Implications of Choice of Form

Labor law follows the basic rule that a merger or sale of stock obligates the acquiring company to assume the liabilities of the acquired or selling company, and this includes Collective Bargaining Agreement (CBAs). But in an asset sale, the CBA is not assumed unless the purchaser voluntarily takes it on, or unless there is another reason to view the buyer as a successor or surrogate of the seller. Yet even if a company is not fully bound by its predecessor's CBA, it may still have a duty to bargain with the existing union in good faith—if there is continuity linking the old and new enterprises.

In addition to situations in which one entity replaces another, two or more enterprises can be viewed as a "single employer" for labor law purposes, or one might be treated as an alter ego (surrogate) of the other. If a parent company and its subsidiary engage in the same line of business, the NLRB will probably treat them as only a single enterprise, not two. Furthermore, "joint employers" that are separate entities that share decision making about labor issues may be treated together by the NLRB.

To summarize, it is important either to be prepared to undertake the predecessor's union contracts and other labor law obligations or to structure the transition in a way that leaves the surviving or successor operation free of these obligations. Also note that a change in corporate ownership (even if corporate structure remains the same) may lead to revocation of state-granted privilege to self-insure for Worker's Compensation claims.

Note that a new company that adopts an existing operation can unilaterally change the wage scale, unless it's "perfectly clear" that the new owner will hire all of the old employees. In a "perfectly clear" case where the new owner does not consult with the union and there is no evidence of what would have emerged if there had been negotiations, the employees are given the benefit of the doubt: It's assumed that the former wage rate would have continued, without diminution. Thus, new ownership in a "perfectly clear" case cannot lead to wage cuts without union acquiescence.

31.8.2 CBA Bars

Generally speaking, the existence of a valid, ongoing collective bargaining agreement will constitute a bar to holding another representation election (although a petition can be filed during a "window" period before the existing contract expires). A CBA bars a new election in a merger or acquisition if the new operation carries on the old business; it is not a bar if the result is an entirely new operation that makes major personnel changes. A CBA is not a bar when a successor employer comes in and the successor does not issue a written assumption of the existing agreement.

31.9 TRANSITIONS AND UNEMPLOYMENT INSURANCE

Although it is a comparatively minor cost, the acquiror of a business may wish to take advantage of amounts of FUTA tax already paid by the transferor of the business during the portion of the year prior to the transfer to the new owner. [See ¶18.15 (main volume) for a more detailed discussion of FUTA compliance.] The successor employer can rely on wages paid by the predecessor employer (and thus on FUTA payments made by the predecessor) if either one of two circumstances exists. The first is that the transferee acquires substantially all the property used in the transferor's entire trade or business (or in a separate unit of the trade or business). The other is that, whether or not the property was acquired, at least one employee from the old business remains employed immediately after the transfer.

The IRS's view (for FICA and tax withholding as well as FUTA) is that, in a statutory merger or consolidation, the surviving corporation is the same taxpayer and the same corporation as the predecessor corporation(s). Of course, that means that the successor will have to pay any taxes due but unpaid by the predecessor—unless the successor gives the local administrative agency adequate written notice. (The form should be available from the agency.)

However, state unemployment laws usually provide that companies remain subject to unemployment insurance laws for at least two years once they have acquired an experience rating—with the result that the transferor may remain liable in a year after it ceases operations, unless it applies to the local administrative agency for a determination that it is no longer an employer.

➠ TIP

Usually, in a multistate operation, wages paid in the various states can be combined for FUTA purposes.

If the predecessor has acquired a good experience rating, the successor will probably be able to acquire the experience rating with the rest of the operation, as long as operations remain more or less the same, at the original business location, and the workforce remains stable. (Altering these important factors in effect means that there is a new enterprise, which must acquire its own experience rating.)

31.10 CORPORATE CULTURE AND HR'S ROLE IN TRANSITION PLANNING

In 1998 alone, there were almost 11,500 merger or acquisition transactions, with an aggregate value over $1.6 trillion. Unfortunately, however, many of these transactions must be "unwound," or remain in force but disappoint one or more participants. According to Mark Herndon of Watson Wyatt Worldwide, 70% of mergers and acquisitions fall short of the financial goals for the deal. Almost half of the executives of acquired companies leave within a year, and by three years posttransaction, 75% of the former managers are gone. The deal can reduce productivity within the target company by 50%, and it can take up to three years to reconcile the corporate cultures.

For instance, the acquired company might have had a highly automated expense processing system, and a low-level manager might be able to spend up to $5000 without approval. Chaos ensues if the acquiring company relies on advance approval, using a paper form, and demands that the paperwork be completed for every purchase over $500.

Sometimes the business logic for the combination is faulty; in many cases, the problem is irreconcilability of corporate cultures. Earlier and deeper involvement of both companies' HR departments could have smoothed the transition. HR also plays a part in transactions that are contemplated but not consummated, by pointing out potential problems.

Transactions that can affect a corporation's continued existence or can change its form require "due diligence": It's the duty of the corporation's board of directors to study the transaction thoroughly, and recommend it only if it is in the best interests of the stockholders (and perhaps of other constituencies, such as employees, retirees, and the community as a whole). So it's important to determine if a potential merger partner is guilty of discrimination, labor law violations (e.g., unlawful union busting), or wage and hour violations. Even if the potential partner has behaved lawfully in every respect, it may have a more generous pension or benefit structure, which may have to be maintained as to current employees. The plan's investment performance could be poor (requiring additional funding from the employer to maintain promised levels); its actuarial assumptions could be defective.

Corporate culture issues are discussed in *HR Magazine's* April 1999 issue, especially Bill Leonard's "Will This Marriage Work?" (p. 35) and Robert J. Grossman's "Irreconcilable Differences," (p. 42).

Chapter 32

FORMS

SPD NOTICE OF PBGC COVERAGE [SOURCE: 63 FR 48386 (9/9/98)]

Your pension benefits under this plan are insured by the Pension Benefit Guaranty Corporation (PBGC), a federal insurance agency. If the plan terminates (ends) without enough money to pay all benefits, the PBGC will step in to pay pension benefits. Most people receive all of the pension benefits they would have received under their plan, but some people may lose certain benefits.

The PBGC guarantee generally covers (1) normal and early retirement benefits; (2) disability benefits if you become disabled before the plan terminates; and (3) certain benefits for your survivors.

The PBGC guarantee generally does not cover (1) benefits greater than the maximum guaranteed amount set by law for the year in which the plan terminates; (2) some or all of benefit increases and new benefits based on plan provisions that have been in place for fewer than five years at the time the plan terminates; (3) benefits that are not vested because you have not worked long enough for the company; (4) benefits for which you have not met all of the requirements at the time the plan terminates; (5) certain early retirement payments (such as supplemental payments that stop when you become eligible for Social Security) that result in an early retirement monthly benefit greater than your monthly benefit at the plan's normal retirement age; and (6) nonpension benefits, such as health insurance, life insurance, certain death benefits, vacation pay, and severance pay.

Even if certain of your benefits are not guaranteed, you still may receive some of those benefits from the PBGC depending on how much money your plan has and on how much the PBGC collects from employers.

For more information about the PBGC and the benefits it guarantees, ask your plan administrator or contact the PBGC's Technical Assistance Division, 1200

K Street NW Suite 930, Washington, DC 20005-4026, or call 202-326-4000 (not a toll-free number). TTY/TDD users may call the federal relay service toll-free at 1-800-877-8339 and ask to be connected to 202-326-4000. Additional information about the PBGC's pension insurance program is available through the PBGC's Web site at http://www.pbgc.gov.

SPD NOTICE OF ERISA RIGHTS [SOURCE: 63 FR 48386 (9/9/98); DELETE ITEMS OF INFORMATION THAT ARE NOT APPLICABLE TO YOUR PLAN]

As a participant in (name of plan) you are entitled to certain rights and protections under the Employee Retirement Income Security Act of 1974 (ERISA). ERISA provides that all plan participants shall be entitled to

> Examine, without charge, at the plan administrator's office and at other specified locations, such as worksites and union halls, all documents governing the plan, including insurance contracts and collective bargaining agreements, and a copy of the latest annual report (Form 5500 Series) filed by the plan with the U.S. Department of Labor.
>
> Obtain, upon written request to the plan administrator, copies of documents governing the operation of the plan, including insurance contracts and collective bargaining agreements, and copies of the latest annual report (Form 5500 Series) and updated summary plan description. The administrator may make a reasonable charge for the copies.
>
> Receive a summary of the plan's annual financial report. The plan administrator is required by law to furnish each participant with a copy of this summary annual report.
>
> Obtain a statement telling you whether you have a right to receive a pension at normal retirement age (age * * *) and, if so, what your benefits would be at normal retirement age if you stop working under the plan now. If you do not have a right to a pension, the statement will tell you how many more years you have to work to get a right to a pension. This statement must be requested in writing and is not required to be given more than once every twelve (12) months. The plan must provide the statement free of charge.
>
> Continue health care coverage for yourself, spouse, or dependents if there is a loss of coverage under the plan as a result of a qualifying event. You or your dependents may have to pay for such coverage. Review this summary plan description and the documents governing the plan on the rules governing your COBRA continuation coverage rights.

Reduction or elimination of exclusionary periods of coverage for preexisting conditions under your group health plan, if you have creditable coverage from another plan. You should be provided a certificate of creditable coverage, free of charge, from your group health plan or health insurance issuer when you lose coverage under the plan, when you become entitled to elect COBRA continuation coverage, when your COBRA continuation coverage ceases, if you request it before losing coverage, or if you request it up to 24 months after losing coverage. Without evidence of creditable coverage, you may be subject to a preexisting condition exclusion for 12 months (18 months for late enrollees) after your enrollment date in your coverage.

In addition to creating rights for plan participants, ERISA imposes duties upon the people who are responsible for the operation of the employee benefit plan. The people who operate your plan, called "fiduciaries" of the plan, have a duty to do so prudently and in the interest of you and other plan participants and beneficiaries. No one, including your employer, your union, or any other person, may fire you or otherwise discriminate against you in any way to prevent you from obtaining a (pension, welfare) benefit or exercising your rights under ERISA. If your claim for a (pension, welfare) benefit is denied in whole or in part, you must receive a written explanation of the reason for the denial. You have the right to have the plan review and reconsider your claim. Under ERISA, there are steps you can take to enforce the above rights. For instance, if you request materials from the plan and do not receive them within 30 days, you may file suit in a federal court. In such a case, the court may require the plan administrator to provide the materials and pay you up to $110 a day until you receive the materials, unless the materials were not sent because of reasons beyond the control of the administrator. If you have a claim for benefits which is denied or ignored, in whole or in part, you may file suit in a state or federal court. In addition, if you disagree with the plan's decision or lack thereof concerning the qualified status of a domestic relations order or medical child support order, you may file suit in federal court. If it should happen that plan fiduciaries misuse the plan's money, or if you are discriminated against for asserting your rights, you may seek assistance from the U.S. Department of Labor, or you may file suit in a federal court. The court will decide who should pay court costs and legal fees. If you are successful the court may order the person you have sued to pay these costs and fees. If you lose, the court may order you to pay these costs and fees: for example, if it finds your claim is frivolous.

If you should have any questions about your plan, you should contact the plan administrator. If you have any questions about this statement or about your rights under ERISA, you should contact the nearest office of the Pension and Welfare Benefits Administration, U.S. Department of Labor, listed in your telephone directory, or the Division of Technical Assistance and Inquiries, Pension and Welfare Benefits Administration, U.S. Department of Labor, 200 Constitution Avenue N.W., Washington, DC 20210.

Form **SS-8**
(Rev. June 1997)
Department of the Treasury
Internal Revenue Service

Determination of Employee Work Status for Purposes of Federal Employment Taxes and Income Tax Withholding

OMB No. 1545-0004

Paperwork Reduction Act Notice

We ask for the information on this form to carry out the Internal Revenue laws of the United States. You are required to give us the information. We need it to ensure that you are complying with these laws and to allow us to figure and collect the right amount of tax.

You are not required to provide the information requested on a form that is subject to the Paperwork Reduction Act unless the form displays a valid OMB control number. Books or records relating to a form or its instructions must be retained as long as their contents may become material in the administration of any Internal Revenue law. Generally, tax returns and return information are confidential, as required by Code section 6103.

The time needed to complete and file this form will vary depending on individual circumstances. The estimated average time is: **Recordkeeping,** 34 hr., 55 min.; **Learning about the law or the form,** 12 min.; and **Preparing and sending the form to the IRS,** 46 min. If you have comments concerning the accuracy of these time estimates or suggestions for making this form simpler, we would be happy to hear from you. You can write to the Tax Forms Committee, Western Area Distribution Center, Rancho Cordova, CA 95743-0001. **DO NOT** send the tax form to this address. Instead, see **General Information** for where to file.

Purpose

Employers and workers file Form SS-8 to get a determination as to whether a worker is an employee for purposes of Federal employment taxes and income tax withholding.

General Information

Complete this form carefully. If the firm is completing the form, complete it for **ONE** individual who is representative of the class of workers whose status is in question. If you want a written determination for more than one class of workers, complete a separate Form SS-8 for one worker from each class whose status is typical of that class. A written determination for any worker will apply to other workers of the same class if the facts are not materially different from those of the worker whose status was ruled upon.

Caution: *Form SS-8 is **not** a claim for refund of social security and Medicare taxes or Federal income tax withholding. Also, a determination that an individual is an employee does not necessarily reduce any current or prior tax liability. A worker must file his or her income tax return even if a determination has not been made by the due date of the return.*

Where to file.—In the list below, find the state where your legal residence, principal place of business, office, or agency is located. Send Form SS-8 to the address listed for your location.

Location:	Send to:
Alaska, Arizona, Arkansas, California, Colorado, Hawaii, Idaho, Illinois, Iowa, Kansas, Minnesota, Missouri, Montana, Nebraska, Nevada, New Mexico, North Dakota, Oklahoma, Oregon, South Dakota, Texas, Utah, Washington, Wisconsin, Wyoming	Internal Revenue Service SS-8 Determinations P.O. Box 1231, Stop 4106 AUSC Austin, TX 78767
Alabama, Connecticut, Delaware, District of Columbia, Florida, Georgia, Indiana, Kentucky, Louisiana, Maine, Maryland, Massachusetts, Michigan, Mississippi, New Hampshire, New Jersey, New York, North Carolina, Ohio, Pennsylvania, Rhode Island, South Carolina, Tennessee, Vermont, Virginia, West Virginia, All other locations not listed	Internal Revenue Service SS-8 Determinations Two Lakemont Road Newport, VT 05855-1555
American Samoa, Guam, Puerto Rico, U.S. Virgin Islands	Internal Revenue Service Mercantile Plaza 2 Avenue Ponce de Leon San Juan, Puerto Rico 00918

Name of firm (or person) for whom the worker performed services		Name of worker	
Address of firm (include street address, apt. or suite no., city, state, and ZIP code)		Address of worker (include street address, apt. or suite no., city, state, and ZIP code)	
Trade name		Telephone number (include area code) ( )	Worker's social security number
Telephone number (include area code) ( )	Firm's employer identification number		

Check type of firm for which the work relationship is in question:
☐ **Individual** ☐ **Partnership** ☐ **Corporation** ☐ **Other** (specify) ▶ ....

Important Information Needed To Process Your Request

This form is being completed by: ☐ Firm ☐ Worker

If this form is being completed by the worker, the IRS **must** have your permission to disclose your name to the firm.

Do you object to disclosing your name and the information on this form to the firm? . . . . ☐ **Yes** ☐ **No**

If you answer "Yes," the IRS cannot act on your request. **Do not complete the rest of this form unless the IRS asks for it.**

Under section 6110 of the Internal Revenue Code, the information on this form and related file documents will be open to the public if any ruling or determination is made. However, names, addresses, and taxpayer identification numbers will be removed before the information is made public.

Is there any other information you want removed? . . . . ☐ **Yes** ☐ **No**

If you check "Yes," we cannot process your request unless you submit a copy of this form and copies of all supporting documents showing, in brackets, the information you want removed. Attach a separate statement showing which specific exemption of section 6110(c) applies to each bracketed part.

Cat. No. 16106T   Form **SS-8** (Rev. 6-97)

Form SS-8 (Rev. 6-97) Page **2**

This form is designed to cover many work activities, so some of the questions may not apply to you. ***You must answer ALL items or mark them "Unknown" or "Does not apply."*** *If you need more space, attach another sheet.*

Total number of workers in this class. (Attach names and addresses. If more than 10 workers, list only 10.) ▶ ______

This information is about services performed by the worker from ______ (month, day, year) to ______ (month, day, year)

Is the worker still performing services for the firm? . . . . . ☐ **Yes** ☐ **No**

- If "No," what was the date of termination? ▶ ______ (month, day, year)

1a Describe the firm's business ......

b Describe the work done by the worker ......

2a If the work is done under a written agreement between the firm and the worker, attach a copy.

b If the agreement is not in writing, describe the terms and conditions of the work arrangement ......

c If the actual working arrangement differs in any way from the agreement, explain the differences and why they occur ......

3a Is the worker given training by the firm? . . . . . ☐ **Yes** ☐ **No**

- If "Yes," what kind? ......
- How often? ......

b Is the worker given instructions in the way the work is to be done (exclusive of actual training in 3a)? ☐ **Yes** ☐ **No**

- If "Yes," give specific examples ......

c Attach samples of any written instructions or procedures.

d Does the firm have the right to change the methods used by the worker or direct that person on how to do the work? . . . . . ☐ **Yes** ☐ **No**

- Explain your answer ......

e Does the operation of the firm's business require that the worker be supervised or controlled in the performance of the service? . . . . . ☐ **Yes** ☐ **No**

- Explain your answer ......

4a The firm engages the worker:

☐ To perform and complete a particular job only

☐ To work at a job for an indefinite period of time

☐ Other (explain) ......

b Is the worker required to follow a routine or a schedule established by the firm? . . . . . ☐ **Yes** ☐ **No**

- If "Yes," what is the routine or schedule? ......

c Does the worker report to the firm or its representative?. . . . . ☐ **Yes** ☐ **No**

- If "Yes," how often? ......
- For what purpose? ......
- In what manner (in person, in writing, by telephone, etc.)? ......
- Attach copies of any report forms used in reporting to the firm.

d Does the worker furnish a time record to the firm? . . . . . ☐ **Yes** ☐ **No**

- If "Yes," attach copies of time records.

5a State the kind and value of tools, equipment, supplies, and materials furnished by:

- The firm ......
- The worker ......

b What expenses are incurred by the worker in the performance of services for the firm? ......

c Does the firm reimburse the worker for any expenses? . . . . . ☐ **Yes** ☐ **No**

- If "Yes," specify the reimbursed expenses ......

Form SS-8 (Rev. 6-97) Page **3**

6a Will the worker perform the services personally? . . . . ☐ **Yes** ☐ **No**

b Does the worker have helpers? . . . . ☐ **Yes** ☐ **No**

- If "Yes," who hires the helpers? ☐ Firm ☐ Worker
- If the helpers are hired by the worker, is the firm's approval necessary? . . . . ☐ **Yes** ☐ **No**
- Who pays the helpers? ☐ Firm ☐ Worker
- If the worker pays the helpers, does the firm repay the worker? . . . . ☐ **Yes** ☐ **No**
- Are social security and Medicare taxes and Federal income tax withheld from the helpers' pay? . . ☐ **Yes** ☐ **No**
- If "Yes," who reports and pays these taxes? ☐ Firm ☐ Worker
- Who reports the helpers' earnings to the Internal Revenue Service? ☐ Firm ☐ Worker
- What services do the helpers perform? ....

7 At what location are the services performed? ☐ Firm's ☐ Worker's ☐ Other (specify) ....

8a Type of pay worker receives:

☐ Salary ☐ Commission ☐ Hourly wage ☐ Piecework ☐ Lump sum ☐ Other (specify) ....

b Does the firm guarantee a minimum amount of pay to the worker? . . . . ☐ **Yes** ☐ **No**

c Does the firm allow the worker a drawing account or advances against pay? . . . . ☐ **Yes** ☐ **No**

- If "Yes," is the worker paid such advances on a regular basis? . . . . ☐ **Yes** ☐ **No**

d How does the worker repay such advances? ....

9a Is the worker eligible for a pension, bonus, paid vacations, sick pay, etc.? . . . . ☐ **Yes** ☐ **No**

- If "Yes," specify ....

b Does the firm carry worker's compensation insurance on the worker? . . . . ☐ **Yes** ☐ **No**

c Does the firm withhold social security and Medicare taxes from amounts paid the worker? . . . . . . ☐ **Yes** ☐ **No**

d Does the firm withhold Federal income tax from amounts paid the worker? . . . . ☐ **Yes** ☐ **No**

e How does the firm report the worker's earnings to the Internal Revenue Service?

☐ Form W-2 ☐ Form 1099-MISC ☐ Does not report ☐ Other (specify) ....

- Attach a copy.

f Does the firm bond the worker? . . . . ☐ **Yes** ☐ **No**

10a Approximately how many hours a day does the worker perform services for the firm? ....

b Does the firm set hours of work for the worker? . . . . ☐ **Yes** ☐ **No**

- If "Yes," what are the worker's set hours? _______ a.m./p.m. to _______ a.m./p.m. (Circle whether a.m. or p.m.)

c Does the worker perform similar services for others? . . . . ☐ **Yes** ☐ **No** ☐ **Unknown**

- If "Yes," are these services performed on a daily basis for other firms? . . . . . . ☐ **Yes** ☐ **No** ☐ **Unknown**
- Percentage of time spent in performing these services for:

  This firm .... % Other firms .... % ☐ **Unknown**
- Does the firm have priority on the worker's time? . . . . ☐ **Yes** ☐ **No**
- If "No," explain ....

d Is the worker prohibited from competing with the firm either while performing services or during any later period? . . . . ☐ **Yes** ☐ **No**

11a Can the firm discharge the worker at any time without incurring a liability? . . . . ☐ **Yes** ☐ **No**

- If "No," explain ....

b Can the worker terminate the services at any time without incurring a liability? . . . . ☐ **Yes** ☐ **No**

- If "No," explain ....

12a Does the worker perform services for the firm under:

☐ The firm's business name ☐ The worker's own business name ☐ Other (specify) ....

b Does the worker advertise or maintain a business listing in the telephone directory, a trade journal, etc.? . . . . ☐ **Yes** ☐ **No** ☐ **Unknown**

- If "Yes," specify ....

c Does the worker represent himself or herself to the public as being in business to perform the same or similar services? . . . . ☐ **Yes** ☐ **No** ☐ **Unknown**

- If "Yes," how? ....

d Does the worker have his or her own shop or office? . . . . ☐ **Yes** ☐ **No** ☐ **Unknown**

- If "Yes," where? ....

e Does the firm represent the worker as an employee of the firm to its customers? . . . . ☐ **Yes** ☐ **No**

- If "No," how is the worker represented? ....

f How did the firm learn of the worker's services? ....

13 Is a license necessary for the work? . . . . ☐ **Yes** ☐ **No** ☐ **Unknown**

- If "Yes," what kind of license is required? ....
- Who issues the license? ....
- Who pays the license fee?

14 Does the worker have a financial investment in a business related to the services performed? . . . ☐ **Yes** ☐ **No** ☐ **Unknown**

• If "Yes," specify and give amount of the investment ....

15 Can the worker incur a loss in the performance of the service for the firm? . . . ☐ **Yes** ☐ **No**

• If "Yes," how? ....

16a Has any other government agency ruled on the status of the firm's workers? . . . ☐ **Yes** ☐ **No**

• If "Yes," attach a copy of the ruling.

b Is the same issue being considered by any IRS office in connection with the audit of the worker's tax return or the firm's tax return, or has it been considered recently? . . . ☐ **Yes** ☐ **No**

• If "Yes," for which year(s)? ....

17 Does the worker assemble or process a product at home or away from the firm's place of business? ☐ **Yes** ☐ **No**

• If "Yes," who furnishes materials or goods used by the worker? ☐ Firm ☐ Worker ☐ Other

• Is the worker furnished a pattern or given instructions to follow in making the product? . . . ☐ **Yes** ☐ **No**

• Is the worker required to return the finished product to the firm or to someone designated by the firm? ☐ **Yes** ☐ **No**

18 Attach a detailed explanation of any other reason why you believe the worker is an employee or an independent contractor.

Answer items 19a through o only if the worker is a salesperson or provides a service directly to customers.

19a Are leads to prospective customers furnished by the firm? . . . ☐ **Yes** ☐ **No** ☐ **Does not apply**

b Is the worker required to pursue or report on leads? . . . ☐ **Yes** ☐ **No** ☐ **Does not apply**

c Is the worker required to adhere to prices, terms, and conditions of sale established by the firm? . . ☐ **Yes** ☐ **No**

d Are orders submitted to and subject to approval by the firm? . . . ☐ **Yes** ☐ **No**

e Is the worker expected to attend sales meetings? . . . ☐ **Yes** ☐ **No**

• If "Yes," is the worker subject to any kind of penalty for failing to attend? . . . ☐ **Yes** ☐ **No**

f Does the firm assign a specific territory to the worker? . . . ☐ **Yes** ☐ **No**

g Whom does the customer pay? ☐ Firm ☐ Worker

• If worker, does the worker remit the total amount to the firm? . . . ☐ **Yes** ☐ **No**

h Does the worker sell a consumer product in a home or establishment other than a permanent retail establishment? . . . ☐ **Yes** ☐ **No**

i List the products and/or services distributed by the worker, such as meat, vegetables, fruit, bakery products, beverages (other than milk), or laundry or dry cleaning services. If more than one type of product and/or service is distributed, specify the principal one ....

j Did the firm or another person assign the route or territory and a list of customers to the worker? . . ☐ **Yes** ☐ **No**

• If "Yes," enter the name and job title of the person who made the assignment ....

k Did the worker pay the firm or person for the privilege of serving customers on the route or in the territory? ☐ **Yes** ☐ **No**

• If "Yes," how much did the worker pay (not including any amount paid for a truck or racks, etc.)? $ ....

• What factors were considered in determining the value of the route or territory? ....

l How are new customers obtained by the worker? Explain fully, showing whether the new customers called the firm for service, were solicited by the worker, or both ....

m Does the worker sell life insurance? . . . ☐ **Yes** ☐ **No**

• If "Yes," is the selling of life insurance or annuity contracts for the firm the worker's entire business activity? . . . ☐ **Yes** ☐ **No**

• If "No," list the other business activities and the amount of time spent on them ....

n Does the worker sell other types of insurance for the firm? . . . ☐ **Yes** ☐ **No**

• If "Yes," state the percentage of the worker's total working time spent in selling other types of insurance .... %

• At the time the contract was entered into between the firm and the worker, was it their intention that the worker sell life insurance for the firm: ☐ on a full-time basis ☐ on a part-time basis

• State the manner in which the intention was expressed ....

o Is the worker a traveling or city salesperson? . . . ☐ **Yes** ☐ **No**

• If "Yes," from whom does the worker principally solicit orders for the firm? ....

• If the worker solicits orders from wholesalers, retailers, contractors, or operators of hotels, restaurants, or other similar establishments, specify the percentage of the worker's time spent in the solicitation .... %

• Is the merchandise purchased by the customers for resale or for use in their business operations? If used by the customers in their business operations, describe the merchandise and state whether it is equipment installed on their premises or a consumable supply

Under penalties of perjury, I declare that I have examined this request, including accompanying documents, and to the best of my knowledge and belief, the facts presented are true, correct, and complete.

Signature ▶ **Title ▶** **Date ▶**

If the firm is completing this form, an officer or member of the firm must sign it. If the worker is completing this form, the worker must sign it. If the worker wants a written determination about services performed for two or more firms, a separate form must be completed and signed for each firm. Additional copies of this form may be obtained by calling 1-800-TAX-FORM (1-800-829-3676).

a Control number	22222	Void ☐	For Official Use Only ► OMB No. 1545-0008

b Employer identification number	1 Wages, tips, other compensation	2 Federal income tax withheld
c Employer's name, address, and ZIP code	3 Social security wages	4 Social security tax withheld
	5 Medicare wages and tips	6 Medicare tax withheld
	7 Social security tips	8 Allocated tips
d Employee's social security number	9 Advance EIC payment	10 Dependent care benefits
e Employee's name (first, middle initial, last)	11 Nonqualified plans	12 Benefits included in box 1
	13 See instrs. for box 13	14 Other
f Employee's address and ZIP code	15 Statutory employee ☐ Deceased ☐ Pension plan ☐ Legal rep. ☐ Deferred compensation ☐	

16 State	Employer's state I.D. no.	17 State wages, tips, etc.	18 State income tax	19 Locality name	20 Local wages, tips, etc.	21 Local income tax

Form **W-2** **Wage and Tax Statement** 1998

Department of the Treasury—Internal Revenue Service

For Privacy Act and Paperwork Reduction Act Notice, see separate instructions.

Copy A For Social Security Administration—Send this entire page with Form W-3 to the Social Security Administration; photocopies are **Not** acceptable.

Cat. No. 10134D

Do NOT Cut, Staple, or Separate Forms on This Page **Do NOT Cut, Staple, or Separate Forms on This Page**

DO NOT STAPLE

a Control number	33333	For Official Use Only ▶ OMB No. 1545-0008	
b Kind of Payer: 941 ☐ Military ☐ 943 ☐ CT-1 ☐ Hshld. emp. ☐ Medicare govt. emp. ☐		1 Wages, tips, other compensation	2 Federal income tax withheld
		3 Social security wages	4 Social security tax withheld
c Total number of Forms W-2	d Establishment number	5 Medicare wages and tips	6 Medicare tax withheld
e Employer identification number		7 Social security tips	8 Allocated tips
f Employer's name		9 Advance EIC payments	10 Dependent care benefits
		11 Nonqualified plans	12 Deferred compensation
		13	
g Employer's address and ZIP code		14	
h Other EIN used this year		15 Income tax withheld by third-party payer	
i Employer's state I.D. No.			
Contact person	Telephone number ( )	Fax number ( )	E-mail address

Under penalties of perjury, I declare that I have examined this return and accompanying documents, and, to the best of my knowledge and belief, they are true, correct, and complete.

Signature ▶ Title ▶ Date ▶

Form **W-3 Transmittal of Wage and Tax Statements 1998** Department of the Treasury Internal Revenue Service

Send this entire page with the entire Copy A page of Forms W-2 to the Social Security Administration. Photocopies are NOT acceptable.
DO NOT SEND ANY REMITTANCE (cash, checks, money orders, etc.) WITH FORMS W-2 AND W-3.

Change To Note

New boxes. At the bottom of the form above the signature area, boxes were added to enter the name of a contact person and that person's phone or fax number and e-mail address. This data may be used by the SSA if more information is needed during processing.

Need Help?

For information about the information reporting call site, bulletin board services, substitute forms, and how to get forms and publications, see the **1998 Instructions for Form W-2.**

Where To File

Send the entire first page of this form with the entire Copy A page of Forms W-2 to:

Social Security Administration
Data Operations Center
Wilkes-Barre, PA 18769-0001

Note: *If you use "Certified Mail" to file, change the ZIP code to "18769-0002." Also see* ***Shipping and Mailing*** *on page 2 for additional information. If you use an IRS approved private delivery service, add "ATTN: W-2 PROCESS, 1150 E. Mountain Dr." to the address and change the ZIP code to "18702-7997." See Circular E for a list of IRS approved private delivery services.*

For Privacy Act and Paperwork Reduction Act Notice, see the 1998 Instructions for Form W-2.

Cat. No. 10159Y

DO NOT STAPLE

a Control number	33333	For Official Use Only ▶ OMB No. 1545-0008	
b Kind of Payer ▶	941-SS ☐ Military ☐ 943 ☐ Hshld. emp. ☐ Medicare govt. emp. ☐	1 Wages, tips, other compensation	2 Income tax withheld
		3 Social security wages	4 Social security tax withheld
c Total number of Forms W-2	d Establishment number	5 Medicare wages and tips	6 Medicare tax withheld
e Employer identification number		7 Social security tips	8
f Employer's name		9 Advance EIC payments	10
		11 Nonqualified plans	12
		13	
g Employer's address and ZIP code		14	
h Other EIN used this year		15	
i Employer's state I.D. no.			
Contact person	Telephone number ( )	Fax number ( )	E-mail address

Copy 1—For Local Tax Department

Under penalties of perjury, I declare that I have examined this return and accompanying documents, and, to the best of my knowledge and belief, they are true, correct, and complete.

Signature ▶ Title ▶ Date ▶

Form **W-3SS Transmittal of Wage and Tax Statements 1999** Department of the Treasury Internal Revenue Service

time after employment ends but by January 31. If the employee asks for the form, furnish him or her the completed copies within 30 days of the request or within 30 days of the last wage payment, whichever is later. If an employee loses a form, write "REISSUED STATEMENT" on the new copy, but **do not send Copy A of the reissued statement to the SSA.**

Undeliverable forms. Keep for 4 years any employee copies of Forms W-2AS, W-2GU, W-2CM, or W-2VI that you tried to deliver but could not.

Calendar year basis. You must base all entries on Forms W-2AS, W-2GU, W-2CM, W-2VI, and W-3SS on a calendar year. Use the current year form.

Magnetic media reporting. If you are required to file 250 or more Forms W-2AS, W-2GU, or W-2VI, you must file them on magnetic media. You can get specifications for furnishing this information on magnetic media by contacting the Magnetic Media Coordinator at 787-766-5574 for the Virgin Islands or 510-970-8247 for Guam and American Samoa.

If you file on magnetic media, do not file the same returns on paper.

Note: ***You are encouraged to file*** *on magnetic media (or electronically) even though you are filing fewer than 250 Forms W-2.*

You may request a waiver on **Form 8508,** Request for Waiver From Filing Information Returns on Magnetic Media. Submit Form 8508 to the IRS at least 45 days before the due date of Form W-2. See Form 8508 for filing information.

Taxpayer identification numbers. Social security numbers are used to record employee earnings for future social security and Medicare benefits. Please be sure to show the correct social security number in box d on the Form W-2AS, W-2GU, or W-2VI.

Employers use an employer identification number (EIN) (00-0000000). Employees use a social security number (000-00-0000). When you list a number, please separate the nine digits properly to show the kind of number.

Special Reporting Situations

Corrections. Use **Form W-2c,** Corrected Wage and Tax Statement, to correct errors on previously filed Forms W-2AS, W-2GU, W-2CM, or W-2VI. Generally, send **Form W-3c,** Transmittal of Corrected Wage and Tax Statements, with Forms W-2c to the SSA. Instructions are on the forms. Also, see below for information on correcting an employee's address.

If you are making an adjustment in 1999 to correct social security and Medicare taxes for a prior year, you must file **Form 941c,** Supporting Statement To Correct Information, with your **Form 941-SS,** Employer's Quarterly Federal Tax Return, or **Form 943,** Employer's Annual Tax Return for Agricultural Employees, in the return period you find the error. File Copy A of Form W-2c and W-3c with the SSA and give the employee a copy of Form W-2c for the prior year.

Employee's incorrect address on Form W-2. If you filed a Form W-2 with the SSA showing an incorrect address for the employee but all other information on the Form W-2 is correct, **do not** file Form W-2c with the SSA merely to correct the address.

However, if the address was incorrect on the Form W-2 furnished to the employee, **you must do one of the following:**

- Issue a new Form W-2 containing all correct information, including the new address. Indicate "REISSUED STATEMENT" on the new copies. **Do not** send Copy A to the SSA.
- Issue a Form W-2c to the employee showing the correct address in box b. **Do not** send copy A to the SSA.
- Reissue Form W-2 with the incorrect address to the employee in an envelope showing the correct address.

Notice to Employers in the Commonwealth of the Northern Mariana Islands

If you are an employer in the Commonwealth of the Northern Mariana Islands, you must contact the Division of Revenue and Taxation, Capital Hill, Saipan, MP 96950, to get Form W-2CM and the instructions for completing and filing that form.

General Instructions

Purpose of forms. Use Form W-3SS to transmit Form W-2AS, W-2GU, W-2CM, or W-2VI to the proper authority. Form W-2AS is used to report American Samoa wages, Form W-2GU is used to report Guam wages, Form W-2CM is used to report the Commonwealth of the Northern Mariana Islands wages, and Form W-2VI is used to report U.S. Virgin Islands wages. **Do not** use these forms to report wages subject to U.S. income tax withholding. Instead, use Form W-2 to show U.S. income tax withheld.

Who must file. Employers and other payers in American Samoa, Guam, the Commonwealth of the Northern Mariana Islands, and the Virgin Islands must report wages and withheld income, U.S. social security, and U.S. Medicare taxes to their local tax department and to the U.S. Social Security Administration (SSA).

Household employers, even those with only one household employee, must file Form W-3SS with Form W-2AS, W-2GU, W-2CM, or W-2VI. On Form W-3SS, mark the "Hshld. emp." checkbox in box b.

Where to file Copy 1. File Copy 1 of **Forms W-2AS** and **W-3SS** with the American Samoa Tax Office, Government of American Samoa, Pago Pago, AS 96799.

File Copy 1 of **Forms W-2GU** and **W-3SS** with the Department of Revenue and Taxation, Government of Guam, P.O. Box 23607, GMF, GU 96921.

File Copy 1 of **Forms W-2VI** and **W-3SS** with the V.I. Bureau of Internal Revenue, 9601 Estate Thomas, Charlotte Amalie, St. Thomas, VI 00802.

Contact the Division of Revenue and Taxation, Commonwealth of the Northern Mariana Islands for the address to send Copy 1 of **Forms W-2CM** and **W-3SS.**

Shipping and mailing. If you send more than one kind of form, please group forms of the same kind, and send them in separate groups. For example, send Forms W-2GU with one Form W-3SS and Forms W-2AS with a second Form W-3SS. Forms W-2AS, W-2GU, W-2CM, or W-2VI are printed two forms to a page. Send the whole page of Copies A and 1 even if one of the forms is blank or void. Do not staple or tape the forms together.

If you have a large number of forms with one Form W-3SS, you may send them in separate packages. Show your name and employer identification number (EIN) on each package. Number them in order (1 of 4, 2 of 4, etc.), and place Form W-3SS in package 1. Show the number of packages at the bottom of Form W-3SS. If you mail them, you must send them First Class.

Furnishing Copies B and C to employees. Furnish Copies B and C of Forms W-2AS, W-2GU, W-2CM, and W-2VI by January 31, 2000. If employment ends before December 31, 1999, you may give the copies any

DO NOT STAPLE

a Control number	33333	For Official Use Only ▶ OMB No. 1545-0008	
b Kind of Payer ▶ 941-SS ☐ Military ☐ 943 ☐ Hshld. emp. ☐ Medicare govt. emp. ☐		1 Wages, tips, other compensation	2 Income tax withheld
		3 Social security wages	4 Social security tax withheld
c Total number of Forms W-2	d Establishment number	5 Medicare wages and tips	6 Medicare tax withheld
e Employer identification number		7 Social security tips	8
f Employer's name		9 Advance EIC payments	10
		11 Nonqualified plans	12
		13	
g Employer's address and ZIP code		14	
h Other EIN used this year		15	
i Employer's state I.D. no.			
Contact person	Telephone number ( )	Fax number ( )	E-mail address

Copy 1—For Local Tax Department

Under penalties of perjury, I declare that I have examined this return and accompanying documents, and, to the best of my knowledge and belief, they are true, correct, and complete.

Signature ▶ Title ▶ Date ▶

Form **W-3SS Transmittal of Wage and Tax Statements 1999** Department of the Treasury Internal Revenue Service

time after employment ends but by January 31. If the employee asks for the form, furnish him or her the completed copies within 30 days of the request or within 30 days of the last wage payment, whichever is later. If an employee loses a form, write "REISSUED STATEMENT" on the new copy, but **do not send Copy A of the reissued statement to the SSA.**

Undeliverable forms. Keep for 4 years any employee copies of Forms W-2AS, W-2GU, W-2CM, or W-2VI that you tried to deliver but could not.

Calendar year basis. You must base all entries on Forms W-2AS, W-2GU, W-2CM, W-2VI, and W-3SS on a calendar year. Use the current year form.

Magnetic media reporting. If you are required to file 250 or more Forms W-2AS, W-2GU, or W-2VI, you must file them on magnetic media. You can get specifications for furnishing this information on magnetic media by contacting the Magnetic Media Coordinator at 787-766-5574 for the Virgin Islands or 510-970-8247 for Guam and American Samoa.

If you file on magnetic media, do not file the same returns on paper.

Note: ***You are encouraged to file*** *on magnetic media (or electronically) even though you are filing fewer than 250 Forms W-2.*

You may request a waiver on **Form 8508,** Request for Waiver From Filing Information Returns on Magnetic Media. Submit Form 8508 to the IRS at least 45 days before the due date of Form W-2. See Form 8508 for filing information.

Taxpayer identification numbers. Social security numbers are used to record employee earnings for future social security and Medicare benefits. Please be sure to show the correct social security number in box d on the Form W-2AS, W-2GU, or W-2VI.

Employers use an employer identification number (EIN) (00-0000000). Employees use a social security number (000-00-0000). When you list a number, please separate the nine digits properly to show the kind of number.

Special Reporting Situations

Corrections. Use **Form W-2c,** Corrected Wage and Tax Statement, to correct errors on previously filed Forms W-2AS, W-2GU, W-2CM, or W-2VI. Generally, send **Form W-3c,** Transmittal of Corrected Wage and Tax Statements, with Forms W-2c to the SSA. Instructions are on the forms. Also, see below for information on correcting an employee's address.

If you are making an adjustment in 1999 to correct social security and Medicare taxes for a prior year, you must file **Form 941c,** Supporting Statement To Correct Information, with your **Form 941-SS,** Employer's Quarterly Federal Tax Return, or **Form 943,** Employer's Annual Tax Return for Agricultural Employees, in the return period you find the error. File Copy A of Form W-2c and W-3c with the SSA and give the employee a copy of Form W-2c for the prior year.

Employee's incorrect address on Form W-2. If you filed a Form W-2 with the SSA showing an incorrect address for the employee but all other information on the Form W-2 is correct, **do not** file Form W-2c with the SSA merely to correct the address.

However, if the address was incorrect on the Form W-2 furnished to the employee, **you must do one of the following:**

- Issue a new Form W-2 containing all correct information, including the new address. Indicate "REISSUED STATEMENT" on the new copies. **Do not** send Copy A to the SSA.
- Issue a Form W-2c to the employee showing the correct address in box b. **Do not** send copy A to the SSA.
- Reissue Form W-2 with the incorrect address to the employee in an envelope showing the correct address.

Educational assistance programs. The $5,250 exclusion for employer-provided educational assistance applies to courses starting before June 1, 2000. However, the exclusion does not apply to graduate courses that started after June 30, 1996. Generally, a course starts on the first regular day of class. See **Pub. 508,** Educational Expenses, and **Pub. 15-A,** Employer's Supplemental Tax Guide, for more information.

Group-term life insurance. If you paid for group-term life insurance over $50,000 for an employee or a former employee, you must report the amount determined by using the table in section 5 of Pub. 15-A in boxes 1, 3, and 5 of Form W-2AS, W-2GU, W-2CM, or W-2VI. Also, show the amount in box 13 with code **C.** For employees, you must withhold social security and Medicare taxes, but not income tax. Former employees must pay the employee part of social security and Medicare taxes on premiums for group-term life insurance over $50,000 on Form 1040. You are not required to collect those taxes. However, you must report the uncollected social security tax with code **M** and the uncollected Medicare tax with code **N** in box 13 of Form W-2.

Moving expenses. For 1998 and later years, **Form 4782,** Employee Moving Expense Information, was **eliminated.** Employers are no longer required to provide this form to employees. However, employers may continue providing similar information to employees in any format they wish if they deem it helpful to employees.

Report moving expenses as follows:

- Qualified moving expenses an employer pays **to a third party on behalf of the employee** (e.g., to a moving company) and services that an employer furnishes in kind to an employee are **not reported** on Form W-2.
- Qualified moving expense reimbursements paid **directly to an employee** by an employer **are** reported only in box 13 with code **P.**
- **Nonqualified** moving expense reimbursements are reported in box 1. These amounts are subject to income tax withholding and social security and Medicare taxes.

Sick pay. Sick pay paid to an employee by a third party, such as an insurance company or trust, requires special treatment because the IRS reconciles Forms 941-SS with the Forms W-2AS, W-2GU, W-2CM, or W-2VI and Form W-3SS filed. See **Sick Pay Reporting** in Pub. 15-A for specific reporting instructions.

Terminating a business. If you terminate your business, you must provide Forms W-2AS, W-2GU, W-2CM, or W-2VI to your employees for the calendar year of termination by the due date of your final Form 941-SS (or 941) or 943. You must also file Forms W-2AS, W-2GU, W-2CM, or W-2VI with the SSA by the last day of the month that follows the due date of your final Form 941-SS (or 941) or 943. However, if any of your employees are immediately employed by a successor employer, see Rev. Proc. 96-60, 1996-2 C.B. 399. Also see Rev. Proc. 96-57, 1996-2 C.B. 389, for information on automatic extensions for furnishing Forms W-2AS, W-2GU, W-2CM, or W-2VI to employees and filing them with the SSA.

Specific Instructions for Completing Forms W-2AS, W-2GU, and W-2VI

Because the forms are read by machine, **please type entries,** if possible. **Send the entire first page of Form W-3SS with Copy A of Forms W-2AS, W-2GU, or W-2VI. Make all dollar entries without the dollar sign and comma but with the decimal point (00000.00).** If an entry does not apply to you, leave it blank. Employers in the Commonwealth of the Northern Mariana Islands should contact the local tax division for instructions on completing Forms W-2CM.

Box a—Control number. You may use this box to identify individual forms. *(Optional)*

Void. Check this box when an error is made on a Form W-2 and you are voiding it because you will complete a new Form W-2. Be careful **not to include** any amounts shown on Void forms in the totals you enter on Form W-3SS.

Box b—Employer identification number. Show the EIN assigned to you by the IRS (00-0000000). This should be the same number that you used on your Form 941-SS or 943. Do not use a prior owner's EIN. If you do not have an EIN, enter "Applied For" in box b, not your SSN. File **Form SS-4,** Application for Employer Identification Number, to get an EIN.

Box c—Employer's name, address, and ZIP code. This entry should be the same as shown on your Form 941-SS or 943.

Box d—Employee's social security number. Enter the number shown on the employee's social security card. If the employee does not have a card, he or she should apply for one by completing **Form SS-5,** Application for a Social Security Card. If the employee has applied for a card, enter "Applied For" in box d.

Boxes e and f—Employee's name and address. Enter the name as shown on the employee's social security card (first, middle initial, last). If the name does not fit, you may show first name initial, middle initial, and last name. **Do not show titles or academic degrees, such as "Dr.," "RN," or "Esq." with the name.** If the name has changed, the employee must get a corrected card from any SSA office. Use the name on the original card until you see the corrected one.

Include in the address the number, street, apt. or suite number, or P.O. Box number if mail is not delivered to a street address.

Third-party payers of sick pay filing third-party sick pay recap Forms W-2AS, W-2GU, or W-2VI must enter "Third-Party Sick Pay Recap" in place of the employee's name in box e. See **Sick Pay Reporting** in Pub. 15-A.

Box 1—Wages, tips, other compensation. Show, before any payroll deductions, the total of **(1)** wages, prizes, awards paid, **(2)** noncash payments, including certain fringe benefits, **(3)** tips reported, **(4)** group-term life insurance over $50,000, and **(5)** all other compensation. Other compensation is amounts you pay the employee from which income tax is not withheld. You may show other compensation on a separate Form W-2AS, W-2GU, or W-2VI.

Note: *Show payments to statutory employees that are subject to social security and Medicare taxes but not subject to income tax withholding in box 1 as other compensation. See* ***Circular SS,*** *Federal Tax Guide for Employers in the U.S. Virgin Islands, Guam, American Samoa, and the Commonwealth of the Northern Mariana Islands (Pub. 80), for the definition of a statutory employee.*

Box 2—Income tax withheld. Show the total amount of American Samoa, Guam, or Virgin Islands income tax withheld. Do not reduce this amount by any advance EIC payments.

Box 3—Social security wages. Show the total wages paid (before payroll deductions) subject to employee social security tax. Do not include tips. The total of boxes 3 and 7 should not be more than $72,600 (1999 maximum social security wage base). Generally, noncash payments are considered wages. (See Circular SS for more information.)

Box 4—Social security tax withheld. Show the total employee social security tax (not your share) withheld or paid by you for the employee, including social security tax on tips. Include only taxes withheld (or paid by you for the employee) for 1999 wages and social security tips. The amount shown should not exceed $4,501.20 ($72,600 × 6.2%).

Box 5—Medicare wages and tips. Show the total wages paid and tips reported subject to employee Medicare tax. There is no wage base limit for Medicare tax.

Box 6—Medicare tax withheld. Show the total employee Medicare tax (not your share) withheld or paid by you for the employee. Include only taxes for 1999 wages and tips. The rate is 1.45% of all wages.

Box 7—Social security tips. Show the amount the employee reported to you even if you did not have enough employee funds to collect the social security tax for the tips. The total of boxes 3 and 7 should not be more than $72,600 (for 1999). Report all tips in box 1 along with wages and other compensation.

Box 8—Benefits included in box 1. Use of this box is optional. You may use it to report taxable fringe benefits that are included in box 1. However, the lease value of a vehicle provided to your employee and reported in box 1 **must** be reported here or in a separate statement to your employee.

Box 9—Advance EIC payment. Forms W-2GU and W-2VI only. Show the total amount of the advance earned income credit (EIC) paid to the employee.

Box 11—Nonqualified plans. Show the amount of **distributions** to an employee from a nonqualified plan or a section 457 plan. Also include these distributions in box 1. If you did not make distributions this year, show the amount of **deferrals** (plus earnings) under a nonqualified or section 457 plan that became **taxable for social security and Medicare taxes during the year** (but were for prior year services) because the deferred amounts were no longer subject to a substantial forfeiture risk. **Do not** report in box 11 deferrals that are included in boxes 3 and/or 5 and that are for current year services.

Note: *If you made distributions and you are also reporting deferrals in box 3 and/or 5, do not complete box 11. See* ***Pub. 957,*** *Reporting Back Pay and Special Wage Payments to the Social Security Administration, and* ***Form SSA-131,*** *Employer Report of Special Wage Payments, for special reporting instructions for these and other kinds of compensation earned in prior years. However,* ***do not*** *file Form SSA-131 if contributions and distributions occur in the same year* ***and*** *the employee will* ***not*** *be age 62 or older by the end of that year.*

Box 13—Codes. Complete and code this box for all items described below. On Copy A, do not enter more than three items in box 13. If more than three items need to be reported in box 13, use a separate Form W-2AS, W-2GU, or W-2VI for additional items. You may enter more than three items on all other copies.

Use the codes shown with the dollar amount. Enter the code using capital letters. Leave at least one blank space after the code, enter the dollar amount on the same line, and use decimal points but not dollar signs or commas, e.g., D 2000.00.

Code A—Uncollected social security tax on tips. Show the employee social security tax on tips that you could **not** collect because the employee did not have enough funds from which to deduct it. Do not include this amount in box 4.

Code B—Uncollected Medicare tax on tips. Show the employee Medicare tax on tips that you could **not** collect because the employee did not have enough funds from which to deduct it. Do not include this amount in box 6.

Code C—Cost of group-term life insurance coverage over $50,000. Show the taxable amount of the cost of group-term life insurance coverage over $50,000 provided to your employee (including former employees). Also include it in boxes 1, 3, and 5.

Codes D through H and S. Use these codes to show the amount of deferrals made to the plans listed. Do not report amounts for other types of plans. The **Example** following code **H** shows how to report an elective deferral to a section 401(k) plan.

Except for section 457(b) plans (code G), report as an elective deferral only the part of the employee's salary (or other compensation) that he or she did not receive because of the deferral. For section 457(b) plans, report both elective and nonelective deferrals.

Nonelective employer contributions on behalf of employees are not elective deferrals. Nor are after-tax contributions, such as voluntary contributions to a pension plan that are deducted from an employee's pay. These amounts are not reported in box 13, but you may report them in box 14.

Code D—Elective deferrals to a section 401(k) cash or deferred arrangement. Also show the amount deferred under a SIMPLE retirement account that is part of a section 401(k) arrangement.

Code E—Elective deferrals under a section 403(b) salary reduction agreement.

Code F—Elective deferrals under a section 408(k)(6) salary reduction SEP.

Code G—Elective and nonelective deferrals to a section 457(b) deferred compensation plan for employees of state and local governments or tax-exempt organizations. Do not report section 457(f) amounts or amounts deferred under section 457(b) that are subject to a substantial risk of forfeiture.

Note: *The section 457 dollar limit should be reduced by deferrals to certain other deferred compensation plans. See section 457(c)(2).*

Code H—Elective deferrals to a section 501(c)(18)(D) tax-exempt organization plan. Be sure to include this amount in box 1 as wages. The employee will deduct the amount on his or her income tax return.

Example. For 1999, Employee A elected to defer $10,300 to a section 401(k) plan and made a voluntary after-tax contribution of $600. In addition, the employer, on Employee A's behalf, made a qualified nonelective contribution of $1,000 to the plan and a nonelective profit-sharing employer contribution of $2,000.

The total elective deferral of $10,300 is reported in box 13 with code **D** (D 10300.00). Even though the 1999 limit for elective deferrals is $10,000, the employer must report the total amount of $10,300 in box 13. Do not report the excess in box 1. The $600 voluntary after-tax contribution may be reported in box 14 but not in box 13. This is optional. The $1,000 nonelective contribution and the $2,000 nonelective profit-sharing employer contribution are not required to be reported on Form W-2AS, W-2GU, or W-2VI but may be reported in box 14.

Check "Deferred compensation" in box 15.

Code J—Nontaxable sick pay. Show any sick pay **not** includible in income because the employee contributed to the sick pay plan. If you issue a separate Form W-2 for sick pay, enter "Sick Pay" in box 13.

Code M—Uncollected social security tax on cost of group-term life insurance coverage over $50,000 (for former employees). If you provided your former employees (including retirees) more than $50,000 of group-term life insurance coverage for periods during which an employment relationship no longer exists, enter the amount of uncollected social security tax on the coverage in box 13.

Code N—Uncollected Medicare tax on cost of group-term life insurance coverage over $50,000 (for former employees). Enter any uncollected Medicare tax on the cost of group-term life insurance coverage over $50,000 for your **former employees.** See **Code M** above.

Code P—Excludable moving expense reimbursements paid directly to an employee. Show the total moving expense reimbursements you paid directly to your employee for qualified (deductible) moving expenses. See **Moving expenses** on page 4.

Code Q—Military employee basic housing, subsistence, and combat zone compensation. If you are a military employer and provide your employee with basic housing, subsistence allowances, or combat zone compensation, report it in box 13.

Code R—Employer contributions to a medical savings account (MSA). Show any employer contributions to an MSA.

Code S—Employee salary reduction contributions to a section 408(p) salary reduction SIMPLE. Show the amount deferred under a section 408(p) salary reduction SIMPLE retirement account. However, if the SIMPLE is part of a section 401(k) arrangement, use code **D.**

Code T—Adoption benefits. Show the total amount you paid or reimbursed your employee for qualified adoption expenses furnished to your employee under an adoption assistance program.

Box 14—Other. You may use this box for any other information you want to give your employee, such as health insurance premiums deducted, union dues, voluntary after-tax contributions, or nontaxable income. Clearly label each entry.

Box 15—Checkboxes. Check the boxes that apply.

- ***Statutory employee.*** Check this box for statutory employees whose earnings are subject to social security and Medicare taxes but **not** subject to income tax withholding. See Circular SS for more information on statutory employees. Do not check this box for common law employees.
- ***Pension plan.*** Check this box if the employee was an active participant (for any part of the year) in any of the following:

1. A qualified plan described in section 401(a) (including a 401(k) plan).

2. An annuity plan described in section 403(a).

3. An annuity contract or custodial account described in section 403(b).

4. A simplified employee pension (SEP) plan described in section 408(k).

5. A SIMPLE retirement account described in section 408(p).

6. A trust described in section 501(c)(18).

7. A plan for Federal, state, or local government employees or by an agency or instrumentality thereof (other than a section 457 plan).

See **Pub. 1602,** General Rules for Individual Retirement Arrangements Under the Tax Reform Act of 1986, for information on who qualifies as an active participant. **Do not** check this box for contributions made to a nonqualified or section 457 plan. Also check the deferred compensation box.

- ***Deferred compensation.*** Check this box if the employee has made an elective deferral to a section 401(k), 403(b), 408(k)(6), 408(p), or 501(c)(18)(D) retirement plan. Also check this box for an elective or nonelective deferral to a section 457(b) plan. Do not check this box for a nonqualified deferred compensation plan. See also, **Codes D through H and S** under **Box 13.**

Specific Instructions for Completing Form W-3SS

How to complete Form W-3SS. Please type or print entries. Make all entries without the dollar sign and comma but with the decimal point (00000.00). If an entry does not apply, leave it blank.

Box a—Control number. This box is for numbering the whole transmittal. *(Optional)*

Box b—Kind of Payer. Mark only **one** box. If you have more than one type of Form W-2AS, W-2GU, W-2CM, or W-2VI, send each type with a separate Form W-3SS.

941-SS. Mark this box if you file Form 941-SS and no other category applies.

Military. Mark this box if you are a military employer sending Forms W-2AS, W-2GU, W-2CM, or W-2VI for members of the uniformed services.

943. Mark this box if you file Form 943 and are sending forms for agricultural employees. For nonagricultural employees, send their Forms W-2AS, W-2GU, W-2CM, or W-2VI with a separate Form W-3SS.

Hshld. emp. Mark this box if you are a household employer sending Form W-2AS, W-2GU, W-2CM, or W-2VI for household employees.

Medicare government employee. Mark this box if you are a U.S. or a U.S. Virgin Islands government employer with employees subject only to the 1.45% Medicare tax.

Box c—Total number of Forms W-2. Show the number of completed individual Forms W-2AS, W-2GU, W-2CM, or W-2VI filed with this Form W-3SS. Do not count Void forms.

Box d—Establishment number. You may use this box to identify separate establishments in your business. You may file a separate Form W-3SS, with Forms W-2AS, W-2GU, W-2CM, or W-2VI, for each establishment even if they all have the same EIN, or you may use a single Form W-3SS for all Forms W-2 of the same type.

Box e—Employer identification number. If you received a preprinted label from the IRS with Circular SS (Pub. 80), place the label inside the brackets in boxes e, f, and g. Make any necessary corrections on the label. If you are not using a preprinted IRS label, enter the nine-digit number assigned to you by the IRS. The number should be the same as shown on your Form 941-SS or 943 and in the following format: 00-0000000. **Do not use a prior owner's EIN.** If you do not have an EIN, see **Box b** on page 4.

Box f—Employer's name. If you are not using the printed IRS label, enter the same name as shown on your Form 941-SS or 943.

Box g—Employer's address and ZIP code. If you are not using the preprinted IRS label, enter your address.

Box h—Other EIN used this year. If you have used an EIN (including a prior owner's EIN) on Form 941-SS or 943 submitted for 1999 that is different from the EIN reported in box e on this form, enter the other EIN used.

Contact person, telephone number, fax number, and e-mail address. Please enter this information for use by the SSA if questions arise during processing.

Boxes 1 through 7. Enter the totals reported in boxes 1 through 7 of Forms W-2AS, W-2GU, W-2CM, or W-2VI being transmitted with this Form W-3SS.

Box 9—Advance EIC payments. To be shown for Forms W-2GU and W-2VI only. Enter the total amount of EIC payments shown.

Box 11—Nonqualified plans. Enter the total amounts reported in box 11 on Forms W-2AS, W-2GU, W-2CM, or W-2VI being transmitted with this Form W-3SS.

Box 13. Third-party payers of sick pay filing third-party sick pay recap Forms W-2 and W-3SS must enter "Third-Party Sick Pay Recap" in this box. See **Sick Pay Reporting** in Pub. 15-A for details.

Signature. The signature on Copies A and 1 of Form W-3SS should be an **original** (not a copy).

Privacy Act and Paperwork Reduction Act Notice. We ask for the information on Forms W-2AS, W-2GU, W-2CM, W-2VI, and W-3SS to carry out the Internal Revenue laws of the United States. We need it to figure and collect the right amount of tax. Section 6051 and its regulations require you to furnish wage and tax statements to employees and to the Social Security Administration. Section 6109 requires you to provide your employer identification number. Routine uses of this information include giving it to the Department of Justice for civil and criminal litigation, and to cities, states, the District of Columbia, and U.S. possessions for use in administering their tax laws. We may also give this information to other countries pursuant to tax treaties. If you fail to provide this information in a timely manner, you may be subject to penalties.

You are not required to provide the information requested on a form that is subject to the Paperwork Reduction Act unless the form displays a valid OMB control number. Books or records relating to a form or its instructions must be retained as long as their contents may become material in the administration of any Internal Revenue law. Generally, tax returns and return information are confidential, as required by section 6103.

The time needed to complete and file these forms will vary depending on individual circumstances. The estimated average times are:

Form W-2AS — 22 minutes
Form W-2GU — 23 minutes
Form W-2VI — 22 minutes
Form W-3SS — 26 minutes

If you have comments concerning the accuracy of these time estimates or suggestions for making these forms simpler, we would be happy to hear from you. You can write to the Tax Forms Committee, Western Area Distribution Center, Rancho Cordova, CA 95743-0001. **DO NOT** send these tax forms to this address. Instead, see **Where To File Copy A** on page 1.

Form W-4 (1999)

Purpose. Complete Form W-4 so your employer can withhold the correct Federal income tax from your pay. Because your tax situation may change, you may want to refigure your withholding each year.

Exemption from withholding. If you are exempt, complete only lines 1, 2, 3, 4, and 7, and sign the form to validate it. Your exemption for 1999 expires February 16, 2000.

Note: *You cannot claim exemption from withholding if (1) your income exceeds $700 and includes more than $250 of unearned income (e.g., interest and dividends) and (2) another person can claim you as a dependent on their tax return.*

Basic instructions. If you are not exempt, complete the Personal Allowances Worksheet. The worksheets on page 2 adjust your withholding allowances based on itemized deductions, adjustments to income, or two-earner/two-job situations. Complete all worksheets that apply. They will help you figure the number of withholding allowances you are entitled to claim. **However, you may claim fewer allowances.**

Child tax and higher education credits. For details on adjusting withholding for these and other credits, see **Pub. 919,** Is My Withholding Correct for 1999?

Head of household. Generally, you may claim head of household filing status on your tax return only if you are unmarried and pay more than 50% of the costs of keeping up a home for yourself and your dependent(s) or other qualifying individuals. See line **E** below.

Nonwage income. If you have a large amount of nonwage income, such as interest or dividends, you should consider making estimated tax payments using Form 1040-ES. Otherwise, you may owe additional tax.

Two earners/two jobs. If you have a working spouse or more than one job, figure the total number of allowances you are entitled to claim on all jobs using worksheets from only one Form W-4. Your withholding will usually be most accurate when all allowances are claimed on the Form W-4 prepared for the highest paying job and zero allowances are claimed for the others.

Check your withholding. After your Form W-4 takes effect, use Pub. 919 to see how the dollar amount you are having withheld compares to your estimated total annual tax. Get Pub. 919 especially if you used the Two-Earner/Two-Job Worksheet and your earnings exceed $150,000 (Single) or $200,000 (Married).

Recent name change? If your name on line 1 differs from that shown on your social security card, call 1-800-772-1213 for a new social security card.

Personal Allowances Worksheet

A Enter "1" for **yourself** if no one else can claim you as a dependent . . . . A ______

B Enter "1" if:
- You are single and have only one job; or
- You are married, have only one job, and your spouse does not work; or
- Your wages from a second job or your spouse's wages (or the total of both) are $1,000 or less.

. . . B ______

C Enter "1" for your **spouse.** But, you may choose to enter -0- if you are married and have either a working spouse or more than one job. (This may help you avoid having too little tax withheld.). . . . . C ______

D Enter number of **dependents** (other than your spouse or yourself) you will claim on your tax return . . . . D ______

E Enter "1" if you will file as **head of household** on your tax return (see conditions under **Head of household** above) . E ______

F Enter "1" if you have at least $1,500 of **child or dependent care expenses** for which you plan to claim a credit . . F ______

G **Child Tax Credit:** • If your total income will be between $20,000 and $50,000 ($23,000 and $63,000 if married), enter "1" for each eligible child. • If your total income will be between $50,000 and $80,000 ($63,000 and $115,000 if married), enter "1" if you have two eligible children, enter "2" if you have three or four eligible children, or enter "3" if you have five or more eligible children . . G ______

H Add lines A through G and enter total here. **Note:** This amount may be different from the number of exemptions you claim on your return. ▶ H ______

For accuracy, complete all worksheets that apply.
- If you plan to **itemize or claim adjustments to income** and want to reduce your withholding, see the Deductions and Adjustments Worksheet on page 2.
- If you are **single,** have **more than one job** and your combined earnings from all jobs exceed $32,000, OR if you are **married** and have a **working spouse or more than one job** and the combined earnings from all jobs exceed $55,000, see the Two-Earner/Two-Job Worksheet on page 2 to avoid having too little tax withheld.
- If **neither** of the above situations applies, **stop here** and enter the number from line H on line 5 of Form W-4 below.

Cut here and give the certificate to your employer. Keep the top part for your records.

Form **W-4** | **Employee's Withholding Allowance Certificate** | OMB No. 1545-0010 **1999**

Department of the Treasury Internal Revenue Service

▶ **For Privacy Act and Paperwork Reduction Act Notice, see page 2.**

1 Type or print your first name and middle initial	Last name	2 Your social security number
Home address (number and street or rural route)	3 ☐ Single ☐ Married ☐ Married, but withhold at higher Single rate. **Note:** *If married, but legally separated, or spouse is a nonresident alien, check the Single box.*	
City or town, state, and ZIP code	4 If your last name differs from that on your social security card, check here. **You** must call 1-800-772-1213 for a new card . . . ▶ ☐	

5 Total number of allowances you are claiming (from line H above or from the worksheets on page 2 if they apply) . **5** ______

6 Additional amount, if any, you want withheld from each paycheck . . . . **6** $ ______

7 I claim exemption from withholding for 1999, and I certify that I meet **BOTH** of the following conditions for exemption:
- Last year I had a right to a refund of **ALL** Federal income tax withheld because I had **NO** tax liability **AND**
- This year I expect a refund of **ALL** Federal income tax withheld because I expect to have **NO** tax liability.

If you meet both conditions, write "EXEMPT" here . . . . ▶ **7** ______

Under penalties of perjury, I certify that I am entitled to the number of withholding allowances claimed on this certificate, or I am entitled to claim exempt status.

Employee's signature (Form is not valid unless you sign it) ▶ **Date** ▶

8 Employer's name and address (Employer: Complete 8 and 10 only if sending to the IRS)	9 Office code (optional)	10 Employer identification number

Cat. No. 10220Q

Form W-4 (1999) Page **2**

Deductions and Adjustments Worksheet

Note: *Use this worksheet only if you plan to itemize deductions or claim adjustments to income on your 1999 tax return.*

1	Enter an estimate of your 1999 itemized deductions. These include qualifying home mortgage interest, charitable contributions, state and local taxes (but not sales taxes), medical expenses in excess of 7.5% of your income, and miscellaneous deductions. (For 1999, you may have to reduce your itemized deductions if your income is over $126,600 ($63,300 if married filing separately). Get Pub. 919 for details.)	1	$
2	Enter: { $7,200 if married filing jointly or qualifying widow(er); $6,350 if head of household; $4,300 if single; $3,600 if married filing separately }	2	$
3	**Subtract** line 2 from line 1. If line 2 is greater than line 1, enter -0-	3	$
4	Enter an estimate of your 1999 adjustments to income, including alimony, deductible IRA contributions, and student loan interest . .	4	$
5	**Add** lines 3 and 4 and enter the total	5	$
6	Enter an estimate of your 1999 nonwage income (such as dividends or interest)	6	$
7	**Subtract** line 6 from line 5. Enter the result, but not less than -0-	7	$
8	**Divide** the amount on line 7 by $3,000 and enter the result here. Drop any fraction	8	
9	Enter the number from Personal Allowances Worksheet, line H, on page 1	9	
10	**Add** lines 8 and 9 and enter the total here. If you plan to use the Two-Earner/Two-Job Worksheet, also enter this total on line 1 below. Otherwise, **stop here** and enter this total on Form W-4, line 5, on page 1	10	

Two-Earner/Two-Job Worksheet

Note: *Use this worksheet only if the instructions for line H on page 1 direct you here.*

1	Enter the number from line H on page 1 (or from line 10 above if you used the Deductions and Adjustments Worksheet)	1	
2	Find the number in **Table 1** below that applies to the **LOWEST** paying job and enter it here	2	
3	If line 1 is **GREATER THAN OR EQUAL TO** line 2, subtract line 2 from line 1. Enter the result here (if zero, enter -0-) and on Form W-4, line 5, on page 1. **DO NOT** use the rest of this worksheet	3	

Note: *If line 1 is **LESS THAN** line 2, enter -0- on Form W-4, line 5, on page 1. Complete lines 4–9 to calculate the additional withholding amount necessary to avoid a year end tax bill.*

4	Enter the number from line 2 of this worksheet . . . . 4 ______		
5	Enter the number from line 1 of this worksheet . . . . 5 ______		
6	**Subtract** line 5 from line 4	6	
7	Find the amount in **Table 2** below that applies to the **HIGHEST** paying job and enter it here	7	$
8	**Multiply** line 7 by line 6 and enter the result here. This is the additional annual withholding amount needed	8	$
9	Divide line 8 by the number of pay periods remaining in 1999. (For example, divide by 26 if you are paid every other week and you complete this form in December 1998.) Enter the result here and on Form W-4, line 6, page 1. This is the additional amount to be withheld from each paycheck	9	$

Table 1: Two-Earner/Two-Job Worksheet

Married Filing Jointly				All Others			
If wages from **LOWEST** paying job are—	Enter on line 2 above	If wages from **LOWEST** paying job are—	Enter on line 2 above	If wages from **LOWEST** paying job are—	Enter on line 2 above	If wages from **LOWEST** paying job are—	Enter on line 2 above
$0 - $4,000	0	40,001 - 45,000	8	$0 - $5,000	0	65,001 - 80,000	8
4,001 - 7,000	1	45,001 - 54,000	9	5,001 - 11,000	1	80,001 - 100,000	9
7,001 - 12,000	2	54,001 - 62,000	10	11,001 - 16,000	2	100,001 and over	10
12,001 - 18,000	3	62,001 - 70,000	11	16,001 - 21,000	3		
18,001 - 24,000	4	70,001 - 85,000	12	21,001 - 25,000	4		
24,001 - 28,000	5	85,001 - 100,000	13	25,001 - 40,000	5		
28,001 - 35,000	6	100,001 - 110,000	14	40,001 - 50,000	6		
35,001 - 40,000	7	110,001 and over	15	50,001 - 65,000	7		

Table 2: Two-Earner/Two-Job Worksheet

Married Filing Jointly		All Others	
If wages from **HIGHEST** paying job are—	Enter on line 7 above	If wages from **HIGHEST** paying job are—	Enter on line 7 above
$0 - $50,000	$400	$0 - $30,000	$400
50,001 - 100,000	770	30,001 - 60,000	770
100,001 - 130,000	850	60,001 - 120,000	850
130,001 - 240,000	1,000	120,001 - 250,000	1,000
240,001 and over	1,100	250,001 and over	1,100

Privacy Act and Paperwork Reduction Act Notice. We ask for the information on this form to carry out the Internal Revenue laws of the United States. The Internal Revenue Code requires this information under sections 3402(f)(2)(A) and 6109 and their regulations. Failure to provide a **properly** completed form will result in your being treated as a single person who claims no withholding allowances; **providing fraudulent information may also subject you to penalties.** Routine uses of this information include giving it to the Department of Justice for civil and criminal litigation and to cities, states, and the District of Columbia for use in administering their tax laws.

You are not required to provide the information requested on a form that is subject to the Paperwork Reduction Act unless the form displays a valid OMB control number. Books or records relating to a form or its instructions must be retained as long as their contents may become material in the administration of any Internal Revenue law. Generally, tax returns and return information are confidential, as required by Code section 6103.

The time needed to complete this form will vary depending on individual circumstances. The estimated average time is: **Recordkeeping** 46 min., **Learning about the law or the form** 10 min., **Preparing the form** 1 hr., 10 min. If you have comments concerning the accuracy of these time estimates or suggestions for making this form simpler, we would be happy to hear from you. You can write to the Tax Forms Committee, Western Area Distribution Center, Rancho Cordova, CA 95743-0001. **DO NOT** send the tax form to this address. Instead, give it to your employer.

Form **941** (Rev. January 1999) Department of the Treasury Internal Revenue Service

Employer's Quarterly Federal Tax Return

▶ **See separate instructions for information on completing this return.**

Please type or print.

Enter state code for state in which deposits were made ONLY if different from state in address to the right ▶ (see page 2 of instructions).

Name (as distinguished from trade name) | Date quarter ended

Trade name, if any | Employer identification number

Address (number and street) | City, state, and ZIP code

OMB No. 1545-0029

T
FF
FD
FP
I
T

1 1 1 1 1 1 1 1 1 1 2 3 3 3 3 3 3 3 3 4 4 4 5 5 5

If address is different from prior return, check here ▶ ☐ IRS Use

6 7 8 8 8 8 8 8 8 8 9 9 9 9 9 10 10 10 10 10 10 10 10 10 10

If you do not have to file returns in the future, check here ▶ ☐ and enter date final wages paid ▶

If you are a seasonal employer, see **Seasonal employers** on page 1 of the instructions and check here ▶ ☐

1	Number of employees in the pay period that includes March 12th . ▶ 1			
2	Total wages and tips, plus other compensation		2	
3	Total income tax withheld from wages, tips, and sick pay		3	
4	Adjustment of withheld income tax for preceding quarters of calendar year		4	
5	Adjusted total of income tax withheld (line 3 as adjusted by line 4—see instructions)		5	
6	Taxable social security wages	6a ___ × 12.4% (.124) =	6b	
	Taxable social security tips	6c ___ × 12.4% (.124) =	6d	
7	Taxable Medicare wages and tips . . .	7a ___ × 2.9% (.029) =	7b	
8	Total social security and Medicare taxes (add lines 6b, 6d, and 7b). Check here if wages are not subject to social security and/or Medicare tax . . . ▶ ☐		8	
9	Adjustment of social security and Medicare taxes (see instructions for required explanation) Sick Pay $ ______ ± Fractions of Cents $ ______ ± Other $ ______ =		9	
10	Adjusted total of social security and Medicare taxes (line 8 as adjusted by line 9—see instructions)		10	
11	**Total taxes** (add lines 5 and 10)		11	
12	Advance earned income credit (EIC) payments made to employees		12	
13	Net taxes (subtract line 12 from line 11). **If $1,000 or more, this must equal line 17, column (d) below (or line D of Schedule B (Form 941))**		13	
14	Total deposits for quarter, including overpayment applied from a prior quarter		14	
15	**Balance due** (subtract line 14 from line 13). See instructions		15	

16 **Overpayment.** If line 14 is more than line 13, enter excess here ▶ $ ______
and check if to be: ☐ Applied to next return **OR** ☐ Refunded.

- **All filers:** If line 13 is less than $1,000, you need not complete line 17 or Schedule B (Form 941).
- **Semiweekly schedule depositors:** Complete Schedule B (Form 941) and check here . . . ▶ ☐
- **Monthly schedule depositors:** Complete line 17, columns (a) through (d), and check here . . . ▶ ☐

17 Monthly Summary of Federal Tax Liability. Do not complete if you were a semiweekly schedule depositor.

(a) First month liability	(b) Second month liability	(c) Third month liability	(d) Total liability for quarter

Sign Here Under penalties of perjury, I declare that I have examined this return, including accompanying schedules and statements, and to the best of my knowledge and belief, it is true, correct, and complete.

Signature ▶ Print Your Name and Title ▶ Date ▶

For Privacy Act and Paperwork Reduction Act Notice, see back of form. Cat. No. 17001Z Form **941** (Rev. 1-99)

Form 941 (Rev. 1-99) Page **2**

Where to file. In the list below, find the state where your legal residence, principal place of business, office, or agency is located. Send your return to the **Internal Revenue Service** at the address listed for your location. No street address is needed. **Note:** *Where you file depends on whether or not you are including a payment.*

Florida, Georgia, South Carolina

Return without payment: Atlanta, GA 39901-0005

Return with payment: P.O. Box 105703, Atlanta, GA 30348-5703

New Jersey, New York (New York City and counties of Nassau, Rockland, Suffolk, and Westchester)

Return without payment: Holtsville, NY 00501-0005

Return with payment: P.O. Box 416, Newark, NJ 07101-0416

New York (all other counties), Connecticut, Maine, Massachusetts, New Hampshire, Rhode Island, Vermont

Return without payment: Andover, MA 05501-0005

Return with payment: P.O. Box 371493, Pittsburgh, PA 15250-7493

Illinois, Iowa, Minnesota, Missouri, Wisconsin

Return without payment: Kansas City, MO 64999-0005

Return with payment: P.O. Box 970007, St. Louis, MO 63197-0007

Delaware, District of Columbia, Maryland, Pennsylvania, Virginia

Return without payment: Philadelphia, PA 19255-0005

Return with payment: P.O. Box 8786, Philadelphia, PA 19162-8786

Indiana, Kentucky, Michigan, Ohio, West Virginia

Return without payment: Cincinnati, OH 45999-0005

Return with payment: P.O. Box 7329, Chicago, IL 60680-7329

Kansas, New Mexico, Oklahoma, Texas

Return without payment: Austin, TX 73301-0005

Return with payment: P.O. Box 970013, St. Louis, MO 63197-0013

Alaska, Arizona, California (counties of Alpine, Amador, Butte, Calaveras, Colusa, Contra Costa, Del Norte, El Dorado, Glenn, Humboldt, Lake, Lassen, Marin, Mendocino, Modoc, Napa, Nevada, Placer, Plumas, Sacramento, San Joaquin, Shasta, Sierra, Siskiyou, Solano, Sonoma, Sutter, Tehama, Trinity, Yolo, and Yuba), Colorado, Idaho, Montana, Nebraska, Nevada, North Dakota, Oregon, South Dakota, Utah, Washington, Wyoming

Return without payment: Ogden, UT 84201-0005

Return with payment: P.O. Box 7922, San Francisco, CA 94120-7922

California (all other counties), Hawaii

Return without payment: Fresno, CA 93888-0005

Return with payment: P.O. Box 60407, Los Angeles, CA 90060-0407

Alabama, Arkansas, Louisiana, Mississippi, North Carolina, Tennessee

Return without payment: Memphis, TN 37501-0005

Return with payment: P.O. Box 70503, Charlotte, NC 28272-0503

If you have no legal residence or principal place of business in any state

All returns: Philadelphia, PA 19255-0005

Privacy Act and Paperwork Reduction Act Notice. We ask for the information on this form to carry out the Internal Revenue laws of the United States. We need it to figure and collect the right amount of tax. Subtitle C, Employment Taxes, of the Internal Revenue Code imposes employment taxes on wages, including income tax withholding. This form is used to determine the amount of the taxes that you owe. Section 6011 requires you to provide the requested information if the tax is applicable to you. Section 6109 requires you to provide your employer identification number (EIN). Routine uses of this information include giving it to the Department of Justice for civil and criminal litigation, and to cities, states, and the District of Columbia for use in administering their tax laws. If you fail to provide this information in a timely manner, you may be subject to penalties and interest.

You are not required to provide the information requested on a form that is subject to the Paperwork Reduction Act unless the form displays a valid OMB control number. Books and records relating to a form or instructions must be retained as long as their contents may become material in the administration of any Internal Revenue law. Generally, tax returns and return information are confidential, as required by section 6103.

The time needed to complete and file this form will vary depending on individual circumstances. The estimated average time is:

For Form 941:

Recordkeeping	11 hr., 44 min.
Learning about the law or the form	40 min.
Preparing the form	1 hr., 47 min.
Copying, assembling, and sending the form to the IRS	16 min.

For Form 941TeleFile:

Recordkeeping	5 hr., 1 min.
Learning about the law or the Tax Record	6 min.
Preparing the Tax Record	11 min.
TeleFile phone call	11 min.

If you have comments concerning the accuracy of these time estimates or suggestions for making this form simpler, we would be happy to hear from you. You can write to the Tax Forms Committee, Western Area Distribution Center, Rancho Cordova, CA 95743-0001. **DO NOT** send the tax form to this address.

Form 941 Payment Voucher

Purpose of Form

Complete Form 941-V if you are making a payment with **Form 941,** Employer's Quarterly Federal Tax Return. We will use the completed voucher to credit your payment more promptly and accurately, and to improve our service to you.

If you have your return prepared by a third party and make a payment with that return, please provide this payment voucher to the return preparer.

Making Payments With Form 941

Make payments with Form 941 only if:

1. Your net taxes for the quarter (line 13 on Form 941) are less than $1,000 or

2. You are a monthly schedule depositor making a payment in accordance with the **accuracy of deposits** rule. (See section 11 of **Circular E,** Employer's Tax Guide, for details.) This amount may be $1,000 or more.

Otherwise, you must deposit the amount at an authorized financial institution or by electronic funds transfer. (See section 11 of Circular E for deposit instructions.) Do not use the Form 941-V payment voucher to make Federal tax deposits.

Caution: *If you pay amounts with Form 941 that should have been deposited, you may be subject to a penalty. See Circular E.*

Specific Instructions

Box 1—Amount paid. Enter the amount paid with Form 941.

Box 2. Enter the first four characters of your name as follows:

- **Individuals (sole proprietors, estates).** Use the first four letters of your last name (as shown in box 5).
- **Corporations.** Use the first four characters (letters or numbers) of your business name (as shown in box 5). Omit "The" if followed by more than one word.
- **Partnerships.** Use the first four characters of your trade name. If no trade name, enter the first four letters of the last name of the first listed partner.

Box 3—Employer identification number (EIN). If you do not have an EIN, apply for one on **Form SS-4,** Application for Employer Identification Number, and write "Applied for" and the date you applied in this entry space.

Box 4—Tax period. Darken the capsule identifying the quarter for which the payment is made. Darken only one capsule.

Box 5—Name and address. Enter your name and address as shown on Form 941.

- Make your check or money order payable to the United States Treasury. Be sure to enter your EIN, "Form 941," and the tax period on your check or money order. Do not send cash. Please do not staple this voucher or your payment to the return or to each other.
- Detach the completed voucher and send it with your payment and Form 941 to the address provided on the back of Form 941.

(Detach here)

Form 941-V
Department of the Treasury
Internal Revenue Service

Form 941 Payment Voucher

▶ Use this voucher when making a payment with your return.

OMB No. 1545-0029

1999

1 Enter the amount of the payment you are making
▶ $.

2 Enter the first four letters of your last name (business name if corporation or partnership)

3 Enter your employer identification number

4 Tax period

1st Quarter	3rd Quarter
2nd Quarter	4th Quarter

5 Enter your business name (individual name if sole proprietor)

Enter your address

Enter your city, state, and ZIP code

For Privacy Act and Paperwork Reduction Act Notice, see back of Form 941.

Form **940**

Department of the Treasury
Internal Revenue Service (99)

Employer's Annual Federal Unemployment (FUTA) Tax Return

▶ **See separate instructions for information on completing this return.**

OMB No. 1545-0028

1998

T	
FF	
FD	
FP	
I	
T	

Name (as distinguished from trade name) — Calendar year

Trade name, if any

Address and ZIP code — Employer identification number

A	Are you required to pay unemployment contributions to only one state? (If "No," skip questions B and C.) .	☐ **Yes**	☐ **No**
B	Did you pay all state unemployment contributions by February 1, 1999? ((1) If you deposited your total FUTA tax when due, check "Yes" if you paid all state unemployment contributions by February 10. (2) If a 0% experience rate is granted, check "Yes." (3) If "No," skip question C.)	☐ **Yes**	☐ **No**
C	Were all wages that were taxable for FUTA tax also taxable for your state's unemployment tax?	☐ **Yes**	☐ **No**

If you answered "No" to any of these questions, you must file Form 940. If you answered "Yes" to all the questions, you may file Form 940-EZ, which is a simplified version of Form 940. (Successor employers see **Special credit for successor employers** on page 3 of the instructions.) You can get Form 940-EZ by calling 1-800-TAX-FORM (1-800-829-3676) or from the IRS's Internet Web Site at **www.irs.ustreas.gov.**

If you will not have to file returns in the future, check here, and complete and sign the return . . . . ▶ ☐
If this is an Amended Return, check here . . . . ▶ ☐

Part I Computation of Taxable Wages

1	Total payments (including payments shown on lines 2 and 3) during the calendar year for services of employees			**1**	
2	Exempt payments. (Explain all exempt payments, attaching additional sheets if necessary.) ▶	**2**			
3	Payments for services of more than $7,000. Enter only amounts over the first $7,000 paid to each employee. Do not include any exempt payments from line 2. The $7,000 amount is the Federal wage base. Your state wage base may be different. **Do not use your state wage limitation** .	**3**			
4	Total exempt payments (add lines 2 and 3)			**4**	
5	**Total taxable wages** (subtract line 4 from line 1) . . . . ▶			**5**	

Be sure to complete both sides of this return, and sign in the space provided on the back.

For Privacy Act and Paperwork Reduction Act Notice, see separate instructions. Cat. No. 11234O Form **940** (1998)

DETACH HERE

Form **940-V**

Department of the Treasury
Internal Revenue Service

Form 940 Payment Voucher

Use this voucher only when making a payment with your return.

OMB No. 1545-0028

1998

Complete boxes 1, 2, 3, and 4. Do not send cash, and do not staple your payment to this voucher. Make your check or money order payable to the "United States Treasury". Be sure to enter your employer identification number, "Form 940", and "1998" on your payment.

1 Enter the amount of the payment you are making	**2** Enter the first four letters of your last name (business name if partnership or corporation)	**3** Enter your employer identification number
▶ $		

Instructions for Box 2

—Individuals (sole proprietors, trusts, and estates)—Enter the first four letters of your last name.

—Corporations and partnerships—Enter the first four characters of your business name (omit "The" if followed by more than one word).

4 Enter your business name (individual name for sole proprietors)

Enter your address

Enter your city, state, and ZIP code

Form 940 (1998) Page **2**

Part II **Tax Due or Refund**

1	Gross FUTA tax. Multiply the wages in Part I, line 5, by .062	1	
2	Maximum credit. Multiply the wages in Part I, line 5, by .054 . . . | 2 |		
3	**Computation of tentative credit (Note:** *All taxpayers must complete the applicable columns.*)		

(a) Name of state	(b) State reporting number(s) as shown on employer's state contribution returns	(c) Taxable payroll (as defined in state act)	(d) State experience rate period From	To	(e) State experience rate	(f) Contributions if rate had been 5.4% (col. (c) x .054)	(g) Contributions payable at experience rate (col. (c) x col. (e))	(h) Additional credit (col. (f) minus col.(g)). If 0 or less, enter -0-.	(i) Contributions paid to state by 940 due date
3a Totals . . . ▶									

3b	**Total tentative credit** (add line 3a, columns (h) and (i) only—for late payments also see the instructions for Part II, line 6 . . . . ▶		
4			
5			
6	**Credit:** Enter the smaller of the amount in Part II, line 2 or line 3b; or amount from the worksheet in the line 6 instructions	6	
7	**Total FUTA tax** (subtract line 6 from line 1). If the result is over $100, also complete Part III . .	7	
8	Total FUTA tax deposited for the year, including any overpayment applied from a prior year . .	8	
9	**Balance due** (subtract line 8 from line 7). Pay to the "United States Treasury". If you owe more than $100, see "Depositing FUTA Tax" on page 3 of the instructions . . . . ▶	9	
10	**Overpayment** (subtract line 7 from line 8). Check if it is to be: ☐ **Applied to next return** or ☐ **Refunded** . . . . ▶	10	

Part III **Record of Quarterly Federal Unemployment Tax Liability** *(Do not include state liability.)* Complete only if line 7 is over $100. See page 6 of the instructions.

Quarter	First (Jan. 1–Mar. 31)	Second (Apr. 1–June 30)	Third (July 1–Sept. 30)	Fourth (Oct. 1–Dec. 31)	Total for year
Liability for quarter					

Under penalties of perjury, I declare that I have examined this return, including accompanying schedules and statements, and, to the best of my knowledge and belief, it is true, correct, and complete, and that no part of any payment made to a state unemployment fund claimed as a credit was, or is to be, deducted from the payments to employees.

Signature ▶ **Title (Owner, etc.)** ▶ **Date** ▶

Form **945**

Department of the Treasury
Internal Revenue Service

Annual Return of Withheld Federal Income Tax

▶ For withholding reported on Forms 1099 and W-2G.

▶ See separate instructions. For more information on income tax withholding, see Circular E.

Please type or print.

OMB No. 1545-1430

1998

IRS USE ONLY
T
FF
FD
FP
I
T

Enter state code for state in which deposits were made only if different from state in address to the right (see page 3 of instructions). ▶ ☐

Name (as distinguished from trade name) — Employer identification number

Trade name, if any

Address (number and street) — City, state, and ZIP code

If address is different from prior return, check here ▶ ☐

IRS Use

If you do not have to file returns in the future, check here ▶ ☐ and enter date final payments paid ▶ ....

1	Federal income tax withheld from pensions, annuities, IRAs, gambling winnings, etc.	1	
2	Backup withholding	2	
3	Adjustment to correct administrative errors (see instructions)	3	
4	**Total taxes.** If $500 or more, this must equal line 8M below or line M of Form 945-A	4	
5	Total deposits for 1998 from your records, including overpayment applied from a prior year	5	
6	**Balance due** (subtract line 5 from line 4). See instructions	6	

7 **Overpayment.** If line 4 is less than line 5, enter overpayment here ▶ $ ____________ and check if to be:

☐ Applied to next return **OR** ☐ Refunded

- **All filers:** If line 4 is less than $500, you need not complete line 8 or Form 945-A.
- **Semiweekly schedule depositors:** Complete Form 945-A and check here ▶ ☐
- **Monthly schedule depositors:** Complete line 8, entries A through M, and check here ▶ ☐

8 Monthly Summary of Federal Tax Liability. Do not complete if you are a semiweekly schedule depositor.

	Tax liability for month		Tax liability for month		Tax liability for month
A January		F June		K November	
B February		G July		L December	
C March		H August		M Total liability for year (add entries A through L)	
D April		I September			
E May		J October			

Sign Here

Under penalties of perjury, I declare that I have examined this return, including accompanying schedules and statements, and to the best of my knowledge and belief, it is true, correct, and complete.

Signature ▶ ____________ Date ▶ ____________

Print Your Name and Title ▶ Telephone Number (optional) ▶

For Privacy Act and Paperwork Reduction Act Notice, see separate instructions. Cat. No. 14584B Form **945** (1998)

Form 945-V
Payment Voucher

Purpose of Form

We will credit your payment more promptly and accurately, and improve our service to you if you use Form 945-V to make a payment with **Form 945,** Annual Return of Withheld Federal Income Tax.

Making Payments With Form 945

Make payments with your 1998 Form 945 only if:

1. Your total taxes for the year (line 4 on Form 945) are less than $500 or

2. You are a monthly schedule depositor making a payment in accordance with the **Accuracy of Deposits** rule (see section 11 of **Circular E,** Employer's Tax Guide, for details). This payment may exceed $500.

Otherwise, you are required to deposit the payment at an authorized financial institution or by electronic funds transfer (see section 11 of Circular E for deposit instructions). Do not use the Form 945-V payment voucher to make Federal tax deposits.

Caution: *If you make payments with Form 945 that should have been deposited, you may be subject to a penalty. See Circular E.*

Note: *Beginning with your 1999 Form 945, if your total taxes for the year (line 4) are less than $1,000, you are not required to make deposits. You may pay the total tax with Form 945.*

Specific Instructions

• Make your check or money order payable to the "United States Treasury." Be sure to enter your EIN, "Form 945," and "1998" on your check or money order. Do not send cash. Please do not staple your payment to the voucher or the return.

• Detach the completed voucher and send it with your payment and Form 945 to the address provided in the separate **Instructions for Form 945.**

Box 1—Enter the amount paid with Form 945.

Box 2—Enter the first four characters of your name as follows:

• **Individuals (sole proprietorships, estates).**—Use the first four letters of your last name (as shown in box 4).

• **Corporations.**—Use the first four characters (letters or numbers) of your business name (as shown in box 4). Omit "The" if followed by more than one word.

• **Partnerships.**—Use the first four characters of your trade name. If no trade name, enter the first four letters of the last name of the first listed partner.

Box 3—If you do not have an EIN, apply for one on **Form SS-4,** Application for Employer Identification Number, and write "Applied for" and the date you applied in this entry space.

Box 4—Enter your name and address as shown on Form 945.

(Detach at this line) Cat. No. 20563G

Form 945-V
Department of the Treasury
Internal Revenue Service

Form 945 Payment Voucher

▶ **Use this voucher when making a payment with your return.**

OMB No. 1545-1430

1998

1 Enter the amount of the payment you are making

▶ $

2 Enter the first four letters of your last name (business name if corporation or partnership)

3 Enter your employer identification number

4 Enter your business name (individual name for sole proprietors)

Enter your address

Enter your city, state, and ZIP code

For Privacy Act and Paperwork Reduction Act Notice, see the Instructions for Form 945.

PBGC Form 500
Approved OMB 1212-0036
Expires 12/31/2000

Standard Termination Notice
Single-Employer Plan Termination

Use this form for terminations for which all notices of intent to terminate are issued on or after January 1, 1998.

PART I. IDENTIFYING INFORMATION

1a Plan name

b Last day of plan year MM/DD ☐☐-☐☐

2a Contributing sponsor

Name

Full Address

City State Zip Code

Telephone Area Code

b Employer identification and plan numbers 9 digit EIN 3 digit PN

c If you used a different EIN or PN for this contributing sponsor/plan in previous filings with the PBGC, also show the number(s) previously reported. 9 digit EIN 3 digit PN

d Industry code 4 digit IC

500-2

3a Plan administrator (If same as 2a, enter "same".)

Name
Company
Full Address
City / State / Zip Code
Telephone (Area Code) - -

3b Name, address, & telephone number of person to be contacted for more information. (If same as 3a, enter "same".)

Name
Company
Full Address
City / State / Zip Code
Telephone (Area Code) - -

PART II. GENERAL PLAN INFORMATION

4a Have you filed, or will you file, with the Internal Revenue Service for a determination letter on the termination of this plan? YES ☐ NO ☐

b If "Yes", enter the district: District

and the filing date: MM/DD/YYYY - -

5a Is this a multiple employer plan? YES ☐ NO ☐

b If "Yes", attach a list of the names and employer identification numbers of all contributing sponsors.

6 Reason for plan termination (if more than one, rank in order of significance, beginning with "1" for the most important).

a Adverse business conditions — a ☐

b Plan administration too costly — b ☐

c Plan benefits too costly — c ☐

d Restructuring of retirement program — d ☐

e Other Specify: — e ☐

500-3

7 Changes in contributing sponsor associated with plan termination.

a No change — a ☐

b Reorganization as part of bankruptcy or similar proceeding — b ☐

c Merger of existing subsidiaries or divisions not involving bankruptcy — c ☐

d Sale or closing of subsidiaries or divisions not involving bankruptcy — d ☐

e Acquisition *by* another business — e ☐

f Acquisition *of* another business — f ☐

g Liquidation — g ☐

---

8 Number of plan participants

a Active participants — a ☐,☐☐☐,☐☐☐

b Retirees or beneficiaries receiving benefits — b ☐,☐☐☐,☐☐☐

c Separated vested participants entitled to benefits — c ☐,☐☐☐,☐☐☐

d Total — d ☐,☐☐☐,☐☐☐

---

9 Estimated percent of currently employed participants covered under the terminated plan you expect to be covered under:

a New or existing defined benefit plan, other than cash balance plan — a ☐☐☐ %

b New or existing cash balance plan — b ☐☐☐ %

c New or existing profit-sharing plan — c ☐☐☐ %

d New or existing 401(k) plan — d ☐☐☐ %

e New or existing simplified employee plan — e ☐☐☐ %

f Other new or existing defined contribution plan — f ☐☐☐ %

Specify:

g No plan — g ☐☐☐ %

---

10 If item 9a or 9b is greater than zero, will the types and levels of benefits under the new or existing defined benefit plan be substantially the same as under the old plan for all groups of participants? YES ☐ NO ☐

500-4

11a Proposed termination date MM/DD/YYYY ☐☐-☐☐-☐☐☐☐

b Proposed termination date stated in notice of intent to terminate (if different from 11a) MM/DD/YYYY ☐☐-☐☐-☐☐☐☐

12a Earliest date notices of intent to terminate issued to affected parties MM/DD/YYYY ☐☐-☐☐-☐☐☐☐

b Latest date notices of intent to terminate issued to affected parties MM/DD/YYYY ☐☐-☐☐-☐☐☐☐

---

13 Latest date notices of plan benefits issued to participants or beneficiaries MM/DD/YYYY ☐☐-☐☐-☐☐☐☐

14a Has a formal challenge to the termination been initiated under an existing collective bargaining agreement? YES ☐ NO ☐ N/A ☐

b If "Yes", attach a copy of the formal challenge and a statement describing the challenge.

---

15 Have all PBGC premiums been paid to date? YES ☐ NO ☐

PART III. RESIDUAL ASSETS

16a Will residual assets be returned to the employer as a result of this termination? YES ☐ NO ☐

b If "No", do not complete the rest of Part III; go to Part IV. If "Yes", enter the estimated amount: $ ☐,☐☐☐,☐☐☐,☐☐☐

17a Is there a plan provision permitting a reversion of residual assets to the employer? YES ☐ NO ☐

b If "Yes", was the provision adopted prior to December 18, 1988? YES ☐ NO ☐

c If you checked "No" in item 17b, enter:

i) Adoption date of plan provision MM/DD/YYYY ☐☐-☐☐-☐☐☐☐

ii) Effective date of plan MM/DD/YYYY ☐☐-☐☐-☐☐☐☐

18a Has the plan been involved in a spin-off/termination transaction? YES ☐ NO ☐

500-**5**

18b If "Yes", have the requirements set forth in the Guidelines been satisfied? YES ☐ NO ☐ N/A ☐

i) If "Yes", enter date, or latest date, a description of the transaction(s) was issued to participants in the ongoing plan. MM/DD/YYYY ☐☐-☐☐-☐☐☐☐

ii) If "Yes", enter date, or latest date, notices of plan benefits were issued to participants in the ongoing plan. MM/DD/YYYY ☐☐-☐☐-☐☐☐☐

iii) If "Yes", have annuities been purchased or will annuities be purchased, to provide all plan benefits for participants in the ongoing plan at the time of the spin-off? YES ☐ NO ☐

c If you checked "No" or "N/A" in item 18b, attach a statement that describes the transaction(s) and explains why the Guidelines were not, or need not have been, followed.

PART IV. PLAN ADMINISTRATOR CERTIFICATION

I, the Plan Administrator, certify that, to the best of my knowledge and belief:

- I am implementing the termination of the plan in accordance with all applicable laws and regulations; and
- the information contained in this filing and made available to the enrolled actuary is true, correct, and complete.

In making this certification, I recognize that knowingly and willfully making false, fictitious, or fraudulent statements to the PBGC is punishable under 18 U.S.C. 1001.

Plan administrator's name (type or print)

X

Plan administrator's signature

Date

Business Info

Premium Forms and Instructions

1999 PREMIUM INSTRUCTIONS AND SAMPLE FORMS

- **Form 1 Instructions** (HTML)
- **Form 1-ES (Estimated Premium) Instructions** (HTML)

- **Form 1 Sample Form** (PDF)
- **Schedule A Sample Form** (PDF)
- **Form 1-ES Sample Form** (PDF)

The Sample Forms are available in Adobe Acrobat's portable document format (PDF). PDF files must be viewed with the Adobe Acrobat Reader. If you do not presently have this viewer software installed, click here to retrieve the appropriate version of the Adobe Acrobat Reader for your computer (Windows, Macintosh and UNIX versions are available) from Adobe's Website. After completing the viewer installation, return to this page on our Website and click on the form above.

The forms are marked "Sample - Do Not Use" and are provided for your convenience. They are not to be used for the actual filing of your premium payment. Only original forms that are in Optical Character Recognition (OCR) format will enable the PBGC to process your plan information quickly and accurately. We have found that even slight variations in the printing of this form can result in errors.

The original forms to be used for filing purposes may be found within the premium filing instruction booklet that are mailed to you. Should additional forms or booklets be desired, please call 202-326-4242, fax 202-326-4250, TTY/TDD users should call the federal relay service toll-free at 1-800-877-8339 and ask to be connected to 202-326-4242; or write to Pension Benefit Guaranty Corporation, P.O. Box 64916, Baltimore, MD 21264-4916.

Prior Year Instructions and Sample Forms

3107

Sample Do Not Use

PBGC Form 1
Pension Benefit Guaranty Corporation
1999

Annual Premium Payment
For Plan Years Beginning in Calendar Year 1999

Check for Amended Filing ☐ Check for Disaster Relief ☐ (see instructions)

See the 1999 Premium Payment Package for the instructions for Form 1

Approved OMB 1212-0009
412752
Photocopies of this form may not be filed.

1. Plan Sponsor — Check for address change ☐ — Check if you do not want forms and instructions next year ☐

Name
Address
City State Zip

2. Plan Administrator — Check for address change ☐ — Check if same as plan sponsor and go to Item 3 ☐

Name
Address
City State Zip

3. Employer Identification Number/Plan Number (EIN/PN)

(a) Enter 9-digit EIN ☐ (b) Enter 3-digit PN ☐

(c) Does EIN/PN match entry on 1998 Form 5500? ☐ Yes ☐ No If no, attach explanation, check box in item 19, and enter EIN/PN from 1998 Form 5500: 9-digit EIN ☐ 3-digit PN ☐

4. If EIN and PN in item 3 (a) and (b) above are NOT BOTH the same as on the most recent premium filing, enter both prior EIN and prior PN.

(a) Prior 9-digit EIN ☐ (b) Prior 3-digit PN ☐ (c) Effective Date of Change M M D D Y Y Y Y ☐

5. Plan Coverage Status (check one) (a) ☐ Covered (b) ☐ Uncertain (If uncertain, you should file. See instructions, page 11.)

6. Is this the first premium filing for this plan? ☐ No ☐ Yes If yes, enter the following dates.

(a) Plan effective date M M D D Y Y Y Y ☐ (b) Plan adoption date M M D D Y Y Y Y ☐ (c) Plan coverage date M M D D Y Y Y Y ☐

7. Transfers from disappearing plans:
Has a plan other than yours ceased to exist in connection with any transfer of assets or liabilities from that plan to this plan since the most recent premium filing? (See instructions, page 12.) ☐ No ☐ Yes
If yes, give EIN/PN of each disappearing transferor plan and effective date of transfer, and indicate whether it was a merger (M), consolidation (C), or spinoff (S).

Transferor's 9-digit EIN	3-digit PN	M M D D Y Y Y Y	Transfer Type M	C	S
			☐	☐	☐
			☐	☐	☐

(If more than 2, attach a separate sheet that lists the additional EIN/PNs, dates, and transfer types, and check the box in item 19.)

8. Industry Code: ☐ (enter 4 digits)

9. Name of Plan: ☐

continue on page 2

Sample Do Not Use

1999 PBGC Form 1 — Page 2

412752 — EIN/PN from Form 1 line 3 (a) and (b) — 9-digit EIN — 3-digit PN

10. Name and Phone Number of Plan Contact
(a) Name: ______ (b) Area Code and Phone Number ______

11. Plan Type (Check appropriate box to indicate type of plan and type of filing.)
(a) ☐ Multiemployer plan (b) ☐ Single-Employer plan (Includes Multiple-Employer plan)

12. (a) This premium is for the plan year beginning: MM DD YYYY **1999**
(b) This premium is for the plan year ending: MM DD YYYY
(c) ☐ Check here if the plan year beginning date has changed since last filing with PBGC
(d) Adoption date of plan year change: MM DD YYYY

13. (a) Enter PARTICIPANT COUNT for the plan year specified in Item 12 .... 13(a)
(b) If this count does not equal the count on your 1998 Form 5500, enter the count from your 1998 Form 5500 .... 13(b)

14. MULTIEMPLOYER plans:
Multiply line 13(a) by the $2.60 premium rate and enter amount 14

15. SINGLE-EMPLOYER plans: Compute your premium as indicated below:
(a) Flat rate premium: Multiply the participant count on line 13(a) by $19 .... 15(a)
(b) Variable rate premium: From Schedule A, line 5 .... 15(b)
(c) Total premium: Add lines 15(a) and 15(b). Enter amount .... 15(c)

16. Premium credits (See instructions, page 15)
(a) Amount paid by check or wire transfer with 1999 Form 1-ES (line 8 of Form 1-ES) .... 16(a)
(b) Other credit (including any credit claimed on line 7 of the 1999 Form 1-ES). (See instructions, page 15) .... 16(b)
(c) Total credit: Add lines 16(a) and 16(b). Enter amount .... 16(c)

17. Amount due. If the amount on line 14 or 15(c) is LARGER than the amount on line 16(c), subtract line 16(c) from line 14 or 15(c) and enter the amount due on line 17 17
See page 15 of instructions for payment methods. Indicate how you are paying the amount due:
☐ by check enclosed with this form, or ☐ by wire transfer.

18. Overpayment. If the amount on line 14 or 15(c) is SMALLER than the amount on line 16(c), subtract line 14 or 15(c) from line 16(c) and enter the overpayment on line 18 18
See page 15 of instructions for application of overpayments. An amount of overpayment not otherwise applied may be refunded (by wire transfer only) or credited against the plan's next premium filing. If you want a refund, enter the bank routing number ______ and bank account number for the refund ______

19. If you have attachments other than Schedule A, check here: ☐ Put EIN/PN (item 3(a) and (b)) and date premium payment year commenced (PYC) on each.

20. Multiemployer Plan Declaration (NOTE: All SINGLE-EMPLOYER Plan Administrators MUST sign the certification in item 6 of Schedule A.)

Under penalties of perjury (18 U.S.C. 1001), I declare that I have examined this filing, and to the best of my knowledge and belief it is true, correct and complete.

Signature of Multiemployer Plan Administrator ______ Date MM DD YYYY ______

Print or type first name of individual who signs ______ Print or type last name of individual who signs ______

SCHEDULE A (PBGC Form 1) **Sample Do Not Use** Page 2

1999 **412760** EIN/PN from Form 1 line 3 (a) and (b): EIN ______ PN ______

SECTION FOUR: CERTIFICATIONS

6. Certification of Plan Administrator. All Single-Employer plan administrators must sign and complete this line. See instructions, Part H.7. I certify, under penalties of perjury (18 U.S.C. 1001), that I have examined the completed PBGC Form 1 (including Schedule A and attachments) and, to the best of my knowledge and belief, the Form 1 (including Schedule A and attachments) and this certificate are in conformance with the premium regulations and instructions, complete, and accurate, and any information I made available to the enrolled actuary is true, correct, and complete.

I further certify, under penalties of perjury (18 U.S.C. 1001), that, for the plan year preceding the premium payment year, a Participant Notice as provided for in ERISA section 4011 (29 U.S.C. 1311) and the PBGC's regulation on Disclosure to Participants (29 CFR Part 4011):

(a) ☐ Was not required to be issued; Or, (b) ☐ Was issued as required; Or, (c) ☐ An explanation is attached.

NOTE: Check box (a), (b), or (c). If you check box (c), attach an explanation and check the box in item 19 on Form 1. Check box (a) if no variable rate premium was required for the plan year preceding the premium payment year or the plan was otherwise exempt (see instructions).

Signature of Single-Employer Plan Administrator ______ Date (M M D D Y Y Y Y) ______

Print or type first name of individual who signs Print or type last name of individual who signs

7. Certification of Enrolled Actuary. An Enrolled Actuary must sign and complete the certification below if: (1) the box on line 1(b)(1) is checked; or (2) any one or more of boxes (a) through (e) below is applicable. (See the **Certification Requirements** instructions in Part H, Item 4 for the filing method you selected to determine which of boxes (a) through (e) below are applicable.)
NOTE: If any one or more of boxes (a) through (e) below is applicable, the Enrolled Actuary must also initial the applicable box(es). Initial, do not check, the applicable box(es).

I certify, under penalties of perjury (18 U.S.C. 1001), that I have examined the completed Schedule A and to the best of my knowledge and belief, the schedule and this certificate are in conformance with the premium regulations and instructions, complete and accurate, and any information I made available to the plan administrator is true, correct, and complete, and further that:

(a) ______ (Initials) The plan had 500 or more participants as of the premium snapshot date; the actuarial value of plan assets equals or exceeds the value of all accrued benefits under the plan (valued at the Required Interest Rate); and the entry on line 2(a) is the present value of accrued benefits.

(b) ______ (Initials) The plan had no unfunded vested benefits and fewer than 500 participants both as of the premium snapshot date.

(c) ______ (Initials) The adjusted value of vested benefits on line 2(b) is the same as the plan value of vested benefits entered on line 2(a), Schedule A, because the plan interest rate used to value the vested benefits entered on lines 2(a)(1) and 2(a)(2) was equal to or less than the Required Interest Rate.

(d) ______ (Initials) The adjusted unfunded vested benefits reported on Schedule A reflect, in a manner consistent with generally accepted actuarial principles and practices, the occurrence, if any, of any of the significant events described in the premium regulation and instructions. (NOTE: If you initial this box, you must complete the following information.)

(1) Check each significant event (S.E.) that occurred between the determination date entered on line 2 of this Schedule A and the premium snapshot date (see Part H 5(d) of instructions for definitions):

☐ S.E. (1) ☐ S.E. (2) ☐ S.E. (3) ☐ S.E. (4) ☐ S.E. (5) ☐ S.E. (6) ☐ S.E. (7) ☐ No Significant Events

(2) Total amount included in line 4 due to significant events
(If this amount is negative, please check this box:) ☐ .... ______

(e) ______ (Initials) The plan meets the requirements for the exemption applicable to plans at the full funding limit.

Enrollment Number ______ Signature of Enrolled Actuary ______ Date (M M D D Y Y Y Y) ______

Print or type first name of individual who signs Print or type last name of individual who signs

Street Address ______ City ______ State ______ Zip Code ______

PBGC Form 10

ADDITIONAL INFORMATION TO BE FILED

Active Participant Reduction

- ☐ Statement explaining the cause of the reduction (e.g., facility shutdown or sale)
- ☐ Number of active participants at the date the event occurs, at the beginning of the current plan year, and at the beginning of the prior plan year

Failure to Make Required Contributions

- ☐ Due date and amount of both the missed contribution and the next payment due
- ☐ Most recent actuarial valuation report
- ☐ Description of the plan's controlled group structure, including the name of each controlled group member
- ☐ Name of each plan maintained by any member of the plan's controlled group, its contributing sponsor(s) and EIN/PN

Inability to Pay Benefits When Due

- ☐ Date of any missed benefit payment and amount of benefits due
- ☐ Next date on which the plan is expected to be unable to pay benefits, the amount of the projected shortfall, and the number of plan participants expected to be affected
- ☐ Amount of the plan's liquid assets at the end of the quarter, and the amount of its disbursements for the quarter
- ☐ Most recent actuarial valuation report
- ☐ Name, address and phone number of plan trustee (and of any custodian)

Distribution to a Substantial Owner

- ☐ Name, address and phone number of person receiving the distribution(s)
- ☐ Amount, form and date of each distribution
- ☐ Most recent actuarial valuation report

Transfer of Benefit Liabilities

- ☐ Name, contributing sponsor and EIN/PN of transferee plan(s)
- ☐ Explanation of the actuarial assumptions used in determining the value of benefit liabilities (and, if appropriate, plan assets) transferred
- ☐ Estimate of the assets, liabilities, and number of participants whose benefits are transferred

Note: To the extent this information is filed with the IRS Form 5310A, PBGC will accept a copy of that filing.

Change in Contributing Sponsor or Controlled Group

- ☐ Description of the plan's old and new controlled group structures, including the name of each controlled group member
- ☐ Name of each plan maintained by any member of the plan's old and new controlled groups, its contributing sponsor(s) and EIN/PN

Liquidation

- ☐ Description of the plan's controlled group structure before and after the liquidation, including the name of each controlled group member
- ☐ Name of each plan maintained by any member of the plan's controlled group, its contributing sponsor(s) and EIN/PN

Extraordinary Dividend or Stock Redemption

- ☐ Name and EIN of person making the distribution
- ☐ Date and amount of cash distribution(s) during fiscal year
- ☐ Description, fair market value, and date or dates of any non-cash distributions
- ☐ Statement whether the recipient was a member of the plan's controlled group

Application for Minimum Funding Waiver

- ☐ Copy of waiver application, with all attachments

Loan Default

- ☐ Copy of the relevant loan documents (e.g., promissory note, security agreement)
- ☐ Due date and amount of any missed payment
- ☐ Copy of any written notice of default or any notice of acceleration from lender

Bankruptcy or Similar Settlement

- ☐ Copy of bankruptcy petition or similar document
- ☐ Docket sheet or other list of documents filed
- ☐ Last date for filing claims, if known
- ☐ Name, address and phone number of any trustee, receiver or similar person
- ☐ Most recent actuarial valuation report for each plan in the controlled group
- ☐ Description of the plan's controlled group structure, including the name of each controlled group member
- ☐ Name of each plan maintained by any member of the plan's controlled group, its contributing sponsor(s) and EIN/PN

SCHEDULE A
(PBGC Form 1)
1999

Single-Employer Plan

Variable Rate Premium
(See Part H for General Instructions and Part I for Line-By-Line Instructions)

Photocopies of this form may not be filed.

Approved OMB 1212-0009

412760

(a) Plan Year from Form 1 line 12(a): M M D D Y Y Y Y 1 9 9 9

(b) EIN/PN from Form 1 line 3 (a) and (b): 9-digit EIN 3-digit PN

(c) Plan Name:

SECTION ONE: FILING STATUS. All Single-Employer plans must complete this section.

1. **(a) Plans Exempt from Variable Rate Premium:** Check a single box, go to line 5 and enter $0. See Section Four for required certifications.
   (1) ☐ No Vested Participants. (2) ☐ 412(i) Plan. (3) ☐ Fully funded plan with fewer than 500 Participants.
   (4) ☐ Standard Termination with a pre-1999 Plan Year proposed termination date of: M M D D Y Y Y Y
   (5) ☐ Plan at Full Funding Limit.

   (b) Filing Method If Plan Is Not Exempt: Check a single box and go to line 2. See Section Four for required certifications.
   (1) ☐ General Rule. (2) Alternative Calculation Method (ACM).
   (i) ☐ Plan with fewer than 500 Participants. (ii) ☐ Plan with 500 or more Participants.
   (3) ☐ Modified ACM for Plan Terminating in Distress or Involuntary Termination with a pre-1999 Plan Year termination date of: M M D D Y Y Y Y

SECTION TWO: UNFUNDED VESTED BENEFITS. Complete this section if you checked a box in Section 1.(b).

2. **Present Value of Vested Benefits:** Plan Values are determined as of: M M D D Y Y Y Y
   The assumed retirement age is ☐ years. The adjusted values are based on a
   Required Interest Rate of ☐ % and an accrual factor of ... ☐

	(a) Plan Value of Vested Benefits: Value	Interest Rate	(b) Adjusted Value of Vested Benefits
(1) Retirees/beneficiaries receiving payments		%	
(2) Participants not receiving payments		%	
(3) Total (Line (1) plus line (2))			

3. **Value of Plan Assets:**
   (a) Enter value of Plan Assets as of M M D D Y Y Y Y
   (b) Enter contribution receivables included in line 3(a)
   (c) Discounted paid contributions.
   (Note: For plans with fewer than 500 participants, this line is optional)
   (d) Enter adjusted value of plan assets (Line 3(a) minus line 3(b) plus line 3(c))
4. **Adjusted Unfunded Vested Benefits:** Enter adjusted unfunded vested benefits. (ACM filers see instructions for this line in Part I, Subpart 7, for interest and significant events adjustments.)

SECTION THREE: VARIABLE RATE PREMIUM. All Single-Employer plans must complete this section.

5. **Variable Rate Premium:** Enter here and on Form 1, line 15(b), either
   (a) $0, if any box on line 1(a) was checked or if line 4 was $0; or
   (b) the amount on line 4 multiplied by 0.009.

POST-EVENT NOTICE OF REPORTABLE EVENTS

PBGC Form 10
Approved OMB #1212-0013
Expires 9/30/99

This form may be used by a plan administrator or contributing sponsor of a single-employer plan when notifying the Pension Benefit Guaranty Corporation that a reportable event has occurred.

IDENTIFYING INFORMATION

Name of filer ______________________

Street address of filer ______________________

City, State, Zip ______________________

EIN of contributing sponsor ______________ Plan number ________

Filer is: ☐ Plan administrator ☐ Contributing sponsor

Plan name ______________________

Name / title of individual to contact ______________________

Street address of contact ______________________

City, State, Zip ______________________

Telephone number of contact ______________________

REPORTABLE EVENTS

See instructions for descriptions of these events. Check all boxes that apply.

☐ Active participant reduction
☐ Failure to make required contributions
☐ Inability to pay benefits when due
☐ Distribution to a substantial owner
☐ Transfer of benefit liabilities
☐ Change in contributing sponsor or controlled group
☐ Liquidation
☐ Extraordinary dividend or stock redemption
☐ Application for minimum funding waiver
☐ Loan default
☐ Bankruptcy or similar settlement

BRIEF DESCRIPTION

Briefly describe the pertinent facts relating to the event.

The reverse side lists additional information that must be submitted with this form, if not included above.

ADVANCE NOTICE OF REPORTABLE EVENTS

PBGC Form 10-Advance
Approved OMB #1212-0013
Expires 9/30/99

This form may be used by a contributing sponsor of a single-employer plan required to notify the Pension Benefit Guaranty Corporation in advance that a reportable event will occur.

IDENTIFYING INFORMATION

Name of plan

Name of contributing sponsor	Name / title of individual to contact
Street address of contributing sponsor	Street address of contact
City, State, Zip	City, State, Zip
EIN of contributing sponsor Plan number	Telephone number of contact

REPORTABLE EVENTS

See instructions for descriptions of these events. Check all boxes that apply.

- ☐ Change in contributing sponsor or controlled group
- ☐ Liquidation
- ☐ Extraordinary dividend or stock redemption
- ☐ Transfer of benefit liabilities
- ☐ Application for minimum funding waiver
- ☐ Loan default
- ☐ Bankruptcy or similar settlement

BRIEF DESCRIPTION

Briefly describe the pertinent facts relating to the event.

The reverse side lists additional information that must be submitted with this form, if not included above.

PBGC Form 10

ADDITIONAL INFORMATION TO BE FILED

Active Participant Reduction

- ☐ Statement explaining the cause of the reduction (e.g., facility shutdown or sale)
- ☐ Number of active participants at the date the event occurs, at the beginning of the current plan year, and at the beginning of the prior plan year

Failure to Make Required Contributions

- ☐ Due date and amount of both the missed contribution and the next payment due
- ☐ Most recent actuarial valuation report
- ☐ Description of the plan's controlled group structure, including the name of each controlled group member
- ☐ Name of each plan maintained by any member of the plan's controlled group, its contributing sponsor(s) and EIN/PN

Inability to Pay Benefits When Due

- ☐ Date of any missed benefit payment and amount of benefits due
- ☐ Next date on which the plan is expected to be unable to pay benefits, the amount of the projected shortfall, and the number of plan participants expected to be affected
- ☐ Amount of the plan's liquid assets at the end of the quarter, and the amount of its disbursements for the quarter
- ☐ Most recent actuarial valuation report
- ☐ Name, address and phone number of plan trustee (and of any custodian)

Distribution to a Substantial Owner

- ☐ Name, address and phone number of person receiving the distribution(s)
- ☐ Amount, form and date of each distribution
- ☐ Most recent actuarial valuation report

Transfer of Benefit Liabilities

- ☐ Name, contributing sponsor and EIN/PN of transferee plan(s)
- ☐ Explanation of the actuarial assumptions used in determining the value of benefit liabilities (and, if appropriate, plan assets) transferred
- ☐ Estimate of the assets, liabilities, and number of participants whose benefits are transferred

Note: To the extent this information is filed with the IRS Form 5310A, PBGC will accept a copy of that filing.

Change in Contributing Sponsor or Controlled Group

- ☐ Description of the plan's old and new controlled group structures, including the name of each controlled group member
- ☐ Name of each plan maintained by any member of the plan's old and new controlled groups, its contributing sponsor(s) and EIN/PN

Liquidation

- ☐ Description of the plan's controlled group structure before and after the liquidation, including the name of each controlled group member
- ☐ Name of each plan maintained by any member of the plan's controlled group, its contributing sponsor(s) and EIN/PN

Extraordinary Dividend or Stock Redemption

- ☐ Name and EIN of person making the distribution
- ☐ Date and amount of cash distribution(s) during fiscal year
- ☐ Description, fair market value, and date or dates of any non-cash distributions
- ☐ Statement whether the recipient was a member of the plan's controlled group

Application for Minimum Funding Waiver

- ☐ Copy of waiver application, with all attachments

Loan Default

- ☐ Copy of the relevant loan documents (e.g., promissory note, security agreement)
- ☐ Due date and amount of any missed payment
- ☐ Copy of any written notice of default or any notice of acceleration from lender

Bankruptcy or Similar Settlement

- ☐ Copy of bankruptcy petition or similar document
- ☐ Docket sheet or other list of documents filed
- ☐ Last date for filing claims, if known
- ☐ Name, address and phone number of any trustee, receiver or similar person
- ☐ Most recent actuarial valuation report for each plan in the controlled group
- ☐ Description of the plan's controlled group structure, including the name of each controlled group member
- ☐ Name of each plan maintained by any member of the plan's controlled group, its contributing sponsor(s) and EIN/PN

TECHNICAL UPDATE

Pension Benefit Guaranty Corporation

1200 K Street, N.W., Washington, D.C. 20005-4026

TECHNICAL UPDATE 98-1

July 16, 1998

1998 Model Participant Notice

The Retirement Protection Act of 1994 requires certain underfunded plans annually to notify participants and beneficiaries of the plan's funding status and the limits of PBGC's guarantee. (*See* Section 4011 of ERISA and 29 CFR Part 4011.) The regulation includes a model notice that plans can use to meet this requirement.

For the convenience of plan administrators, this Technical Update provides the Model Participant Notice, updated to reflect the 1998 maximum guaranteed benefits. Technical Update 98-1 also reflects the increase from $3,500 to $5,000 in the maximum value of benefits that PBGC may pay in the form of a single, lump-sum payment to participants in pension plans that have been terminated and taken over by the agency. (*See* 63 Fed. Reg. 38,305, July 16, 1998.) This increase is effective with respect to Participant Notices issued on or after August 17, 1998. However, for a reasonable time period, PBGC will not treat a Participant Notice as failing to satisfy the Participant Notice requirement merely because it refers to the $3,500 threshold.

Model Participant Notice

The following is an example of a Participant Notice that satisfies the requirements of § 4011.10 when the required information is filled in.

Notice to Participants of [Plan Name]

The law requires that you receive information on the funding level of your defined benefit pension plan and the benefits guaranteed by the Pension Benefit Guaranty Corporation (PBGC), a federal insurance agency.

YOUR PLAN'S FUNDING

As of [DATE], your plan had [INSERT NOTICE FUNDING PERCENTAGE DETERMINED IN ACCORDANCE WITH § 4011.10(c)] percent of the money needed to pay benefits promised to employees and retirees.

To pay pension benefits, your employer is required to contribute money to the pension plan over a period of years. A plan's funding percentage does not take into consideration the financial strength of the employer. Your employer, by law, must pay for all pension benefits, but your benefits may be at risk if your employer faces a severe financial crisis or is in bankruptcy.

[INCLUDE THE FOLLOWING PARAGRAPH ONLY IF, FOR ANY OF THE PREVIOUS FIVE PLAN YEARS, THE PLAN HAS BEEN GRANTED AND HAS NOT FULLY REPAID A FUNDING WAIVER.]

Your plan received a funding waiver for [LIST ANY OF THE FIVE PREVIOUS PLAN YEARS FOR WHICH A FUNDING WAIVER WAS GRANTED AND HAS NOT BEEN FULLY REPAID]. If a company is experiencing temporary financial hardship, the Internal Revenue Service may grant a funding waiver that permits the company to delay contributions that fund the pension plan.

[INCLUDE THE FOLLOWING WITH RESPECT TO ANY UNPAID OR LATE PAYMENT THAT MUST BE DISCLOSED UNDER § 4011.10(b)(6):]

Your plan was required to receive a payment from the employer on [LIST APPLICABLE DUE DATE(S)]. That payment [has not been made] [was made on [LIST APPLICABLE PAYMENT DATE(S)]].

PBGC GUARANTEES

When a pension plan ends without enough money to pay all benefits, the PBGC steps in to pay pension benefits. The PBGC pays most people all pension benefits, but some people may lose certain benefits that are not guaranteed.

The PBGC pays pension benefits up to certain maximum limits.

The maximum guaranteed benefit is $2,880.68 per month or $34,568.16 per year for a 65-year-old person in a plan that terminates in 1998.

The maximum benefit may be reduced for an individual who is younger than age 65. For example, it is $1,296.31 per month or $15,555.72 per year for an individual who starts receiving benefits at age 55.

[IN LIEU OF AGE 55, YOU MAY ADD OR SUBSTITUTE ANY AGE(S) RELEVANT UNDER THE PLAN. FOR EXAMPLE, YOU MAY ADD OR SUBSTITUTE THE MAXIMUM BENEFIT FOR AGES 62 OR 60. THE MAXIMUM BENEFIT IS $2,275.74 PER MONTH OR $27,308.88 PER YEAR AT AGE 62; IT IS $1,872.44 PER MONTH OR $22,469.28 PER YEAR AT AGE 60. IF THE PLAN PROVIDES FOR NORMAL RETIREMENT BEFORE AGE 65, YOU MUST INCLUDE THE NORMAL RETIREMENT AGE.]

[IF THE PLAN DOES NOT PROVIDE FOR COMMENCEMENT OF BENEFITS BEFORE AGE 65, YOU MAY OMIT THIS PARAGRAPH.]

The maximum benefit will also be reduced when a benefit is provided for a survivor.

The PBGC does not guarantee certain types of benefits. [INCLUDE THE FOLLOWING GUARANTEE LIMITS THAT APPLY TO THE BENEFITS AVAILABLE UNDER YOUR PLAN.]

The PBGC does not guarantee benefits for which you do not have a vested right when a plan ends, usually because you have not worked enough years for the company.

The PBGC does not guarantee benefits for which you have not met all age, service, or other requirements at the time the plan ends.

Benefit increases and new benefits that have been in place for less than a year are not guaranteed. Those that have been in place for less than 5 years are only partly guaranteed.

Early retirement payments that are greater than payments at normal retirement age may not be guaranteed. For example, a supplemental benefit that stops when you become eligible for Social Security may not be guaranteed.

Benefits other than pension benefits, such as health insurance, life insurance, death benefits, vacation pay, or severance pay, are not guaranteed.

The PBGC does not pay lump sums exceeding $5,000.

WHERE TO GET MORE INFORMATION

Your plan, [EIN-PN], is sponsored by [CONTRIBUTING SPONSOR(S)]. If you would like more information about the funding of your plan, contact [INSERT NAME, TITLE, BUSINESS ADDRESS AND PHONE NUMBER OF INDIVIDUAL OR ENTITY].

For more information about the PBGC and the benefits it guarantees, you may request a free copy of ``Your Guaranteed Pension" by writing to Consumer Information Center, Dept. YGP, Pueblo, Colorado 81009. [THE FOLLOWING SENTENCE MAY BE INCLUDED:] ``Your Guaranteed Pension" is also available from the PBGC Homepage on the World Wide Web at http://www.pbgc.gov/ygp.htp.

Issued: [INSERT AT LEAST MONTH AND YEAR]

NOTICE OF GROUP HEALTH PLAN'S EXEMPTION FROM THE MENTAL HEALTH PARITY ACT

*** DESCRIPTION OF THE ONE PERCENT INCREASED COST EXEMPTION — This notice is required to be provided to you under the requirements of the Mental Health Parity Act of 1996 (MHPA) because the group health plan identified in Line 1 below is claiming the one percent increased cost exemption from the requirements of MHPA. Under MHPA, a group health plan offering both medical/surgical and mental health benefits generally can no longer set annual or aggregate lifetime dollar limits on mental health benefits that are lower than any such dollar limits for medical/surgical benefits. In addition, a plan that does not impose an annual or aggregate lifetime dollar limit on medical/surgical benefits generally may not impose such a limit on mental health benefits. However, a group health plan can claim an exemption from these requirements if the plan's costs increase one percent or more due to the application of MHPA's requirements.**

This notice is to inform you that the group health plan identified in Line 1 below is claiming the exemption from the requirements of MHPA. The exemption is effective as of the date identified in Line 4 below. Since benefits under your group health plan may change as of the date identified in Line 4 it is important that you contact your plan administrator or the plan representative identified in Line 5 below to see how your benefits may be affected as a result of your group health plan's election of this exemption from the requirements of MHPA.

Upon submission of this notice by you (or your representative) to the plan administrator or the person identified in Line 5 below, the plan will provide you or your representative, free of charge, a summary of the information upon which the plan's exemption is based.

1. Name of the group health plan and the plan number (PN): ______________________

2. Name, address, and telephone number of plan administrator responsible for providing this notice:

   ____

   ____

   ____

3. For single-employer plans, the name, address, telephone number, (if different from Line 2) and employer identification number (EIN) of the employer sponsoring the group health plan:

   ____

   ____

   ____

4. Effective date of the exemption (at least 30 days after the notices are sent): ______________________

5. For further information, call: ______________________

BILLING CODE 4830-01-C; 4510-29-C; 4120-01-C

66938 Federal Register / Vol. 62, No. 245 / Monday, December 22, 1997 / Rules and Regulations

NOTICE OF GROUP HEALTH PLAN'S USE OF TRANSITION PERIOD

*** IMPORTANT — This notice is required to be provided if a group health plan uses the transition period under the requirements of the Mental Health Parity Act (MHPA). Under MHPA, a group health plan offering both medical/surgical and mental health benefits generally can no longer set annual or aggregate lifetime dollar limits on mental health benefits that are lower than any such dollar limits for medical/surgical benefits. In addition, a plan that does not impose an annual or aggregate lifetime dollar limit on medical/surgical benefits generally may not impose such a limit on mental health benefits. However, a group health plan can claim an exemption from these requirements if the plan's costs increase one percent or more due to the application of MHPA's requirements. Under MHPA, a plan that claims the one percent increased cost exemption prior to the issuance of the MHPA interim regulations based on assumptions inconsistent with the MHPA interim regulations may delay compliance with the parity requirements of MHPA until a date no later than March 31, 1998.**

This notice is to inform you that the plan is utilizing the MHPA transition period and that the plan is delaying compliance with the parity requirements of MHPA until a time no later than March 31, 1998.

1. Name of the group health plan and the plan number (PN): ______________________

2. Name, address, and telephone number of plan administrator responsible for providing this notice:

____

____

____

3. For single-employer plans, the name, address, telephone number, (if different from Line 2), and employer identification number (EIN) of the employer sponsoring the group health plan:

____

____

____

4. For further information, call: ______________________

5. Signature of plan administrator: ______________________ Date: __________

BILLING CODE 4830-01-C; 4510-29-C; 4120-01-C

Form **5500**
Department of the Treasury
Internal Revenue Service
Department of Labor
Pension and Welfare Benefits Administration
Pension Benefit Guaranty Corporation

Annual Return/Report of Employee Benefit Plan
(With 100 or more participants)
This form is required to be filed under sections 104 and 4065 of the Employee Retirement Income Security Act of 1974 and sections 6039D, 6047(e), 6057(b), and 6058(a) of the Internal Revenue Code, referred to as the Code.
▶ See separate instructions.

OMB Nos. 1210-0016
1210-0089
1996
This Form Is Open to Public Inspection.

For the calendar plan year 1996 or fiscal plan year beginning 1996, and ending , 19

If *A(1)* through *A(4)*, *B*, *C*, and/or *D*, do not apply to this year's return/report, leave the boxes unmarked.

For IRS Use Only
EP–ID

A This return/report is: *(1)* ☐ the first return/report filed for the plan; *(2)* ☐ an amended return/report; *(3)* ☐ the final return/report filed for the plan; or *(4)* ☐ a short plan year return/report (less than 12 months).

IF ANY INFORMATION ON A PREPRINTED PAGE 1 IS INCORRECT, CORRECT IT. IF ANY INFORMATION IS MISSING, ADD IT. PLEASE USE RED INK WHEN MAKING THESE CHANGES AND INCLUDE THE PREPRINTED PAGE 1 WITH YOUR COMPLETED RETURN/REPORT.

B Check here if any information reported in 1a, 2a, 2b, or 5a changed since the last return/report for this plan . . . . ▶ ☐
C If your plan year changed since the last return/report, check here . . . . ▶ ☐
D If you filed for an extension of time to file this return/report, check here and attach a copy of the approved extension . . . . . ▶ ☐

1a Name and address of plan sponsor (employer, if for a single-employer plan) (Address should include room or suite no.)

1b Employer identification number (EIN)

1c Sponsor's telephone number

1d Business code (see instructions, page 20)

1e CUSIP issuer number

2a Name and address of plan administrator (if same as plan sponsor, enter "Same")

2b Administrator's EIN

2c Administrator's telephone number

3 If you are filing this page without the preprinted historical plan information and the name, address, and EIN of the plan sponsor or plan administrator has changed since the last return/report filed for this plan, enter the information from the last return/report in line **3a** and/or line **3b** and complete line **3c.**

a Sponsor .... EIN .... Plan number ....
b Administrator .... EIN ....
c If line **3a** indicates a change in the sponsor's name, address, and EIN, is this a change in sponsorship only? (See line **3c** on page 8 of the instructions for the definition of sponsorship.) Enter "Yes" or "No." ▶

4 **ENTITY CODE.** (If not shown, enter the applicable code from page 8 of the instructions.) ▶

5a Name of plan ▶ ....

5b Effective date of plan (mo., day, yr.)

5c Three-digit plan number ▶

All filers must complete 6a through 6d, as applicable.

6a ☐ Welfare benefit plan **6b** ☐ Pension benefit plan
(If the correct codes are not preprinted below, enter the applicable codes from page 8 of the instructions in the boxes.)

6c Pension plan features. (If the correct codes are not preprinted below, enter the applicable pension plan feature codes from page 8 of the instructions in the boxes.)

6d ☐ Fringe benefit plan. Attach Schedule F (Form 5500). See instructions.

Caution: *A penalty for the late or incomplete filing of this return/report will be assessed unless reasonable cause is established.*

Under penalties of perjury and other penalties set forth in the instructions, I declare that I have examined this return/report, including accompanying schedules and statements, and to the best of my knowledge and belief, it is true, correct, and complete.

Signature of employer/plan sponsor ▶.................... Date ▶....................
Type or print name of individual signing above ....
Signature of plan administrator ▶.................... Date ▶....................
Type or print name of individual signing above

For Paperwork Reduction Act Notice, see page 1 of the instructions. Cat. No. 13500F Form **5500** (1996)

Form 5500 (1996) Page **2**

6e Check all applicable investment arrangements below (see instructions on page 9):
(1) ☐ Master trust *(2)* ☐ 103-12 investment entity
(3) ☐ Common/collective trust *(4)* ☐ Pooled separate account

f Single-employer plans enter the tax year end of the employer in which this plan year ends ▶ Month .... Day .... Year ....
g Is any part of this plan funded by an insurance contract described in Code section 412*(i)*? . . . . ☐ **Yes** ☐ **No**
h If line **6g** is "Yes," was the part subject to the minimum funding standards for either of the prior 2 plan years? . . . . ☐ **Yes** ☐ **No**

7 Number of participants as of the end of the plan year (welfare plans complete only lines 7a(4), 7b, 7c, and 7d):
a Active participants: *(1)* Number fully vested . . . . **a(1)**
(2) Number partially vested . . . . **a(2)**
(3) Number nonvested . . . . **a(3)**
(4) Total . . . . **a(4)**
b Retired or separated participants receiving benefits . . . . **b**
c Retired or separated participants entitled to future benefits . . . . **c**
d Subtotal. Add lines **7a(4), 7b,** and **7c** . . . . **d**
e Deceased participants whose beneficiaries are receiving or are entitled to receive benefits . . . . **e**
f Total. Add lines **7d** and **7e** . . . . **f**
g Number of participants with account balances. (Defined benefit plans do not complete this line item.). . . **g**
h Number of participants that terminated employment during the plan year with accrued benefits that were less than 100% vested . . . . **h**

		Yes	No
i *(1)* Was any participant(s) separated from service with a deferred vested benefit for which a Schedule SSA (Form 5500) is required to be attached? (See instructions.)	**i(1)**		
(2) If "Yes," enter the number of separated participants required to be reported ▶			
8a Was this plan ever amended since its effective date? If "Yes," complete line **8b** . . . . If the amendment was adopted in this plan year, complete lines **8c** through **8e.**	**8a**		
b If line **8a** is "Yes," enter the date the most recent amendment was adopted ▶ Month .... Day .... Year			
c Did any amendment during the current plan year result in the retroactive reduction of accrued benefits for any participants?	**c**		
d During this plan year did any amendment change the information contained in the latest summary plan descriptions or summary description of modifications available at the time of amendment?	**d**		
e If line **8d** is "Yes," has a summary plan description or summary description of modifications that reflects the plan amendments referred to on line **8d** been both furnished to participants and filed with the Department of Labor? . . .	**e**		
9a Was this plan terminated during this plan year or any prior plan year? If "Yes," enter the year ▶....................	**9a**		
b Were all the plan assets either distributed to participants or beneficiaries, transferred to another plan, or brought under the control of PBGC?	**b**		
c Was a resolution to terminate this plan adopted during this plan year or any prior plan year?	**c**		
d If line **9a** or line **9c** is "Yes," have you received a favorable determination letter from the IRS for the termination? . .	**d**		
e If line **9d** is "No," has a determination letter been requested from the IRS?	**e**		
f If line **9a** or line **9c** is "Yes," have participants and beneficiaries been notified of the termination or the proposed termination?	**f**		
g If line **9a** is "Yes" and the plan is covered by PBGC, is the plan continuing to file a PBGC Form 1 and pay premiums until the end of the plan year in which assets are distributed or brought under the control of PBGC?	**g**		
h During this plan year, did any trust assets revert to the employer for which the Code section 4980 excise tax is due?	**h**		
i If line **9h** is "Yes," enter the amount of tax paid with Form 5330 ▶ $			

10a In this plan year, was this plan merged or consolidated into another plan(s), or were assets or liabilities transferred to another plan(s)? If "Yes," complete lines **10b** through **10e** . . . . ▶ ☐ **Yes** ☐ **No**

If "Yes," identify the other plan(s)	**c** Employer identification number(s)	**d** Plan number(s)
b Name of plan(s) ▶		

e If required, has a Form 5310-A been filed? . . . . ▶ ☐ **Yes** ☐ **No**

11 Enter the plan funding arrangement code from page 10 of the instructions . . . . ▶

12 Enter the plan benefit arrangement code from page 10 of the instructions ▶

		Yes	No
13a Is this a plan established or maintained pursuant to one or more collective bargaining agreements?	**13a**		
b If line **13a** is "Yes," enter the appropriate six-digit LM number(s) of the sponsoring labor organization(s) (see instructions): *(1)* *(2)* *(3)*			
14 If any benefits are provided by an insurance company, insurance service, or similar organization, enter the number of **Schedules A (Form 5500)**, Insurance Information, attached. If none, enter "-0-." ▶			

Form 5500 (1996) Page **3**

Welfare Plans Do Not Complete Lines 15 Through 24. Go To Line 25 On Page 4.

			Yes	No
15a	If this is a defined benefit plan subject to the minimum funding standards for this plan year, is **Schedule B** (Form 5500) required to be attached? (If this is a defined contribution plan leave blank.)	**15a**		
b	If this is a defined contribution plan (i.e., money purchase or target benefit), is it subject to the minimum funding standards? (If a waiver was granted, see instructions.) (If this is a defined benefit plan, leave blank.)	**b**		
	If "Yes," complete *(1)*, *(2)*, and *(3)* below:			
	(1) Amount of employer contribution required for the plan year under Code section 412 — **b(1)** $			
	(2) Amount of contribution paid by the employer for the plan year — **b(2)** $			
	Enter date of last payment by employer ▶ Month......... Day........ Year......			
	(3) If *(1)* is greater than *(2)*, subtract *(2)* from *(1)* and enter the funding deficiency here; otherwise, enter -0-. (If you have a funding deficiency, file Form 5330.) — **b(3)** $			
16	Has the annual compensation of each participant taken into account under the current plan year been limited as required by section 401(a)(17)? (See instructions.)	**16**		
17a	*(1)* Did the plan distribute any annuity contracts this year? (See instructions.)	**a(1)**		
	(2) If *(1)* is "Yes," did these contracts contain a requirement that the spouse consent before any distributions under the contract are made in a form other than a qualified joint and survivor annuity?	**a(2)**		
b	Did the plan make distributions or loans to married participants and beneficiaries without the required consent of the participant's spouse?	**b**		
c	Upon plan amendment or termination, do the accrued benefits of every participant include the subsidized benefits that the participant may become entitled to receive subsequent to the plan amendment or termination?	**c**		
18	Is the plan administrator making an election under section 412(c)(8) for an amendment adopted after the end of the plan year? (See instructions.)	**18**		
19	If a change in the actuarial funding method was made for the plan year pursuant to a Revenue Procedure providing automatic approval for the change, indicate whether the plan sponsor agrees to the change	**19**		
20	Is the employer electing to compute minimum funding for the plan year using the Transition rule of Code section 412(l)(11)?	**20**		
21	Check if you are applying the substantiation guidelines from Revenue Procedure 93-42, in completing lines **21a** through **21o** (see instructions) ☐			
	If you checked the box, enter the first day of the plan year for which data is being submitted ▶ Month ....Day ....Year			
a	Does the employer apply the separate line of business rules of Code section 414(r) when testing this plan for the coverage and discrimination tests of Code sections 410(b) and 401(a)(4)?	**21a**		
b	If line **21a** is "Yes," enter the total number of separate lines of business claimed by the employer ▶ .... If more than one separate line of business, see instructions for additional information to attach.			
c	Does the employer apply the mandatory disaggregation rules under Income Tax Regulations section 1.410(b)-7(c)? If "Yes," see instructions for additional information to attach.	**c**		
d	In testing whether this plan satisfies the coverage and discrimination tests of Code sections 410(b) and 401(a), does the employer aggregate plans?	**d**		
e	Does the employer restructure the plan into component plans to satisfy the coverage and discrimination tests of Code sections 410(b) and 401(a)(4)?	**e**		
f	If you meet either of the following exceptions, check the applicable box to tell us which exception you meet and do NOT complete the rest of question **21**: *(1)* ☐ No highly compensated employee benefited under the plan at any time during the plan year; *(2)* ☐ This is a collectively bargained plan that benefits only collectively bargained employees, no more than 2% of whom are professional employees.			
g	Did any leased employee perform services for the employer at any time during the plan year?	**g**		
			Number	
h	Enter the total number of employees of the employer. Employer includes entities aggregated with the employer under Code section 414(b), (c), or (m). Include leased employees and self-employed individuals	**h**		
i	Enter the total number of employees excludable because of: *(1)* failure to meet requirements for minimum age and years of service; *(2)* collectively bargained employees; *(3)* nonresident aliens who receive no earned income from U.S. sources; and *(4)* 500 hours of service/last day rule	**i**		
j	Enter the number of nonexcludable employees. Subtract line **21i** from line **21h**	**j**		
k	Do 100% of the nonexcludable employees entered on line **21j** benefit under the plan? ☐ **Yes** ☐ **No** If line **21k** is "Yes," do NOT complete lines **21l** through **21o**.			
l	Enter the number of nonexcludable employees (line **21j**) who are highly compensated employees	**l**		
m	Enter the number of nonexcludable employees (line **21j**) who benefit under the plan	**m**		
n	Enter the number of employees entered on line **21m** who are highly compensated employees	**n**		
o	This plan satisfies the coverage requirements on the basis of (check one): *(1)* ☐ The average benefits test *(2)* ☐ The ratio percentage test—Enter percentage ▶ ☐☐☐.☐ %			

Form 5500 (1996) Page **4**

Welfare Plans Go To Line 25 On This Page. | Yes | No

22a Is it or was it ever intended that this plan qualify under Code section 401(a)? If "Yes," complete lines **22b** and **22c**. . **22a**

b Enter the date of the most recent IRS determination letter . . . . ▶ Month .... Year ....

c Is a determination letter request pending with the IRS?. . . . . **c**

23a Does the plan hold any assets that have a fair market value that is not readily determinable on an established market? (If "Yes," complete line **23b**) (See instructions) **23a**

b Were all the assets referred to in line **23a** valued for the 1996 plan year by an independent third-party appraiser? . . **b**

c If line **23b** is "No," enter the value of the assets that were not valued by an independent third-party appraiser for the 1996 plan year. ▶ ____________

d Enter the most recent date the assets on line **23c** were valued by an independent third-party appraiser. (If more than one asset, see instructions.) ▶ Month .... Day .... Year ....

(If this plan does not have ESOP features leave line **23e** blank and go to line **24.**)

e If dividends paid on employer securities held by the ESOP were used to make payments on ESOP loans, enter the amount of the dividends used to make the payments . . . | **23e** |

24 Does the employer/sponsor listed on line **1a** of this form maintain other qualified pension benefit plans? **24**
If "Yes," enter the total number of plans, including this plan ▶

25a Did any person who rendered services to the plan receive directly or indirectly $5,000 or more in compensation from the plan during the plan year (except for employees of the plan who were paid less than $1,000 in each month)? . . **25a**
If "Yes," complete Part I of **Schedule C** (Form 5500).

b Did the plan have any trustees who must be listed in Part II of **Schedule C** (Form 5500)? . . . . **b**

c Has there been a termination in the appointment of any person listed on line **25d** below? . . . . **c**

d If line **25c** is "Yes," check the appropriate box(es), answer lines **25e** and **25f**, and complete Part III of **Schedule C** (Form 5500):
(1) ☐ Accountant *(2)* ☐ Enrolled actuary *(3)* ☐ Insurance carrier *(4)* ☐ Custodian
(5) ☐ Administrator *(6)* ☐ Investment manager *(7)* ☐ Trustee

e Have there been any outstanding material disputes or matters of disagreement concerning the above termination?. . **e**

f If an accountant or enrolled actuary has been terminated during the plan year, has the terminated accountant/actuary been provided a copy of the explanation required by Part III of **Schedule C** (Form 5500) with a notice advising them of their opportunity to submit comments on the explanation directly to the DOL?. . . . . **f**

g Enter the number of **Schedules C** (Form 5500) that are attached. If none, enter -0- ▶

26a Is this plan exempt from the requirement to engage an independent qualified public accountant? (see instructions). . **26a**

b If line **26a** is "No," attach the accountant's opinion to this return/report and check the appropriate box. This opinion is:
(1) ☐ Unqualified
(2) ☐ Qualified/disclaimer per Department of Labor Regulations 29 CFR 2520.103-8 and/or 2520.103-12(d)
(3) ☐ Qualified/disclaimer other *(4)* ☐ Adverse *(5)* ☐ Other (explain) ....
....
....

c If line **26a** is "No," does the accountant's report, including the financial statements and/or notes required to be attached to this return/report disclose (1) errors or irregularities; (2) illegal acts; (3) material internal control weaknesses; (4) a loss contingency indicating that assets are impaired or a liability incurred; (5) significant real estate or other transactions in which the plan and (A) the sponsor, (B) the plan administrator, (C) the employer(s), or (D) the employee organization(s) are jointly involved; (6) that the plan has participated in any related party transactions; or (7) any unusual or infrequent events or transactions occurring subsequent to the plan year end that might significantly affect the usefulness of the financial statements in assessing the plan's present or future ability to pay benefits? **c**

d If line **26c** is "Yes," provide the total amount involved in such disclosure ▶

27 If line **26a** is "No," complete the following questions. (You may NOT use "N/A" in response to lines **27a** through **27i**):
If line **27a, 27b, 27c, 27d, 27e,** or **27f** is checked "Yes," schedules of these items in the format set forth in the instructions are required to be attached to this return/report. **Schedule G** (Form 5500) may be used as specified in the instructions.
During the plan year:

a Did the plan have assets held for investment? **27a**

b Were any loans by the plan or fixed income obligations due the plan in default as of the close of the plan year or classified during the year as uncollectible? . . . . **b**

c Were any leases to which the plan was a party in default or classified during the year as uncollectible? . . . . . **c**

d Were any plan transactions or series of transactions in excess of 5% of the current value of plan assets? . . . . **d**

e Do the notes to the financial statements accompanying the accountant's opinion disclose any nonexempt transactions with parties-in-interest? . . . . **e**

f Did the plan engage in any nonexempt transactions with parties-in-interest not reported on line **27e?**. . . . . . **f**

g Did the plan hold qualifying employer securities that are not publicly traded? . . . . **g**

h Did the plan purchase or receive any nonpublicly traded securities that were not appraised in writing by an unrelated third party within 3 months prior to their receipt? . . . . **h**

i Did any person manage plan assets who had a financial interest worth more than 10% in any party providing services to the plan or receive anything of value from any party providing services to the plan? . . . . **i**

Form 5500 (1996) Page **5**

			Yes	No
28	Did the plan acquire individual whole life insurance contracts during the plan year?	28		
29	During the plan year:			
a (1)	Was this plan covered by a fidelity bond? If "Yes," complete lines 29a(2) and 29a(3)	29a(1)		
(2)	Enter amount of bond ▶ $			
(3)	Enter the name of the surety company ▶			
b (1)	Was there any loss to the plan, whether or not reimbursed, caused by fraud or dishonesty?	29b(1)		
(2)	If line **29b(1)** is "Yes," enter amount of loss ▶ $			

30a Is the plan covered under the Pension Benefit Guaranty Corporation termination insurance program?

☐ **Yes** ☐ **No** ☐ **Not determined**

b If line **30a** is "Yes" or "Not determined," enter the employer identification number and the plan number used to identify it.

Employer identification number ▶ Plan number ▶

31 Current value of plan assets and liabilities at the beginning and end of the plan year. Combine the value of plan assets held in more than one trust. Allocate the value of the plan's interest in a commingled trust containing the assets of more than one plan on a line-by-line basis unless the trust meets one of the specific exceptions described in the instructions. Do not enter the value of that portion of an insurance contract that guarantees, during this plan year, to pay a specific dollar benefit at a future date. **Round off amounts to the nearest dollar; any other amounts are subject to rejection.** Plans with no assets at the beginning and the end of the plan year, enter -0- on line **31f.**

		(a) Beginning of Year	**(b)** End of Year
Assets			
a Total noninterest-bearing cash	a		
b Receivables: **(1)** Employer contributions	b(1)		
(2) Participant contributions	(2)		
(3) Income	(3)		
(4) Other	(4)		
(5) Less allowance for doubtful accounts	(5)		
(6) Total. Add lines **31b(1)** through **31b(4)** and subtract line **31b(5)** ▶	(6)		
c General Investments: **(1)** Interest-bearing cash (including money market funds)	c(1)		
(2) Certificates of deposit	(2)		
(3) U.S. Government securities	(3)		
(4) Corporate debt instruments: **(A)** Preferred	(4)(A)		
(B) All other	(4)(B)		
(5) Corporate stocks: **(A)** Preferred	(5)(A)		
(B) Common	(5)(B)		
(6) Partnership/joint venture interests	(6)		
(7) Real estate: **(A)** Income-producing	(7)(A)		
(B) Nonincome-producing	(7)(B)		
(8) Loans (other than to participants) secured by mortgages: **(A)** Residential	(8)(A)		
(B) Commercial	(8)(B)		
(9) Loans to participants: **(A)** Mortgages	(9)(A)		
(B) Other	(9)(B)		
(10) Other loans	(10)		
(11) Value of interest in common/collective trusts	(11)		
(12) Value of interest in pooled separate accounts	(12)		
(13) Value of interest in master trusts	(13)		
(14) Value of interest in 103-12 investment entities	(14)		
(15) Value of interest in registered investment companies	(15)		
(16) Value of funds held in insurance company general account (unallocated contracts)	(16)		
(17) Other	(17)		
(18) Total. Add lines **31c(1)** through **31c(17)** ▶	(18)		
d Employer-related investments: **(1)** Employer securities	d(1)		
(2) Employer real property	(2)		
e Buildings and other property used in plan operation	e		
f **Total** assets. Add lines **31a, 31b(6), 31c(18), 31d(1), 31d(2),** and **31e** ▶	f		
Liabilities			
g Benefit claims payable	g		
h Operating payables	h		
i Acquisition indebtedness	i		
j Other liabilities	j		
k **Total** liabilities. Add lines **31g** through **31j** ▶	k		
Net Assets			
l Subtract line **31k** from line **31f** ▶	l		

Form 5500 (1996) Page 6

32 Plan income, expenses, and changes in net assets for the plan year. *Include all income and expenses of the plan, including any trust(s) or separately maintained fund(s), and any payments/receipts to/from insurance carriers.* **Round off amounts to the nearest dollar; any other amounts are subject to rejection.**

Income		(a) Amount	(b) Total
a Contributions:			
(1) Received or receivable from:			
(A) Employers	a(1)(A)		
(B) Participants	(B)		
(C) Others	(C)		
(2) Noncash contributions	(2)		
(3) Total contributions. Add lines **32a(1)(A), (B), (C)** and line **32a(2)** ▶	(3)		
b Earnings on investments:			
(1) Interest			
(A) Interest-bearing cash (including money market funds)	b(1)(A)		
(B) Certificates of deposit	(B)		
(C) U.S. Government securities	(C)		
(D) Corporate debt instruments	(D)		
(E) Mortgage loans	(E)		
(F) Other loans	(F)		
(G) Other interest	(G)		
(H) Total interest. Add lines **32b(1)(A)** through **(G)** ▶	(H)		
(2) Dividends: **(A)** Preferred stock	b(2)(A)		
(B) Common stock	(B)		
(C) Total dividends. Add lines **32b(2)(A)** and **(B)** ▶	(C)		
(3) Rents	(3)		
(4) Net gain (loss) on sale of assets: **(A)** Aggregate proceeds	(4)(A)		
(B) Aggregate carrying amount (see instructions)	(B)		
(C) Subtract **(B)** from **(A)** and enter result	(C)		
(5) Unrealized appreciation (depreciation) of assets	(5)		
(6) Net investment gain (loss) from common/collective trusts	(6)		
(7) Net investment gain (loss) from pooled separate accounts	(7)		
(8) Net investment gain (loss) from master trusts	(8)		
(9) Net investment gain (loss) from 103-12 investment entities	(9)		
(10) Net investment gain (loss) from registered investment companies	(10)		
c Other income	c		
d Total income. Add all amounts in column **(b)** and enter total ▶	d		
Expenses			
e Benefit payment and payments to provide benefits:			
(1) Directly to participants or beneficiaries	e(1)		
(2) To insurance carriers for the provision of benefits	(2)		
(3) Other	(3)		
(4) Total payments. Add lines **32e(1)** through **32e(3)** ▶	(4)		
f Interest expense	f		
g Administrative expenses: **(1)** Salaries and allowances	g(1)		
(2) Accounting fees	(2)		
(3) Actuarial fees	(3)		
(4) Contract administrator fees	(4)		
(5) Investment advisory and management fees	(5)		
(6) Legal fees	(6)		
(7) Valuation/appraisal fees	(7)		
(8) Trustees fees/expenses (including travel, seminars, meetings, etc.)	(8)		
(9) Other	(9)		
(10) Total administrative expenses. Add lines **32g(1)** through **32g(9)**	(10)		
h Total expenses. Add lines **32e(4), 32f,** and **32g(10)** ▶	h		
i Net income (loss). Subtract line **32h** from line **32d** ▶	i		
j Transfers to (from) the plan (see instructions)	j		
k Net assets at beginning of year (line **31l**, column **(a)**)	k		
l Net assets at end of year (line **31l**, column **(b)**) ▶	l		

	Yes	No
33 Did any employer sponsoring the plan pay any of the administrative expenses of the plan that were not reported on line **32g?**		

U.S. DEPARTMENT OF LABOR

EMPLOYMENT STANDARDS ADMINISTRATION

Wage and Hour Division
Washington, D.C. 20210

NOTICE

EMPLOYEE POLYGRAPH PROTECTION ACT

The Employee Polygraph Protection Act prohibits most private employers from using lie detector tests either for pre-employment screening or during the course of employment.

PROHIBITIONS

Employers are generally prohibited from requiring or requesting any employee or job applicant to take a lie detector test, and from discharging, disciplining, or discriminating against an employee or prospective employee for refusing to take a test or for exercising other rights under the Act.

EXEMPTIONS*

Federal, State and local governments are not affected by the law. Also, the law does not apply to tests given by the Federal Government to certain private individuals engaged in national security-related activities.

The Act permits *polygraph* (a kind of lie detector) tests to be administered in the private sector, subject to restrictions, to certain prospective employees of security service firms (armored car, alarm, and guard), and of pharmaceutical manufacturers, distributors and dispensers.

The Act also permits polygraph testing, subject to restrictions, of certain employees of private firms who are reasonably suspected of involvement in a workplace incident (theft, embezzlement, etc.) that resulted in economic loss to the employer.

EXAMINEE RIGHTS

Where polygraph tests are permitted, they are subject to numerous strict standards concerning the conduct and length of the test. Examinees have a number of specific rights, including the right to a written notice before testing, the right to refuse or discontinue a test, and the right not to have test results disclosed to unauthorized persons.

ENFORCEMENT

The Secretary of Labor may bring court actions to restrain violations and assess civil penalties up to $10,000 against violators. Employees or job applicants may also bring their own court actions.

ADDITIONAL INFORMATION

Additional information may be obtained, and complaints of violations may be filed, at local offices of the Wage and Hour Division, which are listed in the telephone directory under U.S. Government, Department of Labor, Employment Standards Administration.

THE LAW REQUIRES EMPLOYERS TO DISPLAY THIS POSTER WHERE EMPLOYEES AND JOB APPLICANTS CAN READILY SEE IT.

**The law does not preempt any provision of any State or local law or any collective bargaining agreement which is more restrictive with respect to lie detector tests.*

U.S. DEPARTMENT OF LABOR

EMPLOYMENT STANDARDS ADMINISTRATION

Wage and Hour Division
Washington, D.C. 20210

WH Publication 1462
September 1988

Equal Employment Opportunity is THE LAW

Employers Holding Federal Contracts or Subcontracts

Applicants to and employees of companies with a Federal government contract or subcontract are protected under the following Federal authorities:

RACE, COLOR, RELIGION, SEX, NATIONAL ORIGIN

Executive Order 11246, as amended, prohibits job discrimination on the basis of race, color, religion, sex or national origin, and requires affirmative action to ensure equality of opportunity in all aspects of employment.

INDIVIDUALS WITH DISABILITIES

Section 503 of the Rehabilitation Act of 1973, as amended, prohibits job discrimination because of disability and requires affirmative action to employ and advance in employment qualified individuals

Private Employment, State and Local Government, Educational Institutions

Applicants to and employees of most private employers, state and local governments, educational institutions, employment agencies and labor organizations are protected under the following Federal laws:

RACE, COLOR, RELIGION, SEX, NATIONAL ORIGIN

Title VII of the Civil Rights Act of 1964, as amended, prohibits discrimination in hiring, promotion, discharge, pay, fringe benefits, job training, classification, referral, and other aspects of employment, on the basis of race, color, religion, sex or national origin.

DISABILITY

The Americans with Disabilities Act of 1990, as amended, protects qualified applications and employees with disabilities from discrimination in hiring, promotion, discharge, pay, job training, fringe benefits, classification, referral, and other aspects of employment on the basis of disability. The law also requires that covered entities provide qualified applicants and employees with disabilities

Programs or Activities Receiving Federal Financial Assistance

RACE, COLOR, NATIONAL ORIGIN, SEX

In addition to the protection of Title VII of the Civil Rights Act of 1964, Title VI of the Civil Rights Act prohibits discrimination on the basis of race, color or national origin in programs or activities receiving Federal financial assistance. Employment discrimination is covered by Title VI if the primary objective of the financial assistance is provision of employment, or where employment discrimination causes; or may cause discrimination in providing services under such programs. Title IX of the Education Amendments of 1972 prohibits employment discrimination on the basis of sex in educational programs or activities which receive Federal assistance.

with disabilities who, with reasonable accommodation, can perform the essential functions of a job.

VIETNAM ERA AND SPECIAL DISABLED VETERANS

38 U.S.C. 4212 of the Vietnam Era Veterans Readjustment Assistance Act of 1974 prohibits job discrimination and requires affirmative action to employ and advance in employment qualified Vietnam era veterans and qualified special disabled veterans.

Any person who believes a contractor has violated its nondiscrimination or affirmative action obligations under the authorities above should contact immediately:

The Office of Federal Contract Compliance Programs (OFCCP), Employment Standards Administration, U.S. Department of Labor, 200 Constitution Avenue, N.W., Washington, D.C. 20210 or call (202) 219-9430, or an OFCCP regional or district office, listed in most telephone directories under U.S. Government, Department of Labor.

with reasonable accommodations that do not impose undue hardship.

AGE

The Age Discrimination in Employment Act of 1967, as amended, protects applicants and employees 40 years of age or older from discrimination on the basis of age in hiring, promotion, discharge, compensation, terms, conditions or privileges of employment.

SEX (WAGES)

In addition to sex discrimination prohibited by Title VII of the Civil Rights Act (see above), the Equal Pay Act of 1963, as amended, prohibits sex discrimination in payment of wages to women and men performing substantially equal work in the same establishment.

Retaliation against a person who files a charge of discrimination, participates in an investigation, or opposes an unlawful employment practice is prohibited by all these Federal laws.

If you believe that you have been discriminated against under any laws, you immediately should contact:

The U.S. Equal Employment Opportunity Commission (EEOC), 1801 L. Street, N.W., Washington, D.C. 20507 or an EEOC field office by calling toll free (800) 669-4000. For individuals with hearing impairments, EEOC's toll free TDD number is (800) 800-3302.

INDIVIDUALS WITH DISABILITIES

Section 504 of the Rehabilitation Act of 1973, as amended, prohibits employment discrimination on the basis of disabilities in any program or activity which receives Federal financial assistance. Discrimination is prohibited in all aspects of employment against disabled persons who, with reasonable accommodation, can perform the essential functions of a job.

If you believe you have been discriminated against in a program of any institution which receives Federal assistance, you should contact immediately the Federal agency providing such assistance.

*U.S. GOVERNMENT PRINTING OFFICE 1994-0-368-769

Your Rights
Under The
Family and Medical Leave Act of 1993

FMLA requires covered employers to provide up to 12 weeks of unpaid, job-protected leave to "eligible" employees for certain family and medical reasons.

Employees are eligible if they have worked for a covered employer for at least one year, and for 1,250 hours over the previous 12 months, and if there are at least 50 employees within 75 miles.

Reasons For Taking Leave:

Unpaid leave must be granted for *any* of the following reasons:

- to care for the employee's child after birth, or placement for adoption or foster care;
- to care for the employee's spouse, son or daughter, or parent, who has a serious health condition; or
- for a serious health condition that makes the employee unable to perform the employee's job.

At the employee's or employer's option, certain kinds of *paid* leave may be substituted for unpaid leave.

Advance Notice and Medical Certification:

The employee may be required to provide advance leave notice and medical certification. Taking of leave may be denied if requirements are not met.

- The employee ordinarily must provide 30 days advance notice when the leave is "foreseeable."
- An employer may require medical certification to support a request for leave because of a serious health condition, and may require second or third opinions (at the employer's expense) and a fitness for duty report to return to work.

Job Benefits and Protection:

- For the duration of FMLA leave, the employer must maintain the employee's health coverage under any "group health plan."
- Upon return from FMLA leave, most employees must be restored to their original or equivalent positions with equivalent pay, benefits, and other employment terms.
- The use of FMLA leave cannot result in the loss of any employment benefit that accrued prior to the start of an employee's leave.

Unlawful Acts By Employers:

FMLA makes it unlawful for any employer to:

- interfere with, restrain, or deny the exercise of any right provided under FMLA:
- discharge or discriminate against any person for opposing any practice made unlawful by FMLA or for involvement in any proceeding under or relating to FMLA.

Enforcement:

- The U.S. Department of Labor is authorized to investigate and resolve complaints of violations.
- An eligible employee may bring a civil action against an employer for violations.

FMLA does not affect any Federal or State law prohibiting discrimination, or supersede any State or local law or collective bargaining agreement which provides greater family or medical leave rights.

For Additional Information:

Contact the nearest office of the Wage and Hour Division, listed in most telephone directories under U.S. Government, Department of Labor.

U.S. Department of Labor
Employment Standards Administration
Wage and Hour Division
Washington, D.C. 20210

WH Publication 1420
June 1993

U.S. GOVERNMENT PRINTING OFFICE:1996 171-169

JOB SAFETY & HEALTH PROTECTION

The Occupational Safety and Health Act of 1970 provides job safety and health protection for workers by promoting safe and healthful working conditions throughout the Nation. Provisions of the Act include the following:

Employers

All employers must furnish to employees employment and a place of employment free from recognized hazards that are causing or are likely to cause death or serious harm to employees. Employers must comply with occupational safety and health standards issued under the Act.

Employees

Employees must comply with all occupational safety and health standards, rules, regulations and orders issued under the Act that apply to their own actions and conduct on the job.

The Occupational Safety and Health Administration (OSHA) of the U.S. Department of Labor has the primary responsibility for administering the Act. OSHA issues occupational safety and health standards, and its Compliance Safety and Health Officers conduct jobsite inspections to help ensure compliance with the Act.

Inspection

The Act requires that a representative of the employer and a representative authorized by the employees be given an opportunity to accompany the OSHA inspector for the purpose of aiding the inspection.

Proposed Penalty

The Act provides for mandatory civil penalties against employers of up to $7,000 for each serious violation and for optional penalties of up to $7,000 for each nonserious violation. Penalties of up to $7,000 per day may be proposed for failure to correct violations within the proposed time period and for each day the violation continues beyond the prescribed abatement date. Also, any employer who willfully or repeatedly violates the Act may be assessed penalties of up to $70,000 for each such violation. A minimum penalty of $5,000 may be imposed for each willful violation. A violation of posting requirements can bring a penalty of up to $7,000.

There are also provisions for criminal penalties. Any willful violation resulting in the death of any employee, upon conviction, is punishable by a fine of up to $250,000 (or $500,000 if the employer is a corporation), or by imprisonment for up to six months, or both. A second conviction of an employer doubles the possible term of imprisonment. Falsifying records, reports, or applications is punishable by a fine of $10,000 or up to six months in jail or both.

Voluntary Activity

While providing penalties for violations, the Act also encourages efforts by labor and management, before an OSHA inspection, to reduce workplace hazards voluntarily and to develop and improve safety and health programs in all workplaces and industries. OSHA's Voluntary Protection Programs recognize outstanding efforts of this nature

Where there is no authorized employee representative, the OSHA Compliance Officer must consult with a reasonable number of employees concerning safety and health conditions in the workplace.

Complaint

Employees or their representatives have the right to file a complaint with the nearest OSHA office requesting an inspection if they believe unsafe or unhealthful conditions exist in their workplace. OSHA will withhold, on request, names of employees complaining.

The Act provides that employees may not be discharged or discriminated against in any way for filing safety and health complaints or for otherwise exercising their rights under the Act.

Employees who believe they have been discriminated against may file a compliant with their nearest OSHA office within 30 days of the alleged discriminatory action.

Citation

If upon inspection OSHA believes an employer has violated the Act, a citation alleging such violations will be issued to the employer. Each citation will specify a time period within which the alleged violation must be corrected.

The OSHA citation must be prominently displayed at or near the place of alleged violation for three days, or until it is corrected, whichever is later, to warn employees of dangers that may exist there.

OSHA has published Safety and Health Program Management Guidelines to assist employers in establishing or perfecting programs to prevent or control employee exposure to workplace hazards. There are many public and private organizations that can provide information and assistance in this effort, if requested. Also, your local OSHA office can provide considerable help and advice on solving safety and health problems or can refer you to other sources for help such as training.

Consultation

Free assistance in identifying and correcting hazards and in improving safety and health management is available to employers, without citation or penalty, through OSHA-supported programs in each State. These programs are usually administered by the State Labor or Health department or a State university.

Posting Instructions

Employers in States operating OSHA approved State Plans should obtain and post the State's equivalent poster.

Under provisions of Title 29, Code of Federal Regulations, Part 1903.2(a)(1) employers must post this notice (or facsimile) in a conspicuous place where notices to employees are customarily posted.

More Information

Additional information and copies of the Act, specific OSHA safety and health standards, and other applicable regulations may be obtained from your employer or from the nearest OSHA Regional Office in the following locations:

Atlanta, GA	(404) 347-3573
Boston, MA	(617) 565-7164
Chicago, IL	(312) 353-2220
Dallas, TX	(214) 767-4731
Denver, CO	(303) 391-5858
Kansas City, MO	(816) 426-5861
New York, NY	(212) 337-2378
Philadelphia, PA	(215) 596-1201
San Francisco, CA	(415) 744-6670
Seattle, WA	(206) 553-5930

Washington, DC
1995 (Reprinted)
OSHA 2203

Robert B. Reich, Secretary of Labor

U.S. Department of Labor

Occupational Safety and Health Administration

Washington, DC 1995 (Reprinted) OSHA 2203

This information will be made available to sensory impaired individuals upon request. Voice phone: (202) 219-8615; TDD message referral phone: 1-800-326-2577

| HOME | INDEX | SEARCH | STATISTICS & DATA |

Injury and Illness Rate Chart 1973-1997

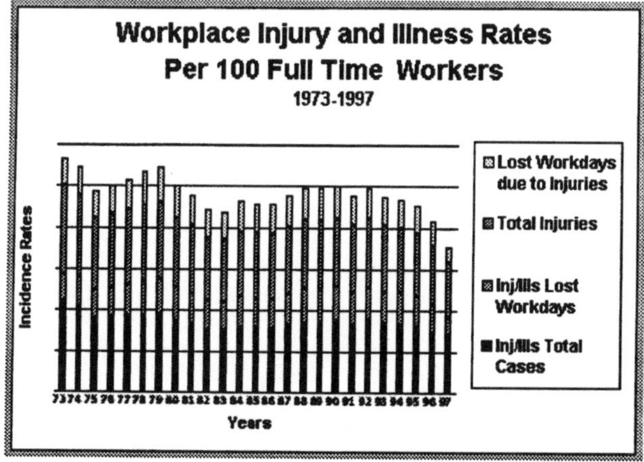

Data Source: Bureau of Labor Statistics Press Release USDL 98-494, Thursday, December 17, 1998.

| USDOL | CONTACT INFORMATION | DISCLAIMER |

INDEX